THE INDISPENSABLE ENEMY

"THE FIRST BLOW AT THE CHINESE QUESTION"
The Wasp [San Francisco] 2 (1878): 289.

The Indispensable Enemy

LABOR AND THE ANTI-CHINESE MOVEMENT
IN CALIFORNIA

ALEXANDER SAXTON

FOREWORD BY WILLIAM DEVERELL

UNIVERSITY OF CALIFORNIA PRESS
BERKELEY   LOS ANGELES   LONDON

Cover Illustration:
Chinese Rail Road Laborers, filling in Secrettown Trestle.
California, 1877 (Courtesy of the Bancroft Library,
University of California, Berkeley).

University of California Press
Berkeley and Los Angeles, California

University of California Press, Ltd.
London, England

© 1971, 1995 by
The Regents of the University of California

First Paperback Printing, 1975

Library of Congress Cataloging-in-Publication Data
Saxton, Alexander.
    The indispensable enemy : labor and the anti-Chinese movement in
California / Alexander Saxton.
        p.   cm.
    Includes bibliographical references and index.
    ISBN 0-520-02905-4 (alk. paper)
    1. Alien labor, Chinese—California—History.   2. Chinese—
California—History.   3. Trade-unions—California—Political
activity—History.   4. California—Politics and
government—1850–1950.   I. Title.
HD8081.C5S3   1995   95-24926
331.6′21510794—dc20   CIP

Printed in the United States of America

08   07   06   05   04   03   02   01
9   8   7   6   5   4   3   2

The paper used in this publication meets the minimum requirements
of ANSI/NISO Z39.48-1992 (R 1997) (*Permanence of Paper*). ∞

To my wife,

WHO CARRIED MORE THAN HALF
OF THIS UNDERTAKING

CONTENTS

FOREWORD

On the 24th of March, 1855, somewhere in northern California's gold country, Charles De Long "shot a Chinaman." He entered this terse, matter-of-fact phrase in one of his little leatherbound journals. Other than admitting that he "had a hell of a time," De Long, then in his early twenties, tells us no more about the incident. Instead, his mention of the assault sounds no different than other curt citations of daily tasks, chores, observations. "Prospected the creek." "Found a ring." "Had stiff neck." "Bought goods." "Shot a Chinaman."[1]

Shot a Chinaman. The phrase says so little, and yet it reveals so much. What is shocking (even one hundred and forty years later) is how ordinary the attack seems to have been. Such banality is itself emblematic of the generality and anonymity of racial conflict and racial violence in the history of California. Charles De Long obviously felt little need to explain his diary entries.[2] He would not expect to be called upon to justify his shooting of a Chinese man. He would not expect to be asked why he found Chinese women erotic and mysterious. He would not expect to be questioned about his revelation that cutting the hair of Chinese men was sporting and fun.[3]

Charles De Long looked for gold and, in his words, "hunted Chinamen." As a deputy sheriff in the gold country, he enforced the ugly Foreign Miner's tax, collecting fees and issuing licenses with violence and impunity, and without apology. And let it not escape notice that this is a man who would later graduate from playing the part of Everyman Gold Rush Miner to United States Minister to Japan. Astonishing, ironic . . . and somehow not surprising.

How to begin to explain the unrepentent racism directed at the Chi-

---

[1] See Carl Wheat, ed., "California's Bantam Cock: The Journals of Charles E. De Long, 1854–1863," *Quarterly of the California Historical Society* 8 (September 1929): 194–213; continued in *Quarterly of the California Historical Society* 8 (December 1929): 337–363. Journal entries selected at random with corrected punctuation, capitalization.

[2] This despite the fact that editor Wheat points out several times that De Long expected the journals eventually to be read.

[3] Other journal entries note randomly that "Chinese women [are] quite a fancy . . . . went down the river in the night . . . had a great time, Chinamen tails cut off. . . . loafing around doing nothing but picking up a few Chinamen whom their bad luck and my good threw in my way."

nese in California history? A good start is with this book. First published in 1971, one hundred years after a brutal massacre of Chinese
in Los Angeles, *The Indispensable Enemy: Labor and the Anti-Chinese
Movement in California* immediately became an important book. Re-
viewers praised Alexander Saxton's research, his accessible (and often
very moving) prose, and his tough-minded critique of racial exclusion
by those trying to build white labor solidarity. Nearly twenty-five
years later, *The Indispensable Enemy* remains a critical case study of
American labor, American politics, and American racism. If a classic is
that kind of book which changes the way people look at and think
about something, and continues to be of real importance ten, twenty,
fifty years after it is written, then *The Indispensable Enemy* is just that
sort of work.

   One reason this book is still significant is that it anticipated many
scholarly insights and preoccupations. A model study of the intersec-
tion of race and class in American history, *The Indispensable Enemy* appeared at least a decade before historiographical stirrings from the
"new western history" insisted that race and ethnicity occupy center
stage in analyses of the American West. Though less about California's
Chinese population than about white response to the Chinese, *The Indispensable Enemy* must also rank as an extremely important early study
of Asian American history.[4] Even the book's historical vantage point—
the worldviews of white labor leaders, Democratic party functionaries
and organizers—foreshadowed much of current scholarly fascination
with whiteness and white culture(s). Saxton knew that the criss-cross-
ing tensions of class, labor, race, and politics produced the complex
stuff of California and American history, and this book has continued
to remind succeeding generations of historians of that complexity. Despite the fact that they often suggest different arguments *vis a vis* class
and race, such recent works as Tomás Almaguer's *Racial Fault Lines*

----

   [4] I would place Saxton alongside such path-breaking studies as E.C. Sandmeyer's
1939 book *The Anti-Chinese Movement in California* (Urbana: University of Illinois Press)
and Roger Daniels, *The Politics of Prejudice: The Anti-Japanese Movement in California
and the Struggle for Japanese Exclusion* (Berkeley: University of California Press, 1978).
Saxton helps to bridge such earlier studies with more recent works such as Ronald
Takaki, *Iron Cages: Race and Culture in Nineteenth Century America* (New York: Knopf,
1979) and Sucheng Chan, *This Bittersweet Soil: Chinese in California Agriculture, 1860–
1910* (Berkeley: University of California Press, 1986).
   [5] Tomás Almaguer, *Racial Fault Lines: The Historical Origins of White Supremacy in
California* (Berkeley: University of California Press, 1994); David R. Roediger, *The
Wages of Whiteness: Race and the Making of the American Working Class* (London and
New York: Verso, 1991); Alexander Saxton, *The Rise & Fall of the White Republic: Class
Politics & Mass Culture in Nineteenth Century America* (London and New York: Verso,
1991). I would also suggest that Saxton can be read in tandem with R. Hal Williams'
contemporary study of late nineteenth century California party politics; both works

and David R. Roediger's *Wages of Whiteness*, as well as Saxton's own later work, are indebted to *The Indispensable Enemy*.[5]

But the reissue of *The Indispensable Enemy* is not simply an act of tribute or commemoration. On the contrary, this is a book to be read and read again, to be engaged right alongside those works of more recent vintage. A new generation of students is entitled to this book and to its arguments, entitled to know its rich, committed scholarship. Entire classes of students will now be able to encounter Saxton's work anew, will now dog-ear these pages and write in these margins.

Yet it must be noted that *The Indispensable Enemy* is not an easy book to read. It tells a sad and disturbing story, and its pages reveal a history of hatred every bit as obvious as Charles De Long's cavalier notation that he had "shot a Chinaman." From the opening chapters, which help to set demographic and ideological stages, Alexander Saxton moves to his critical task: an examination of the ways in which organized (white) labor in nineteenth and early twentieth century California utilized the presence of Chinese workers to fashion hierarchies of racial exclusion. As simple and as brutal as such categorization (and its attendant violence) might have been, Saxton is careful to note that the story, like any such story in American history, is more complex than it might first appear.

Saxton notes that the Chinese in nineteenth century California were not viewed as complete anathema. Chinese immigrants were, instead, quite literally indispensable to an economy in transition from raw extraction to something approaching industrial capitalism. Whether for purchasing old and worn-out mining claims in the 1850s or for shouldering the hardest and most lethal labor of the construction of the Central Pacific Railroad through the 1860s, the Chinese proved themselves a vital component of the working class.[6] California's industrial growth through the mining era and into the railroad era simply cannot be explained without regard to the massive contribution of Chinese labor.

And while the Big Four of the Central Pacific and construction foremen may have celebrated Chinese work and a Chinese work ethic (and paid them slightly more than half what others earned along the

focus particular attention upon the organization and platforms of the post-Civil War Democratic Party. See R. Hal Williams, *The Democratic Party and California Politics, 1880–1896* (Stanford: Stanford University Press, 1973).

[6] The Chinese, already 9 percent of the state's population in 1860, proved especially valuable to the corporate and construction heads of the Central Pacific. "I like the idea of your getting over more Chinamen," Collis P. Huntington of the Central Pacific wrote to a company official in the midst of transcontinental rail construction; "it would be all the better for us and the State if there should a half million come over in 1868." Quoted in William Deverell, *Railroad Crossing: Californians and the Railroad, 1850–1910* (Berkeley: University of California Press, 1994), p. 15.

way), rising sentiment within white working-class circles was of resentment, hatred, and mistrust. Saxton is brilliant at describing the inherent instability of California's version of racialized democracy. White
workers had initially perceived that the Chinese actually elevated the
status of Caucasian labor, since whites could claim that skilled jobs
were race specific and that, in essence, the employment of mass numbers of unskilled Chinese at the bottom of the labor ladder forced white
workers up a rung or two. For this to continue, the Chinese would have
to be shunted off to work at the most dangerous and least skilled jobs,
and the economy had to produce enough skilled jobs for white laborers.[7] White society determined the Chinese to be inferior (they could
even, apparently, occasionally be shot without so much as explanatory
comment), it had determined that the Chinese had particular and isolated roles to play in the workforce, and it had determined that Chinese labor was but a necessary evil that might someday be proven dispensable. With the state's native Indian population already decimated
by disease and genocidal warfare, the Chinese became a critical mass
of exploitable (often expendable) labor.

But demographic expansion and economic retraction helped render
the Chinese indispensable for other, equally despicable, reasons. Simple racist formulas about "Chinese work" and "white work" were
bound to break down once the state's economy, now tied to the east by
the iron thread of the Central Pacific, began to show signs of depression
and "less work." Stress prompted by unemployment and a rapidly strati-
fying industrial order led to increased demagoguery. Anti-coolie "clubs"
and organizations arose, agitated, and in turn prompted more concerted
efforts toward racial exclusion and outright violence.

Saxton's depiction of Bay Area organized labor falling under the
spell of Denis Kearney's "The Chinese Must Go!" exhortations remains one of the best scholarly treatments of the rise of the Workingmen's Party. By perpetuating anti-Chinese rhetoric and actions, white
workers fashioned a short-lived, but important, political movement
which tried to attack land and industrial monopoly at the same time it
stomped on Chinese laborers. Nor was the power of racist demagoguery lost on mainstream parties: Saxton's work reveals how deeply
the stain of racist exclusion marked the *post bellum* Democratic Party's
efforts to gain working-class support.

The explanation, the poignant lesson (even the warning) is as clear
today as it was twenty-five years ago when Alexander Saxton wrote it

---

[7] For instance, Saxton notes that the Chinese probably had little competition for the
most deadly railroad labor (p. 63): "No man who had any choice would have chosen to
be a common laborer on the Central Pacific during the crossing of the High Sierra."

on the first page of this book. "Racial identification cut at right angles to class consciousness." How else to explain Denis Kearney, or, for that matter, Henry George, the man who worried most about the class ramifications of the arriving transcontinental railroad while simultaneously railing, Kearney-like, against the continued presence of the Chinese?[8] There's the rub, a complex set of ironies and energies expended that men like Frank Roney, whose hopes for racial egalitarianism fell victim to Kearney's racist rallying cries, could never surmount.

California capital has always found workers to exploit; and organized California labor has not always been able to distance itself from that history. Once California had filled, pushed, and pulled the cart of Chinese exclusion to its legislative destination (at last complete by the turn of the century), no sleight of hand was needed to turn attention to the Japanese. Similarly, the "indispensibilty" of undocumented Mexican and other Latino labor in this century has revealed many of the same faultlines and conflicts which Saxton elucidates here.[9] And at a time in which organized labor in the state struggles anew with the challenges of ethnic and racial diversity, it seems entirely appropriate to add this book to the discussions, to utilize its rich historical perspective and its deeply contextualized analysis.

Recall that Charles De Long felt no need to explain himself after noting that he shot a Chinese man in 1855. Nor did the ugly statement receive comment seventy years ago, when the *California Historical Society Quarterly* published the De Long diary. I would hope this would be different today. Words change, and words change meaning. Charles De Long's commonplace acts of racist categorization and violence leap from the pages of his journal today, demanding comment and, if possible, explanation. Reconciliation of the pains and hatreds, divisions and conflicts within California and American society requires as much understanding as we can possibly bring to the task. Alexander Saxton clearly hoped that *The Indispensable Enemy* would be for the classroom and outside of it; reissue of this justly classic work is both fulfillment of that wish and an appropriate sign that the hard work of understanding continues.

William Deverell
June 1995
Los Angeles

[8] Saxton's discussion of George's path to anti-Chinese statements is brilliant. It was as if George could not stifle the racism that burbled out from beneath his ostensibly rigorous economic arguments. See, especially, chapter five.

[9] See Almaguer, *Racial Fault Lines* and David G. Gutiérrez, *Walls & Mirrors: Mexican Americans, Mexican Immigrants & the Politics of Ethnicity* (Berkeley: University of California Press, 1995).

ACKNOWLEDGEMENTS

I am deeply indebted to Ira Cross. Professor Cross was a student of John R. Commons at Wisconsin, and when he came to California he brought with him not only Commons' dedication to scholarship, but his conviction that industrial America could be democratized through the practice of trade unionism. Cross and his students at Berkeley have done for western labor history what Commons and his associates did for labor history nationally. More than thirty years after its first publication, Cross' *History of the Labor Movement in California* remains the major work in the field. Its pages still offer the researcher long vistas together with extraordinarily accurate detail. To him also we owe the invaluable autobiography of Frank Roney, *Irish Rebel and California Labor Leader*. Few workingmen in America have found the time or the energy to record their own experience; it is certainly due to the patient insistence of his friend Ira Cross that Frank Roney did so. Finally there is the treasury of documents, letters, pamphlets, notes, clippings and newspapers which Cross left in Bancroft Library, University of California, Berkeley, for the use of subsequent historians. I have met Professor Cross only once, yet through his work and his students, I feel as if I had known him well. He will doubtless disagree with much of my interpretation. Nonetheless I have traveled in his company for many miles which I could scarcely have got through otherwise.

This study could not have been undertaken without the assistance and criticism of Professor Walton Bean of the University of California at Berkeley. Once undertaken, I think it would never have been finished except for the leads and cues afforded by his knowledge of western history; and the unfailing encouragement which he and his wife Beth Bean provided. To Professors Henry Nash Smith, Lawrence Levine, and Michael Rogin I am grateful for patient readings, for errors avoided due to their admonitions, and for improvements made thanks to their suggestions. The many errors I have doubtless failed to avoid I claim as my own. To Professor Henry May I am indebted for the generous sharing of his scholarship, and for his confidence and good counsel at several dubious turnings.

I was for many months almost a fulltime boarder at the Bancroft Library. The enthusiastic assistance of the staff of that library proved inexhaustible. In addition, I have leaned heavily on the expert guidance of librarians and staff of the California State Library at Sacramento, the California Historical Society in San Francisco, the public libraries of San Francisco, Detroit and New York, of Harvard's Widener Library, and of the libraries of the universities of Nevada and Michigan, and of the University of California at Berkeley and Los Angeles. May they prosper and multiply. Mrs. Susan Goldstein and Mr. Charles Slosser helped with many troublesome problems of research. Portions of chapters 3 and 11 appeared first as articles in the *Pacific Historical Review*, which has consented to their being reprinted here. Portions of chapter 12 appear in somewhat different form in my essay, "Race and the House of Labor," in *The Great Fear: Race in the Mind of America*, edited by Gary Nash and Richard Weiss (New York: Holt, Rinehart, and Winston, 1970). My own continuing work on this project has been made possible in large measure by a Research Fellowship of the John Randolph and Dora Haynes Memorial Foundation, and by research grants from the Academic Senate of the University of California at Los Angeles.

There is one other debt I wish to acknowledge, although I cannot repay it because the man to whom it is owing died probably six or seven years before I was born. He was a Polish Jew named Sigismund Danielewicz, a Socialist who worked as a barber and sailor and union organizer in California in the 1880s. If this book had a hero, it would be Danielewicz. He was one of the founders of the Sailors' Union of the Pacific and helped to build the labor movement in the West. He might have had ships and high schools—even union halls— named for him, except that he chose to stand for the principle of interracial equality. The last reference I found to him indicates that he was out of work in the winter of 1910 and set out out on foot for the East. One of my colleagues, when I told him what little I knew about Danielewicz, said, "He restores my faith." I think he meant that Danielewicz reminds us there was (and perhaps still is) a tradition of humane and humanist radicalism in America. No star is lost.

INTRODUCTION

Having broken from the old circumference in search of new territory, European explorers and entrepreneurs found themselves involved in a quest for labor to work the lands they had laid open. A large segment of the history of the Americas could be bracketed within this context.

The first effort at labor recruitment was the impressment of Indians, an attempt generally unsuccessful north of the Rio Grande. The second effort was the importation of African slaves. The third, beginning as the slave trade tapered off, was the coolie traffic from South China. Out of that hungry and overpopulated region, Chinese laborers were carried to the ocean islands, reached the Pacific coasts of North and South America, and passed on across the Isthmus to the sugar plantations of the Caribbean. The Chinese were followed—briefly and in much smaller numbers—by Japanese, Hindus, and Filipinos. Immigration of Chinese to the United States, then, from its earliest beginnings during the Gold Rush through flood tide in the early eighties and rapid decline thereafter, formed only one phase of a more extended historical episode.

In another respect also the half century of Chinese labor in the West was contained within a larger historical context. North Americans of European background have experienced three great racial confrontations: with the Indian, with the African, and with the Oriental. Central to each transaction has been a totally one-sided preponderance of power, exerted for the exploitation of nonwhites by the dominant white society. In each case (but especially in the two that began with systems of enforced labor), white workingmen have played a crucial, yet ambivalent, role. They have been both exploited and exploiters. On the one hand, thrown into competition with nonwhites as enslaved or "cheap" labor, they suffered economically; on the other hand, being white, they benefited by that very exploitation which was compelling the nonwhites to work for low wages or for nothing. Ideologically they were drawn in opposite directions. Racial identification cut at right angles to class consciousness.

Clearly, the importation of indentured workers from an area of relatively depressed living standards constituted a menace to a society developing, at least after 1865, on the basis of free wage labor. This will be taken for granted. Yet America's hostile reception of Chinese cannot be explained solely by the "cheap" labor argument, although many historians have endeavored to do so. The dominant society responded differently to Irish or Slavic than to Oriental cheap workers, not so much for economic as for ideological and psychological reasons. What happened to Orientals in America, while similar in many ways to what happened to other immigrants, is generally more like what happened to blacks, who were certainly not immigrants in the usual meaning of the term.

The purpose of this study is to examine the Chinese confrontation on the Pacific Coast, as it was experienced and rationalized by the white majority. For reasons which will be evident in what follows, the main body of the work (chapters 3 through 11) will focus on the Democratic party and the labor movement of California through the forty-year period after the Civil War. The two opening chapters turn back to explore aspects of the Jacksonian background which appear crucial to an understanding of what occurred in California. The final chapter looks beyond the turn of the century to trace certain results of the sequence of events in the West for the labor movement as a whole, and to suggest the influence of those events upon the crystallization of an American concept of national identity.[1]

[1] For general accounts of the Chinese in America, see Gunther Barth, *Bitter Strength: A History of the Chinese in the United States, 1850–1870* (Cambridge, Mass., 1964); Mary Roberts Coolidge, *Chinese Immigration* (New York, 1909); S. W. Kung, *The Chinese in American Life: Some Aspects of Their History, Status, Problems and Contributions* (Seattle, 1962); Rose Hum Lee, *The Chinese in the United States of America* (Hong Kong, 1960); Kwang-Ching Lin, *Americans and Chinese: A Historical Essay and Bibliography* (Cambridge, Mass., 1963); Stuart C. Miller, *The Unwelcome Immigrant: American Images of Chinese, 1785–1882* (Berkeley and Los Angeles, 1969). On the background of the coolie trade: Persia Crawford Campbell, *Chinese Coolie Emigration to Countries Within the British Empire* (London, 1923); Harley Farnsworth MacNair, *The Chinese Abroad, Their Position, and Protection: A Study in International Law and Relations* (Shanghai, 1924); Watt Stewart, *Chinese Bondage in Peru: A History of the Chinese Coolie in Peru, 1849–1874* (Durham, N.C., 1951); Wing Yung, *My Life in China and America* (New York, 1909), 191–196.

1

THE LABOR FORCE IN
CALIFORNIA

The Chinese

The census of 1870 showed just under fifty thousand Chinese in California. Their number had increased at an accelerating pace since before the Civil War and would continue to rise till after 1880; but the rate of increase was less rapid than that for the population as a whole. In 1860 Chinese had represented slightly more than 9 percent of all Californians; ten years later the proportion had dropped to 8.6 percent and in 1880 to 7.5 percent.

Distribution throughout the state was uneven and shifted with changing occupational patterns. Most Chinese immigrants were laborers. The majority reaching California in the early fifties had joined the rush to the foothills. There they had found themselves in competition with white miners, who frequently resolved their own differences sufficiently to join in evicting Chinese from the camps. Already, however, the golden days were passing; by the end of the decade, as surface deposits were stripped away, most white miners went hunting richer territory elsewhere or drifted into other pursuits. The Chinese then returned to work out low-yield diggings and comb over the abandoned tailings. Thus, the census of 1860 for California found more than two-thirds of all Chinese in the mining regions of the Sierra Nevada and Trinity Alps.[1]

1 United States, Bureau of the Census, *Eighth Census: Population of the United States in 1860* (Washington, 1864), 25, 28, 31, 34; *Ninth Census*, Pt. I, (Washington, 1872), 91, 328, 338, 386. Davis McEntire, "An Economic Study of Population Movements in California, 1850–1944" (PhD. diss., Harvard University, 1947), 154, Table 27; Warren S. Thompson, *Growth and Changes in California's Population* (Los Angeles, 1955), 75, Table VII-6; Ping Chiu, *Chinese Labor in California, 1850–1880: An Economic Study* (Madison, 1963), 27–30; Mary Roberts Coolidge, *Chinese Immigration* (New York, 1909), 498–504.

But even under Chinese methods of extraction, the placers were finally giving out, and through the sixties a large number of Chinese moved into heavy construction. The Central Pacific Railroad provided the transition for this shift. From 1866 through 1869, the railroad kept some 10,000 Chinese at work boring the Sierra tunnel and driving the line east across the deserts of Nevada and Utah.[2] One result—aside from the golden spike at Promontory—was the assembly of an army of experienced Chinese construction workers. Afterward some stayed with the railroad, which, upon completion of the transcontinental link, began pushing its lines out to the northern and southern extremities of the state. Others moved into agriculture. California ranchers, having come through their pastoral stage, were now demanding enormous supplies of labor for clearing, diking, ditching, draining, irrigating, and harvesting the new crops.

As most of this activity centered in the great valleys, a corresponding shift of Chinese population occurred. By 1870 the mining districts had lost half their Chinese residents of ten years earlier, while the valley counties were showing a rapid increase. In Sacramento, for example, the number of Chinese tripled in the twenty-year period from 1860 to 1880; in San Joaquin their number rose from 139 to almost 2,000; in Santa Clara from 22 to 2,695; in Yolo from 6 to over 600.[3]

While these movements in the interior were under way, a second and more important concentration of Chinese population was developing at San Francisco. Here, until 1860, the resident community had comprised little more than 8 percent of Chinese in the state. By 1870, this percentage had risen to 26 and climbed through the seventies to just under 30 percent. Primary cause of the increase was the growth of manufacture. San Francisco's *Alta*, in 1877, estimated that there were 18,000 Chinese in the city's factories. Aside from manufacture, there were two other pursuits in which Chinese traditionally engaged:

[2] E. L. Sabin, *Building the Pacific Railway* (Philadelphia, 1919), 110–111; United States, Pacific Railway Commission, *Report and Testimony Taken*, 50th Cong. 1st Sess., Sen. Ex. Doc. 51 (Washington, 1888), VI, 3139.

[3] Paul Victor DeFord, "In Defense of Empire: The Southern Pacific versus the Texas Pacific" (M.A. thesis, History, University of California, Berkeley, 1948), 36, 40–41, 51–55; Robert Glass Cleland, *A History of California: The American Period* (New York, 1922), 397; John W. Caughey, *California*, 2d ed. (Englewood Cliffs, N.J., 1953), 260–264; Stuart Jamieson, *Labor Unionism in American Agriculture*, U.S. Bureau of Labor Statistics, *Bulletin No. 836* (Washington, 1945), 45–46; Carey McWilliams, *Factories in the Field* (Boston, 1939), 49–51; Elmer Clarence Sandmeyer, *The Anti-Chinese Movement in California* (Urbana, Ill., 1939), 19, Table 4; Thompson, *Growth and Changes*, 75, Table VII-6; George F. Seward, *Chinese Immigration in its Social and Economical Aspects* (New York, 1881), 30–36; the San Francisco *Daily Alta California*, June 16, August 8, 1867; July 12, 1869; May 2, August 19, 1870; August 30, 1877.

washing and domestic service. Since clothes in need of cleansing and middle class families able to hire servants were probably most plentiful in the metropolis, these also tended to further the urban concentration of Chinese. A police department survey for 1876 reported 5,000 serving as domestics while another 3,000 were employed in washhouses. Wildly inaccurate as these figures apparently are (they add up to more Chinese than the census of 1880 found in the city), they at least warrant a conclusion that large numbers of Chinese actually did follow these lines of work.[4]

Viewing the state as a whole, then, Chinese were found in occupations which required little or no skill, in occupations stigmatized as menial, and in manufacturing. In a general way, the division between Chinese and non-Chinese corresponded to lines of skill or prestige. In the country these lines remained fairly simple, but in the city they became extraordinarily complex. Manufacturing had begun in San Francisco to supply the mining camps; during the Civil War, it flourished under the artificial protection of short supply in the East, lack of transport, and high shipping insurance rates. By 1867, however, and even more disastrously after completion of the railroad in 1869, eastern goods came flooding back into the market. The infant manufactories of the Pacific port either went under or found ways of reducing costs; but the only cost that could really be cut was labor cost. Happily for the industrialists, Chinese were available; and Chinese contract labor seemed to provide an answer to the more advanced techniques and cheaper production costs of the East.[5]

Meanwhile, demobilization and postwar recession, followed by the opening of the railroad, brought a westward migration of workingmen. San Francisco manufacturers, therefore, initiated employment of Chinese under circumstances quite different from those that had prevailed in the hinterland when first the railroad and then the agriculturalists began hiring Chinese. In the country there had been a shortage of labor.[6] In the city, on the contrary, white laborers were seeking

4 In San Francisco County, with a population in 1870 of 149,473, Chinese represented 8 percent of the total; in the state as a whole they were 8.7 percent. The Census of 1880 reported 21,745 Chinese in San Francisco. Sandmeyer, *Anti-Chinese Movement*, 17, 19, 21; Thompson, *Growth and Changes*, Appendix, 333, Table 1. On the development of the Chinese urban community, see Gunther Barth, *Bitter Strength: A History of the Chinese in the United States, 1850–1870* (Cambridge, Mass., 1964), 105–114; *Alta*, May 27, 1876; December 27, 28, 1877.

5 Hubert Howe Bancroft, *History of California* (Vol. XXIV, *Works*, San Francisco, 1890), VII; Ira B. Cross, *A History of the Labor Movement in California* (Berkeley, 1935), 30–31, 63–64, 79–86; *Alta*, May 6, 1867; June 24, 1869.

6 Cross, 61, 69; U.S., Pacific Railway Commission, *Report and Testimony*, VI, 3224; U.S., Congress, *Report of the Special Joint Committee to Investigate Chinese*

work. Because they could not live as cheaply as Chinese, they were unable to compete directly; but their organizational skills partially compensated for this disability. They had succeeded, by 1867, in mounting a campaign of moral, political, and economic pressure against the employment of Chinese which was proving moderately effective. Employers who could afford to yield generally preferred to do so. The line between those who could yield and those who could not was simply the line between those whose products sold in a market that was only locally competitive and those whose products came into competition with wares shipped from the East.

Cigar making and building construction offer an example of this separation. Despite the dissimilarity of their products, the two industries had several characteristics in common: small employers predominated in both due to the low threshold of necessary investment; these employers were dependent on skilled craftsmen, yet had work as well for apprentices or unskilled laborers. In cigar making, Chinese took over the trade almost completely. In construction, on the other hand, Chinese were totally excluded. The moment of decision in this respect seems to have occurred during the winter of 1867 when some four hundred white workingmen attacked a group of Chinese who were excavating for a street railway. The crowd stoned the Chinese, maimed several, and burned their shanties. Afterward, alleged leaders of the riot were jailed and the Chinese resumed work under armed guard.[7] But the demonstration had made its point. Throughout the long record of anti-Oriental agitation which followed, there appears little if any reference to Chinese as construction laborers in San Francisco or its environs. The evidence is negative, but conclusive: had there been Chinese in this line of work their presence would have been stressed rather than minimized.

Thus in the national market industry—cigar making—Chinese took over both skilled and unskilled operations; in the local market industry—building—they were excluded from both. This became the urban pattern. In the country, however, where white workers remained in short supply, white unemployed seldom gathered into crowds large enough to be intimidating or were concentrated in sufficient numbers to exert much voting power. Lines of skill and prestige, in the country, continued more decisive than conditions of market competition; consequently, Chinese laborers were able to play a prominent part in

Immigration, 44th Cong., 2nd Sess., Senate Report 689 (Washington, 1877), 723–728; Chiu, *Chinese Labor*, 46–47.

[7] Cross, 136–137, 147, 169–172; Coolidge, *Chinese Immigration*, 359, 399; *Alta*, February 13, 14, 17, 19, 1867; May 27, 1876.

agricultural work and heavy construction for another twenty years at least.[8]

In summary, the Chinese during the seventies and early eighties comprised about one-twelfth of the inhabitants both of California and of San Francisco. Having earlier been largely occupied at placer mining, they were moving now into heavy construction and farm labor, and into manufacturing. These changes of occupation caused shifts in concentration of Chinese population from the mountain districts to the great valleys and to the San Francisco Bay area. In the hinterland, Chinese were generally restricted to unskilled positions as agricultural and construction workers; in the city they were generally restricted to "sweated" trades, the products of which entered tightly competitive national markets.

Before turning, however, to the non-Chinese components of the labor force, it may be well to consider two additional factors which deeply affected the relations between Chinese and non-Chinese.

First, while Chinese were only one-twelfth of total population, they comprised a much larger fraction of the labor force. The 1870 census estimated California's gainfully employed as 239,000 in a population of somewhat over 570,000. There were, by the same count, slightly fewer than 50,000 Chinese, almost all of whom must, as a necessary condition of their coming to California, have been gainfully employed. If we exclude Chinese women (one in every thirteen), we find that Chinese males constituted approximately one-fifth of the total number of persons gainfully employed. But even this figure is too small. The census category included entrepreneurs, independent farmers, supervisors, businessmen—and these we can assume to have been more numerous among non-Chinese than among the Chinese. If then our concern is primarily with wage workers, it would probably not be far wrong to estimate that one-quarter of all available for hire in the early seventies must have been Chinese.[9]

The second factor is that the large contingent of Chinese within the labor force was tightly and exclusively organized. All accounts seem to agree that the Chinese came to California in organized groups; that they were received by the Six Companies in San Francisco and housed, fed, and sent off to their various places of employment. At the

8 Jamieson, *Labor Unionism*, 43–50; *Alta*, May 26, 1873.

9 McEntire, "Economic Study of Population Movements" (above, n. 1), 186; Sandmeyer, *Anti-Chinese Movement*, 17. My own estimate is based on McEntire, 154, and Robert Joseph Pitchell, "Twentieth Century California Voting Behavior" (Ph.D. diss., Political Science, University of California, Berkeley, 1955), 68. Pitchell's tabulation is credited to Frank L. Kidner, *California Business Cycles* (Berkeley, 1946), 15.

bottom of this organizational structure were the laborers. Above them was an assortment of gang foremen, agents, and interpreters. At the top were the Chinese merchants of San Francisco who, as directors of the Six Companies, represented or were associated with even wealthier merchants and businessmen in China. The resident merchants in San Francisco dealt, more or less on a basis of equality, with American interests desirous of securing contract labor. Most spectacular of such recruitments were those undertaken for the western railroads beginning with the Central Pacific; but an extraordinary variety of employers—including San Francisco factory owners, California farmers, land improvement companies, Southern planters, railroad promoters in Southern states, even a shoe manufacturer in North Adams, Massachusetts, and a laundry operator in New Jersey—entered into similar arrangements.[10]

Essential to such a system of recruitment and employment was strict internal discipline. Contracts had to be honored and advances of passage money repaid. Yet any legal machinery for the enforcement of labor contracts was lacking. The Chinese organization therefore enforced its own regulations, adjudicated disputes, punished transgressors. While all this was, in terms of American law, not only extralegal but illegal, the American courts and police authorities actually served as bulwarks for the entire structure. For many years the Six Companies kept a special Chinatown contingent of San Francisco policemen on their payroll. They also retained competent lawyers who were frequently in court seeking the apprehension of runaway laborers or sing-song girls on complaints of petty theft which would later be withdrawn. As final capstone to this structure, the Six Companies maintained an unwritten protocol with shipping lines to the effect that no Chinese would be booked passage *out* of California unless he carried a clearance from the Six Companies. It was a tight system.[11]

But had the sole function been that of requiring obedience, the apparatus probably would not have lasted long in America. Actually it conveyed many positive benefits. It served as insurance society and bank. It made the years of labor in exile tolerable by providing a social club, companionship, recreation, women occasionally, familiar food, a link with the homeland. It offered protection against the menace from outside. When four Chinese woodcutters were shot to death near

10 Barth, *Bitter Strength,* 99–100, 189–209; U.S., Senate Report 689, pp. 674–676; Stanford M. Lyman, "The Structure of Chinese Society in Nineteenth Century America" (Ph.D. diss., University of California, Berkeley, 1961), 78–80, 217–218, 399–403; Robert L. Fulton, *Epic of the Overland* (Los Angeles, 1924), 33–35; *Alta,* June 24, 1869; July 21, 1870.

11 U.S., Senate Report 689, pp. 82, 675–676; Barth, 98–100, 136–139; Sandmeyer, *Anti-Chinese Movement,* 62; *Alta,* March 31, 1876.

Chico in 1877, the Six Companies offered a reward for the names of the killers and sent a private detective into the area, who, with the assistance of Colonel Frederick A. Bee, the Companies' attorney, played a leading part in the arrest and conviction of the murderers. Bee, in addition to frequent rounds in court, appeared for the Chinese before various governmental agencies and was appointed Chinese consul in San Francisco. From top to bottom, the Chinese establishment in America had something in it for everybody. To the Cantonese peasant it offered escape from a depressed and hopelessly overcrowded country-side—and always the distant chance of coming home again with enough California gold to redeem all the lost promises of youth. As one ascended the levels of the apparatus, benefits became less promissory and more tangible, till at the highest level the merchant entrepreneurs on both sides of the Pacific seem to have been impounding very real profits indeed.[12]

Essentially this structure was vertical. Stressing the common heritage of language and culture, it linked individual members from top to bottom across class lines. Yet clearly the prime purpose of the entire apparatus was the exploitation of cheap labor in a high-priced labor market. One would expect, therefore, to find horizontal fault lines in the vertical structure; and there were in fact hints of such fissures. During construction of the Central Pacific, for example, Chinese laborers conducted a brief strike which Charles Crocker ascribed to paid agitators sent in by the rival railroad, the Union Pacific.[13] San Francisco's *Daily Alta* in the summer of 1873 reported a successful strike by Chinese crewmen on steamers of the Pacific Mail Line. Both these cases involved conflicts with white employers; yet given the nature of the contract system, a dispute with the white employer would be likely to lead to a collision between Chinese workingmen and the Chinese labor contractor.

This seems to have been the situation that brought on a "bloody fight" one March afternoon in Dupont Street, when the Chinatown police detail had to send for reinforcements and later for an express wagon to carry away the wounded. A Chinese trading company, which doubled as a labor contractor, had agreed to place some 750 men in the shoe factories of Einstein Brothers and of Buckingham, Hecht, and Company. As guarantee of performance, the shoe manufacturers required a sizable deposit, which the contractor in turn extracted from

---

12 Barth, 98, 120–128; San Francisco *Examiner*, March 27, 29; May 26, 1877; *The Bay of San Francisco, the Metropolis of the Pacific Coast, a History*, 2 vols. (Chicago, 1892), II, 491–493; F. A. Bee, *Opening Argument of F. A. Bee before the Joint Committee of the Two Houses of Congress on Chinese Immigration* (San Francisco, 1876).
13 Barth, 93–107, 120; U.S., Senate Report 689, p. 669; *Alta*, May 26, 1873.

his laborers in sums ranging from twenty-five to one hundred dollars apiece. Afterward, in the opinion at least of the laborers, Einstein Brothers and Buckingham, Hecht reneged on the terms of the agreement. The laborers struck the jobs, then attempted to recover their deposits. Neither the manufacturers nor the labor contractor would return the money. Apparently this dispute had been carried to higher tribunals within the Chinese establishment, but without resolution. The laborers finally armed themselves and attempted settlement by direct action.[14]

These three episodes, though of no great importance in themselves, when taken together make up a revealing microcosm of the way in which the system operated and of the social roles played by the various participants. Undoubtedly there were class conflicts within this structure; and these, under certain circumstances, might have shattered it. Meanwhile, on all sides, the non-Chinese contingents of the labor force were organizing along horizontal lines; that is, they were setting up trade unions and political bodies which rallied workingmen as opposed to employers. One of the accusations frequently made by non-Chinese against their Asiatic fellow workers was that they were too docile, too slave-like, to be able ever to stand on their own feet in a free society.[15] But the greater the pressure from outside, the more cohesive became the vertical structure of the Chinese establishment, and the more unlikely any horizontal cleavage within it.

The Non-Chinese

If one-quarter of California's wage workers were Chinese, who were the other three-quarters? Again we are reduced to rather rough estimates. Excluding Chinese, approximately 28 percent of the inhabitants of the state in 1870 were foreign-born—one-third of these being Irish, one-fifth German or Austrian, and another fifth of generally Anglo-Scotch extraction. But the proportion of foreign-born (still leaving aside Chinese) would certainly have been higher among wage earners than for the general population. This would apply with particular force to the Irish, who being latecomers had less opportunity than others to move out of the working class by acquiring farms or businesses.[16]

14 *Alta*, March 1, 1876.
15 *Examiner*, March 19, 1877.
16 McEntire, "Economic Study of Population Movements," 80–86, 154. J. D. Borthwick, in his journal of travels in California first published in Edinburgh, 1857, was struck by the absence of Irish workingmen, which he ascribed to the

On the basis of these figures and assumptions, it becomes possible to make a reasonable guess as to the composition by nativity of the wage-earning labor force in California in 1870:

Native American	40%
Chinese	25%
Irish	15%
German (or Austrian)	6%
English, Scotch, Welsh, Anglo-Canadian	6%
Other foreign-born	8%

But in this context place of birth is less significant than linguistic and ethnic background. The category of native American included many children of immigrant parents. Especially this must have been true for those from the New England and central Atlantic areas where immigration had been heaviest. Perhaps, then, the best answer that can be given to the question regarding the origins of California's non-Chinese wage earners is that, as of 1870, well over half must have been immigrant or first generation, with Irish and Germans strongly predominating, and that the old stock Americans would have formed a rather small minority, perhaps not more than 30 percent. The most striking aspect is diversity. And yet, contained within that diversity, were experiences held profoundly in common.

An Irish-American aged forty-five in 1870 would have been twenty at the time of the potato famine. Had he then been in Ireland, he would have seen and might have experienced starvation. His voyage to America would have been made in the cargo hold of some New England lumber scow or more elegantly in the steerage of a paddle wheel steamer; and not more than 10 percent of the passengers on the average would have died in transit. If he were luckier he might have arrived in America before the famine years, yet was inevitably involved in that disaster. He would have encountered the refugees, heard their stories, known them individually when they came to roost in his already Irish neighborhood.[17]

For Germans the pattern was much the same. Germany too had its peasant population subsisting on fractional holdings, burdened with a complex structure of rents and tithes, dependent on the potato. There too, in the late forties, the blight struck. The journey to the

general poverty of Irish immigrants and their inability to finance the journey to the Pacific Coast. (Borthwick, *The Gold Hunters* [New York, 1917], 68; and see Coolidge, *Chinese Immigration*, 359.)

[17] Oscar Handlin, *The Uprooted* (Boston, 1951), 37–62; Marcus Lee Hansen, *The Atlantic Migration, 1607–1860: A History of the Continuing Settlement of the United States* (New York, 1961), 243–251, 256–258.

sea was longer for the Germans and involved crossing borders where
they might be held up at the checkpoints or turned back as indigents.
Those who reached the ports faced the same delays while savings and
health eroded, and the steerage passage, and confrontation with America at last—and their ordeal had only begun.[18]

This experience of uprooting, Oscar Handlin wrote, was one that
"each mind would forever mark as its most momentous. . . . The
crossing immediately subjected the immigrant to a succession of shattering shocks and decisively conditioned the life of every man that survived it." [19] A great many did, in fact, survive it. The total foreign-born
in the population of the United States rose from two and a quarter
million in 1850 to more than four million at the start of the Civil
War. Of these, a million and a half were Irish, approximately a million
and a quarter German.[20] The remaining million and a quarter were
of many different origins, languages, religions; but the impact of uprooting and alienation would have been much the same for all. This
was part of the baggage of all foreign-born who came to California.

But it was not all. Nothing so provokes man's inhumanity to his fellow men as their misfortunes. Native Americans regarded the influx
of foreigners first with anxiety, then with hatred. Throughout three
decades prior to the Civil War a barrage of sermons, books, newspaper
articles made known to immigrants that their religion, their language,
their food and dress, their very existence as willing wage earners were
objects of offense and contempt. Propaganda of the word was generously salted with propaganda of the deed. A mob in the summer of
1834 destroyed the Ursuline school and convent at Charleston, Massachusetts. Ten years later native Philadelphians were burning down
Catholic churches and blocks of houses in the Irish suburbs. Through
the mid-fifties, Americans in Ohio and Indiana raided German picnics,
stormed meeting halls, fought pitched battles with Germans in the
streets.[21] These were only the notorious episodes; the background of
petty violence, endlessly condoned and renewed, became one of the
circumstances of urban life in the cities of the eastern seaboard and
midwest. For the immigrants, after their bad luck in the old country,
and after having read or at least heard the rumor that in America

[18] Hansen, 211–225, 252.
[19] Handlin, 38.
[20] Hansen, 280.
[21] Ray Allen Billington, *The Protestant Crusade, 1800–1860: A Study of the
Origins of American Nativism* (Gloucester, Mass., 1963), 1–14, 22–37, 53–84; John
Higham, *Strangers in the Land: Patterns of American Nativism, 1860–1925* (New
York, 1963), 3–11; Carl Wittke, *Refugees of Revolution: The German Forty-Eighters
in America* (Philadelphia, 1952), 177–189.

all men could engage equally in the pursuit of happiness, it came inevitably as a crowning shock to find themselves among the pursued rather than the pursuers.

Old stock Americans also were traveling to California (where they would furnish, as noted earlier, between one-quarter and one-third of the non-Chinese labor force); so that the tension between immigrant and old stock became part of the western scene as it had been of the eastern. Yet California seems to have exerted a curiously cosmopolitan effect upon these newcomers. Superficially at least the tension was muted, and this permitted what was shared by all in common to make itself felt. What was shared was the sense of displacement and victimization. For the fact was that any native American still working for wages in California in 1870 had also suffered a displacement, albeit less violent than that of the immigrants.

Of the old stock from rural backgrounds, most would have come from that portion which had been rolling westward through several generations, in flight from constant encroachment of a more complex and commercialized community. Displacement had been turned into a way of life, each man's sons moving out to the adjacent counties at the western fringe till they made the final jump, which was California. But agriculture in California was already more complex and commercialized than anything they had left behind. For many of them, failure was foreordained.

Those who came from the cities were likely to have been displaced by industrialization. The expansion of markets which followed the successive transportation revolutions of the forties and fifties had demanded reorganization of small-scale shop work into mass production. Reorganization led into technological change; and these together wiped out many established skills and pushed great segments of the production process into the hands of unskilled workers. A classic example of this sequence is furnished by the shoemaking industry. Here, within a period of seven years, an organization of craftsmen, the Knights of St. Crispin, rose to national membership of 50,000, then totally disintegrated. The dynamic of the union's rise and the cause of its destruction were the same: introduction of new machinery and the employment of unskilled hands.[22]

In less dramatic form, many other industries—among them the metal trades, typesetting, clothing manufacture, window glass, and bottle making—showed similar tendencies. The unskilled labor market, during earlier years, had been largely supplied by the children of already established urban workers and by the flow of young people from the country into the city. But in the forties and fifties this market was invaded by immigrants, especially Irish, who in their desperation had no choice but to underbid any going wage level. The result was that the old stock had faced a double squeeze. If skilled, they frequently found their skills rendered obsolete by technological change; if unskilled, they were forced to compete with an ever-growing army of hungry foreigners. Here was the economic basis of nativist hostility to the European immigrant.[23]

Yet in California, where even the nativist was a stranger and newcomer, these hostilities were transferred and largely focused upon other objects.[24]

Since the white population of the state had increased by 88 percent between 1860 and 1870, it would seem reasonable to suppose that most of the non-Chinese labor force, as of the early seventies, must have come west during or after the Civil War. But there remained a portion which had come earlier and which was perhaps more influential than its numbers would imply; the forty-niners. Actually the significance is not in the year of arrival, but in the experience of that brief arcadian interlude, the first surface mining of the foothills. The moment itself was gone in a flash, say by 1854; but the men who took part in it were marked. What became of them? Some gave up and went home.[25] A few (among them, for example, Leland Stanford and Charles Crocker) emerged as prosperous businessmen. Others got out of mining early enough to acquire handsome tracts of California land. As easy pickings dwindled in the foothills, a large number moved on, searching for new bonanzas in Nevada, Colorado, Montana. Finally, there was a residue that failed to get out, or perhaps crossed the mountains with the first backwash to try their luck on the Comstock and failed to get out there. For these men the only path was the descent from the status of gold hunters—independent entrepreneurs—to that of wage workers.

After the exhaustion of California's surface diggings, mining had shifted to deep quartz operations or to fluming and hydraulicking. Capital investment necessary for these processes was far beyond the

23 Maldwyn Allen Jones, *American Immigration* (Chicago, 1960), 130; Billington, 334, 338.

24 Leonard Pitt, "The Beginnings of Nativism in California," *Pacific Historical Review*, XXX (February, 1961), 23–38.

25 McEntire, "Economic Study of Population Movements," 154; Jaquelin Smith Holliday, "The California Gold Rush in Myth and Reality" (Ph.D. diss., History, University of California, Berkeley, 1959), 348–356.

capability of individual miners or even such partnerships as had been customary during the pan and placer period. In San Francisco enormous sums were raised for excavation and timbering, for setting up quartz mills, for building water systems. The heyday of the joint stock company was beginning; within less than two decades the capitalists from the city had taken over the mines in the mountains.[26] For the miner this descent was like the fall of Adam. The garden would appear to him in the remembered images of California as it had been in the early fifties:

> After prospecting a little we soon found a spot on the bank of a stream which we judged would yield us pretty fair pay for our labor; . . . we soon got everything in working order, and pitched in. The gold which we found here was of the finest kind. . . . It was a wild rocky place where we now located. . . . The nearest village or settlement was about ten miles distant; and all the miners on the Creek . . . living in isolated cabins, tents and brush houses, or camping out on the rocks, resorted for provisions to the small store already mentioned. . . . The sky was always bright and cloudless. . . . In the hottest weather in California it is always agreeably cool at night.[27]

Yet less than twenty years later the real world had come to stay:

> The morning shift goes on at seven o'clock. Before descending the shaft the men go to the office of the time-keeper, situated in the hoisting works, and give their names at a window that resembles that of the ticket-office at a railroad station. . . . Our underground streets are not wanting in life. . . . We meet with the people of the place at every turn. Our mine connects with another and so we have streets three miles long. There are employed in a single mine from five hundred to seven hundred men, a number sufficient to populate a town of considerable size. . . . We seem to have been suddenly brought face to face with a new and strange race of men. All are naked to the waist . . . drenched with perspiration, and their bodies glisten in the light of the candles as though they had just come up through the waters of some subterranean lake.[28]

It is impossible to describe this transition without oversimplifying it. Different strands of experience merge and interact. For the hard-rock miner, checking his time card, working his shift, collecting his weekly

[26] Dan De Quille [William Wright], *The Big Bonanza* (New York, 1953), 115–124, 377–384, 399–408.
[27] Borthwick, *Gold Hunters*, 141–143.
[28] De Quille, 247–248.

wage, the sense of the earlier period was still present. Prospectors were
always drifting through town; he could meet them in the bars; occasionally they struck something good. More than likely he himself had
not reached the West Coast till the placer mining days were long
passed, yet he knew them vicariously because the recollections of others
remained so intense. Afterward, in retrospect, it was not so much the
gold, which had all slipped through the fingers anyway; it was the
freedom of movement, the newness, the magnificent bounty and opportunity. Illusions though these may have been, their vanishing left
a taste of tragedy.

In 1870 almost every adult in California had come a journey to get
there. These journeys may have varied in difficulty, but they had all
involved labor and sacrifice. In a psychological sense, a journey is a
moratorium: so long as the journey continues the traveler may reasonably believe that something new and a great deal better will crop
up at the next turning. He therefore strains every effort; but once
arrived, he is brought face to face with his real situation. He must
either make the best of it, whatever it is, or keep on traveling. For
most Californians, however, there was no place further to go. Literally
and symbolically, San Francisco was the end of the line. The euphoria
of the early days had veiled this meaning; but as San Francisco grew
into a city, and the great valleys developed into agricultural empires;
as the routines of factory and farm became the norm; and as, after the
war and completion of the railroad, hard times settled over the state,
frustration replaced euphoria.[29] Small farmers and workingmen especially were embittered because they felt themselves once already displaced and deprived. Here too it was to be the same story over again.
And as for that vicariously remembered image in which the land and
its good things were supposed to have lain open to all comers, how
could that have been taken away unless some enemy had conspired
against them?

> The land is fast passing into the hands of the rich few; great
> money monopolies control congress, purchase the state legisla-
> tures, and have perverted the great republic of our fathers into
> a den of dishonest manipulators. This concentration and con-
> trol of wealth has impoverished the people, producing crime
> and discontent.[30]

[29] Holliday, "California Gold Rush."
[30] From a resolution adopted by the first state convention of the Workingmen's
Party of California, January 24, 1878. (See Winfield J. Davis, *History of Political
Conventions in California* [Sacramento, 1893], 379.)

Boundaries of Consensus

Displacement, then, and deprivation whether real or fancied, and the psychological pitch of the westward journey and its ensuing frustration—these were common denominators underlying the multiplicity of the non-Chinese labor force. Men who could not understand each other's talk—Irish and German, Catholic and Protestant, urban and rural, immigrant and native—all shared these elements of experience.

But so did the Chinese. They too had suffered deprivation and displacement; they had come a long journey, and some of them had good reason to be disappointed in California after they got there. Yet they were not included in the developing unity of the California labor force. Why?

One reason lay within the Chinese themselves. They viewed their journey as a round trip. Most Chinese were birds of passage, "sojourners" in America,[31] whose conscious intent was to stay a little while, save a little money, and return to the nest. Whatever happened to them in California would be incidental to a further goal, and they were therefore less vulnerable to frustration than their non-Chinese fellow workers and less impelled to expend energy in resisting abuses. The greater the abuse, the stronger would be their inclination to hurry along to the final destination. But the most promising road in that direction led through the Chinese establishment. Thus the sojourner frame of mind reinforced the vertical structure of Chinese organization; and this stood diametrically opposed to those horizontal forms through which non-Chinese workingmen were attempting to express their hopes and their anger.

But the basic factor was lack of communication. Common denominators of past experience could have no meaning apart from some shared understanding of them, and between Chinese and non-Chinese there was none. The absence was not solely due to language and cultural differences. Many such differences existed between groups of European immigrants, as well as between new and old stock Americans. Nor was it due only to economic rivalry. The same accusations of cheapness directed against Chinese were also made against immigrant laborers, especially Irish, in the East. And even with respect to California, it would be difficult to argue that Chinese were a great deal cheaper than some of the European newcomers.

What lay beneath all these rationalizations was a psychological bar-

[31] Barth, *Bitter Strength* (above, n. 4) 1–4.

rier which foreclosed any exchange of experience. The barrier resulted from a concept of fundamental differentness. How this idea had
taken shape, in the minds at least of non-Chinese workingmen, will be
the subject of the next chapter. Here it need simply be pointed out
that the concept, later to be gigantically reinforced, was present from
the earliest days. Colville's *Gazeteer of San Francisco,* published in
1856 but referring to the year 1851, described the Chinese as "unique."
Their appearance seemed devised "to make people wonder"—the
writer thus established a dichotomy between *Chinese* on one hand and
people on the other—"to make people wonder that nature and custom
should so combine to manufacture so much individual ugliness." On
the same page he spoke of Chinese women as "the most degraded and
beastly of all human creatures." [32] He had apparently not yet made
up his mind whether Chinese were or were not of the human condition; but that they were different and "degraded" was beyond question.

Among workingmen especially this proposition became self-evident.
The outstanding common characteristic of all those disparate elements
which composed the non-Chinese labor force was that they were not
Chinese. Aspirant leaders engaged in a search for facts or fictions to
express the values of non-Chineseness. Christianity would be stressed in
contrast to the earlier (and eastern) focus on the Catholic-Protestant
cleavage. Assimilability was on the point of being discovered—that
mysterious substance which resided in the circulatory systems of persons having certain ancestries and which rendered them desirable as
neighbors, sons-in-law, fellow workers, even as voters. The words
assimilable, white, and the pseudo-scientific term *caucasian,* just then
coming into fashion, would be taken as equivalents. Before the decade
of the seventies was out, there would be California workingmen,
styling themselves brothers in the Order of Caucasians, who would
undertake the systematic killing of Chinese in order to preserve their
assimilable fellow toilers from total ruin.[33]

[32] Samuel Colville, *Colville's San Francisco Directory and Gazetteer, 1856–1857*
(San Francisco, 1856), xxv.
[33] *Examiner,* March 23, 27–31, April 2, 3, 5, 10, 21, 25, 26, May 29, 1877.

2

IDEOLOGICAL BAGGAGE

The impression of Chinese quoted at the end of the last chapter from a San Francisco gazeteer of the mid-1850s indicates the speed and precision with which uniqueness could be equated with racial inferiority. Hinton Helper, the North Carolina yeoman soon to become a chief Republican polemicist against slavery, wrote of the Chinese he saw on the Pacific Coast in 1852 that they were "semibarbarians" having no more business to be in California than "flocks of blackbirds have in a wheat field." "No inferior race of men can exist in these United States without becoming subordinate to the will of the Anglo-Americans. . . . It is so with the Negroes in the South; it is so with the Irish in the North; it is so with the Indians in New England; and it will be so with the Chinese in California. . . . I should not wonder, at all," he predicted, "if the copper of the Pacific yet becomes as great a subject of discord and dissension as the ebony of the Atlantic." [1]

Helper, it seems clear, was proceeding not by discovery but by analogy. He was replaying the script of an older drama. Rather abundant evidence indicates that most newcomers from the East to California reacted in the same manner as Helper. Their responses were largely shaped by previous responses to Indians, to immigrants, and especially to Negroes and Negro slaves. The numerous expulsions of Chinese from mine camps and the anti-Chinese ordinances written into the codes of local mining districts duplicated actions already taken against blacks. One of the earliest efforts to exclude Chinese from California by state law was passed in the Assembly as companion piece to a measure barring entry of Negroes. Both were modeled on the black codes of midwestern states which had been widely discussed in California at least since the debates over slavery and Negro exclusion in

1 Hinton R. Helper, *The Land of Gold: Reality versus Fiction* (Baltimore, 1855), 94–96.

the Constitutional Convention of 1849.[2] Or, turning to a different line of evidence, the well-known stereotype of the "Heathen Chinee" found its way into the American theater (almost twenty years before Bret Harte's famous poem) by way of black face minstrel shows; and comic Chinese characters in wild west melodrama were experimentally paired with black sambos.[3]

Deeply enmeshed in traditional value systems and behavioral patterns, the social experience underlying these identifications formed part of the enormous ideological baggage of Jacksonian America. It would be convenient if the content of this baggage could be sorted in accordance wtih some useful classification of the men who carried it. What would be most helpful, of course, in order to round out the examination undertaken in the last chapter of conflict and consensus within the California labor force, would be a classification by economic status. Unfortunately, that seems impractical. There was too much upward and downward mobility, and moreover there was nothing in America, or in California, in those years that could be described as the exclusive outlook of a particular class. Some patterns of behavior and some sets of ideas would spread more widely than the labor force; others would be restricted to smaller groups within it. Since the subject under consideration centrally involves political ideas and activities, it seems reasonable to begin by arranging the major and minor tendencies which comprised this ideological baggage in terms of political affinities.

"Americans of all classes," wrote the English traveler Borthwick, who visited California in 1852, "are particularly *au fait* at the ordinary routine of public meetings." Impressed by what seemed to him the remarkable ability of miners at improvising parliamentary pro-

[2] Eugene H. Berwanger, *The Frontier Against Slavery: Western Anti-Negro Prejudice and the Slavery Extension Controversy* (Urbana, Ill., 1967), 60–77; Carl Wheat (ed.), "California's Bantam Cock: The Journal of Charles E. De Long, 1854–1863," *California Historical Society Quarterly*, IX (September, 1930) 256–258, 281–283; below, pp. 50–60. Stuart C. Miller in *The Unwelcome Immigrant: American Images of Chinese, 1785–1882* (Berkeley, 1969), argues that the response to Chinese immigration was shaped by a negative image of the Chinese imprinted in the American mind since colonial times by the hostile accounts of travelers, traders, missionaries and editors. Miller's evidence is interesting and persuasive; but I remain convinced, as I have argued in this chapter, that the main dynamic came from the historic experience with blacks and slavery.

[3] Stuart W. Hyde, "The Chinese Stereotype in American Melodrama," *California Historical Society Quarterly*, XXXIV (December, 1955), 357–365; George C. D. Odell, *Annals of the New York Stage*, 15 vols. (New York, 1931), VI, 585–586; James J. McCloskey, "Across the Continent, or, Scenes from New York Life and the Pacific Railroad," in Isaac Goldberg and Hubert Heffner (eds.), *Davy Crockett and Other Plays* (Princeton, 1940), 65–114; Augustin Daly, "Horizon," in Allan Gates Halline (ed.), *American Plays* (New York, 1935), 339.

cedure and drawing up codes to govern everything from horse stealing to riparian rights, Borthwick speculated on how they came by so much political know-how: "They are trained to it from their youth in their innumerable, and to a foreigner unintelligible, caucus meetings, committees and conventions, and so forth, by means of which they bring about the election of every officer in the State." [4] Many witnesses have corroborated this impression of the public focus of American life.[5] Politics was a language in which most Americans were fluent and in which they were accustomed to express their economics, their ethics, their emotions, even their religions.

The Major Traditions: Democratic

In 1869 most Californians were Democrats or Republicans. The Democratic tradition was oldest. It took Jefferson for its father figure and the Declaration of Independence as revelation. What was revealed was necessarily self-evident, and this included the proposition that nature's reasonable and benevolent deity had created all men equal—not in every respect, but in the moral sense, as human beings. Consequently, all men were endowed with certain inalienable rights, among them life, liberty, and pursuit of happiness. Did the "all" include blacks? Jefferson himself had been uncertain or negative on this point.[6] Yet he had written no exclusion into the Declaration and that was how the mandate stood—*all*. Aside from this ambiguity the Jeffersonian vision was crystal clear: Independent small farmers would comprise the majority in the Republic; these being close to the earth and therefore incorruptible would serve as value carriers, as champions against the constant encroachment of urban wealth and special privilege.

But as the young Republic grew older, its cities gained population more rapidly than the countryside and interests other than agrarian rose to prominence. It became necessary to expand the concept of value carriers to include not only yeomen farmers but producers of all sorts—"the productive and burthen-bearing classes," in the words of

---

[4] J. D. Borthwick, *The Gold Hunters* (New York, 1917), 155, 347–348.

[5] For example, see Charles Howard Shinn, *Mining Camps: A Study in American Frontier Government* (New York, 1948), 215–216; Josiah Royce, *California, from the Conquest in 1846 to the Second Vigilance Committee in San Francisco: A Study of American Character* (Boston and New York, 1891), 327–328; Alexis de Tocqueville, *Democracy in America*, 2 vols. (New York, 1961), I, 216–226.

[6] Nathan Schachner, *Thomas Jefferson: A Biography* (New York, 1957), 153–155, 231–232; Thomas Jefferson, *Notes on the State of Virginia* (New York, 1964), 132–138.

Senator Thomas Hart Benton, the great Missouri agrarian. What was intended by the term "productive" remained flexible, and here was one of its chief advantages. Clearly, it included farmers, independent artisans, workingmen. Yet it might also comprise businessmen, promoters, manufacturers, especially if they had ever laid hands on a tool and if their politics tended in the right direction. Lumped with the enemy were most bankers and all monopolists—those masters of "great moneyed corporations" against which the "bone and sinew of our country" must wage relentless warfare.[7]

This producer concept was one of the works of the Jacksonian "revolution" in that it described elements of society among which Jacksonians hoped to find support. Whether the "revolution" really was a revolution, and whether it was Jacksonian, and whether its driving force came from frontier farmers, from workingmen, or from aspiring entrepreneurs are questions that need not detain us here. The point is that city dwellers, including craftsmen and laborers, assumed a new importance in politics. During the first Jackson administration, through local unions and independent workingmen's parties, they pressed for higher wages and shorter hours of labor; and they campaigned for such egalitarian goals as free public education, mechanics' lien laws, abolition of imprisonment for debt and of prison labor contracting. They supported the removal of property qualifications from the suffrage and echoed the arguments of western agrarians like Benton for free land as a cure-all of the nation's ills. Workingmen's parties and unions both quickly disintegrated; but the disintegration was in part a process of absorption by the major parties. The main flux, drawn by the bank war, by hard money slogans, by the crusade against monopoly, merged into the Democratic apparatus. In New York, labor politicians briefly won control of Tammany and afterward kept a strong foothold there; while the name of one of their factions, Locofoco, entered the national vocabulary as a term (usually applied invidiously by its enemies) to describe the alliance of the northern Democracy with workingmen in the cities.[8]

[7] Thomas Hart Benton to a Democratic convention in Mississippi, 1834, cited in William Nisbet Chambers, *Old Bullion Benton, Senator from the New West* (Boston, 1956), 203; "Jackson's Farewell Address," in James D. Richardson, *A Compilation of the Messages and Papers of the Presidents* (New York, 1897–), IV, 1524.

[8] In the many-sided debate over the relationship between labor and Jacksonian Democracy, there seems at least to have been agreement on the growing importance of urban working-class politics. A convenient summary of the literature will be found in Edward Pessen, *Most Uncommon Jacksonians* (Albany, N.Y., 1967), 3–51. See also Walter E. Hugins, *Jacksonian Democracy and the Working Class* (Stanford, 1960); Helene Zahler, *Eastern Workingmen and National Land Policy, 1829–1862* (New York, 1941); Arthur M. Schlesinger, Jr., *The Age of Jackson* (Boston, 1945),

The tone of all this was egalitarian. It stemmed from the Declaration and the original Jeffersonian vision. And it was contagious if for no other reason than because it was politically successful. By the 1850s the concept of the producers' Republic embattled against monopolists was firmly planted in the Middle West and was making its way to the Pacific with every wagon train that crossed the plains.[9] It would shape the style of the nascent Republican party as well as renovate that of the old Democracy.

In human affairs, however, there seems to be a law of the dissipation of principle according to which the daily life of any established organization tends to erode its declaratory faith. By the time California entered the union, the Democratic party had been in existence a great many years. Unmistakably the dominant party, it had controlled the federal government with only two exceptions since 1829 and would continue its control for another decade. Yet it remained in a sense prisoner of its own success. The southern wing of the party, having virtually eliminated effective opposition within its own region, held the key to each national election. For southerners this control seemed crucial to the preservation of their slave-plantation economy. Slavery itself, obviously, was incompatible with the egalitarian mandate of the Declaration upon which the entire party had its ideological foundation. Endeavoring to escape this dilemma, the South had worked out its series of rationalizations, economic, political, moral, and religious.[10] But the net result of all rationalizations, and in fact the only thing that could make any of them tenable, was the conclusion that the Declaration had been mistaken. The Negro was not created equal. Sad to say, he lacked the abilities to compete with superior white men in the pursuit of happiness, and it therefore became the moral obligation of white men to protect him from his own weakness and from exploitation by other whites less scrupulous than themselves.

This argument needs no repeating except to point out the effect on Democratic partisans in the North. The attack upon slavery, emanating from whiggish social bases in New England, upstate New York, and the Old Northwest, posed an increasingly divisive threat to north-

---

177–209. On early labor ideology, see Maurice Neufeld, "Realms of Thought and Organized Labor in the Age of Jackson," *Labor History*, X (Winter, 1969), 5–43.

[9] Chester M. Destler, *American Radicalism, 1865–1901: Essays and Documents* (New London, Conn., 1946), "Western Radicalism," 1–31; Schlesinger, *Age of Jackson*, 283, 294–305.

[10] For a readily available sampling, see Eric McKitrick (ed.), *Slavery Defended: Views of the Old South* (Englewood Cliffs, N.J., 1963). See also Louis Hartz, *The Liberal Tradition in America* (New York, 1955), 145–200; and Clement Eaton, *The Growth of Southern Civilization, 1790–1860* (New York, 1961), 295–324.

ern ranks of the Democracy. National election victories, however—and all good things which flowed from the federal apparatus—depended on a continuing alliance with the southern wing. Regardless of their private views, therefore, northern party leaders were for the sake of organizational unity required to justify the southern interest. For this reason the defense of slavery remained until the outbreak of the Civil War a national preoccupation of the Democratic party. Here was the political meaning of the term "doughface"—a northern man who espoused southern principles.[11] One of the earliest full dress presentations of this position was James K. Paulding's *Slavery in the United States,* published in 1836. Paulding, a friend and relative by marriage of Washington Irving, had played a leading role in New York literary circles and, from 1812 at least till the war against Mexico, figured as an eminent American man of letters. He was also a successful officeholder. From his first appointment to a civilian post in the Navy Department in 1815 until his retirement from public service at the end of Van Buren's administration, Paulding remained continuously on the federal payroll.

His treatise on slavery echoed the defense already elaborated in the South. For his northern audience, however, Paulding shifted from the southern emphasis on the plantation as a system of benevolent social control to a direct evocation of racial anxiety. Enemies of the Republic, he warned, were at work throughout the North, fanatics who spoke in grand moral terms against slavery yet were really intent upon destroying the white race through amalgamation with blacks. "That there are such men, and—shame on the sex—such women, is but too evident. . . . They are traitors to the white skin, influenced by mad-brained fanaticism, or the victims of licentious, ungovernable passions, perverted into an unnatural taste by their own indulgence." Loyal Americans must stand firm against these wreckers, remembering that to meddle with the domestic institutions of another state was to fly in the face of the Constitution. If any evil attached to the system of slavery, it was insignificant by contrast to those disasters which must certainly follow upon an attempt to change it from outside. The Union itself was at stake; the "great principle" Paulding wished to convey was that "no beneficial consequences to any class of mankind, or to the whole universe, can counterbalance the evils that will result to the people of the United States from the dissolution of the Union." This happened also to be the message of the Democratic party. Van

---

[11] Apparently first used by John Randolph of Virginia to describe northern congressmen who voted for the Missouri Compromise in 1820. Richard B. Morris, *Encyclopedia of American History* (New York, 1953), 160.

Buren triumphed as heir to President Jackson in 1836; and two years later raised Paulding to the highest office of his long career, that of secretary of the navy.[12]

Paulding's handling of the slavery question remained in substance the official party dogma until the secession of the southern states. Even George Bancroft, the New England Brahmin, who certainly outranked Paulding as a Jacksonian ideologist, never took issue with him on this matter. Bancroft, to judge by his earlier writings, had at first been negatively disposed toward the peculiar institution. About 1834, however, he fell discreetly silent and stayed so throughout the next twenty years. Meanwhile, he became party boss of Massachusetts, helped to engineer the nomination of James K. Polk, served as secretary of the navy during the first part of the Mexican War, and was later appointed ambassador to England.[13]

Both these literary politicians flourished through the success of their party. Yet one need not assume that they were motivated simply by desire for political office. They had perhaps concluded, as had Ralph Waldo Emerson, that the Democracy offered the better cause. "The philosopher, the poet or the religious man," Emerson wrote in 1843, "will of course wish to cast his vote with the democrat for free trade, for wide suffrage, for the abolition of legal cruelties in the penal code, and for facilitating in every manner the access of the young and the poor to the sources of wealth and power." [14] Here was a generous statement of the Jacksonian persuasion, albeit written by an adversary; yet even these high principles comprised only one part of the cause which was really at issue. It was, certainly, no accident that both Paulding and Bancroft served Democratic administrations as secretaries of the navy; nor that Paulding had titled one of his most widely read books *Westward Ho!;* nor that Bancroft helped to devise that sequence of devious maneuvers which ended with American occupation of California. The two men were pilgrims of manifest destiny. The 1830s and 1840s had been decades of expansion for the United States and of national revolution in Europe. On both sides of the Atlantic these movements were accompanied by crescendoes of romantic nationalism.

The Democratic party not only had preached the egalitarian gospel

12 Amos L. Herold, *James Kirke Paulding, Versatile American* (New York, 1926), 30–128; James Kirke Paulding, *Slavery in the United States* (New York, 1836), 62, 7–8.

13 Russel B. Nye, *George Bancroft, Brahmin Rebel* (New York, 1944), especially 81, 103–106.

14 "Politics" (1844), in Stephen Whicher (ed.), *Selections from Ralph Waldo Emerson* (Boston, 1966), 246–247.

of equal access for "the young and the poor" to "sources of wealth and power," it had sought to open up for the benefit of every citizen that potential wealth which lay waiting in the West. Democrats had fashioned the Texas policy, the Oregon policy, the war against Mexico. Doubtless, to a majority of Americans until well into the fifties, the party appeared as champion of individual opportunity and the national interest—as "perpetuator [in the words of Walt Whitman] of all that is really good and noble and true in our institutions." Whitman in 1846 and 1847 was editing a Jacksonian party paper, the Brooklyn *Daily Eagle;* "We hope that the United States will keep a fast grip on California," he wrote. "We have lofty views of the scope and destiny of our American Republic. It is for the interest of mankind that its power and territory should be extended—the farther the better." Might not certain concessions on the question of slavery be justifiable for the sake of such a splendid vista as this? "Come, let us be candid with ourselves," he admonished his readers. "The mad fanaticism of the ultra 'Abolitionists' has pretty well spent its fury—and by the by, has done far more harm than good to the cause it professed to aid." In any case, the evil was vastly exaggerated. By contrast to the misery of wage workers in England, "the South Carolinian Negro is in paradise." [15] Thus the Jacksonian party pursuing the manifest destiny of the nation carried slavery under its southern wing.

What has been said so far tends to the conclusion that northern Democrats were subject to various pressures and inducements to justify the southern position on slavery, which in turn involved an assertion of the racial inferiority of Negroes. Perhaps most white Americans had always believed, really, in the inferiority of the black. This was at first an emotional response which conflicted with the rationalism of the Declaration and stood in direct opposition to fundamental teachings of Christianity. Where it came from is beyond the scope of this study. Certainly it was not created by the southern defense of slavery nor by the Democratic party's justification of that defense. What these factors added was the sanction of respectability and long custom. An ideology need not be internally consistent to be strongly held; all that matters is that the inconsistencies be ignored with approval of recognized higher authority. By the mid-fifties it had become not only possible but easy for an American, from the North or South, to assert

[15] Henry Seidel Canby, *Walt Whitman, an American* (Boston, 1943), 1–51; Brooklyn *Daily Eagle,* November 3, 1847, July 7, 1846, December 2, 1847, December 5, 1846, February 10, 1847, in Walt Whitman, *The Gathering of the Forces,* ed. Cleveland Rogers and John Black, 2 vols. (New York, 1920), I, 219–220, 246–247, 265–266, 192, 42–43

that he believed in the Declaration of Independence, in the teachings of Christianity, and in the inferiority of colored races. All three statements carried the same sort of authority; they were self-evident. Of course it was not only Democrats who adhered to these views. But the will to believe tended to be stronger among them than others precisely because their party was so deeply enmeshed in the defense of slavery.

Moreover, for northern workingmen, attracted as a great many were by the egalitarianism and nationalism of the Democracy, this will to believe sanctioned and reinforced powerful preexisting factors of racial antagonism. Workingmen alone of the northern white population came into direct competition with free Negroes, and as antislavery agitation increased so did their fear of such competition. They had, in several industries, their first encounter with blacks in the role of imported strikebreakers. Workingmen frequently regarded the antislavery cause as a stalking horse put forward by their class enemies. At the least it would serve to distract attention from their own plight and at worst might conjure a horde of Negro freedmen out of the South to take their jobs and deliver them into starvation. To this theme Ely Moore, New York labor leader and Locofoco congressman, was speaking in 1839 when he denounced antislavery petitions as part of a Federalist-Whig conspiracy gotten up for "the especial purpose of humbling and degrading the Democracy." Their real purpose, Moore charged, was to bring "the Southern negro to compete with the Northern white man"; and if that should occur, then "the moral and political character, the pride, power and independence of the latter are forever gone." [16]

Immigrants and children of immigrants (who together comprised a majority of the white labor force in California) were particularly vulnerable to the compulsions of race hostility. Every aspect of the immigrant laborer's situation converged at this focal point. His earliest lesson in American politics had been that Democrats were more hospita-

[16] Winthrop D. Jordan, *White over Black: American Attitudes Toward the Negro, 1550–1812* (Chapel Hill, N.C., 1968). *Congressional Globe*, 25th Cong., 3rd Sess. (Washington, 1839), Appendix, 241; Walter E. Hugins, "Ely Moore, the Case History of a Jacksonian Labor Leader," *Political Science Quarterly*, LXV (March, 1950), 105–125; Leon F. Litwack, *North of Slavery: The Negro in the Free States, 1790–1860* (Chicago, 1965), 160, 165; Philip S. Foner, *History of the Labor Movement in the United States*, 4 vols. (New York, 1947), I, 266–276. Foner (272) quotes the climactic verse of a poem that was reprinted in several labor papers during the decade 1834–1844. As a white factory girl lies dying of cold and starvation, the factory owner and his daughters pass by in their carriage on the way to an antislavery meeting: "Their tender hearts are sighing/As Negroes' woes are told:/While the white slave lay dying/Who gained their father's gold."

ble to foreigners and Catholics than were Whigs or Know-Nothings. He could, in turn, respond enthusiastically to the Jacksonian message. Since regional attachments in the new country held little meaning for him, his first loyalty would be personal—to the man (or party) that found him a job, to immigrant neighbors and fellow workingmen— and beyond that he would identify with the Jacksonian vision of the ever-expanding white republic. Yet white though he surely was himself, he found himself *almost* at the bottom of the social and economic hierarchy. This seeming paradox the Democratic party interpreted for him in terms of the productive classes (of which he was a part) and those great moneyed corporations against which all honest men must do battle. He easily grasped the mortal danger of any increase in the number of free blacks. Meanwhile, the trauma of his own uprooting and the intensity of his desire to grow in the new land fired his dread of these competitors. Abolitionists therefore became his enemies. His friends the Democrats assured him that it was permissible by the established custom of the country for white men to hate and despise Negroes; and he made the most of whatever security was thereby conveyed.

Pressure on the Irish in this connection became doubly severe. Of all immigrant groups, they were the most poverty ridden, the most pathetically unequipped with salable skills. Few had industrial experience even as unskilled hands; the vast majority had been landless agricultural laborers or cotters on worked-out, overpopulated tenancies. What they knew of farming as it was pursued in the new world would have been less on the average than what the black slave knew. Having neither knowledge nor money for a start in farming, the Irish in America were confined to cities and to unskilled and casual occupations.[17] The contrast here with the Germans, who formed the second largest immigrant group, is striking. Germans moved in large numbers, for example, into the agricultural Northwest, financing themselves either with their own savings or with aid from friends and relatives who had settled their earlier. The German migration also included craftsmen; and from as early as the 1860s in the East (a decade later in California), one finds references to all-German local unions of skilled workingmen. On the other hand an all-Irish craftsmen's local was virtually unheard of. The Irish, for three decades prior to the Civil War, furnished a disproportionate share of that unskilled and partially

[17] Marcus Lee Hansen, *The Atlantic Migration, 1607–1860: A History of the Continuing Settlement of the United States* (New York, 1961), 243–251; Maldwyn Allen Jones, *American Immigration* (Chicago, 1960), 130–131; Wayne G. Broehl, Jr., *The Molly Maguires* (Cambridge, Mass., 1964), 70–75.

surplus army which was endlessly expendable in the rise of American industry.[18]

Although Irish immigrants during the early years were not much found in labor unions, they were by no means without organization. Their organizations were vertical rather than horizontal and in this respect resembled those of the Chinese in the West. Visible Irish organizations were of three types: the church; immigrant aid societies, of which the Ancient Order of Hibernians was the outstanding example; and nationalist clubs, notably the Fenians.[19] Within these, occasional groups gathered in the tradition of secret societies like the Ribbonmen and the Molly Maguires, which in the old country had carried on the battle against landlords and Protestants. Given benign circumstances, they would probably have dissolved into social and fraternal activity; but circumstances were not always benign. There was the sporadic warfare with nativist and Protestant gangs. There were strong-arm tactics of political factions in the big cities. Records naturally are in short supply; yet the ease with which Irish mobs could be raised against abolitionists, the New York draft riots, and the story of the Molly Maguires—all suggest a submerged pattern not of formal organization, but of shared attitudes and common tradition. The record for the Molly Maguires, at least, is fairly clear. Even the name of one of the old secret societies had been resurrected out of the past. So pervasive was acceptance of the meanings implicit in the name that the Mollies were able to function almost openly in the coal mining community and to make use of the Ancient Order of Hibernians for what would now be described as a front organization.[20]

18 Foner, I, 228–234; John Rogers Commons et al., *History of Labour in the United States*, 4 vols. (New York, 1960–1961) II, 223–227; California Bureau of Labor Statistics, *Third Biennial Report* (Sacramento, 1888), 119; Jones, *American Immigration*, 130–134.

19 Richard B. Morris, "Andrew Jackson, Strikebreaker," *American Historical Review*, LV (October, 1949), 54–68. Evidence cited in this article on the organization of Irish canal-workers suggests at least as much resemblance to county or regional societies (a vertical structure) as to unionism. Albert C. Stevens, *Cyclopedia of Fraternities* (New York, 1907), 211–213, 515; John O'Dea, *History of the Ancient Order of Hibernians and Ladies Auxiliaries*, 4 vols. (Philadelphia, 1923), II, 884–913.

20 Harry J. Carman and Reinhard H. Luthin, "Some Aspects of the Know-Nothing Movement Reconsidered," *South Atlantic Quarterly*, XXXIX (January, 1940), 213–234; Jones, *American Immigration*, 159–169; Roger W. Shugg, *Origins of Class Struggle in Louisiana* (Baton Rouge, 1939), 146–168; Leon Soulé, *The Know-Nothing Party in New Orleans, 1858–1860* (Baton Rouge, 1961), 43–60; Broehl, *Molly Maguires*, 98–100, 167–168; Stevens, *Cyclopedia;* 212–213, 415; F. P. DeWees, *The Molly Maguires: The Origin, Growth and Character of the Organization* (Philadelphia, 1877); *William Lloyd Garrison, 1805–1879: The Story of his Life Told by His Children*, 4 vols. (New York, 1885), II, 1–72; John Jay Chapman, *William Lloyd Garrison*, 2nd ed. rev. (Boston, 1921), 59–96, 199–218; Ralph Korngold, *Two Friends*

Inevitably, in America this line of secret violence became linked to
hatred for the Negro; and the same line, when it reached California,
would be woven into the anti-Chinese web.

The Major Traditions: Republican

The Republican tradition was more complex than the Democratic.
It sprang from the same origins, Locke through Jefferson; then came
the Federalist bifurcation, which flowed back into the mainstream and
emerged as the Whig party. Early Whigs, like the Federalists before
them, had set great store by property qualifications for public office
and exercise of the franchise. This did not mean, however, that they
abandoned the Declaration. A good Whig need have had no more
difficulty accepting the mandate of the Declaration than Hamilton had
in 1776. He simply restated the well-known argument: that life, liberty,
and pursuit of happiness, inalienable rights though they might be,
were worthless without stable government; stable government depended on responsibility of the governors to society as a whole; and
such responsibility was characteristic of citizens having a stake in
society—that is, men of property. "Political power naturally and
necessarily goes into the hands which hold the property," Daniel
Webster explained to the Massachusetts Constitutional Convention of
1820. "If the nature of our institutions be to found government on
property, and that it should look to those who hold property for its
protection, it is entirely just that property should have its due weight
and consideration in political arrangements." [21]
   On this front the Whigs were routed by the Jacksonian Democrats.
But they regrouped, briefly captured the standards of their opponents,
and came back to win in the famous Log Cabin and Hard Cider
campaign of 1840. Thenceforth, political egalitarianism shaped the
styles of both major lines. Throughout the fifties, the dying Whigs, the
divided Democrats, the *nouveaux* Republicans were all to this extent
Jacksonian. Yet the battles of the earlier years had left a permanent
effect—the memory of them lent substance to the notion of the
Democracy as representative of the "productive and burthen-bearing
classes." [22] and on this notion in large measure depended that long

of Man: The Story of William Lloyd Garrison and Wendell Phillips, Their Rela-
tionship with Abraham Lincoln (Boston, 1950), 82–104; and see also O'Dea, *History,*
II, 884–913, III, 1027–1047; Fergus MacDonald, *The Catholic Church and the*
Secret Societies in the United States (New York, 1946), 32–100.
   [21] *The Writings and Speeches of Daniel Webster*, 18 vols. (Boston, 1903), V, 15.
   [22] See above, p. 21.

Democratic dominance which ended only with the election of Lincoln in 1860.

While the Whig line provided a major component of the Republican tradition, there were several other elements of crucial importance. One was nativism. It seems unmistakable that Federalist and Whig championship of the property concept of responsible government struck a common harmonic with fear of foreign immigration. At all events, subsequent antiforeign, anti-Catholic agitation was associated with whiggishness. An early manifestation in northern and western states took the form of temperance law crusades in which the use of alcoholic beverages and sabbath-breaking were seen as expressions of the evil that inhered in foreignness and Catholicism. The dynamic of this agitation seems to have come in part from native-born and especially old-stock workingmen who felt themselves threatened with displacement. Nativism flared up in the mid-forties, partially subsided, then rose to a crescendo between 1852 and 1856. During those years the American (Know-Nothing) party won control of a number of state governments, including those of Massachusetts, Maryland, and California, and polled for their candidate Millard Fillmore a quarter of the total vote cast in the presidential election of 1856. But the American party was, in one sense, only the last gasp of dying whiggery. By 1860 most of the nativists had followed most of their whiggish colleagues into the Republican movement, where they played an apparently decisive role in throwing the nomination from Seward (tainted by his supposed sympathy for Catholics and foreign-born) to the as yet uncommitted Lincoln.[23]

There are three points of particular interest in connection with the nativist element of Republicanism. The first is that nativism, unlike other elements of the Republican coalition, exercised a strong attraction for certain groups of workingmen. The second point is that this attraction did not necessarily diminish as immigrants and their children came to form a larger proportion of the urban working class. Once arrived, the immigrant was as much menaced by further immigration as was the native American; and in the case of the immigrant (especially perhaps in the case of his children), economic hos-

[23] Joel H. Silbey, *The Transformation of American Politics, 1840–1860* (Englewood Cliffs, N.J., 1967), 1–34; Hubert Howe Bancroft, *History of California*, VI, 691–700; Carman and Luthin, *South Atlantic Quarterly*, XXXIX, 215–234; Ray Allen Billington, *The Protestant Crusade, 1800–1860: A Study of the Origins of American Nativism* (Gloucester, Mass., 1963), 1–14, 22–37, 53–84, 334–338, 389–397; W. Darrell Overdyke, *The Know-Nothing Party in the South* (Baton Rouge, 1950).

tility was reinforced by the longing for security and acceptance.[24] The third point is that the nativist line carried with it a pattern of organized violence which paralleled and complemented that of the immigrants.

Secret societies under patriotic titles—like the Order of United Americans, United American Mechanics (with membership restricted to American-born laborers), and Order of the Star Spangled Banner—sprouted during the two decades prior to the Civil War.[25] These, with their widely read newspapers and magazines, "convinced many workingmen that . . . prosperity depended on restricted immigration" and "played a prominent part in creating the anti-Catholic, anti-foreign sentiment upon which the Know Nothing Party was nurtured." [26] Disruption and violence, ranging all the way from petty heckling to riot and arson, provided a continual counterpoint to the antiforeign agitation. In larger cities, violence actually became institutionalized into the political structure. Armed clubs of workingmen and native American Know-Nothings, on one hand, and Democrats, largely immigrants, on the other, fought for control of the registration machinery and the polling places.[27] Here were lessons in organizational technique that would not soon be forgotten.

The Republican tradition, then, included the dominant Whig line as well as the somewhat less pervasive nativist line. And there was one other, antislavery. But with this, as usual, comes the troublesome necessity of dividing the subject matter. Antislavery itself was composed of three main elements—abolition, free soil, and unionism.

The first was essentially religious. For those who accepted the authority of scripture, its argument was unassailable; it might be ignored or forgotten, but never refuted. Appropriately, in his study of antislavery, Dwight Dumond selected a New England Congregational sermon as keynote for the abolitionist message. "God hath made of one blood all nations of men to dwell on the face of the earth," the

---

[24] See, for example, John Francis Maguire, The Irish in America (New York, 1868), 438–439. Maguire, an Irish member of Parliament, was incensed to discover that second-generation Irish had taken part in anti-Irish agitation. "Absurd instances might be told of the sons of Irish Catholic immigrants boasting of their American birth, and expressing their sympathy with the Know Nothings' hatred of foreigners. . . . Such spectacles have been witnessed to the infinite shame of the poor creatures whose vanity was too much for a weak head and a poor heart. But that such melancholy spectacles were witnessed . . . is a proof of the madness that seized on the public mind" (450–451).

[25] Billington, Protestant Crusade, 335–338, 381–382; Stevens, Cyclopedia, 311–318, 326.

[26] Billington, 335–336, 420.

[27] Billington, 420; W. Darrell Overdyke, "History of the American Party in Louisiana," Louisiana Historical Quarterly, XVI (April, 1933), 257–277; Shugg, Origins of Class Struggle, 128, 146–148.

Reverend Josephus Wheaton of Holliston, Massachusetts, had declared on the annual fast day in the year of the Missouri Compromise, 1820. He then went on to derive the necessary consequences of his scriptural proposition:

> This passage not only teaches us that mankind have a common origin and are united by a common nature, but suggests that they are originally equal. . . . Mankind are naturally equal in respect to their moral characters. . . . Mankind are equal in respect to their immortality. . . . Mankind are equal in respect to their native rights. As they are united by a common nature, and are all members of the same great family, each individual possesses certain rights which others are bound to respect. In reference to these, superiority is unknown. Every person has a perfect right to his life, to his liberty, to the property which he lawfully acquires, and to whatever happiness he may enjoy without injuring himself and others.[28]

Here, in religion terms, was the counterpart to the mandate of the Declaration of Independence. It permitted no compromise, left little elbow room for politics, and perhaps for this reason abolitionists were few in number. Yet because of the sanctified origins of the message and because of their dedication to its fulfillment, they became— outside the South at least—extraordinarily influential in national affairs. Their influence, however, was always at a minimum among northern workingmen. Once again the relation to the Democratic party was at the crux of the matter, in that the commitment of politically active workingmen to the party, and its supposed commitments to them, involved a justification of slavery which rendered them emotionally deaf to abolitionist appeals.

Beyond abolition and more inclusive in scope was the free-soil impulse. The thrust in this case was not against slavery itself, but to open the territories for development by non-slave-holding settlers— an objective virtually identical with that of the homestead and free-land schemes which had stirred some enthusiasm among urban workingmen in the thirties and early forties. Ironically, it was harnessed in tandem to that conviction of black inferiority which James Kirke Paulding (along with many others) had exploited as a means of unifying the Democratic party in defense of slavery. There seems little doubt that hostility to blacks became a major factor in resistance to

---

[28] Josephus Wheaton, *The Equality of Mankind and the Evils of Slavery Illustrated: A Sermon Delivered on the Day of the Annual Fast, April 6, 1820* (Boston, 1820). Cited in Dwight W. Dumond, *The Anti-Slavery Impulse: The Crusade for Freedom in America* (Ann Arbor, 1961), 147–148.

34

the extension of slavery, especially in the Midwest and on the Pacific Coast.[29] "I plead the cause and the rights of white freemen," David Wilmot—a Pennsylvania Democrat—told the House of Representatives in arguing for his proviso to exclude slavery from territory acquired as a result of the war against Mexico. "I would preserve to free white labor a fair country, a rich inheritance, where the sons of toil of my own race and my own color can live without the disgrace which association with Negro slavery brings upon free labor." [30]

While the free-soil impulse—as David Wilmot's political affiliation suggests—was in considerable measure of Democratic origin, its *effect* on Democrats who came under its influence was to move them out of their own party and into the Union-Republican coalition. Certainly no great upsurge of the "productive and burthen-bearing classes" greeted the Free Soil party in 1848; yet precisely the same issues and slogans proved massively effective when taken over by the Republicans in the late fifties. By this time, the South must to a great many have appeared to be blocking development of the nation's western lands. Free soil therefore took on an aura of nationalism which it had lacked in the earlier period, and so merged with the largest component of antislavery, unionism.

During the decade that followed the Compromise of 1850, the Democratic party, while it continued to win presidential elections, was separating into a national and a southern wing. The South became more and more aggressively sectional. Step by step through the debates over California and the Mexican cession territories, over Kansas-Nebraska and homesteads, and over the transcontinental railroad, southern leaders assumed (in the eyes at least of many northerners and westerners) a disruptive role with respect to continental development. From having been an essential ingredient of national unity, the defense of slavery became tantamount to the advocacy of separation. The result was that nationalist sentiment, which earlier had drawn laborers along with vast numbers of others to the party of manifest destiny, would now work in the opposite direction and push them into the Republican (or Union-Republican) party. A case in point is the political career of Walt Whitman.[31] The son of a carpenter, Whitman

---

[29] Commons et al., *History* (above, n. 18), I, 522–535; Zahler, *Eastern Workingmen* (above, n. 8); and Berwanger, *The Frontier Against Slavery* (above, n. 2).

[30] *Congressional Globe*, 29th Cong., 2nd Sess. (Washington, 1847), Appendix, 317.

[31] Walt Whitman, Henry George (below, pp. 92–97), and Andrew Johnson are all case examples of the effect of free-soil doctrine on men of Jacksonian background. For this examination of the major party traditions with respect to racial attitudes in the context of 1865–1870, I have placed free soil on the Republican side of the line, regardless of its several points of origin. For the Free Soil and

himself became a journeyman printer and editor of a Democratic party newspaper—a post from which he was expelled in 1848 because of his free-soil proclivities. Yet as late as 1860 (and a good deal later, too), Whitman was still uttering the rhetoric of the old spread-eagle Democracy:

> Americanos! conquerors! marches humanitarian!
> Foremost! century marches! Libertad! masses!
> For you a program of chants.
>
> Chants of the prairies,
> Chants of the long-running Mississippi, and down
>   to the Mexican sea. . . .

Indeed it was precisely this vision which bound him to the Republican Lincoln: "O powerful western fallen star! . . . O western orb sailing the heaven . . . the sweetest wisest soul of all my days and lands." [32]

One clear demonstration of the force of the issue of unionism (aside from the fact that the Union itself survived the war) was Republican reluctance to give it up afterward. For almost three decades beyond Appomatox, Republicans reenacted at least once every four years the passion and resurrection of the Union. This was to have profound effects on the Democratic party; in seeking a counterweapon it would turn again to that racism which had partially been sublimated through the war years.

Of the three elements of antislavery, only the first (abolition) involved an assertion that all mankind was created equal. Neither the second nor third (free soil and unionism) required acceptance of the first. Yet an alliance of these two with abolition had proved expedient. The reason was that the crises of war, burning out the middle ground, had driven men to seek refuge on heights of fundamental conviction, even though such convictions were not always their own. Lincoln, previously hostile to abolition, became an abolitionist in 1863. And by 1865, in the Second Inaugural, his tone resembled that of John Brown's final message five years earlier. [33] It may be that the ironsides

Republican platforms, see Kirk H. Porter and Donald Bruce Johnson, *National Party Platforms, 1840–1960*, 2nd ed. (Urbana, 1961), 27–29, 30–31.

[32] John Kouwenhoven, "Biographical Introduction," Walt Whitman, *Leaves of Grass and Selected Prose* (New York, Modern Library Paperback, 1950), viii-ix. See also James D. Hart, *The Oxford Companion to American Literature*, 4th ed. (New York, 1965), 918. The lines quoted are from "Starting from Paumanok," stanza 3, and "When Lilacs last in the Dooryard Bloom'd," stanzas 2, 8, 16.

[33] James D. Richardson (ed.), *Messages and Papers of the Presidents* (New York, 1897-), VII, 3477–3478; *The Life, Trial and Execution of Capt. John Brown, Being a Full Account of the Attempted Insurrection at Harpers Ferry, Va.* (New York, 1859), 94–95.

spirit of abolition was indispensable in saving the Union. But afterward it seemed equally necessary for preservation of the Republican party. In the complicated politics of Reconstruction, Republican control of the national government had seemingly come to depend on enfranchisement of black freedmen in the South.[34] This was a step for which the expedient antislavery of the free-soilers and unionists was totally unprepared. Again, as during the war, abolition provided the ideological iron; and again the abolitionist persuasion appeared more widely held than it actually was. Meanwhile, thousands of Americans, including workingmen and immigrants, passed through the free-soil and unionist phases of antislavery without modifying their previously held attitudes toward the Negro. Not much of abolition rubbed off on them.

As for the Republicans, as soon as they dared give way, their retreat from their forward position was precipitate. Long before the collapse of Reconstruction, the fate of blacks in the South was foreshadowed in the first full-dress debate on the status of Chinese in the West. Charles Sumner of Massachusetts had moved to amend the naturalization clause of the Immigration Act by deleting the adjective "white" wherever it occurred. Western senators, Republicans and Democrats united, led the counterattack.[35] The climax came on July 4, 1870, when Sumner, taking advantage of the date, read into the record the mandate of the Declaration. Then, precisely as had the Reverend Wheaton fifty years earlier from the corresponding scriptural text, Sumner drew the obligatory conclusions:

> It is "all men" and not a race or color that are placed under the protection of the Declaration, and such was the voice of our fathers on the fourth day of July, 1776. . . . Now, Sir, what better thing can you do on this anniversary than to expunge from the statutes that unworthy limitation which dishonors and defiles the original Declaration? . . . The word "white" wherever it occurs as a limitation of rights, must disappear. Only in this way can you be consistent with the Declaration.[36]

[34] William A. Dunning, *Reconstruction, Political and Economic, 1865–1877* (New York, 1962), 133–135; Fawn M. Brodie, *Thaddeus Stevens, Scourge of the South* (New York, 1959), 296–304; Paul H. Buck, *The Road to Reunion, 1865–1900* (New York, 1959), 82–88.

[35] *Alta California*, "Senate Has Gone and Done It," July 4, 1870; "Looking One Way and Rowing Another," July 15, 1870.

[36] Charles Sumner, *Works of Charles Sumner*, 15 vols. (Boston, 1875–1883), XIII (1880), 482. Sumner's adherence to the Declaration was fundamentally religious. Later in the debate (July 8, 1870) he said: "There can be but one rule for all. Because the Almighty made him [the Chinese] of a color slightly different from

His opponents remained unmoved. In the Republican Senate of 1870 Sumner was defeated 30 to 14.[37]

Ideology Within the Labor Force

While the Republican and Democratic traditions doubtless comprised the major portion of ideological baggage carried to California, they were not by any means all of it. Other tendencies, narrower in scope, characterized particular groups within the labor force.

Among European immigrants, especially perhaps among men who assumed political leadership, republicanism (with the lower case *r*) was a standard pattern. This was so particularly with respect to the Germans. Though few of them actually had fought in the revolution of 1848, the radical style was preponderant. Scarcely arrived in America, they had begun to organize for the next round in the old country. Carl Wittke described these refugees as "German Fenians," [38] and their activities did for a time parallel those of the Irish nationalists, many of whom also envisioned national liberation in republican terms. But the Germans did not rally quite so unanimously as the Irish to the Democratic party's justification of slavery. Their republicanism was still linked directly to its origins in revolutionary egalitarianism. They had by their defeat been spared any such experience of political power as had eroded the Jeffersonianism of the American Democracy; and they had to a degree been spared those agonies through which the Irish had passed and which darkened and narrowed their vision. The Germans were bumptious, enthusiastic—and naive. Looking back, it is sad even to recall the names of their *Gesangvereine,* their workers' cultural and athletic associations, their *Volksbünde* for the new world and the old: the new world was to be ushered in by brass bands and demonstrations of close-order drill. And it would turn out before long that some of these romantic exiles who had studied the Prussian manual of arms hoping to overthrow the Prussians would march in defense of the American Republic—while others would march for the Confederacy.

my friend the Senator from Oregon, I know not why he should not be equal to that Senator in rights—I know not why he should not enter into the same citizenship." (See Edward L. Pierce, *Memoir and Letters of Charles Sumner,* 4 vols. [Boston, 1894], IV, 424–425.)

[37] Sumner, *Works,* XIII, 493, 498. Final disposition of the matter in 1870 was to extend naturalization to persons of African descent but to continue the ban against all other nonwhites.

[38] Hansen, *Atlantic Migration* (above, n. 17), 274; Carl Wittke, *Refugees of Revolution: The German Forty-Eighters in America* (Philadelphia, 1952), 92–110; 186–200.

The difference was largely their port of entry.[39] In the fifties, however, it was still the radicalism of the newcomers that was most striking. This they demonstrated—with rather dramatic results—on the occasion of Louis Kossuth's famous visit to America in 1851.

Revolutionary in the old down-with-tyrants spirit of '76, Kossuth, so long as he remained in Europe, was everybody's hero in America. No one, North or South, could do other than wish him well. When things went poorly for him abroad, the Senate in one of its rare moments of harmony during those troubled years, invited Kossuth to visit Washington and President Fillmore sent a warship to fetch him over. Naturally immigrants in America gave Kossuth an enthusiastic reception. When, however, northern abolitionists and free-soilers turned out to hail him as a champion of the rights of man, the South took alarm. And when Protestants, especially the New England variety, rallied to Kossuth as an anti-Catholic, the Catholic clergy marshaled their largely Irish parishioners in opposition. The result was a sectional and party division. Democrats in Congress fought successfully to damp down the official welcome. Touring the South, Kossuth was ignored (except by Germans) and southern legislatures passed resolutions condemning his visit and warning of the perils of foreign entanglement.[40]

The significance of this controversy can be summed up in the response of Orestes Brownson. Brownson, who came of a poverty-ridden old stock New England family, had been a sansculotte himself in earlier days, a friend of Frances Wright and advocate of the New York Workingmen's Party. That was in the 1820s. In the thirties he was a Jacksonian Democrat. In the forties, still believing himself "to be working for the laborers" (the words are Arthur Schlesinger, Jr.'s), Brownson had supported John C. Calhoun for the presidency. In 1842 he gave up Unitarianism to become a Catholic. And of Kossuth,

[39] Billington, *The Protestant Crusade*, 329; Samuel Colville, *Colville's San Francisco Directory and Gazetteer, 1856–1857* (San Francisco, 1856), xxviii. The leading German newspaper of New Orleans, *Täglich Deutsche Zeitung*, commenting on Lincoln's election, wrote (November 21, 1860): "We have known for a long time that a great part of our German population of the North and West is raving about Nigger-freedom. We wish them joy—joy from our whole heart, and hope that through a successful amalgamation of the German element with the Nigger element of the North and West there may arise a doughty race to hold the political balance against the barbarism of the rest of the world. We assure them that they may visit us without written permission from the police. We shall recognize them—by the wool of their heads—by the whites of their eyes, and by the disgusting odor, by which Goethe's Mephistopheles is recognized." (Quoted by Robert T. Clark, "The New Orleans German Colony in the Civil War," *Louisiana Historical Quarterly*, XX [October, 1937], 990–1015.) A substantial number of Germans served in the Confederate armies.

[40] Billington, 330–334.

the revolutionary, Brownson wrote that he was "one of the most dangerous characters now living." [41] Here, epitomized, was the ideological history of the working-class wing of the Democracy.[42] It was clear that republicanism with the lower case *r* would find scant shelter in the party of Jefferson and Jackson. Probably a majority of Germans, for this and perhaps some other reasons as well, went with Karl Schurz into the Republican party. But a substantial number, who were workingmen, turned to socialism.

To be more precise, they had brought socialism with them. Yet socialism was not confined to Germans, nor to immigrants. Although its spread was slow among native American workmen, it seems to have appealed primarily to the most active, or else to have activated those to whom it most appealed. At all events, socialism as a tendency within the labor force took on considerable importance not only in California but in the nation at large during the decades of industrial conflict which followed the war. Here again the case of a single individual will serve to pinpoint some general conclusions.

Frank Roney was an Irish immigrant who became one of the pioneers of union organization in California. In several respects Roney was nontypical of the majority of his uprooted countrymen. He came from an urban background; he had learned a skilled trade (that of iron molder) before leaving the old country; he had abandoned Catholicism; and he had taken part as a leader of second rank in the ill-fated rebellion of 1867. Roney's emigration from Ireland in fact was the condition of his release from prison and may have saved him from hanging. As an Irish republican during the years of the American Civil War, his sympathies had been profoundly with the North. Reaching New York in 1868, he was angered by the effort of local Democrats to recruit him in exchange for immediate (and illegal) naturalization. Roney's first affiliation was with the Republican party, the leader he most admired being Thaddeus Stevens. But Stevens was seven years dead by the time Roney had made his way to the Pacific Coast. Finding in California Republicanism little to hold his loyalty, he turned to socialism; and more lastingly, to the cause of labor organization.[43]

This account of the poitical and geographical wanderings of an im-

---

[41] Arthur M. Schlesinger, Jr., *Orestes Brownson: A Pilgrim's Progress* (Boston, 1939), 160–161; Billington, 331.

[42] Schlesinger, *Brownson*, 1–26, 34, 155–157, 160–162, 179–182, 207; Billington, 330–334; Richard Hofstadter, *The American Political Tradition* (New York, 1948), 88; H. J. Brownson, *Orestes A. Brownson*, 2 vols. (Detroit, 1898–1900), II, 418–419.

[43] Frank Roney, *Frank Roney, Irish Rebel and California Labor Leader*, ed. Ira B. Cross (Berkeley, 1931), 29–32, 53–57, 93–95, 112–118, 148–149, 155–168, 176–179, 206-207, 215–225, 262.

migrant workingman we owe to the fact that Roney, happily, was induced to write down his recollections before he died.[44] How *typical*
was he? There is no way of answering with certainty because so few
other workers, even skilled craftsmen, found time or energy to record
their experiences. Clearly, Roney did not typify the majority of Irish;
but he expressed an important trend of working class radicalism, and
his case does suggest an affinity that linked abolitionism with republicanism and socialism. Each proclaimed the equality of man; and for
each it was necessarily forbidden to exclude on account of race any
group of men from the republic, or of laborers from the consensus of
workingmen. The labor situation of the Pacific Coast was likely to
provide a troublesome dilemma for persons of Frank Roney's persua-
sions.

But socialism and republicanism, though strongly held, were narrowly held. The major tendency in the labor force, nationally and in
California, was the line that descended through the Democratic party
and especially through its radical wing. Central to this tendency was
the concept of the producer ethic which had informed the labor politics of the thirties, the cooperative experiments of the forties, and the
beginnings of labor union organization in the fifties. After the Civil
War it continued dominant. The Knights of Labor, founded in 1869,
required the master workman of each local assembly to initiate new
members with the words: "On behalf of the toiling millions of the
earth, I welcome you to this Sanctuary, dedicated to the service of God,
by serving humanity." [45] The Knights even tried to carry their aspira-
tion into organizational practice. Farmers, unskilled laborers, women,
Negroes—all, as producers, were invited into the local assemblies. Only
at accepting Chinese did the Knights generally draw the line.[46] The
National Labor Union, established three years before the Knights as
an annual convention of labor and reform organizations, had set forth
its guiding principles as follows:

> What is then wanted is for every union to help inculcate the
> grand, ennobling idea that the interests of labor are one; that
> there should be no distinction of race or nationality; no classi-
> fication of Jew or Gentile, Christian or Infidel; that there is

[44] *Frank Roney,* "Introduction," xv-xxii, xxxix.
[45] John R. Commons et al., *A Documentary History of American Industrial
Society,* 10 vols. (New York, 1958), X, 23.
[46] Philip Taft, *Organized Labor in American History* (New York, 1964), 665;
John R. Commons, et al., *History of Labour in the United States,* 4 vols. (New York,
1918), III, 336–337, 396–397. Nicholas A. Somma, "The Knights of Labor and
Chinese Immigration" (M.A. thesis, Catholic University of America, Washington,
1952), 21–23; Foner, *History of the Labor Movement* (above, n. 16), II, 59–60.

but one dividing line—that which separates mankind into two great classes, the class that labors and the class that lives by others' labors. . . . The interest of all on our side of the line is the same, and should we be so far misled by prejudice or passion as to refuse to aid the spread of union principles among any of our fellow toilers, we would be untrue to them, untrue to ourselves and to the great cause we profess to have at heart. If these general principles be correct, we must seek the cooperation of the African race in America.[47]

It appears, then, with respect to the three tendencies of labor-force ideology so far discussed—the producer ethic, socialism, and republicanism—that their messages were in certain important respects similar, yet by no means identical. What they agreed on was the republican assertion of the equality of mankind, morally as human beings. The producer ethic went beyond this to designate the "productive and burthen-bearing classes" as the value carriers of society, but then assumed that political egalitarianism would adequately insure equal opportunities for these producers. Socialism stressed the necessity of economic egalitarianism as well, through the sharing of property. The more rigorous view of Marxian socialists further narrowed the definition of value carriers to wage workers, and invoked a potential class unity that would bridge racial and national differences. There was, in addition, one other tendency within the labor force which has not yet been dealt with. This was trade unionism.

During the period immediately following the Civil War, trade unionism seemed a minor trend. It would not emerge as the main form of American labor organization until twenty years afterward. But already a number of national unions had established themselves. They concentrated on defending the economic interest of their members who were the skilled operatives of particular trades. What was the ideology of the trade unions? Actually, they had as yet none of their own and would be obliged to await the presidency of Samuel Gompers and the scholarship of John R. Commons and Selig Perlman before they developed one. In the interim they simply borrowed the ideological language of other tendencies. For the most part trade unionists based themselves on the producer ethic; although later, as Perlman has shown, they adapted to their own usage a nonrevolutionary version of socialist class consciousness.[48] Yet there was an obvious conflict between

47 Andrew C. Cameron, *The Address of the National Labor Congress to the Workingmen of the United States* (Chicago, 1867), in Commons et al., *Documentary History*, IX, 141–168; for the portion quoted, 158–159.

48 Lloyd Ulman, *The Rise of the National Trade Union* (Cambridge, Mass., 1955), 3–7. Selig Perlman, *A Theory of the Labor Movement* (New York, 1949), 182–207.

craft orientation on the one hand, and *either* the producer ethic or working-class loyalty on the other.

That this dichotomy was already apparent in 1867 is evident from the National Labor Union manifesto referred to above. "Even among workingmen," the manifesto acknowledged, there was widespread hostility toward trade unionism; and this opposition was due to the "vindictive, arbitrary spirit" sometimes displayed by trade union organizations. Yet such was not their real character. The true character of trade unionism, the manifesto went on, was expressed by the producer ethic. Always in the long run a broader view would prevail over narrow craft interest; and therefore, it was proper to urge skilled workers to join appropriate trade unions because the success of those unions would accrue to the advantage of all producers.[49] These views represented the outlook not only of non-trade-unionists in the labor movement (like Andrew Cameron, Chicago labor editor and author of the *Address* just quoted), but of trade union pioneers such as Richard Trevellick of the Ships' Carpenters and William Sylvis, president of the Molders International Union. And—to speak of one other—Frank Roney, the immigrant republican who became a member of Sylvis' union and held Sylvis in highest esteem, would have been in general agreement.[50]

But although trade unionism of that period carried no separate ideological message, its practice tended to narrow the producer ethic and, therefore, reinforced the process of erosion which was already under way. After the National Labor Union's ringing statement in its *Address* of 1867 about the unity of all mankind, the next convention stalled at dead center on the Negro question. A committee, having wrestled at length with the problem, reported that "we find the subject involved in so much mystery, and upon it so wide a diversity of opinion among our members, we believe that it is inexpedient to take action on the subject in this National Labor Congress." The debate which followed revealed the lines of division within the convention:

> In New Haven [said Mr. Phelps, chairman of the reporting committee] were a number of respectable colored mechanics, but they had not been able to induce the trades' unions to admit them. He asked was there any union in the States which would admit colored men? Mr. Gibson said it would be time enough to talk about admitting colored men to trades' unions and to the Congress when they applied for admission.

[49] Commons et al., *Documentary History*, IX, 152–154.
[50] Commons et al., *History*, II, 29, 129–131; Jonathan Grossman, *William Sylvis, Pioneer of the American Labor Movement: A Study of the Labor Movement during the Era of the Civil War* (New York, 1945), 189–191, 220–237; Roney, *Frank Roney,* 90, 177–201, 206–208, 228–229.

> Mr. Sylvis [William Sylvis of the Molders' Union] said this question had already been introduced in the South, the whites striking against the blacks, and creating antagonism which will kill off the trades' unions unless the two be consolidated. . . . "If the workingmen of the white race do not conciliate the blacks, the black vote will be cast against them." [51]

The timing of this exchange is crucially important—1868. The war was over; slavery was ended; Radical Reconstruction with its declared goal of converting the black freedman into an independent producer and voting citizen was at high tide. Older leaders, like Sylvis, devoted to the producer ethic and to the dream of a workingman's party, now saw no alternative but to seek the "cooperation of the African race." The younger men from the trades locals which had burgeoned during the war and were already coalescing into national craft organizations, claimed the right to judge every question in terms of their own local membership of skilled craftsmen.

Needless to say, it was the younger men who won. The matter was tabled in 1868. Later, several black delegates gained entrance to the national gatherings, but nothing was done about admission to local unions. Negroes were allowed to go unorganized or to form their own associations. This in fact they endeavored to do, and in 1869 a National Colored Labor Convention sent the following plea in a memorial to the United States Congress: "The exclusion of colored men, and apprentices, from the right to labor in any department of industry or workshops, in any of the states and territories of the United States, by what is known as 'trades' unions' is an insult to God, injury to us, and disgrace to humanity." [52] The congressional session to which this appeal was directed was the same that defeated Charles Sumner in his Fourth of July argument for the naturalization of Chinese.

Yet the quotation of memorials to Congress and minutes of long-forgotten conventions scarcely touches the heart of the matter. In 1863 the first federal conscription act roused widespread opposition. Aside from being a Republican measure aimed at hastening the defeat of the Confederacy, the draft law was patently unfair. It permitted rich men to buy out of military service or hire substitutes, thus throwing the burden of sacrifice unequally on the poor, and especially on workingmen. There were good Jeffersonian and Jacksonian reasons for objecting to this measure; and workingmen and others did object very strenuously in demonstrations that cropped out from New York to the Middle Border and south to the fringes of the Confederacy in Indiana and in the Pennsylvania anthracite fields. The New York dem-

---

[51] Commons et al., *Documentary History*, IX, 185, 186–187.
[52] Ibid., 250.

onstration turned into a four-day battle bloodier than many engagements of the war itself. The point is that what had begun, somewhat in the tradition of the Boston Tea Party, as a protest against the unequal application of governmental power, went on to the burning of a Negro orphanage and the torture and murder of Negroes in the streets.[53] Such were the new meanings added by half a century of social habituation to the self-evident truths of the producer ethic.

Resources to Draw On

Each of the ideological tendencies which might be supposed to have shaped the thoughts of white Californians, and especially of those included within the labor force during the early seventies, contained an assertion of the equality of all mankind. In socialism and republicanism these assertions remained central, and there had as yet been little opportunity for erosion. But they were minor trends.

The two major trends were those that came down through the Republican and Democratic parties. Both acknowledged a rather distant allegiance to the original mandate of the Declaration. The Democratic tradition had translated this mandate into the producer ethic and had thereby won lasting popular support, both urban and rural. Then, first through its defense of slavery and second through its efforts to stage a comeback after the Civil War, the Democracy had stressed a concept of race superiority which excluded Africans—and by implication other colored races as well—from the meaning of the Declaration.[54]

The Republican tradition was less influential with labor than the Democratic. Of the various elements in the Republican tradition, one only, abolition, had strongly reasserted a belief in human equality. But abolition had elicited scant enthusiasm from organizations of working people. The Republican party's broadest and most successful appeal was the plea for national unity. Although this had led to the circumscription and finally abolition of slavery, it was by no means inconsistent with hostility to blacks.

---

[53] Joseph Rayback, *A History of American Labor* (New York, 1961) 109; James B. Fry, *New York and the Conscription Act of 1863: A Chapter in the History of the Civil War* (New York, 1885), 67; A Volunteer Special [William Osborn Stoddard], *The Volcano under the City* (New York, 1887), 50–51, 85, 95, 106, 112–113, 224, 235, 247, 292–293.

[54] Attitudes of California's early literary men toward the Chinese seem to have been shaped largely by the twin mandates of equality. For a survey in this connection of the works of Mark Twain, Joaquin Miller, Bret Harte, Ambrose Bierce, and others, see William Purviance Fenn, *Ah Sin and His Brethren in American Literature. Delivered before the Convocation of the College of Chinese Studies,* June, 1933 (Peking, China, 1933).

A small number of workingmen had encountered direct competition from Negroes prior to or during the war; a great many more had learned to fear such competition. The newly developing trade unions, although they might frequently honor the producer ethic in words, in practice generally sanctioned exclusion of blacks from their trades.

These were the resources of ideology and previous experience which the various components of California's labor force had to draw on. Underneath, tending to unify these components (and to separate them from the Chinese) was an intense shared conviction of displacement and deprivation. And there were, finally, ingrained patterns of organized violence, carried on the one hand by nativist groups, largely Republicans, and on the other by immigrant groups, largely Democratic. Each had reinforced and reactivated the other; but in California, as the antagonism between old stock and European immigrant subsided, they would tend to coalesce.

3

MINES AND RAILROADS

The Mines

As the survey of the labor force undertaken in the first chapter suggests, California mining camps rapidly developed forms of social organization within which were areas of consensus and lines of conflict. Along these lines occurred the first confrontations with Chinese. But the whole matter of miners' organization has been silted over with layers of poetry and legend which convert any exploration of these early communities into something of a mining operation in itself. And here it is not sufficient simply to uncover what lies beneath; for the layers of legend and poetry have themselves become historical factors. Certainly the first step is to sink some kind of shaft through this accumulated mystique.

One of the most mystical among miners' historians was Charles Howard Shinn whose book, *Mining Camps: A Study in American Frontier Government,* first published in 1884, has run through several editions. Shinn's qualifications for this work were impeccable. Born in the course of his parents' trek to the Pacific, he grew up during the slow afterglow of the California gold rush. His first undertakings were teaching, poetry, and newspaper reporting. In his study of mining camps, Shinn found confirmation for his own optimistic and pragmatic view of the human condition. The miners, as he saw them, had created spontaneously from their own need a model of mining regulation and social order which not only shaped subsequent mining frontiers but contributed a democratizing influence to American society as a whole. "Nowhere in the mines," he wrote, "was there any planning ahead; men were too busy and time too precious for that. The result was a degree and quality of unhampered, untroubled freedom to which it is hard to find a historical parallel." [1]

[1] Charles Howard Shinn, *Mining Camps: A Study in American Frontier Government* (New York, 1948). For a sketch of Shinn, see Joseph Henry Jackson's "Intro-

This was written ten years before publication of Frederick Jackson Turner's essay on the frontier in American history; the concept of something new and splendid emerging from the atomization of the old society on the rocks of frontier experience had already a long incarnation in legend before Turner put it into the language of social science. Shinn had merely tapped some of the same sources that Turner tapped; and Shinn quickly ran on to some of the same logical difficulties that Turner's thesis was to encounter. Among these was the problem of the origin of new values. Did they reside in the virgin land?[2] How then could they be transmitted into the frontier settlements? Or did they reside in the state of primitiveness? In that case the values ought to be found in their highest form among Indians or mountain men, which obviously they were not. The only other alternative—aside from spontaneous generation which might as well have occurred anywhere—was that somehow these values were brought along by the frontiersmen. But this led into a contradiction with the original concept.

Shinn discovered his solution to the dilemma in a set of ideas which Charles Beard later referred to as the Teutonic theory of history. At the newly founded Johns Hopkins University in Baltimore, these ideas were very much in vogue; and Shinn, now past thirty, enrolled there to take his A.B. degree. He completed his work on mining camps while a student at Johns Hopkins. What the Teutonic theory revealed to Shinn was a much earlier frontier, deep in the primeval German forest. Democracy, perhaps mystically, had come to birth there; and the ancestors of most forty-niners, and of the Shinns, and of all Anglo-Saxons, Teutons, and Scandinavians, had practised self-government based on individualism tempered by a reasonable willingness to compromise. Of all this, of course, no direct record remained. But there was the indirect evidence of such Anglo-Saxon triumphs as the Magna Carta, the Glorious Revolution, and the Constitution of the United States. Moreover, Johns Hopkins scholarship was disclosing that the land tenure

---

duction" to the 1948 Harper Torchbook edition. Shinn, "Land Laws of Mining Districts," *The Johns Hopkins Studies in Historical and Political Science*, II (Baltimore, 1884), 547–613; Shinn, *Mining Camps*, 258–274. Rodman Paul, in *California Gold: The Beginning of Mining in the Far West* (Cambridge, Mass., 1947), 193–196, agrees with Shinn that California precedents were important in shaping the development of later mine districts, but argues that the California precedents were themselves shaped by Mexican practices which derived from European law and custom. See also R. Paul, "The Origins of the Chinese Issue in California," *Mississippi Historical Review*, XXV (September, 1938), 181–196. The quotation is from Shinn, *Mining Camps*, 105.

[2] Henry Nash Smith, *Virgin Land, the American West as Symbol and Myth* (New York, 1961), especially 291–305.

system of early New England towns repeated the pattern of ancient Anglo-Saxon villages, and that the New England town meeting was in fact a reincarnation of the primitive German tribal council.[3] Thus the "instinct" of self-government was racially transmitted. Shinn simply extended the argument several thousand miles westward:

> It was the miners' court, that our Norse and Saxon ancestors, could they have risen from burial mounds like Beowulf's "on the steep, seen by sea-goers from afar," reared there by the "battle-brave companions of the dead," would undoubtedly have recognized as akin to those folk-moots held of old in primeval German and Scandinavian forests. In both alike were the right of free speech for all freemen, the right of unhampered discussion, the visible earnestness, the solemn judgement.[4]

Oddly, at almost the same time that Shinn was trying to fortify his frontier concept by means of Teutonic theory, Frederick Jackson Turner, who completed his doctorate at Johns Hopkins in 1890, was trying to break away from Teutonic theory (which he considered too much oriented to Europe) and to establish a nationally autonomous interpretation of American history. The frontier served this purpose. Thus, the two men seemed to be traveling in opposite directions. But their movement constituted a *dos-à-dos* between corners of the same square—which suggests some sort of affinity of opposites. Each in fact complemented the other. The frontier thesis, aside from the old romantic adulation of primitivism, lacked any explanation for the origin of its values until the Teutonic theory furnished one; while the Teutonic theory, to be serviceable in America, needed precisely that certificate of naturalization which the frontier provided. Of logical necessity for this marriage there may have been little enough; but there was at least an emotional congruity. The German forest and

[3] Charles A. Beard, *An Economic Interpretation of the Constitution of the United States* (New York, 1914), 2–3; Joseph Henry Jackson, "Introduction," Shinn, *Mining Camps*. The first volume, *Local Institutions* (Baltimore, 1883), of the *Johns Hopkins Studies in Historical and Political Science*, edited by Herbert Baxter Adams, contains the following papers by Adams: "The Germanic Origin of New England Towns," "Saxon Tithingmen in America," and "Norman Constables in America." Volume II, *Institutions and Economics* (Baltimore, 1884), contains Shinn's "Land Laws of Mining Districts." Frederick Jackson Turner, also a student of Adams's, completed his doctorate at Johns Hopkins in 1890 with a dissertation entitled, "Character and Influence of the Indian Trade in Wisconsin." (Dumas Malone and Allen Johnson (eds.), *Dictionary of American Biography*, 22 vols. (New York, 1928–1944), XVI (1936), 205–211.) Josiah Royce (below, p. 49) had taken his doctorate in literature and philosophy at Johns Hopkins in 1878. (*Dictionary of American Biography*, XIX, 62–64.)

[4] Shinn, *Mining Camps*, 167–168.

the American frontier would walk hand in hand for a good many decades through the visions and revisions of the West.[5]

Meanwhile, however, Shinn was encountering a formidable critic in the person of another Californian who had grown up not only during the afterglow of the gold rush, but in the very heart of the gold rush country. This was Josiah Royce, born in Grass Valley. Royce, like Shinn a product of the University of California, had also journeyed eastward in pursuit of scholarship. But Royce pushed beyond Shinn to the summits of academic life. After a pilgrimage to Germany in philosophy and literature, he returned to take his doctorate at Johns Hopkins in 1878; and by 1880 was ensconced at Harvard as a protégé of William James. Two years after the appearance of Shinn's *Mining Camps*, Royce published an essay on California subtitled, *A Study of American Character*.[6]

The admirable aspects of American character, for Royce, resided in the fabric of habit, education, and shared responsibility—that outer and inner garment which the Puritans had called civility. Despite his own allegiance to German scholarship, Royce ignored the mystique of the German forest; and he angrily rejected the frontier mystique. All that was worst in California sprang from the frontier. The frontier bred irresponsibility. Frontiersmen, having left settled communities behind them, felt themselves freed of social obligation and therefore at liberty to concentrate every energy on their search for gold. Such a totally individual focus became immoral and disastrous. One result was license for the criminal elements to run wild, since it was no man's obligation to control them. A second result was license for the vicious and irrational proclivities existing even in honest men, and of which, in California, the chief manifestation was brutal treatment of foreigners.[7]

[5] Richard Hofstadter, "Turner and the Frontier Myth," *American Scholar*, XVIII (Autumn, 1949), 433–443. For a few examples, see Lucille Eaves, *A History of California Labor Legislation* (Berkeley, 1910), 1–6; Jack London, in *The Valley of the Moon* (New York, 1913), 50, "All the old tales trooped before Saxon's eyes. . . . Shimmering in the sun-flashed dust of ten thousand hoofs, she saw pass, from East to West across a continent, the great hegira of the land-hungry Anglo-Saxon. It was part and fiber of her . . ."; Carl I. Wheat, in an editor's comment on a description of a lynching in Louise Amelia Clappe [Dame Shirley], *The Shirley Letters from the California Mines, 1851–1852* (New York, 1949), 101, "It is a tribute to the political genius of the miners and to their Anglo-Saxon traditions that the young men who in large part made up the mining population in a few short years brought order out of the chaos of this middle period of California's development."

[6] *Dictionary of American Biography*, XVI, 205–211; Josiah Royce, *California, from the Conquest in 1846 to the Second Vigilance Committee: A Study of American Character* (Boston, 1891).

[7] Royce, 275, 277.

Royce acknowledged all the evidence (of which Shinn presented a great deal) of miners' meetings and miners' courts. These men did indeed have, from their previous experience, an aptitude in political organization. But under frontier conditions the aptitude itself became corrupt. A miners' court might conduct a splendidly fair and "earnest" trial. Then having convicted the accused, say of theft, the court would either hang him, which was immoral, or whip and banish him, which was equally immoral since it turned him loose, hurt and embittered, to prey on other camps. These punishments were the only alternatives likely to receive much consideration since no one cared to spend the time or trouble necessary for building jails, or for sending prisoners and witnesses down to some distant place where regular trials might be held.[8] Social irresponsibility led inevitably to social immorality.

As for attacks against foreigners, the situation became worse yet. In some cases the entire community participated in criminal action. In other cases the law-abiding citizens sanctioned by their noninterference the acts of a criminal minority which most likely they had themselves helped to incite: "Ours were the crimes of a community consisting largely of honest but cruelly bigoted men, who encouraged the ruffians of their own nation to ill-treat the wanderers of another, to the frequent destruction of peace and good order. We were favored of heaven with the instinct of organization; and so here we organized brutality, and, so to speak, asked God's blessing upon it." [9]

Royce, then, took a somber and perhaps realistic view of the mining frontier. But although he rejected Shinn's (and Turner's) mystiques, he nonetheless had one of his own. This was the mystique of civility. The frontier for Royce was not a result of civilization, but an interruption of it. After the interruption (and it was a brief one in California), civilization would grow again like new flesh over the wound and the ills of the frontier would be healed: "Our true pride . . . must be . . . that the moral elasticity of our people is so great, their social vitality so marvelous, that a community of Americans could sin as fearfully as, in the early years, the mining community did sin, and could yet live to purify itself within so short a time, not by a revolution, but by a simple progress from social foolishness to social steadfastness." [10] In the long run Royce's view was as adamantly and optimistically progressive as was Shinn's.

Setting aside for the time being these several mystiques, common sense will suggest that any frontier must be shaped in part by the society behind it, and that the frontier experience would to some degree

[8] Royce, 313–325.
[9] Royce, 363.
[10] Royce, 375–376.

modify that society. On the California mining frontier, therefore, one might expect to find traces of those patterns of thought and organization which we have explored in previous chapters. Viewed in this light, the miners' community appears not at all surprisingly as a model of the Jacksonian producer ethic. Land, being the property of the United States government, belonged to everyone and was in itself, temporarily at least, valueless. Value lay in the opportunity to exploit the land, and this, the miners' codes declared, must be shared equally. Each man's portion was limited to an amount he could work himself. "A full claim for mining purposes, on the flats or hills in this district, shall consist of an area equal to that of one hundred feet square. . . . No person or persons shall be allowed to hold more than one full claim, within the bounds of this district, by location. . . . Claims shall be forfeited when parties holding them have neglected . . . working them for five days after water can be procured at the usual rates, unless prevented by sickness or unavoidable accident." [11] So ordered the laws of Columbia Camp, Tuolomne County, in language almost identical with that of scores of other mining districts.

Shinn apparently felt there was something unique, perhaps even socialistic in a positive or Christian sense, about this arrangement. Actually the Homestead Act of 1862 was founded on precisely the same principle. There was of course a difference in that the Homestead Act conveyed title to real property, whereas the miners' codes conveyed merely a use right which would terminate when the use ended. But to American producers, urban or agrarian, there was nothing exotic in the concept of use right. Generations of farmers from the Atlantic seaboard to the Pacific Coast had used their land, and mined it, and moved on to new holdings. Fur traders, cattle grazers, lumbermen cared very little for title to land, so long as they had its use. In this respect certainly the miners were following long-established precedents. Title to real property might actually prove a hindrance; it might cost money; it might involve taxes and responsibilities. It might limit mobility and thus reduce a miner's opportunity to stake out new and potentially richer claims. Long after United States law permitted the patenting of claims as real property, most miners neglected to do so. But from this it did not by any means follow that claims were not property. Claims were bought and sold, traded, capitalized, subdivided, combined. The courts always treated them as property.[12]

11 John S. Hittell, *Mining in the Pacific States of North America* (San Francisco, 1861), 192–193.

12 Shinn, *Mining Camps*, 103–104, 221–225, 264; Samuel P. Hays, *Conservation and the Gospel of Efficiency: The Progressive Conservation Movement, 1890–1920* (Cambridge, Mass., 1959), 27–90; Rodman Paul, *California Gold*, 211–239; Hittell, 187. Apparently some of the earliest camp codes attempted to equalize not only

Shinn was right, however, in feeling that there was a new and unique aspect of the California miners' communities. What that uniqueness consisted in was not the definition of property, but the fact that here, almost singly in American experience, the producer ethic found a basis of genuinely equal opportunity. In other fields of endeavor there had always been preliminary qualifications. The entrepreneur, for example, must have accumulated his capital, or at least an adroitness in borrowing money; the craftsman needed his skill; the farmer was helpless without his previously acquired knowledge of farming and some financial reserve as well. But for miners, once they had managed to reach the California foothills, such elements of inequality were largely wiped away. Education, experience, skills, even a bank full of money back home counted for relatively little in the early period of prospecting and placer mining. What technology there was could be learned in a few days; every man had the same chance as his neighbor.[13] Here, briefly, the Jacksonian dream came true; and in this lies one of the chief reasons for the extraordinary impact of these years.

Circumstances, then, gave substance to the equality of opportunity which was legislated by the miners' codes. But how far would such equality reach? In practice it would reach no further than the number of workable claims into which any given district could be divided. This raised immediately a distinction between insiders and outsiders. Such a line of demarcation, however, was not at all inharmonious with the producer ethic. Jacksonianism had reached California as a complex of emotionally charged ideas which included a romantic and spread-eagle nationalism together with a conviction of racial superiority. The first victims were Latin Americans. In many camps the native Californians, Sonorans, a few groups of Chileans were evicted from their claims for nonpayment of the state miners' tax or simply driven out as an undesirable element. Frenchmen also suffered occasionally, while English, Scotch, Irish, and Germans seem generally to have been included within the consensus of insiders. But the Chinese were the main victims. Prohibitions against the holding of claims by Asiatics were widespread, and probably in most districts Chinese were ousted regularly or sporadically from their diggings.[14]

discovery claims but purchase claims. For an example, see the laws of New Kanaka Camp, Tuolumne County, quoted in Hittell, 197–198. Since this tendency ran counter to the entrepreneurial aspect of equal opportunity, it quickly proved recessive.

[13] Hittell, 115–120, 127–153; Royce, 282–289.

[14] Hubert Howe Bancroft, *Works*, XXXV, *California Inter Pocula* (San Francisco, 1888), 560; Clappe, *Shirley Letters*, 141–142, 158–168; Robert Glass Cleland, *A His-*

MINES AND RAILROADS

53

Yet the matter was not so simply resolved. A producer who believed he had fortune in his grasp was not anxious to take time off for cooking food and washing shirts. Chinese were said to be expert at these tasks; and so while they were being run out of camp on one side, they were invited back in on the other. The exhaustion of easy surface deposits further complicated the situation. As good claims became scarce, the pressure against Chinese miners increased. At the same time, however, American miners, discouraged, began to think of picking up stakes and trying their luck elsewhere. In order to move, a miner needed money, and naturally he hated to abandon work already put into his old diggings. He therefore looked around for a buyer and found that the only prospective buyers of second-hand merchandise in mine claims were the Chinese.[15]

To this extent they became indispensable if American miners were to exploit their equality of opportunity to the full. The outcome was a tacit regularization of status for Chinese in the camps. They could come in and stay. They could work at tasks other than mining, especially if these were menial or unskilled; and they could comb out low-yield or worked-over sites. Reporting the purchase by Chinese of a

tory of California; The American Period (New York, 1922), 281–282; Royce, California, 356–368; Shinn, Mining Camps, 203–204, 208. J. D. Borthwick, in The Gold Hunters (New York, 1917), testified to the ready acceptance in California of the Scotch-English. He also noted the easier assimilation (233) of Germans than of French. On the French in the mines, see Shirley Letters, 112, and Royce, 365–366. Shirley Letters (163–164) tells of a fight over a prostitute between an Irish immigrant and a Spanish American of unspecified origin. When the Irishman was felled by a knife thrust, the American community rose in arms to avenge "poor Tom" against the foreigners. Paul, California Gold, 320–321; Royce, 366–367. For examples of exclusion clauses in camp codes, see Hittell, 179, 194, 198; Eliot Lord, Comstock Mines and Miners, Monographs of the United States Geological Survey, IV (Washington, 1883), 44. Royce and Shinn, on the subject of the Chinese, are a study in themselves. Shinn viewed the problem of antiforeignism solely in terms of the ill-treatment of the French and of Spanish Americans, especially the native Californians. "This tendency to despise, abuse, and over-ride the Spanish-Americans may well be called one of the darkest threads in the fabric of Anglo-Saxon frontier government" (208). Royce, more sensitive on the issue than Shinn, expressed indignation in behalf of Spanish Americans, the French, and "Digger" Indians (363, 365–366). But like Shinn, he seemed scarcely to see the treatment of Chinese as part of the same question. In a twelve-page chapter (346–358) titled "The Warfare Against the Foreigners," Royce mentioned the Chinese only once, and then in a peripheral reference to an episode in which a Canadian miner was able to rally his camp to defend several Chinese holders of purchase claims against some "gaunt, long-haired" claim jumpers from Arkansas (366–367).

15 On the ubiquity of Chinese washers in the mines, see Shirley Letters, 185; Shinn, Mining Camps, 204; Chauncey L. Canfield (ed.), The Diary of a Forty Niner (Stanford, 1947), 167–168, 175–176. Oscar Lewis in his introduction (v–x), contends that this fictional "diary" offers a reasonably accurate account of the general social background.

supposedly worthless claim for $2,200, the Nevada County *Transcript* commented that if the claim had remained in the hands of the original holder, it would probably never have been worked. But the Chinese would do well: "They appear to have reduced this kind of mining to a science. Old abandoned claims that nobody thought had enough gold in them to buy salt, have been purchased by Chinamen and worked with profit." [16] Through the sixties, Chinese in California were largely replacing Americans in placer and riverbed operations.[17]

Meanwhile, the organization of the miners' community was changing its character. What had begun as an undifferentiated democracy had first drawn the line against certain types of outsiders. Insiders, simply, were those who held (and were permitted to continue holding) claims. The result was something which resembled a joint stock company rather more than it did Charles Shinn's folk-moot. And presently, divisions developed among insiders as well. The camp was growing, it needed supplies; merchants and traders arrived, preempted town lots, threw up buildings. As placer operations expanded, the principal diggings moved out of the creek bottoms up into dry gulches to which water had to be brought from a distance. The first water companies were partnerships of miners who pooled their own labor. But soon the projects outgrew the initial resources; labor had to be hired, and this in turn required cash outlay. Cash was largely in the hands of the merchants and these became the major investors in the water companies. When gold production began to decline, as it very soon did, the miners demanded lower water rates; but the companies by this time were struggling to meet dividends on capital invested during the years of maximum labor cost.[18]

Here was a conflict of interest which resulted in a series of strikes by working miners against the water companies. Rodman Paul, in his study of California mining, makes the valid point that these actually were consumer boycotts rather than strikes.[19] But whatever name one calls them by, the reality was a head-on collision within the community. Clearly it was impossible to resolve such an issue in the old style— by calling the camp to assembly and taking a majority vote. The reign of equal opportunity had been short-lived indeed.

But an even more fundamental cleavage was taking shape. A few claims were rich, and many were poor. Large numbers of miners found

[16] Quoted in *Alta California*, "Industrial Condition of the State," July 12, 1869.
[17] Paul, *California Gold*, 129–130, 320–321; Ping Chiu, *Chinese Labor in California, 1850–1880: An Economic Study* (Madison, 1963), 27–30.
[18] Paul, *California Gold*, 60, 324–326.
[19] Paul, 324.

it more advantageous to work at the prevailing wage for their luckier neighbors, or for the water companies, than to go on scratching their own barren claims.[20] At the same time, a similar process as between rich and poor districts was bringing wage workers—American miners, not Chinese—into the bonanza camps. The old camp assemblies had without too much difficulty been able to handle such matters as size of claims, methods of registration and transfer; but how would they deal with disagreement over rates of pay and hours of labor? Whom would the assembly represent—the miners or the claim holders?

Resolution of this problem was interrupted in California by the rapid decline of placer mining and by discovery of the Comstock Lode, which in 1859 swept the surplus population out of the foothills and across the mountains into Nevada.[21] The next act would be played in Virginia City and Gold Hill. Here, surface mining yielded to deep quartz excavation. With extraordinary speed the original claimants were bought out, their holdings consolidated and capitalized—not as in the case of the foothill water companies by the money of local merchants, but by large investments funneled through the San Francisco stock exchange. The cleavage which had begun in California was now complete. Absentee and depersonalized, the claim holders had become employers. When the miners of the Comstock assembled, there could be no question whom the gathering would speak for; there was none among them except wage workers.

So long as flush times held, no collision occurred. But the effects of the increasing depth of shafts, drainage problems, the pinching out of promising leads were cumulative; and by the spring of 1864 profits fell sharply. Next came the collapse of stock prices. Inevitably, the owners, trying to reduce costs, whittled away at the prevailing wage rate which at that time was four dollars a day: [22] "On the evening of July 31, 1864, a long procession was formed, including in its ranks nearly all the miners and mill hands of the district, and marched through the streets of Virginia City and Gold Hill, headed by a band of music playing all the defiant airs in their score books." Several days later, "the miners again met in a body and completed the organization of a Miners' League. . . . By the laws of this society every member was

20 The prevailing rate varied with the optimism of individual miners as to what they thought they could earn working for themselves. Paul, in *California Gold*, 349–350, estimates that wages averaged ten dollars a day in 1850–1851, leveled off at five dollars a day till 1858, then dropped down toward three dollars a day and lower, through the sixties.

21 Paul, 174–181.

22 Zoeth Skinner Eldredge (ed.), *History of California*, 5 vols. (New York [1915]), IV, 242; Lord, *Comstock Mines* (above, n. 14), 77–79, 131–132, 181–183, 186.

required to pledge his word of honor 'never to work in the County of Storey for less than $4 per day in gold and silver coin.' " [23]

The mine owners retaliated by hiring non-league members at piece rates and under individual contracts. They thwarted an effort to impose the closed shop, and then in a series of counteroffensives virtually drove the league off the Comstock. But this apparent debacle for the miners turned out to be no more than a tactical retreat. The exploratory shafts and tunnels, now hundreds of feet deep in the mountainside, presently broke into chambers of high grade ore. Bonanza days returned, throwing the labor market into short supply. The league, reorganized on the Fourth of July 1867, promptly renewed its demand for a four-dollar daily wage.[24] Again the owners tentatively gave in, waiting meanwhile to see how one of their number would fare in defying the miners. A "committee" of some three hundred men

> quietly formed in column and marched to the Savage mine works, where the foreman . . . was persuaded to hoist out the working miners in order that it might be ascertained how many were receiving less than $4 per day. Fourteen of the seventy miners thus brought to the surface admitted that their wages were less than the union standard and were ordered to stand aside as black sheep. . . . The Savage Mining Company bowed to the decision, and thus the arbitrary standard of wages became again a binding law on the Comstock Lode.[25]

The metamorphosis of miners' assembly into an industrial and closed shop union was complete.[26]

It remains to examine the status of Chinese with respect to these transformations in the community of miners. In California, miners had learned to regard the opportunity of finding and exploiting gold

---

[23] Lord, 184–185.

[24] Lord, 187–190, 266–267.

[25] Lord, 267–268.

[26] The closed shop, which seems to have existed de facto from 1867, was not officially declared until ten years later. (Lord, 357; Virginia City (Nevada) *Territorial Enterprise*, September 7, 1877.) It was typical of miners' organization that it took industrial form, although no distinction between "industrial" and "trade" unionism was drawn until a good many years later. Herbert R. Northrup, in *Organized Labor and the Negro* (New York, 1944), 162, attributed the tendency of miners to industrial unionism to the absence of wide skill differentials among the bulk of the workers. The few high-skilled employees, because of the isolation of most mining communities, would be cut off from contact with their fellow craftsmen. Beyond this, the hazards of the work, and the single-industry character of mine towns, would tend to sharpen class consciousness and minimize craft consciousness. For whatever reasons, miners' unions—from the Miners' Leagues of the Comstock down through the Knights of Labor, to the Mine, Mill and Smelter Workers and the United Mine Workers—have been industrial in structure.

deposits as a kind of property right, inherent in Anglo-Saxon descent and American nationality. The right was extended by courtesy to "assimilable" aliens; the Chinese, of course, were excluded from its exercise. There had been, however, a tacit acceptance of Chinese as menial or unskilled laborers, and as purchasers of second-hand surface claims. This entire fabric was carried across the mountains with the first rush to the Comstock. Here, placer mining was of only slight importance; the miners' community became a community of wage earners; and the concept of property right was transferred from entrepreneurial opportunity to job opportunity. As for the Chinese, they were barred from employment in Comstock quartz mining just as they had been from the exploitation of discovery claims in California. Yet here too they were ushered in by the side entrance. They performed their traditional functions as cooks, house servants, washermen; and most important of all, perhaps, they fetched in firewood—an occupation which during the winters at seven thousand feet of altitude in that sparsely timbered country may well have proved almost as lucrative as mining itself.[27]

While the deep mines of the Comstock were building cities and creating millionaires, early experiments with quartz mining in California had turned out disastrously. Later, as the placer deposits were mined out, quartz exploration continued and finally brought several groups of deep shafts into profitable operation. Miniscule in comparison with the diggings of the Comstock, these California mines continued locally owned and for the most part locally financed. Moreover they developed in regions already showing some occupational diversity. The result was that the process of class polarization remained ragged and incomplete. Instead of enunciating law for the land, as hard-rock miners were doing across the Sierra, those in California found themselves an alienated minority within an increasingly hostile community.[28]

California quartz mining was in almost every respect imitative of the Nevada model. Owners learned from the Comstock how to cope with problems of drainage and ventilation in deep shafts, while their workmen were studying the Comstock pattern of unionism. As in Nevada, the first confrontation was triggered by efforts of the owners to reduce a previously accepted wage level. The California scale had leveled off at three dollars, the differential from Nevada's four-dollar rate being the measure of relative labor scarcity on the far side of the mountains. Coupled with the wage issue was a conflict over technologi-

27 Dan De Quille [William Wright], *The Big Bonanza* (New York, 1953), 40, 291–295; Lord, 44, 199, 204, 355.
28 Paul, *California Gold*, 132, 143–144, 183–186, 322–323.

cal change. Dynamite, thanks to the efforts of Nobel in Sweden, was just then making its appearance and provided a more effective explosive for hard rock than the old style black powder. In addition it fitted a smaller bore hole, requiring less labor time. Whereas it had been customary for two-man teams to prepare charges of black powder, one turning the drill as the other swung the sledge hammer, in drilling for dynamite one worker with a diamond bit could do the job by himself. California quartz miners bitterly opposed this innovation. From 1869 to 1873, Nevada and Amador counties were shaken by a series of strikes and lockouts. Buildings were burned, strikers and nonstrikers beat and sometimes killed one another. The governor in 1871 called out the state militia.[29]

Always in the background of this dispute was the question of Chinese labor. Completion of the Central Pacific in 1869 released a formidable number of Chinese construction workers, trained in tunneling, drilling—and handling dynamite. They were employed by water companies and increasingly by quartz mines for work at the surface and in the stamping mills.[30] Mine owners (and newspapers supporting them) threatened to let the Chinese take over the entire industry. This, wrote the San Francisco *Daily Alta California* in 1869, was the only way. Because the cost of extraction was prohibitively high, the state's mining regions had fallen into depression and decay. Yet white miners refused to use the new explosive; and white miners demanded three dollars a day, whereas Chinese asked only a dollar and a half and doubtless within a year or two would be working for less than that. The *Daily Alta* predicted that Chinese labor in the vein mines of California and Nevada would boost the output of precious metals by more than 100 percent: "The Chinamen are ploughmen, laundrymen, placer miners, woollen spinners and weavers, domestic servants, cigar makers, shoemakers, and railroad builders to the great benefit of the State, and why should they not be quartz miners?"[31]

The outcome was a kind of stalemate. For most underground work the miners managed to salvage the old three-dollar scale, although they yielded to a second class rating at $2.50 a day. And they largely succeeded in holding the line against the Chinese. But here the price was total surrender on the issue that actually had touched off the conflict—dynamite—and this in turn guaranteed a narrowing of their job opportunity.[32] It is unlikely that they could for long have resisted

29 Paul, 326–327, 350–351. *Alta,* June 14, 17, 28, July 5, 16, 19, 1869.
30 Paul, 326–333.
31 *Alta,* May 22, June 17, 1869.
32 Grass Valley *Daily National,* May 25, 27, 31, June 2, 4, 9, 11, 16, October 2, 1869.

technological innovation under any circumstances; but the result was that they blamed the Chinese for their defeat. What ensued in the quartz districts of California was an uneasy balance, heavy with potential violence.

Yet already this potential was being institutionalized. In June 1869 the miners' unions of Virginia City and Gold Hill adopted an address to the workingmen of Nevada in which they warned of impending crisis:

> Capital has decreed that Chinese shall supplant and drive hence the present race of toilers. . . . Every branch of industry in the State of California swarms with Chinese. . . . Can we compete with a barbarous race, devoid of energy and careless of the State's weal? Sunk in their own debasement, having no voice in government, how long would it be ere ruin would swamp the capitalist and the poor man together? . . . Here, then, upon the threshold of a conflict which, if persevered in, will plunge the State into anarchy and ruin, we appeal to the working men to step to the front and hurl back the tide of barbarous invaders.

Although this language, as San Francisco's *Daily Alta* at once pointed out, seemed "to suggest the use of unlawful and criminal means," [33] the address itself was not to be taken quite at face value. Its real intent was as an opening bid in a rather tricky game the miners' unions were playing with the Bank of California's Nevada agent, William Sharon, and the Comstock kings.[34] That summer, following the junction of transcontinental railways in Salt Lake Basin, a short line was under construction to link the bonanza cities of the Comstock to the Central Pacific at Reno. This was the Virginia and Truckee, a fifty-mile spur which, like the Central, depended largely on Chinese labor. Engineering problems were formidable, requiring a gigantic investment in cuts, trestles, tunnels; and through the summer of 1869 some twelve or fifteen hundred Chinese laborers camped on the slopes below Virginia City. The miners waited till the railhead came within easy walking distance. They then marched out with a brass band, defied the sheriff, and drove the highest encampment of Chinese into the sage brush. Here matters rested at deadlock for several days until William Sharon, who was chief promoter of the railroad project, persuaded the "members of the unions" to let the work go on. In order to gain this concession, he was obliged to sign "an

33 *Alta*, June 17, 1869.
34 Gold Hill (Nev.) *Evening News*, July 7, September 29, October 2, 7, 1869.

agreement which barred him from employing Chinese within the limits of Virginia City and Gold Hill." [35]

The point was, not that the miners cared to take over the tasks of the Chinese, but to make certain that Mr. Sharon and his friends would entertain no notion of keeping Chinese on afterward for deep shaft work. Despite the inflammatory address, there was no general boycott or proscription. The new railroad obviously benefitted the miners' community through its enhancement of their "property" in job opportunities. They were therefore as willing to tolerate Chinese labor in its construction as they were to accept the services of Chinese in cooking, washing, scrounging firewood, and digging water supply ditches. Thus on both sides of the Sierra, however ominous the potential of violence, the fact was that a balance, a regularization, had been established. The Chinese lived and functioned in the hard-rock mining towns very much as they had lived and functioned in the earlier placer camps.

The Railroads

While this pattern of mingled acceptance and exclusion was taking shape in the mining districts, a parallel development was occurring on the railroads. The transcontinental line had begun as a wartime undertaking. Prior to the Civil War, a number of engineering studies and a great deal of agitation had inspired certain preliminary steps of organization; but it was only the threatened dismemberment of the Union, coupled with removal of southern opposition to the north-central route, which finally brought Congress in 1862 to the point of voting out franchises and federal money. Appropriately since the railroad had been a major plank of the Republican platforms, the franchise for the western portion went to a group of rising young California Republicans. None of them had much experience in railroad building. They had come west as gold hunters in 1849 or soon after, and like many others had done better at storekeeping than at mining. But they had helped hold the state against the secessionists; and one of them, Leland Stanford, was serving simultaneously as first Republican governor of California and first president of the Central Pacific Railroad.[36]

Two gigantic problems immediately confronted the young entrepreneurs: scarcity of capital and scarcity of labor. These they must resolve somehow or other before they could come to grips with the

[35] Lord, *Comstock Mines* (above, n. 14), 355–357.

[36] E. L. Sabin, *Building the Pacific Railway* (Philadelphia, 1919), 11–40; George T. Clark, *Leland Stanford* (Stanford, 1931), 194.

third and even larger problem, the Sierra Nevada. As to the first difficulty, Congress had partially solved it for them by loans of government bonds and outright grants of public land along both sides of the
projected right of way. Here was security for borrowing needed capital.
But the solution of the first difficulty tended to aggravate the second.
Because the bonds and land grants were to be issued per mile of track
cons'·ucted, and because no meeting point for the eastern and western
lines was designated in the act of Congress, the two companies were
thrown into a race for mileage, and for survival.[37] Success would hinge
on speed of construction. In a time of national crisis such an arrangement doubtless seemed appropriate; but construction speed in that
prebulldozer era varied more or less directly with the size of the labor
force. And the labor force in California in the early 1860s appeared
meager indeed. Of the men offering for hire—white men, that is—
most were, like the promoters of the railroad themselves, slightly over-
age forty-niners, still gold-diggers at heart. There was in addition a
sprinkling of laborers and skilled mechanics beginning to drift out
from the East. But they too seem to have been infected upon arrival
in the golden state with a touch of the poet. "Mining was more to
their taste than the discipline of railroad work," wrote Lewis Clement,
who served as assistant chief in the Central Pacific Engineering Department. "They were indifferent, independent and their labor high-priced.
. . . The first mining excitement meant a complete stampede and
consequent abandonment of all work." [38] The company would hire
men in San Francisco, pay their expenses to the railhead, where
promptly they vanished over the skyline in the direction of the latest
diggings.[39]

Responsibility for solving the Central's construction problems fell
to one of its four top directors, Charles Crocker. Innocent though
Crocker was of any training in engineering, he believed he held a firm
grip on the essential ingredient: knowledge of how to handle workingmen. "There was no need for sympathy for those men," he reminisced
afterward. "Why I used to go up and down that road in my car like
a mad bull, stopping along the way wherever there was anything amiss
and raising old Nick." [40] Even Crocker's assaults, however, failed to
squeeze much mileage out of the boomers and grubstakers who were

[37] Sabin, 13–40. U.S., Pacific Railway Commission, *Report and Testimony Taken*,
9 vols. 50th Cong., 1st Sess., Sen. Ex. Doc. 51 (Washington, 1888), V, 2523.

[38] Quoted in John D. Galloway, *The First Transcontinental Railway* (New York,
1950), 144.

[39] Pacific Railway Commission, VI, 3225–3226.

[40] Charles Crocker, "Facts . . . regarding . . . identification with the Central
Pacific Railroad," dictated to H. H. Bancroft, (typescript in the Bancroft Library,
University of California, Berkeley), 49–52.

willing to dandle an occasional shovel for the transcontinental line. Months rolled into years and the great California project seemed to have bogged down hopelessly in the mud flats and oak thickets of the lower foothills. After two years of effort, the railhead stood less than fifty miles from its starting point. The High Sierra was not yet even in sight.

To make matters worse, the Central's eastern rival the Union Pacific, which had gotten off to a slow start, was now hitting full throttle. With easy access to materials by way of the Missouri River and ample labor supply from waves of Irish immigrants coming through the Atlantic seaports, the Union in the spring of 1866 was laying track at the pace of a mile a day. It was outbuilding the Central by something like eight to one. The Central Pacific directors had engaged in endless discussions of their labor problem. Before Appomattox they had toyed with the idea of having Confederate prisoners shipped out under guard. Later they investigated the possibility of importing black freedmen from the South. One of the first suggestions for using Chinese seems to have come from Crocker's brother, E. B. Crocker, former chief justice of the Supreme Court of California and legal counsel to the railroad. The construction department, however, was unimpressed. Chinese might do well enough as cigarmakers and houseboys or might even be successful in combing out the tailings of abandoned placer mines; but for heavy construction they were too small and too frail.[41]

The decision to hire Chinese was finally taken in 1865. There were, by that time, considerable numbers available, since placer mining, even for the Chinese, was at last giving out. According to the legend, Charles Crocker ordered up a gang of fifty, mainly for the purpose of frightening his white workers who had threatened a strike.[42] The results were so gratifying to Crocker that he sent out a general call. Up from the gold camps and the valley towns, and from Sacramento and San Francisco, they came trooping into the mountains. Crocker had three thousand at work before the end of the year. "Without them," wrote the Central's president, Leland Stanford, "it would be impossible to complete the western portion of this great national highway within the time required by the acts of Congress." Stanford described the Chinese as "quiet, peaceable, industrious, economical—ready and apt to learn all the different kinds of work required in railroad building." [43] They were in fact a construction foreman's dream.

[41] Galloway, 160, 299–300; Oscar Lewis, *The Big Four* (New York, 1938), 69–70; Dutch Flat *Enquirer*, July 5, 1867.

[42] Chiu, *Chinese Labor in California* (above, n. 17), 27–30, 44.

[43] Figures on employment of Chinese in 1865 and the Stanford statement are quoted in Sabin, *Building the Pacific Railway* (above, n. 36), 110–111.

In applying the adjective "economical" to his Chinese laborers, Stanford apparently was speaking of them individually. He meant that each worker was thrifty and was therefore, in the Protestant sense, morally deserving of employment. But it was perhaps equally true that the Chinese en masse were "economical" for the railroad. As of 1865, the going rate for unskilled white workers was thirty dollars a month plus board and lodging. Chinese received the same sum in cash but fed and housed themselves. While the Central's estimate of seventy-five cents to one dollar a day as the cost of maintaining white workers was probably a good deal too high, it would appear, even if the dollar were cut in half, that the company was able to purchase Chinese labor for something like two-thirds the price of white. And the comparison remains incomplete since Chinese must have been used, perhaps rather frequently, on jobs falling within the skilled ratings such as masonry, tracklaying, blacksmithing, handling explosives; and these, for white men, would have commanded a wage of three to five dollars a day.[44]

Yet even if we accept the modest two-thirds ratio, it follows that the company in three years saved approximately five and a half million dollars by hiring Chinese instead of white unskilled laborers.[45] Why did the whites acquiesce in this? Among the more obvious reasons are two previously noted: that white workers were in short supply, and that the mining districts offered attractive alternatives. But there were other factors as well. One was that the hiring of Chinese resulted not in displacement of non-Chinese, but in their upgrading. To the unskilled white railroad laborer of 1865, the coming of the Chinese meant his own advancement into that elite one-fifth of the labor force which was composed of strawbosses, foremen, teamsters, skilled craftsmen. This in itself was no small bonanza. And there was one final reason, perhaps more cogent than all the others. No man who had any choice would have chosen to be a common laborer on the Central Pacific during the crossing of the High Sierra.

Crocker's army laid siege to the summit of the range late in 1866. The railhead was still fourteen miles below the unfinished tunnel and there in December the first snows bogged it down. Normal procedure would have been to withdraw for the winter. But each week lost meant a loss to the Central Pacific of hundreds of thousands in land and subsidy, and beyond this was the overriding question of control. For the California line to be operable afterward as an independent enterprise, it would have to have something better within its territory than

44 Robert L. Fulton, *Epic of the Overland* (Los Angeles, 1924), 33–35; Pacific Railway Commission, VI, 3139–3140; Dutch Flat *Enquirer*, December 28, 1867.

45 If Chinese laborers at $30 a month cost two-thirds as much as white, the difference was $15 per man per month. Ten thousand white workers for three years would then have cost $5,400,000 more than the same number of Chinese.

mountains and desert. Eastward, the nearest lands of sufficient fertil-
ity to provide some volume of freight and passenger traffic were the
Mormon settlements of Utah. Whichever road reached Salt Lake Basin
first would come to dominate the transcontinental system. Crocker, ridden raw by his fellow directors who assailed him over the telegraph
from rose-arbored Sacramento, hurled his forces into this battle in a
continuing frenzy.[46]

The portals of the summit tunnel were buried under fantastic drifts,
the Chinese encampments were snowed under. The Chinese dug
chimneys and air shafts, lived by lantern light. They tunneled in from
the camps to reach the bore of the tunnel itself, and the work continued, although materials now had to be lowered forty feet or more
by steam hoist from the surface of the snow, and the waste from the
digging taken out in the same way.[47] On Christmas Day, 1866, the
Dutch Flat *Enquirer* reported that "a gang of Chinamen employed by
the railroad were covered up by a snow slide and four or five died
before they could be exhumed. . . . The snow fell to such a depth
that one whole camp of Chinamen was covered up during the night
and parties were digging them out when our informant left." [48]

All that winter and through the following summer Donner Summit
held fast. Boring the tunnel required thirteen months and it was well
into September when the drillers finally holed through.[49] But before
tracks could be laid, winter had shut in and the camps were snowed
under again. This second winter was, if anything, worse than the preceding. Crocker's chief lieutenant, James Strobridge, testifying twenty
years later before a federal investigating commission, recalled the details of both those winters with an almost agonized clarity:

> That was the winter when the Dutch Flat stage stuck in the
> mud for six weeks in the streets of Gold Run. . . . There was
> a good deal of that winter when the [rail]road was blocked,
> and then in those bad winters we did not keep it open. . . .
> We hauled over that snow to Donner Lake the material for a
> railroad track of forty miles, with all the trimmings, three
> locomotives and forty cars. We built forty miles of railroad
> in the Truckee Canyon before the connection was made by
> way of the summit. . . . In that manner we forced our way

[46] Sacramento *Union*, November 29, December 12, 1866; Dutch Flat *Enquirer*, January 26, February 3, 1867; testimony of Leland Stanford, Pacific Railway Commission, V, 2523; Clark, *Leland Stanford*, 223.

[47] Pacific Railway Commission, V, 2577–2579.

[48] Reprinted in the Sacramento *Union*, December 28, 1866.

[49] Pacific Railway Commission, VI, 3150; Sabin, *Building the Pacific Railway*, 160; Lewis, *The Big Four*, 77; Dutch Flat *Enquirer*, October 30, 1867.

across the mountains at an enormous cost. It cost nearly three times what it would have cost to have done it in the summertime when it should have been done. But we shortened the time seven years from what Congress expected when the act was passed.

And then, although the commission had made clear that it was inquiring only into the cost in dollars, James Strobridge told them: "The snow slides carried away our camps and we lost a good many men in those slides; many of them we did not find until the next season when the snow melted." [50]

How many men was "a good many"? Perhaps even Crocker and Strobridge had no very clear idea. All laborers in heavy construction in those days had to be to a degree expendable; and Chinese were more so than most. By Crocker's own reckoning, the Central kept ten or eleven thousand on the line from 1866 to 1869, but what the rate of replacement may have been he did not specify. The railroad obtained most of its gang labor through the agency of Sisson and Wallace, a firm in which, by convenient coincidence, another of the Crocker brothers, Clark W., had become a leading member. [51] Where did Sisson and Wallace procure their Chinese? The evidence summarized in chapter 1 indicates that by 1865 large numbers of Chinese were available due to the decline in placer mining. But apparently these were insufficient to meet the need. "We had a good deal of difficulty getting labor," Lewis Clement, the assistant chief in the Engineering Department testified afterward. "The labor was not in the country and had to be imported." [52] Arrangements for such importation—a tricky business—were usually handled by brokers; and the most prominent of these seems to have been a Dutch merchant by the name of Cornelius Koopmanschap with headquarters in San Francisco. Koopmanschap told a convention of southern planters meeting at Memphis in 1869 that he could secure laborers for them direct from China, under five-year contract, for as little as ten or twelve dollars a month. He boasted that his firm had brought 30,000 Chinese into California. [53] There is no

[50] Pacific Railway Commission, V, 2580–2581; VI, 3150. For accounts of the winter construction, see V, 2522–2523; and Fulton, *Epic*, 36–37.

[51] U.S., Congress, Senate, *Report of the Special Joint Committee to Investigate Chinese Immigration*, 44th Cong., 2d Sess., Senate Report 689 (Washington, 1877): testimony of Charles Crocker, 674–676; former Governor Low of California, 82; James Strobridge, 724. See H. L. Wells, *History of Nevada County* (Oakland, California, 1880), 215–216.

[52] Pacific Railway Commission, VI, 3224.

[53] Gunther Barth, *Bitter Strength: A History of the Chinese in the United States, 1850–1870* (Cambridge, Mass., 1964), 117–118, 191–193. On the background of the Pacific coolie traffic, Stanford M. Lyman, "The Structure of Chinese Society in

need to take Koopmanschap's figures as accurate. The point is simply that recruitment was heavy because losses were heavy.

In view of all this it is scarcely surprising that there was no great clamor among western workingmen for the privilege of replacing Chinese on the Central Pacific. The attacks against the railroad for its hiring practices came later and for different reasons. What had taken shape during the years of construction was a pattern similar in many respects to the pattern developing simultaneously in mining. Chinese employment was tolerated—perhaps even welcomed—for unskilled, menial, or otherwise undesirable tasks, the performance of which would enhance the job opportunity and earning capacity of non-Chinese workers. On the railroads especially this arrangement turned out to be extraordinarily enduring. Chinese gangs helped build the Central and Southern Pacific's main line down the San Joaquin Valley in 1870 and 1871. They worked on the hook-up to Los Angeles and the famous loop over Tehachapi Pass, both completed in 1876. By the early eighties when the California system was fighting the Texas Pacific for a direct route to the Gulf of Mexico, Chinese moved east through Yuma to Tucson and beyond El Paso. At the same time they were working north from Sacramento along the Shasta route which connected through to Portland in 1887.[54]

More than a hundred years of tumultuous change in railroading have left this basic division of labor almost unaltered. As if in a daguerreotype from the first decade after the Civil War, the characteristic picture appears: the face of the engineer, always white, capped and goggled at his cab window, one gloved hand raised in casual greeting to the gandy dancers along the trackside—formerly Chinese or Irish, now generally Negro and Mexican—as they stand back to let the express roll through.

Nineteenth Century America" (Ph.D. diss., University of California, Berkeley, 1961), 392–404; and Persia Crawford Campbell, *Chinese Coolie Immigration to Countries within the British Empire* (London, 1923). *Alta,* July 15, 1869.

[54] Paul Victor DeFord, "In Defense of Empire: The Southern Pacific versus the Texas Pacific" (M.A. thesis, History, University of California, Berkeley, 1948), 36, 40–41, 51–55; Cleland, *History of California,* 397. For an example of the division of labor outlined in this chapter, see Bodie (California) *Daily Free Press,* May 25, 28, June 2, 3, 1881.

4

REHABILITATION OF THE
DEMOCRATIC PARTY

Restoration of the Democratic party after Appomattox must have
seemed to California Democrats almost as difficult a task as the tran-
sit of the Sierra had seemed to some of their Republican opponents.
The old party was split and it was tainted with secession. One of
California's two Democratic senators had been arrested by federal
officers, other top-ranking Democrats had departed to fight for the
Confederacy, and throughout the war the political atmosphere in the
West had been thick, if not with plots, at least with rumors of plots.
When news of Lincoln's death reached San Francisco, mobs sacked
the offices of the city's Democratic and "disloyal" newspapers. The
military were called out. Montgomery Street that night from Clay
to Market "was illuminated by 'camp fires' around which were groups
of soldiers 'bivouacking.'" But the soldiers made few arrests and no
compensation was ever paid for damages suffered during the rioting.[1]
"The imperfection . . . of the law is sometimes felt so keenly as to
prompt to its violation for the promotion of natural justice," wrote
the Republican *Chronicle,* apparently undismayed by the elimination
of several of its competitors. "The people performed certain acts of
'irregular justice,' which though not sanctioned by the courts will
not be severely condemned by even the most moderate and law-abiding citizens." [2]

Against these adverse tides, however, the party of Pierce and
Buchanan was still holding steerage way. It had after all been dominant in California before the war. The bulk of its membership had
stood by the Union; and although a good many had voted for Union-

---

[1] Hubert Howe Bancroft, *History of California,* 7 vols. (San Francisco, 1890), VII,
312. San Francisco *Chronicle,* April 17, 1865; John P. Young, *Journalism in California* (San Francisco, 1915), 63.
[2] *Chronicle,* April 17, 1865.

Republican candidates, this by no means made them Republicans. They were willing enough to be weaned from their temporary political alliance as soon as the integrity of the Union seemed secure. What was then wanted was a set of new, or at least different, issues so that Democratic keynoters could say something other than "me too"; and a structure of uncontaminated political machinery. In the hour of need party leaders were scanning the horizon; and there they noted, among other developments, two of outstanding interest. The first was the emergence of a crop of labor unions reassuringly similar to the old locofoco variety; the second was something new—an organizational type apparently unique to the Pacific slope—the anticoolie club. Signals were exchanged and it presently appeared that each of these three—the party, the unions, and the anticoolie clubs—required assistance from the others. However different their goals might be, they shared the same enemies.

Trade Unions

There were probably a few trade unions in San Francisco before the Civil War, but it was during the war years and immediately after that unionism encountered its first far-western bonanza. Imports from the East had largely been cut off, and local industries flourished, one of the chief among them being shipbuilding for the coastal trade. Meanwhile, the silver mines of the Comstock, in first flush of prosperity, were demanding pipe, cable, pumps, hoisting engines, milling machinery. San Francisco's foundries and machine shops worked at capacity. These simultaneous booms triggered a demand for commercial and residential construction. The city was bursting at the seams. Nor did all this come to a halt with the armistice. Prior to completion of the railroad, the Far West was set apart by an economic time lag; as the eastern portion of the nation entered its brief postwar recession, California still rode the ascending spiral.

The same conditions which cut down imports had reduced immigration. Labor, especially skilled labor, was in short supply. Wages went up. Yet prices were rising even faster and the result was an explosive impetus to trade union organization. The first city central had been founded in San Francisco in the year of Gettysburg and Vicksburg. During the next four years, building and shipyard workers enforced the eight-hour day, and several trades achieved closed shop conditions. To protect these gains against employer counterattack, the unionists turned to politics. In 1868, after a two-year pressure campaign, they won from the state legislature an eight-hour law as well as mechanic's lien legislation.[3] This was the high point. Scarcely a year afterward, the cars were rolling across the junction at Promontory Point and the Pacific slope found itself dragged into the national economy. What resulted from that will be the subject of a later chapter; the remainder of this one will be devoted to examining the composition of the labor movement in its first heyday, and to the electoral campaign of 1867.

The House Carpenters' Eight-Hour Leagues (there were two in San Francisco) had set June 3, 1867, as date for their inauguration of the shorter workday. In honor of this occasion some 2,000 workingmen and their friends paraded up Market Street, "showing the community," as the *Daily Alta* put it, "the determination that prevails among a large and intelligent body of workingmen to adopt eight hours as a day's work, and also, in a measure to protest against Chinese labor being introduced so as to interfere with the rights of white workingmen." [4]

The *Daily Alta* found it worth recording that one of the contingents, the Stonecutters, carried a bust of the late Senator David Broderick, with flowers, and a sign proclaiming, "Broderick was one of us." [5] Broderick had in fact been the son of an Irish stonecutter and had worked at his trade in New York before entering Tammany politics. Selection of this detail by the *Daily Alta* reporter served for a kind of shorthand rendering of the political implications of the parade. Broderick had embodied the locofoco tradition, the alliance of urban workingmen with the Democracy. In the split of the party before the war, Broderick had sided with Douglas; the split had triggered a struggle for control of the Democratic organization in California, and Broderick had been killed in a duel by a leader of the opposite faction, the southern fire eater and State Supreme Court justice David Terry.[6] Broderick was therefore remembered as a martyr to the cause of national unity; his image bore witness to the loyalty of antisecession Democrats.

The parade of June 3 ended in a mass meeting at Union Square. Here again it fell to the Stonecutters to sound the keynote. Cornelius Hickey, a leader of that union and one of the selected orators of the

[3] San Francisco *Evening Bulletin*, March 11, 1867; *Alta California*, July 15, 17, 20, August 4, 8, 1867. On the importance of shipbuilding, see *Alta*, July 15. For a summary of economic developments, see Ira B. Cross, *A History of the Labor Movement in California* (Berkeley, 1935), 29–32, 41–43, 48–52, 58.

[4] *Alta*, February 12, June 2, 4, 1867.

[5] *Alta*, June 4, 1867.

[6] Robert Glass Cleland, *A History of California: The American Period* (New York, 1922), 353–356.

day, demanded for the "mechanics of San Francisco" representation in the conventions of both political parties. Capital, he warned, was planning to block the eight-hour movement by importing to California "the lowest caste of the human race in China" and imposing the "vilest system of slavery that was ever enforced in the swamps of the South." [7]

Among organizations participating in this demonstration were the Ship and Steamboat Joiners, Bricklayers, Laborers' Protective and Benevolent Association (these were the hodcarriers), Stonecutters, Lathers, Riggers, Gasfitters, House Carpenters, Plasterers, Lumber Stevedores, Painters. Since places on the line of march had been assigned roughly in accordance with the date of establishing the shorter work day in each trade, this list offers a glimpse into the order of power and prestige within the labor movement. All but two of the groups mentioned were composed of skilled tradesmen, and all were connected with shipbuilding or with construction. But the metal trades soon afterward entered the hierarchy. Early in 1868 when unionists were celebrating passage of the state eight-hour law, delegations of machinists, ironworkers, brass finishers, and their apprentices, furnished the rear guard for the procession. These reports, taken with recorded attendance at other labor gatherings, suggest that three industries—shipbuilding, construction, and metal work—provided the solid base of the urban labor movement as it existed in the late sixties. [8]

Labor organization, however, by no means reflected actual industrial growth. While the wartime interruption of supply from the East stimulated consumer goods manufacture in San Francisco, the expansion of manufacturing came up against the problem of labor shortage. New factories were forced to hire anyone they could get, including women and children—and especially Chinese. [9] Precisely because these were *new* enterprises there was no displacement of white males and the situation in the city resembled (briefly) the pattern prevalent in the hinterland, where employment of Chinese enhanced job opportunities for non-Chinese. It would seem apparent, therefore, that no upsurge of unionism had occurred among factory hands because they were for the most part women, children, and Chinese, and because

---

[7] *Alta,* June 4, 1867.

[8] The two unskilled groups were hod carriers and lumber stevedores, both apparently bracketed into the eight-hour movement by their ties to construction and shipbuilding. For participation by various unions in labor gatherings, see Cross, *History of Labor Movement,* 32–33, 36, 43, 50, 52, 306 note 52.

[9] For a survey of the ready-made clothing industry and its employment practices, see *Alta,* April 4, 1867.

the few white males among them probably were earning premium rates. "Employers," the *Alta* wrote in the summer of 1867, being able to " 'work in' cheap Chinese labor" could "afford better wages to skilled Americans." [10] This bonanza, however, would not last long.

While the onset of depression in the West was delayed till after completion of the railroad, there were some earlier harbingers of what was to come, and these were felt especially in manufacturing. The woolens trade provides a notable example. During the war, New England textile manufacturers, short of cotton, had concentrated largely on woolens which went into army uniforms. They had counted on a large postwar southern demand, but this failed to materialize. The bottom fell out of the market, and by 1867 investors were buying up eastern woolens by the shipload to dump in California. In San Francisco, meanwhile, the Mission and the Pioneer woolen mills had been hard pressed to keep up with the rapidly expanding ready-made clothing industry. But under the impact of dumping from the East, both mills were forced to cut back production by 50 percent in the summer of 1867. The result was an immediate squeeze on the workers. Wages were cut. Chinese contract laborers moved into skilled and semiskilled positions, and even began replacing women. The same sequence was occurring in other consumer industries. Here was the point at which organizational efforts began; but it was already too late. The boot and shoemakers, for example, rose in violent resistance against wage cuts and Chinese competition. They were defeated and Chinese, under police protection, continued their incursion into the shoe factories.[11]

This disastrous outcome for the white shoemakers, who were, after all, highly skilled craftsmen, suggests that the situation of the organized trades immediately following the war was less secure than it appeared. Not only in manufacturing, but in shipbuilding and construction, employers were reported to be damping down production.[12] Labor's successful campaign for a shorter work day may have been in part a defensive response to rising unemployment and pressure on the high wage level achieved during the war. The degree of insecurity which this implies helps to explain the relationship that was developing between trade unions and the anticoolie clubs.

[10] *Alta*, July 17, 1867. The *Alta* was describing a state of affairs that was on the point of ending. The context was a warning to white workingmen not to push their luck too far by excessive demands for high wages and shorter hours.

[11] *Alta*, April 4, May 6, 1867; July 9, August 11, 1870.

[12] *Alta*, July 15, 17, August 4, 8, 1867.

Anticoolie Clubs

There has been a good deal of debate in California historiography over when the first anticoolie clubs made their appearance. The dispute is largely a matter of semantics. If one focuses on function rather than name, it seems clear that the miners' assemblies which evicted Chinese from their diggings were anticoolie clubs; that the quartz miners' union of the Comstock, when it marched out to confront the Virginia and Truckee Railroad, was an anticoolie club; that the San Franciscans who in the winter of 1867 drove a gang of Chinese laborers from their work on the Potrero Street railway were functioning as an anticoolie club.[13] From the time, then, of the earliest encounters of Chinese and non-Chinese in California, groupings appeared which undertook systematic anti-Chinese activities.

What were the origins of these groups? Here too the answer appears most readily from a consideration of their functions. In the attack on the Potrero laborers, a crowd of some four hundred had rolled down rocks injuring a dozen Chinese, destroyed barracks and sheds at the job site, then roamed off through the city burning shanties threatening to storm the ropewalk and the Mission Woolen Mills, both of which had Chinese employees. Various alleged leaders of this riot were arrested. Shortly before their trial opened, an assembly of "workingmen and others" met to set up a continuations committee which included one of the attorneys engaged for the defense. The trial resulted in conviction for ten of the accused, who received stiff jail sentences—an outcome hailed by the *Alta* as "deserved" but which roused resentment elsewhere. An "immense gathering of workingmen and representatives of many industrial associations" then convened upon call of the previously established continuations committee to lay plans for permanent organization. Within a week after this meeting the San Francisco Board of Supervisors voted six to three to appeal on behalf of the convicted rioters for a trial review and executive clemency. Two months and two days later, in response to a plea of habeas corpus filed by a San Francisco attorney, S. B. Axtell, the State Supreme Court released all ten prisoners on the ground that there had been technical errors in the "judgements of commitment." They had each served two months of an eleven-month sentence.[14]

These confused proceedings ran their course against a background

---

[13] On early anticoolie clubs, see Lucille Eaves, *A History of California Labor Legislation* (Berkeley, 1910), 8, 14–15; *Alta*, January 9, 1860.

[14] *Alta*, February 13, 14, 21, 24, 26, March 1, 5, 7, 12, May 14, 15, 1867.

REHABILITATION OF THE DEMOCRATIC PARTY

of scattered violence. Chinese were stoned, beaten, run down on the streets. And there were hints of more ominous actions. In April a stocking factory belonging to the firm of Goldstone and Sharp, employers of Chinese, burned for a total loss. Newspaper reports called the origin of the blaze a mystery since there had been no fire under the boilers for many hours. In the view of the *Alta,* at least, arson was a strong possibility.[15]

Without attempting to untangle the separate strands of this web, it seems clear that some of the lines ran far back into the American and European past. Men were reenacting what had been done before in tenant villages of Ireland, in slums and suburbs of Boston, Philadelphia, New Orleans, Cincinnati. Their actions flowed into remembered forms: the secret societies and the armed neighborhood gangs of immigrants and native Americans. That same potential which had exploded into the New York draft riots four years earlier and which already was enmeshing Pennsylvania anthracite miners in a counterpoint of killing and reprisal was at work in California. This does not mean that the violence of those months should be attributed entirely to the anticoolie clubs. Rather, the clubs and the acts of violence were symptoms of the same tensions and conflicts. Many anticoolie groups declared strenuously their devotion to legal means.[16] Legal and illegal, peaceful and violent were intertwined and mutually reinforcing. Perhaps the clubs often functioned as public fronts within which terrorist cadres could operate, although not much written evidence to this effect will be found. At least there can be no doubt that legal activity built up to a threshold of violence, while what occurred beyond that threshold enhanced and broadened the legal activities. As public acceptance increased, the interrelationship grew increasingly obvious and the work of the clubs became more effective. It was, however, in their legal role that the clubs submitted themselves to the record. And here too precedent dominated. The activities they undertook were the time-honored Jeffersonian and Jacksonian techniques of consumer boycott and precinct level organization.

The boycott of Chinese-made goods had been invoked at least as early as 1859. At that time, and for a good many years afterward, western cigar makers were organized not as trade unionists but in guilds which included masters and journeymen, and which functioned

15 *Alta,* February 14, 17, 19, 20, April 29, 1867.
16 For examples of legal anticoolie associations (though from a somewhat later period), see Anti-Chinese Union of San Francisco, *Constitution and By-Laws* (San Francisco, 1876); United Brothers of California, *Constitution and By-Laws* (San Francisco, 1876), in *Chinese Immigration Pamphlets,* IV, 14 and 24, Bancroft Library, University of California, Berkeley.

as anticoolie clubs. Anticoolieism thus became a means of promoting their own product. The cigar boycott of 1859 and others undertaken during the sixties failed in part, at least, because of the difficulty of prodùct differentiation. This need gave rise to the white label, which, pasted across the box lid, declared: "The cigars herein contained are made by WHITE MEN. This label is issued by authority of the Cigar Makers' Association of the Pacific Coast." Boot- and shoemakers followed soon after with a stamp for designating the product of white craftsmen. In later years the idea would be expanded into the form of a placard for display on the premises of any businessman who had pledged himself to the anticoolie boycott. Since by that time trade unionism and anticoolieism had entered into a public and lasting marriage, the labels, stamps, and placards gradually came to signify not only white but union as well. Such were the humble beginnings of the shop card and the union label.[17]

Boycotting continued as the major public weapon of the anticoolie clubs. The petition seems to have made its appearance only in the seventies [18] and remained a secondary activity that rose or fell as the intensity of debate on immigration restriction varied in Congress. But boycotts and petitioning both demanded local organization. Organizational models which came most naturally to hand were the trade-based club (as in the case of the cigar workers), and the political ward club which first displayed its full potential during the agitation of 1867. The growth sequence of the ward club apparatus was the following: from the presumably spontaneous attack of four hundred against the Chinese laborers came a legal defense committee; out of the defense committee and the resentment roused by conviction of the riot leaders came a city-wide mass meeting; from the mass meeting emerged a structure roughly analogous to that of a political party. A central committee of twelve was charged with the duty of organizing (or discovering) anticoolie clubs in each of the city's twelve wards. These in turn were expected "to ascertain the names of all persons . . . known to employ Chinamen or to dispose of goods and wares manufactured and prepared by Chinese labor to the detriment of white labor." [19] Such information might be put to several uses. One certainly was the boycott.

An outstanding advantage of the ward club structure was that it could absorb both group and individual participation. There was no

17 Cross, *History of the Labor Movement*, 136; Frank Roney, *Frank Roney, Irish Rebel and California Labor Leader* (ed. Ira B. Cross (Berkeley, 1931), 356–362, 364–368.
18 *Alta*, May 25, 1873.
19 *Alta*, March 7, 1867.

limit to the number, or type, of organizations that might "join in the effort to break down the most dangerous enemy that has yet threatened the interests of the working man." And as for individuals, all were welcome simply upon taking the membership pledge to the effect that they would resist, by legal means, further importation of Chinese and would advocate, by legal means, the removal of those already in California. The name adopted for this organization by its founding convention was the Central Pacific Anti-Coolie Association.[20] There is no evidence that the association outlived the year of its birth. Yet it was remarkably predictive. Structurally and programmatically, explicitly and implicitly, everything was already in it; here was the blueprint for three decades of anti-Chinese organization and agitation to follow.

Interconnections

Trade unionism had by 1867 successfully established itself among skilled craftsmen in three major industries: metal trades, shipbuilding, and construction. These were old industries in San Francisco, which meant that they entered the period of wartime labor shortage with an existing pool of experienced workers. They were geared to the local market, which meant that they could pass along high labor costs to the public.[21] Here were optimum circumstances for unionism: the unions could, and did, devote themselves to pushing up wages, shortening hours, and improving job conditions. Driving out Chinese, however, was not one of their functions because there were few if any Chinese to be driven out. This was due to a combination of causes. The three industries already had their own labor force; and as more men were needed, higher wage levels tended to attract white workingmen from other occupations. And there was, moreover, a decisive factor relating to the productive process itself. Metal trades, shipbuilding, and construction all required close integration of numerous workers practicing different skills. Consequently, it was difficult for an employer to break in new hands without willing agreement by the entire community of his workingmen. The combined effect of these circumstances had been to discourage employers from attempting to bring in Chinese.

But the situation with respect to the new manufacturing industries was altogether different. Here, by contrast, there had been no union

---

20 Ibid.

21 Since it was wartime conditions that had encouraged West Coast entrepreneurs to enter national market industries, these were necessarily "new" industries in San Francisco. Conversely, local market industries were for the most part "old."

growth whatever. In fact the normal goals of trade unionism were impossible, because the employers, hard pressed in their competitive national markets, could neither absorb additional labor costs nor pass them along to the public. And finally, in several of these industries, the production process served not as a barrier, but as an incentive to the introduction of new hands. A major portion of the work was unskilled, and there was no limit to possible decentralization. Thus a manufacturer of undergarments, for example, might hire one Chinese, teach him the art, and set him up in any basement in Chinatown to pass along this knowledge to others. Obviously such an approach would not have served for building hoisting engines or lumber schooners.

The inability of trade unionism to survive under these circumstances is amply evidenced in the cases of the cigar makers and the shoemakers. The cigar makers made no effort to function as a union, while the shoemakers made such an effort and were defeated.[22] What both groups in effect became were anticoolie clubs. Since white workers were being forced out, the base of activity in each trade was reduced to a scattering of white wage earners and to a small but influential group of marginal manufacturers. These were the masters of small shops who lacked capital necessary for large-scale enterprise with Chinese labor. In part at least through their guidance, the main thrust of trade-based anticoolieism was turned to the preservation of a noncompetitive niche for a differentiated product. This was the purpose served by the white label on the cigar box and the white labor stamp on boots and shoes. Probably a number of marginal manufacturers, who under other circumstances would have been swamped in the national market, survived not so much in spite, as because, of the competition of Chinese labor. More than ten years later—deep in the depression of the seventies—what remained of a local shoemakers' league was spending its money not to organize the unorganized, but to hire a wagon and fife and drum with transparencies "two hours every Saturday night, to pass around the town and cry down enemies and advertise friends." [23] To this extent the interests of the marginal manufacturer and his employees were identical. There was no function here for the trade union, but for the anti-coolie club there was.

Resources of such trade-based clubs must have been meager. They would probably soon have disintegrated had they not been reinforced from two different directions: on the one hand by the successful trade unions in shipbuilding, construction, and metal trades; on the other

22 See above, pp. 71, 73–74.
23 *Bulletin,* March 11, 1878, as cited in Cross, 136.

by the ward-based anticoolie clubs which, in 1867, were in process of building their first city-wide apparatus—the Central Pacific Anti-Coolie Association. And to the activities of the association the growing numbers of unemployed (many recently pushed out of the new manufacturing industries), the anxiety-ridden workers still hanging on there, and the embattled marginal manufacturers must have contributed a powerful dynamic. What could better have suited their need—emotional as well as economic—than the Anti-Coolie Association's ward-by-ward boycott of Chinese labor and sellers of Chinese-made goods, together with its vivid undercurrent of selective sabotage?

So far the relationship of anticoolieism in the new manufacturing industries to the ward-based anticoolie clubs seems clear enough. But the role of the trade unions remains ambiguous. They were, as of 1867, still functioning successfully as unions, and they had no direct Chinese problem of their own. How much were they involved in citywide agitation? Early in March, when the Anti-Coolie Association had elected its permanent officers, one of two secretaries chosen was General A. M. Winn, leader of the House Carpenters' Eight-Hour Leagues. Moreover, of fifty-one sponsoring vice-presidents of the association, forty-one were listed as representing the following trades: ships' carpenters; house carpenters, painters, plumbers, masons, plasterers; boilermakers, machinists, blacksmiths, coppersmiths, tinners; cigar makers and shoemakers; carriage makers, coopers, butchers, and lumbermen and stevedores.[24] Undoubtedly, trade unionists were heavily committed. Why?

The answer seems to be that they were already feeling themselves on the defensive. While employers in local market industries would not face the full impact of depression till the summer of 1869, they could easily see what was happening in the new manufacturing industries. Demand for housing and for coastwise shipping was probably tapering off. For whatever reasons it is clear that employers in 1867 were setting up mutual aid societies and pressuring for a return to the ten-hour day.[25] The unions endeavored to defend themselves by political means. Key to the legislature was the massive San Francisco delegation, and control of that delegation lay in the wards and assembly districts. But trade unionists were not numerous enough to exercise such control. In anticoolieism they found common ground with a broader voting bloc. Those forty-one vice-presidents who had sponsored the Central Pacific Association in the spring would be able to speak persuasively to electoral candidates throughout the ensuing summer. In fact, they

24 *Alta*, March 7, 1867.
25 *Alta*, July 15, 20, August 4, 8, 1867; Cross, 48–49.

would succeed in persuading the upcoming legislature to pass their mechanics' lien and eight-hour bills.

But more was at stake in all this than bargains with political candidates. The essential difference between the new manufacturing industries and the older local market industries was that employers of the first group really had no alternative but to hire Chinese, whereas those of the second had an option. Should they opt for Chinese, they might increase their profits but might also encounter difficulties with the anticoolie clubs. It was this continuing threat that gave to workers in the local market industries their privileged sanctuary. Of course, the privilege might work for the benefit of both skilled and unskilled, as the episode of the Potrero street railway laborers had demonstrated; but it was the skilled, because of their trade unions and because they were long-term rather than casual workers, who profited most. They had, therefore, a very real stake in the activities of the anticoolie clubs. Their own security, and consequently their bargaining power, would vary directly with the intensity of agitation.

Leagues and Delegated Councils

Out of the trade unions and anticoolie clubs with their common interests and overlapping membership sprouted a tangled crop of secondary organization. Here, especially, was the environment that shaped and nourished leadership. It formed as vital a part of the picture as the clubs and local unions themselves. To reconstruct this environment in detail would scarcely be possible; yet at least a brief overview is essential to what follows.

The first city central, which came together in the early sixties, had met irregularly until sometime in 1866. In January of the following year appeared an organization known as the Industrial League. This was a secret society (like the Knights of Labor in its early days) apparently intended to function as an inner caucus for guiding and ramrodding broader organizations. The league had had something to do with setting up the Central Pacific Anti-Coolie Association and was publicly thanked by that body for its support. Later, the league summoned a "Workingmen's Convention" to which ward clubs of the Central Pacific Association, as well as most trade unions in the city, named delegates. From its opening session in March, the convention continued through a series of adjourned meetings during the spring and summer. It sponsored the June Eight-Hour Day Parade in which the unions had marched in hierarchical order. Then in July and August it turned its attention to the coming elections and played a not inconsiderable role in the state and congressional campaigns.[26] However, as the Workingmen's Convention became more deeply engrossed in politics, the eight-hour movement was left yawing into the wind. Happily there were others ready to take the helm.

One of these was General Winn, co-secretary of the Central Pacific Anti-Coolie Association. Winn for some time past had been organizing eight-hour leagues, primarily among house carpenters in San Francisco and Oakland. Because in several respects he typified the labor leadership of the period, he is worth pausing over for a moment. General Winn was a man of leisure and some means, an entrepreneur, a politician, a genuine rural Jacksonian. Born in Punkinville, Virginia, he later moved to Mississippi where he pursued the vocation of carpenter and builder and enrolled in the Master Carpenters' and Joiners' Society. He had not, presumably, been christened "general" (although seldom separated from that prefix), but had acquired the title through service in the Mississippi state militia during the forties and, more recently (but after the war), in the California militia.

The general came west with the forty-niners. In Sacramento, aside from his military duties, he served as president of the State Board of Swamp Land Commissioners. Sometime after 1860 he moved to San Francisco, engaged in real estate, and married the widow of James King of William, the newspaper editor whose murder ten years earlier had called into action the Second Vigilance Committee. And in San Francisco, General Winn began his crusade for the shorter work day. He was an energetic organizer. Largely through his efforts, two new bodies were added to the already burgeoning roster of organizations. The first of these, the Mechanics' Eight-Hour League, engaged in quizzing and pledging candidates for the legislature and later arranged to maintain several lobbyists at Sacramento in support of labor-sponsored bills. From the Mechanics' League grew a more permanent organization, the Mechanics' State Council, to the presidency of which General Winn was selected.[27]

There were then, as of 1867, four separate organizations in San Francisco above the local trade union level, each claiming to speak with the voice of labor. Only one of these, the Mechanics' State Council, survived for long. But like the Central Pacific Anti-Coolie Association, they represented types that would prove extraordinarily prolific during the coming years. Organizationally, 1867 was a relatively simple year in San Francisco. Afterward, the tangle always thickened;

26 Cross, 32–36, 44–47; *Alta*, March 7, 10, June 2, 4, 5, 1867. See below, pp. 85–91.
27 For Winn's obituary, *Alta*, August 27, 1883; and a biographical sketch in Cross, 305 note 32.

and it was in this setting that leaders of the workingmen dealt with one another and confronted other leaders in the larger jungle of city and state politics.

The Campaign of 1867

Two closely related events occurring in Sacramento in mid-March of 1867 epitomized the situation of the Democratic party. The regular Democratic Club met and voted *not* to name candidates in the upcoming city elections. On the same night an anti-Chinese society convened in the district court rooms to prepare its own complete list. Apparently several present spoke up in protest, one being a newspaper editor who declared that worthy candidates ought to fight under the true Democratic banner. "The party should not lose its identity on account of temporary discouragement." But the majority, rejecting this counsel, offered their slate to the Sacramento electorate under the title Union-Democratic.[28]

For the fact was that what then remained under the true banner was little more than the old, well-known pro-southern leadership. The bulk of voters, being in favor of preservation of the Union, had supported Republican candidates in 1861 and had moved into the Republican-sponsored Union party in 1863. Now, in 1867, they were still there—but they were deeply divided. They were divided over reconstruction of the South; and they were divided over the role of the Negro, the role of Chinese, and the role of the workingman. In the cities, especially in San Francisco, this split approximated the division between the early Republicans on the one hand—those who had been Whigs and antislavery men during the fifties—and the Douglas Democrats on the other. The old-line politicians who had run the city during the heyday of the Democracy before the war and who hoped to run it again naturally went with the Douglas grouping. This faction in the Union party was variously nicknamed the "Short Hairs" or the "Boys" and was alleged to be in alliance with the railroad. Meanwhile, the Republican Unionists, during their six-year dominance, had also developed a crop of enthusiastic urban politicians; and these with their followers were known as the "Long Hairs." [29]

The fate of the true Democracy, therefore, hung on the possibility of schism in the Union party. Under the circumstances its strategy was

---

28 *Alta*, March 12, 1867.
29 Winfield J. Davis, *History of Political Conventions in California* (Sacramento, 1893), 241–263; Bancroft, *History of California*, VII, 315–327; *The Bay of San Francisco*, 2 vols. (Chicago, 1892), I, 257–261.

ready-made: it would endeavor to preempt, or at least neutralize, the national unity appeal; and it would renew the old war cries of locofoco Jacksonianism. The San Francisco *Examiner,* now official keynoter for the Democracy, summed up these themes in the following terms:

> We have stated before and we again repeat it, that the self-styled Union or Mongrel party have but one principle, if it may be so called, distinguishing them as an organization, and that is the doctrine of universal equality for all races, in all things. Take away the Chinese, negro-suffrage, and negro-brotherhood plank from their platform, and they become simply a plunder-league, banded together to rob the Government and use its powers for the aggrandizement of special interests and favored classes. The war is now passed and there can be no living issue connected with its conduct. The charge of disloyalty, so flippantly preferred against the Democracy is an atrocious lie. . . . The Democracy are, and ever have been, the party of the Constitution, the party of the people. They are for a white man's government, constitutionally administered, against a great Mongrel military despotism, upheld by a union of the purse and the sword, and sought to be perpetuated through negro and Chinese votes.[30]

An opening gambit in the game for the governorship was a letter from the executive board of the Central Pacific Anti-Coolie Association to prospective candidates requesting their views on the Chinese question. At the time (April), the leading aspirant certainly was George C. Gorham, former editor of the Sacramento *Union,* former secretary to the Unionist Governor Low, and currently clerk of the United States Circuit and District Courts of California.[31] Gorham, who would soon demonstrate that he could be devious when circumstances seemed to warrant, returned a blunt answer. He was, he wrote, "opposed to the coolie system," but was not for that reason an enemy of its victims.

> I believe in the Christian religion, and that rests upon the universal fatherhood of God and the universal brotherhood of man. The same God created both Europeans and Asiatics. No man of whatever race has any better right to labor, and receive his hire therefor, than has any other man. . . . As a question, then, of right and wrong, I am as emphatically opposed to all attempts to deny the Chinese the right to labor for pay, as I am to the restoration of African slavery whereby black men were compelled to labor without pay. As a question of policy, I am equally opposed to your movement. . . . The question

30 San Francisco *Examiner,* July 1, July 13, 1867.
31 *Bay of San Francisco,* II, 378–379.

of cheap labor I will not here discuss, but it seems certain to
me that if we could have it in abundance, the state would go
forward at such strides as would make prosperity general
among all deserving classes. Principle and policy, then, both
forbid the attempt to make war upon our Asiatic brethren.[32]

Understandably, this statement was not well received by the anticoolie association. But the Democrats rejoiced in it. Their orators repeated its phrases up and down the state, and for the *Examiner,* which
liked to refer to George C. Gorham as "G. Coolie G.," it provided an
inexhaustible source of ammunition.[33] Since Gorham later gave
ground under this barrage, the question presents itself why he made
such a bold stand in the first place. There are several possible answers.
He may simply have underestimated the potential of the anticoolie
movement. What is more likely, however, is that he was attempting to
set right his image with the "Long Hairs," those old-time Republicans
among whom was his natural base of support.

Born in Long Island, and a forty-niner at the age of seventeen, Gorham was himself one of the elders in the Republican party. But he
had alienated a good many of his colleagues—as well as the *Daily Alta
California* and the *Bulletin*—by his conduct at Sacramento. There,
early in the sixties, Gorham had lent aid to the notorious "Bulkhead"
scheme, a plan according to which control of the San Francisco waterfront was to have been granted by legislative enactment to a syndicate
of promoters. This had been blocked at the eleventh hour through intervention of San Francisco civic leaders, several of them Republicans;
but it had not been forgotten. Nor had Gorham's more recent activities as lobbyist for the Central Pacific. He had succeeded in pushing
through both houses of the legislature a railroad subsidy bill that
would have added between two and three million dollars to the state
debt. While Republicans were inclined to see the transcontinental
line as their own proud venture, they were not altogether eager to
gouge the state's taxpayers for the benefit of the Central Pacific di-
rectorate. Especially was this the case with San Francisco businessmen.
The dismay caused by the subsidy issue within the Republican contingent of the Union party was evident from the fact that Governor
Low, himself an old Republican and Gorham's patron in government
service, had finally vetoed the measure.[34]

[32] *Alta,* July 11, 1867; Davis, 241–242.

[33] *Examiner,* "Negroes in the Senate," July 13, 1867.

[34] Oscar T. Shuck, *Bench and Bar in California: History, Anecdote, Reminiscence*
(San Francisco, 1888), 35c–35d, 169; *Bay of San Francisco,* I, 260–261; II, 120; Bancroft, *History of California,* VII, 322–323; *Bulletin,* June 7, 1867; *Examiner,* July 22,
1867.

While Gorham could not undo this portion of the record—and probably had no wish to, since in the friendship of the railroad lay one of his chief assets—he could at least direct the attention of Republican Unionists to an area where he might show to better advantage. His response to the anticoolie association would have had this effect since it was in harmony with views generally expressed by the *Alta* and the *Bulletin,* the very papers which had been most vociferous in their criticism of his subsidy bills. As to coolieism and forced indenture, the *Bulletin* flatly denied the existence of such practices in California, charging that those who agitated the issue—the Central Pacific Anti-Coolie Association, for example—did so for malicious purposes.[35] The *Alta* took even higher ground. It welcomed the flow of immigration from Asia "until the equilibrium of population is attained." [36] On the matter of race, its editors were outraged by the *Examiner*'s almost daily diatribes against Negroes:

> You cannot expect a bird to fly when its wings are cut off, or a man to walk upright if his legs are broken. It will require time to correct the evil and humanize and enlighten public opinion, and shame unfounded prejudice into something like reason. There is not much approach toward it yet. . . . We cannot force public opinion; but at least until *that* manifests a disposition to give the Negro a fair and equal chance, let us not draw unfair and unjust comparisons, holding the black man up as a moral reprobate, whose vices are all his own and whose virtues are to be credited to our example. The reverse of this boast is much nearer the truth.[37]

Gorham then might have replied as he did to the anticoolie association, because he felt that body represented a relatively small number of voters, mostly Democrats in any case, or because he wished to woo the *Alta* and the *Bulletin* and the Long Hair Republicans whose views those journals presumably expressed. And there was a third consideration, perhaps more compelling than these. In his letter he had asserted the economic advantage to California of cheap labor (see above, p. 82). This was anathema to the Democrats, but it was one point upon which the divergent elements in the Republican contingent would be likely to stick together. Those of the Central Pacific subsidy camp, though perhaps unmoved by religious and moral arguments for racial tolerance, would be strong for a supply of cheap labor. The Long Hairs, on the other hand, while from their stance of civic virtue they might with

35 *Bulletin,* March 12, 1867.
36 *Alta,* April 6, August 13, September 3, 1867.
37 *Alta,* May 4, 1867.

equal fervor condemn bigotry and raids on the state treasury, remained deeply interested in Chinese immigration. This was true not only because completion of the railroad, to which they were committed politically, seemed to depend on it; but because as businessmen and investors they were involved economically in the expansion of San Francisco manufacturing and in the drainage and irrigation of California farmlands. Thus, early in 1867, Gorham could have reasoned that, while his letter would doubtless alienate some already his enemies, it would have the effect of bracing up and uniting his potential supporters.

These probably are reasons enough to explain the letter; yet there may be a final reason underlying all the others and that is that Gorham was simply stating what he believed. During the gilded age, as perhaps in other eras, while every man may have had his price a good many also had their sticking points. Gorham had declared the same conviction that Charles Sumner would defend three years later when the Senate debated Chinese naturalization. He had apparently struck some kind of bedrock at this point.[38]

Early in the summer of 1867 his bid for the governorship still looked like a winning hand. Presumably, the Union nomination would be equivalent to victory as it had been since 1861. The nomination would be made by a state convention and the convention would be controlled by the large bloc of San Francisco delegates, provided this bloc were unanimous. Everything depended, then, on the San Francisco delegation which was to be chosen in the following manner: a city primary open to voters of the Union party would select members of a city-wide convention. This in turn would name delegates to the congressional district and state conventions. Consequently, if any candidate had the support of a simple majority of winners in the city primary, he could take charge of the city apparatus and name a solid slate to the state and district gatherings. Gorham and his political ally, Senator Conness, both known as friends of the railroad, controlled the San Francisco Central Committee of the Union party which would draw up the ground rules for the primary election.[39]

This was done in May, the date of the election being set for June 5. Immediately there came protests from the Long Hairs who complained that the hours scheduled for voting had been deliberately limited, while the voter qualifications had been broadened. The re-

[38] This campaign finished Gorham's political career in California. He went to Washington in 1868 and served for several years as secretary of the Senate. Afterward he returned to California, edited the *National Republican,* and worked on a biography of Edwin A. Stanton. (*Bay of San Francisco,* II, 378–379.)

[39] Davis, *History of Political Conventions,* 241–247; *Bulletin,* June 6, 8, 1867.

sult, they charged, would be that bona fide Union voters would find it difficult to get to the polls, whereas the Gorham machine would be able to send in ringers who were not even members or supporters of the party. The Long Hairs then got up a petition signed by some 4,000 Union voters which led to the nomination of a slate of "unpledged" (meaning anti-Gorham) candidates for the upcoming canvass. With this success to bolster them, they next demanded a second session of the party Central Committee to revise the hours and qualifications of voting. The meeting was held but broke up in a free-for-all of the two factions which had to be sorted out by the police; and no business was transacted. This, then, was how matters stood at the end of May: the Gorham faction, still dominating the San Francisco Union party Central Committee had drawn up the ground rules for the primary election; they had as yet entered no list of candidates. Their opponents, on the other hand, were busy campaigning for the "unpledged" slate and seemed (in the accounts at least of the *Alta* and *Bulletin* which wished them well) to be making considerable progress.[40]

From this point, the drama becomes increasingly opaque and it may be well to backtrack for a moment. It was noted in an earlier section that the Central Pacific Anti-Coolie Association, to which George Gorham directed his forthright and much quoted letter, had originated as a protest against imprisonment of the leaders of an anti-Chinese riot. Forty-one out of fifty-one sponsoring vice-presidents of the association had been trade unionists, and the co-secretary was General Winn, champion of the Carpenters' Eight-Hour Leagues. The association had organized anticoolie clubs on a ward basis. From these clubs, and from the trade unions, had sprung a Workingmen's Convention which continued through a series of adjourned meetings. In May, while the Long Hairs were fighting the Gorham faction for control of their party's Central Committee, the Workingmen's Convention was organizing its Eight-Hour-Day Parade to celebrate inauguration by the house carpenters in Oakland and San Francisco of the shorter work day. The parade was held on June 3, two days before the scheduled primary election; and it was during the course of this parade that the Stonecutters had displayed the bust of Broderick, Democratic martyr to the cause of national unity. Afterward, at the mass meeting in Union Square, over which General Winn presided, the crowd had listened to warnings against the Chinese menace expressed by a speaker

---

40 *Bulletin*, June 4, 1867. Davis, 242–247. Actually the petition was an appeal to a group of leading citizens to meet as a "people's nominating committee." This was done, and the result was the "unpledged" or "people's" ticket, which the Long Hair faction put up for the primary.

for the Stonecutters and to the remarks of a Dr. Rowell, whom the
Alta described simply as an anti-Chinese orator. And there was one
other speaker on the platform as well, Assemblyman John W. Wilcox
of Mariposa County.[41]

Wilcox, whom General Winn introduced to the assembly as a "workingman and blacksmith," centered his attention on the eight-hour day.
He detailed his efforts in labor's behalf at Sacramento, described the
opposition he had encountered there from capitalists, and declared
that he held in his possession a petition of 11,000 San Francisco citizens
for the eight-hour law. Wilcox had served in the Assembly since 1861.[42]
According to the *Bulletin* he had been a tool of the Central Pacific at
Sacramento and had supported George Gorham's railroad subsidy
bills. Worse than this, however, in the *Bulletin*'s indictment, was the
charge that he had voted against endorsement of Congressional Reconstruction and had favored instead a resolution of support for President
Johnson's plan. He had even applauded Johnson's "vulgar denunciation" of Charles Sumner and Thaddeus Stevens, and had gone east
during the previous autumn to take part in the President's ill-starred
"swing 'round the circle." [43] It was already common knowledge that
Wilcox hoped to be sent to Washington to represent the First Congressional District, which in those days included Mariposa as well as
San Francisco. Two weeks before the parade, at a mass meeting called
to ratify a declaration drawn up by the Workingmen's Convention,
"the eloquent Mariposa blacksmith" had appeared as chief speaker;
and the *Alta* noted at the time that he was regarded as a possible
candidate for Congress.[44]

On the evening of June 3, after the parade, the Workingmen's Convention assembled once more and adopted a slate of primary candidates pledged to Wilcox for Congress. This list was published in the
newspapers the following day. A meeting of workingmen that night
heard a speech by Wilcox and endorsed the slate. One day later came
the primary election, and the workingmen's candidates carried the
field. Both the *Bulletin* and the *Alta* charged that these were in reality
Gorham delegates masquerading as Wilcox men.[45]

At all events, the Gorham faction now took full command, and its

41 *Alta,* June 4, 1867; *Bulletin,* June 3, 1867.
42 *Alta,* June 4, 1867; on Wilcox's efforts in the previous session of the legislature
for the eight-hour bill, see Cross, *History of the Labor Movement* (above, n. 3), 38–
39; California, Secretary of State, *California Blue Book or State Roster, 1907* (Sacramento, 1907), 626.
43 *Bulletin,* June 4, 7, 1867.
44 *Alta,* May 15, 1867.
45 *Alta,* June 4–6, 1867; *Bulletin,* June 6, 1867.

maneuvers unfolded with military precision. The city convention assembled, was controlled by the newly elected majority of workingmen's delegates, and chose solid Gorham-Wilcox delegations to the congressional district and to the state conventions. Next, the congressional nominators convened at San Jose. Wilcox went down, called the city delegates into caucus and told them—pledged as they were to his candidacy and having the power to enforce it—that he had decided to withdraw from the race. He had only now learned, he explained, that his old enemies the capitalists had put up $100,000 to beat him; his friends could not begin to match this; and so to save the Union party from defeat and himself from bankruptcy, he had no choice but to step down. He would give them the word whom to support in his stead, he said; and he did. The convention then met and nominated an unexceptionable San Francisco Republican, T. J. Phelps, reasonably acceptable even to the Long Hairs. A few days afterward the state convention assembled at Sacramento. Here too the city bloc easily took control, awarding the first prize to George C. Gorham.[46]

And what became of John Wilcox, the eloquent and obliging blacksmith? The record shows that he returned to Mariposa, was reelected to the Assembly where he served till 1876, being later listed as a Democrat. He was of course bitterly denounced in San Francisco. Charges of bribery passed back and forth in the Workingmen's Convention, and the rumor circulated that Wilcox had been bought off by the Pacific Mail Steamship Company for $10,000.[47] Among some workingmen, at least, the interpretation was that their convention had been duped by the Gorham Unionists; and this seems to have been the view taken by the *Bulletin* as well, although the *Bulletin* spared little enough sympathy for the workingmen. "The only straight-out Union ticket," the *Bulletin* wrote, "was beaten by a combination of unscrupulous candidates and schemers who made a catspaw of the workingmen's organization, very many of whom were notoriously not Union voters." And again: "They [the workingmen] cheated the Union organization for Wilcox, and Wilcox has cheated them. The biter is bit and the people who were not in the swindle laugh at both."[48]

It is not altogether clear, however, who was in the swindle and

46 *Bulletin*, June 10, 1867. Phelps, who had been elected to the legislature on the first California Republican ticket in 1856, had been one of the leaders in the fight against the bulkhead scheme. (*Bay of San Francisco*, II, 120; Bancroft, *History of California*, VII, 322–323.)

47 William Halley, *Directory of the California Legislature. Twenty-First Session, 1875–1876* (Sacramento, n.d.), 41; *Bulletin*, June 10, July 12, 1867.

48 *Bulletin*, June 6, 8, 1867.

who was not. Were the Democrats? The *Bulletin* and *Alta* both claimed that Democratic votes had swung the balance in the Union primary to the workingmen's slate; [49] while on behalf of the Democrats, the *Examiner* offered the following comment:

> As we expected, the Workingmen were manipulated for the benefit of the "ring" and its candidate, little Georgy Gorham. The so-called regular Mongrels have put up no ticket against the People's Ticket [that is, against the "unpledged" slate of the Long Hairs], but to a Boy, indorse and vote the Workingmen's Ticket, so-called; and so far, it is asserted, the Boys are ahead. Hurrah for the Chinese immigration and cheap labor candidate, little Georgy, say we; he is the easiest pin to knock down that the Mongrels can set up. [50]

George Gorham had no sooner cinched his gubernatorial nomination than the Union coalition began to disintegrate under his feet. There was not merely one schism, but two. First came a walk-out by the Long Hair Republicans, who held a rump convention, nominated one of their own for governor (this was Caleb T. Fay, a forty-niner from Massachusetts who had served in 1862 as first Republican mayor of San Francisco), and declared themselves an affiliate of the original national Republican party. [51] The second was a long continuing and massive desertion to the Democracy. For the Republican dissidents, the main issue was railroad domination and political corruption. For the others, the central theme was anticoolieism—a receptacle which contained within itself an extensive baggage of anti-Negroism, opposition to Radical Reconstruction in the South, fear of Negro and Chinese job competition, and an intense desire to exclude blacks and Chinese from any kind of economic, civil, or political equality. The Democrats hammered away at both schisms.

As to the first one, Gorham had been on the defensive from the beginning, because he could neither cut loose from the railroad nor defend his actions in its interests; and he continued on the defensive till the end of the campaign. Yet even so this issue was less costly to him than the other. [52] On the other, the Chinese issue with all its undertones and corollaries, he had by his letter to the anticoolie association early in the year made a bold opening move. But it soon turned

[49] *Alta*, June 6, 1867; *Bulletin*, June 6, 8, 1867.

[50] *Examiner*, June 5, 1867, as quoted in *Bulletin*, June 6, 1867.

[51] Bancroft, *History of California*, VII, 324–325; Davis, *History of Political Conventions* (above, n. 29), 258–263.

[52] In the September election, Gorham lost to his Democratic opponent, Haight, by 8,546 votes. The dissident Republican candidate, Caleb Fay, polled only 2,088 votes. (Bancroft, *History of California*, VII, 327.)

out that he had overestimated the staying power of the Union party on this issue. The same state convention that gave Gorham the gubernatorial nomination repudiated his position on the Chinese. The platform on which he was invited to run declared that "the importation of Chinese or any other people of the Mongolian race . . . is in every respect injurious and degrading to American labor, by forcing it into unjust and ruinous competition, and an evil that should be restricted by legislation and abated by such legal and constitutional means as are in our power." [53]

Here was language at least as rigorous as that adopted by the Democrats.[54] But since Gorham had already committed himself in the opposite direction, the language was ineffective in shielding him from the charge of hostility to white workingmen and merely opened him up to accusations of hypocrisy. He was soon in full retreat, trying to catch up with his vanishing army. Over Gorham's signature, the following notice appeared in San Francisco and Sacramento newspapers:

> Dear Sir: A circular has met my eye in which it is stated that I favor Chinese suffrage. As a final answer to all the din raised on this subject, I wish to say that I am not and never have been in favor of the extension of the suffrage to the Chinese. The Democracy are reduced to desperate straits when they find it necessary to reiterate the oft-exploded falsehood contained in the circular alluded to.[55]

In July, one month and two weeks before the close of the campaign, that sequence of events which had begun with the riot against Chinese street railway laborers in February, came around full circle. The Workingmen's Convention met to hear speeches by the rival congressional candidates. Of these, the first was T. J. Phelps, the Union nominee to whom the Mariposa blacksmith had earlier abdicated his place. Phelps told the workingmen that he favored the eight-hour system on

---

[53] Davis, 248–249. The platform was adopted at the Sacramento convention on June 13, 1867. One can trace a similar shift of position in the *Alta California*. On April 2, 1867, the editors were arguing that it was logical and ultimately desirable that race be removed as a qualification of voting. Only three months later (July 15, 1867), the *Alta* greeted with relief the news that a bill introduced by Sumner to provide for manhood suffrage had been "headed off" in the Senate; and went on to write that Sumner was a "vain theorist, striking out after posthumous fame," but that voting by Mongolians was "what California will never assent to."

[54] The Democratic platform held that it was "impracticable to maintain republican institutions based upon suffrage of negroes, Chinese and Indians" and declared that suffrage regulation belonged to the states, demanding that Congress "protect the Pacific States and Territories from an undue influx of Chinese and Mongolians" (*Alta*, June 21, 1867).

[55] *Alta*, September 1, 1867.

all government projects, opposed coolie labor, and would do what he
could to halt the coolie traffic. All this was courteously received, and
he turned over the rostrum to his opponent, Samuel B. Axtell, incumbent, and at this time California's sole Democratic ambassador to the
national capital. Axtell said substantially the same things Phelps had
said, but then went further. He was opposed to Chinese labor on the
railroad. He was opposed to patronizing any man who employed Chinese in any capacity. Having been a forty-niner himself, he said, he
and his partner had in those days "driven Chinamen out of the
gulches. He acknowledged that it 'wasn't exactly legal,' but it was
effective and no more than he believed to be right." Next he spoke
of the Potrero rioters: he could understand and excuse their action;
had he been police judge, he would have vindicated the law, yet without so much severity. Congressman Axtell had no need to remind his
listeners that it was he himself who had carried the appeal of the
convicted rioters to the State Supreme Court and his plea of habeas
corpus which had gained them their freedom.[56]

So far the tone of the proceedings had been that of earnest and
harmonious nonpartisanship. As soon, however, as the invited speakers
took their departure, the convention plunged into a furious debate
over the Wilcox fiasco. Several committees were supposed to have investigated charges of bribery, but these had little to report. There followed motions and countermotions—to rescind, to file, to lay on the
table, to amend the amendment—until the entire session bogged down
into a morass of parliamentary confusion. An adjournment on call at
last was carried. But no sooner had the president stepped down from
the chair than one Michael Cooney summoned the meeting to order
again. A resolution was offered and adopted to endorse the entire
Democratic ticket. Then with three cheers for the success of its candidates, the assemblage voted to adjourn *sine die;* and so ended the long
labors of the Workingmen's Convention.[57]

In September the Democrats swept the state. They elected the governor and his administration, two of California's three congressmen
(Axtell was reelected), and a gigantic majority in the Assembly which,
during the coming winter, would enact the state's first mechanics' lien

[56] *Bulletin,* July 12, 1867. The double quotes enclose the *Bulletin* reporter's para-
phrase of Axtell's speech. *Alta,* May 14, 1867. Axtell had come to California in 1849
from Ohio, and had been elected to Congress in 1866 as a Democrat. But he seems
to have been of Unionist persuasion and was an admirer of General Grant, who
appointed him territorial governor of Utah and later of New Mexico. Oddly, he
ended his career as Republican Central Committee chairman for the Territory of
New Mexico. (*An Illustrated History of New Mexico* [Chicago, 1895], 87.)

[57] *Alta,* July 12, 1867; *Bulletin,* July 12, 1867.

and eight-hour legislation. After seven years in the wilderness, the Democracy of the Pacific Coast had achieved total rehabilitation. Henry Haight, the new governor, summed up in his victory speech the meaning of the outcome as he saw it:

> I will simply say that in this result we protest against corruption and extravagance in our State affairs—against populating this fair State with a race of Asiatics—against sharing with inferior races the Government of the country—against the military despotism which now exists at the South under the late acts of Congress; and this protest of ours, echoing the voice of Connecticut and Kentucky, will be re-echoed in thunder tones by the great central states until the Southern States are emancipated from negro domination, and restored to their proper places as equals and sisters in the great Federal family.[58]

[58] *Alta*, September 6, 1867.

5

THE ROAD TO REUNION

Henry George and the Chinese

Midway in his term of office, Governor Haight, standard bearer for
the newly rehabilitated Democracy of California, made the acquaint-
ance of a young printer and journalist, Henry George. They met at a
conference on tariff reform in San Francisco; but what probably called
the governor's attention to the young man was the fact that he had
published, only a few months earlier, a letter in the New York
Tribune warning of danger to the entire nation from the incursion of
Chinese in the West. The letter had excited favorable comment in
California not only for what it said but for where it appeared—in the
paper of Horace Greeley, one of the founding fathers of Republicanism. Discovering that he and Henry George saw eye to eye on the Chinese question and the tariff, as well as a good many other issues, the
Governor undertook to push his new friend forward. He secured for
him the editorship of a small daily across the bay, the Oakland *Transcript*. Early in 1870 he brought George up to Sacramento to take
charge of a statewide party organ, the *Reporter,* which thrived in part
at least on a subsidy of legal notices voted for it by the Democratic
majority in the legislature.[1]

Throughout most of the following ten years, Henry George collected, in one form or another, a retainer from the Democratic party.
His first analysis of land problems, *Our Land and Land Policy,* was
written on savings made possible by the success of the *Reporter.* His
chef d'oeuvre, *Progress and Poverty,* in the physical sense at least,
owed its creation to a partial sinecure as state inspector of gas meters
which George enjoyed thanks to the patronage of William Irwin, next

[1] Henry George, "The Chinese on the Pacific Coast," New York *Tribune,* May 1,
1869; and see Charles Albro Barker, *Henry George* (New York, 1955), 131–140; and
Henry George, Jr., *The Life of Henry George,* Vol. IX, *Complete Works of Henry
George,* 10 vols. (Garden City, N.Y., 1911), 197.

Democratic governor after Haight. Along with these major under-takings, George was turning out pamphlets and delivering campaign speeches; and on the fourth of July 1877, he received the highest honor which the California branch of the party could bestow—he was named orator for the annual commemoration of the Declaration of Indepen-dence.[2]

All this was appropriate. Just as Broderick, or the memory of Broderick, had summed up the politics of the far western Democracy, so Henry George epitomized its thought. In both cases the major ingredients were eastern urban locofocoism combined with the vicari-ous experience of the placer mining episode in the West. Henry George had been born in Philadelphia in 1839. He was the son of a customshouse clerk who owed his job to the long dominance of the Democrats before the Civil War, and who lost it with the election of Abraham Lincoln. To this family disaster the son Henry contributed by casting his first vote for Lincoln. He had come out to the Pacific Coast before his twenty-first birthday, working the westward passage as seaman on a naval lighthouse tender, and had jumped ship in San Francisco. By that time George already had made up his mind against slavery; but one suspects that the decisive factor in his vote for Lincoln was not so much the slavery issue as a vein of romanticism, a Whit-manesque concept of the indivisible destiny of the nation. Only a few years later George, with the approval of his young wife, actually signed up for a filibustering expedition to Mexico—not to expand the bound-aries of the United States, but to aid Juárez in liberating the Mexican republic. It may be that the leaders of the undertaking held rather less altruistic views; but (and probably happily for the Georges) a federal revenue cutter intervened and the volunteers never left San Francisco Bay.[3]

It happened that the year in which George cast his first vote was also the year in which he completed his apprenticeship in the Typo-graphical Union. During the period of the war he worked at his trade in San Francisco and Sacramento, preparing for the hoped-for transi-tion, then still fairly common, from printer's bench to editor's desk. Yet none of these steps was to come easy. The family in Philadelphia were hard pressed financially. George had had little formal education. When work was slack in the printing trade he took to the countryside and hired out as a farm hand. He put in part of a year in British Columbia helping a cousin with general store keeping on Vancouver

2 Barker, 145–146, 155–163, 230–240; Henry George, *Complete Works*, VIII, 157–184.
3 George, Jr., *Life*, 165–167; Barker, 3–16, 50.

Island opposite the mouth of the Fraser River.[4] Thus, he had knocked around in the Jacksonian style; he was a workingman and producer before he was an intellectual.

George is usually treated as a political economist—a disciple, albeit self-taught, and critic, of the exponents of classical liberalism. Robert Heilbroner (in a chapter titled "The Underworld of Economics") included him among his "worldly philosophers."[5] Certainly it is true that George devoted his major effort to such economic categories as rent, wages, monopoly—generally handled within the comfortable hypothesis of rational self-interest. *Rational* appears to be the key word; and apart from the coincidence that both were printers and both Philadelphians, there was a good deal of Benjamin Franklin in Henry George. Beneath the surface, however, the real kinship was not to Franklin, but to another printer and editor, Walt Whitman. The filibuster episode, for example, which remains indecipherable in the context of rational self-interest, comes in focus with a reading of Whitman's stanzas on the defeated revolutions of 1848:

> Liberty—let others despair of you—I never despair of you.
> Is the house shut? Is the master away?
> Nevertheless be ready, be not weary of watching,
> He will soon return, his messengers come anon.[6]

This is not to suggest that the young seaman and printer had become a devotee of Whitman; the point is that the source of inspiration was the same for both—urban Jacksonian Democracy. Through all the erosion of time and politics, there could hardly be a more convincing demonstration of the real splendor of that vision than the fact that it left behind *Leaves of Grass* and *Progress and Poverty*. A sense of this emotional tone, this romantic dedication to the ongoing cause of mankind, is essential to understanding the ambivalence in George toward the Chinese—and toward organized labor as well.

But first there is one further point of comparison with Walt Whitman. For both men Abraham Lincoln assumed a messianic value. His triumph and death ("O powerful western fallen star! O shades of night—") became the symbol of their own affirmation. George's first breakthrough into the editorial rooms resulted from a letter he sent unsolicited to the San Francisco *Alta California,* an elegy in prose for the murdered president.[7] On the strength of this he was hired as re-

[4] George, Jr., *Life,* 71–72, 74–82, 99, 107.

[5] Barker, 122–123. Robert L. Heilbroner, *The Worldly Philosophers* (New York: Simon and Schuster paperback, 1953), 155–163.

[6] "Europe, the 72d and 73d Years of these States," written in 1850.

[7] For the text of the letter, and an account of George's stint as reporter on the *Alta California,* see George, Jr., *Life,* 160–164.

porter. He covered the memorial services and eight days after the assassination contributed the lead editorial, an effort to sum up the meaning of Lincoln's presidency: "No common man, yet the qualities which made him great and loved were eminently common. He personified the best, the most general character of the people. . . . Let us thank God for him; let us trust God for him; let us place him in that Pantheon which no statue of tyrant ever sullied—the hearts of a free people!" [8] There was no reference to the ending of slavery. With George as with Whitman, it was not Lincoln the emancipator of black slaves that stirred response, but Lincoln the prophet of the American Oversoul.

George moved rapidly up the ladder of political journalism. Within two years he had taken over the editorship of a new daily, the San Francisco *Times*, which under his direction pursued a policy hostile to President Johnson, favorable to George Julian, Thaddeus Stevens, and the Radicals in Congress. But the young editor was unable to stomach for long the Republicanism of the postwar era. He voted for Grant in 1868; then came the *Tribune* letter, the friendship with Haight; and by 1872 he was supporting the Liberal Republican rebels and campaigning for Horace Greeley as Democratic-Liberal candidate against Grant.[9] All the rest of his life he remained, by his own declaration, a Democrat, although the record would indicate that he was more often at odds with his party than in harmony with it. Years later, in a public indictment of President Cleveland, George described his own political allegiance in these terms: "The Democracy that I am talking about, the Democracy to which I belong and as a representative of which I stand here . . . is the Democracy of Thomas Jefferson! It is not the false Democracy of today, but it is the true Democracy; the Democracy that believes in equal rights to all and special privilege to none; the Democracy that would crush monopolies under its foot." [10]

No mention of Lincoln here. He had long since given up the Republican party; but he was still wrestling for the soul of the Democracy and so groped back to its origins. Jefferson suggested ruralness, the sane and sacred intercourse of man with the earth. Yet this really was at second hand for George; what came to him directly from the childhood environment of small urban enterprise and skilled craftsmanship was the concept of equal rights to all and special privilege to none—the image of the producer as value carrier for society. To this extent he identified with labor. "I am still an honorary member of the union which, while working at my trade, I always fully supported,"

8 *Alta*, April 23, 1865.
9 Barker, 72–104, 106–110, 166–175.
10 George, *Works*, VIII, 336.

he declared in *Progress and Poverty;* [11] and his greatest political campaign, the bid for the mayoralty of New York in 1886, was made as nominee of the Independent Labor party.[12]

Of trade unionism itself, however, George took a skeptical view. The gains a union might win must be at best small and partial. In last resort unions had no recourse except to strike, and a strike was always destructive. "Like all war," he wrote, "it lessens wealth. And the organization for it must, like the organization for war, be tyrannical." [13] Yet this was not the worst of it. Those who most needed improvement were the unskilled, and it was the unskilled precisely whom trade unions were least able and least willing to organize. George saw no great benefit in further gains for the already advantaged. What was needed was a general increase. The only type of organization which might serve that end would be one to "include laborers of all kinds." But he regarded such a combination as "practically impossible." [14] Not unionism but individual enterprise would raise the level of humanity. And George believed he had witnessed this process in action during his years in the West.

Thus, it was California and the Fraser River which furnished the second ingredient of his thought. Arriving in San Francisco in 1858, he was five years too late for the heyday of California placer mining. The legend however was already flourishing more luxuriantly than the reality. Land, according to the legend, had been available to all; it needed only the investment of individual effort and a bit of good luck to make it yield gold; all men's chances were equal; the community would limit each claim to what a man could work for himself, and beyond this rational self-interest would provide whatever motivation and whatever controls were necessary. If placer mining was almost over in California, it was briefly in full flower at the Fraser River, and George found there a scale model of the camp and claim system which had developed earlier in the California foothills.[15]

But the mining camp legend was only the beginning. This same model could be extended to timber and agriculture. And above all George applied it to the new towns springing up along the edges of mining, farming, and lumbering regions and to the great cities which took shape at the points of supply. Here would develop an ever-

[11] Henry George, *Progress and Poverty* (Garden City, N.Y., 1926), 313. This book was first published in 1879.

[12] Philip S. Foner, *History of the Labor Movement in the United States,* 4 vols. (New York, 1947), II, 119.

[13] George, *Progress and Poverty,* 313.

[14] Ibid., 311.

[15] Barker, 34–44; George, Jr., *Life,* 77–83.

increasing demand for the enterprise of producers. Merchants and sailors, machinists and iron molders, carpenters and architects, printers and editors would increase and multiply. Potentially there was no end to the spiral of growth. Population need never outstrip production, because for each additional mouth God had provided two hands and the labor of hands furnished the sole and unlimited source of production.[16]

Population *need* not outrun production, yet seemed constantly to do so. How explain the fact that even in such new cities as San Francisco, Vancouver, Sacramento there were surplus people, accumulations of unemployed, homeless and hungry men and women? The source of these evils, George concluded, lay in the engrossment of land.[17] Although land was still plentiful, it was obvious that gold- and lumber-bearing land, and crop lands adjacent to rivers (or to railroads), and, above all, lots in the cities must come in short supply. No enterpriser could pursue his opportunity unless he had access to a piece of the earth to plant his feet and his workbench on. Those who owned the land therefore held the advantage of monopolists; the more rapid the growth of the community, the greater the price of land and the higher the rents they could extort. Yet this bonanza was due to no labor of their own; they were taxing the labor of others; and the result must be so great a curtailment of income for the real producers that growth of the community would come to a halt. Here, George determined, was the controlling factor in the cycle of expansion and collapse which marked the development of western cities.

The danger was monopoly. Thus the warnings of his own early remembrance were verified—the difference being simply that the octopus of land engrossment and land grant railroads had replaced the ancient bank monster of the Jacksonians. On such familiar ground he could feel certain of his analysis. And there was a further assurance in that this reemphasis on land fetched back full circle to the original Jeffersonian mystique of man and the earth, which as a city dweller he had perhaps not previously understood. "On the land we are born, from it we live," he wrote in 1871, "to it we return again—children of the soil as truly as the blade of grass or the flower of the field." [18]

George's first prescription for land monopoly was the same attempted by the placer miners, limitation of the size of holdings. Clearly, this would not work in the new cities. Land could not be

16 George, *Progress and Poverty*, Book I, chaps. 1, 3, 4.

17 The following analysis is based on Henry George, *Our Land and Land Policy* (San Francisco, 1871). Page references are to the text in George, *Works*, VIII, 3–131.

18 Ibid., 75.

subdivided small enough to go around, yet the price of land and its consequent tariff on the producing classes continued to rise. George's solution to the problem came to him in a flash, he testified later, as he was riding one January morning through the hills, green from the first winter rains, east of Oakland. What the solution actually amounted to was an application of the classical law of rent, which probably he had picked up from John Stuart Mill's *Political Economy*.[19] It will scarcely be necessary to pursue this argument very far; the point is that the law of rent abstracted for George the relative "value" of land from land itself. If land could be conceived as opportunity, as the sine qua non of productive enterprise, then its value could be conceived in the same terms. This led George to the advocacy of value taxation upon land; the effect would be to divide opportunity equally among all members of the community, which was precisely what the miners' camp meetings had attempted by limitation of claims.[20] That value taxation would be equivalent to ending private property in land, George subsequently acknowledged. Such was the price of thwarting monopoly. But he justified himself by arguing that land, the creation of God, not the fruit of any man's labor, must properly be for the *use* of all men equally: "There is in nature no such thing as a fee simple in land. . . . There can be but one title to land recognized—the using of it to satisfy reasonable wants."[21]

George's adoption of the law of rent testified once again to his urban origin. For the boy brought up in a narrow-faced, high-stooped brick house, probably leased from a distant landlord, the abstraction of value from the land itself came as naturally as it would to a London economist or an Irish cotter. Nor was the concept inharmonious with the experience of gold miners or with that of entrepreneurs in new cities. Yet it separated George from that portion of the American tradition which equated private land holding with individual enterprise. Generally this included farmers; for them the land and its value were one. If they were tenants, they had been owners and hoped to be so again. They were also speculators, large and small, and to some extent misers and dreamers of land, and their response to the proposal of value taxation (later sloganized into the "Single Tax") was overwhelmingly negative.

None of this George seems to have understood. While he belongs

[19] Ibid., 87–88, 98–99; Barker, 137–138. In the following discussion the word *value* must be understood in a special sense: George used the word in connection with land only as a concession to the popular vocabulary. By his definition land had no value; labor alone produced value.

[20] Barker, 182–191.

[21] George, *Our Land*, 87.

with the "frontier-lands" school of American interpretation, it was a very special frontier to which he addressed himself. He was philosopher of the *urban* frontier; beyond this, even, of the California urban frontier, where due to special circumstances of geography and mineral deposits the cities developed before the agricultural hinterland. By contrast to Frederick Jackson Turner who found his value carriers among farmers and villagers or to Charles Howard Shinn who found his among miners reenacting the Teutonic myth, Henry George looked to a new yeomanry of Jacksonian producers in the western cities. His urbanism was akin to that of Josiah Royce—an enemy of frontiers— the difference between them being that Royce honored the old cities whereas George trusted especially in new ones.[22] Because these appeared to be entering into a period of unlimited expansion, George could be optimistic, far more so than Turner; for the essence of the urban frontier, George believed, could with all its benefits be abstracted, universalized, and made permanent. All that was needed was the "value" tax on land to exorcise monopoly.

All that was needed, however, was not predetermined. Rational self-interest and religion pointed the way. Man had only to choose; yet his choosing might be misdirected by the false arguments of special interest. Monopoly again. And precisely in California, where the way seemed most obvious, it was, in George's eventual conclusion, least likely to be chosen. This was for two reasons: first, that monopoly was strongest there since such vast lands had been so recently engrossed and, second, because of the Chinese. As early as 1868, while the Pacific slope still basked in the afternoon of boom times, George was writing for the newly established *Overland Monthly* in rather somber tones of California's future.[23]

The railroad was then building at a rate of eight or nine miles a day. Taking as his title the question, "What the Railroad Will Bring Us," George predicted that it would fetch in first of all population, like water seeking its own level. Industry, agriculture would become more productive, more complex. The price of land would rise. Necessarily then it would be harder to get ahead. Poor people would have to save longer to acquire land. They would rent and labor; and their

22 See above, pp. 46–50, for a discussion of Shinn, Turner, and Royce.
23 Barker, 260–264. This is not to suggest that George had worked out his whole system by 1868. There was, however, a Platonic character to his intellectual construction. He kept discovering, or making explicit, what was already there. *Progress and Poverty* (1879) is contained in embryo in *Our Land and Land Policy* (1871). And the *Overland Monthly* article here referred to says nothing that would not fit with the later elaborations. But such definitely is not the case with the New York *Tribune* letter on the Chinese (1869).

competition would further increase the rents and lower the wage rates. In the cities, homes would be out of reach of the workingman. "When liveries appear, look out for barefooted children. A few liveries are now to be seen in our streets." Then he turned a nostalgic glance backward: "The miner, working for himself, owned no master; worked when and only when he pleased. . . . But the 'honest miner' of the placers has passed away in California. The Chinaman, the mill owner and his laborers, the mine superintendent and his gang, are his successors." Doubtless the railroad would bring the culture and luxury of the eastern cities; yet it must bring their social evils as well—those fatal questions "like riddles of a Sphinx, which not to answer is death . . . with one of them, the labor question, rendered peculiarly complex by our proximity to Asia." And concluding, he wrote: "The future of our State, or our nation, of our race, looks fair and bright; perhaps the future looked so to the philosophers who once sat in the porches of Athens—to the unremembered men who raised the cities whose ruins lie south of us." [24]

So far George had touched only lightly on the question of the Chinese. In the following year, 1869, he devoted his full attention to the matter. The New York *Tribune* letter constituted a classic statement of the economic argument against Chinese immigration as it had been developed during the preceding five years by anticoolie clubs, trade unions, and the renascent Democratic party.[25] The reservoir of the Asian mainland, George began, was inexhaustible. So long as immigration from Asia continued, it would be impossible, on the Pacific Coast at least, for the withdrawal of workers from the lowest paid industries to exert any upward pressure on wages in those industries. Rather the result would be that the Chinese would take over one occupation after another. Non-Chinese could not complete because life on the subsistence level of the Asian immigrants was impossible or intolerable for them. Moreover, they were accustomd to establishing homes and raising families, while the Chinese, allegedly, were not. As to the advantages of cheap labor which some claimed would accrue to the entire community, George argued that they were illusory. In the the first place the earnings of Chinese did not go to enrich the American community, but were sent back to China in the form of savings or in payment for imported food and clothing. In the second place,

[24] Henry George, "What the Railroad Will Bring Us," *Overland Monthly*, I (San Francisco, October, 1868), 297–306.

[25] Henry George, "The Chinese on the Pacific Coast," New York *Tribune*, May 1, 1869. Page references are to the letter as reprinted in A. M. Winn, *Valedictory Address, January 11, 1871, at Excelsior Hall, San Francisco, to the Mechanics' State Council of California* (San Francisco, 1871), 13–19.

the competition of Chinese would force all workingmen to accept lower wages. This would reduce demand and set up a depressive spiral. Even more importantly, in George's view, it would shift an increasing portion of total product from the producing classes (labor, plus family-size enterprisers) to the capitalists—and to the landlords.

Thus the heart of the indictment was that Chinese labor accentuated the trend toward monopoly. Was it not the great land engrossers, especially the Central Pacific Railroad, which organized and defended the importation of Chinese? In effect, George's letter was an appeal to the Jacksonian persuasion—scattered as it then was between the Democracy and those dissidents among the Republicans who would set afoot the Liberal schism—to take up the anti-Chinese campaign as a general and *unifying* issue. Above all, George insisted on its national scope. The Chinese would flood across the continent; already they were meeting the Irish in Salt Lake Basin. The states of the North and Midwest would find themselves struggling to establish some kind of Missouri Compromise line against coolieism, as once they had struggled to draw lines against slavery. Inevitably, the result would be "to make the rich richer and the poor poorer; to make nabobs and princes of our capitalists, and crush our working classes into the dust; to substitute (if it goes far enough) a population of serfs and their masters for that population of intelligent freemen who are our glory and strength; to rear an empire with its glittering orders round the throne and its prostrate people below, in place of the Republic of Washington and Jefferson." [26]

This was, and remains, an impressive argument. Charles Barker has shown in his biography how closely the patterns of George's thought were contained within the "Jeffersonian and Jacksonian principles of destroying private economic monopolies and of advancing freedom and equal opportunity." Yet Barker was mistaken when he went on to say that George's "Californian attitude toward Chinese immigration" was an exception to this rule.[27] The fact is that the *Tribune* letter reflected precisely that hostility toward minority racial groups which lay close to the heart of Jacksonianism. George's own account of the origin of the letter bears eloquent witness to this relationship. During

---

[26] Ibid., 19.
[27] Barker, ix. Further along (122-123) Barker suggested that by basing his *Tribune* letter argument on the wage fund theory, which like the law of rent, he had gotten from Mill, George "succeeded in avoiding a racial opposition to Chinese immigration." This too is unconvincing, as the quotations from George's letter will indicate. Later, he rejected the wage fund theory (see George, Jr., *Life*, 195-197); but the most racist phase of his hostility to the Chinese coincided with the time when he accepted it.

the spring of 1869 he had gone east as representative of a small San Francisco paper, his assignment being to break through the monopoly on national and European news transmission established by Western Union and the Associated Press. He was appalled, after his years on the Pacific Coast, at the contrast of wealth and squalor in the eastern cities. One day, walking through a slum district of New York, he experienced what he later described as a religious revelation. "There came to me a thought, a vision, a call—give it whatever name you please. But every nerve quivered. And there and then I made a vow." [28] What he vowed was that he would seek out the cause of poverty and so help to set free these wretched of the earth. The first fruit of his experience was the letter to the *Tribune*.[29]

It appears clearly enough from the text that George preferred the economic argument and tried to confine himself to that level. Yet the emotional thrust breaks the surface. Speaking of Chinese in the mines, George wrote: "Though we do not want these poorer diggings, which the Chinamen are working out, we should have a care for those of our own race who will follow us. The day will come when wages in California will sink to an eastern level, and when white men—white men with families depending on them—will be glad to find and work these poor diggings; and for these men we should see that they are reserved, and not permit them to be despoiled by the long-tailed barbarians, who have no interest in this country, and whose earnings do not add to its wealth." [30] What is fascinating here is that George felt impelled to separate himself from this statement. He placed it in quotes as though transmitting, objectively, the views of a typical mining man.[31] Yet only a few paragraphs further along, speaking in his own voice, he asserted that Chinese were, like Africans, "an infusible element," that they were "utter heathens, treacherous, sensual, cowardly and cruel." And again: "They practice all the unnameable vices of the East, and are as cruel as they are cowardly." [32]

It was for this dichotomy—between the rational economic argument which would focus on importation under servile contract and the emo-

28 Letter, Henry George to Rev. Thomas Dawson, Glencree, Ireland, February 2, 1883; quoted in George, Jr., *Life*, 193.

29 Barker, 121–122; George, Jr., *Life*, 192–194.

30 George, "Chinese on the Pacific Coast," in Winn, *Valedictory*, 15.

31 Apparently there was a real prototype for this "mining man." In a speech made twenty-one years later (Metropolitan Hall, San Francisco, February 4, 1890) George attributed substantially the same statement to an old miner he said he had met on shipboard during his trip to the Fraser River. But interestingly the seaborne miner's remarks did not contain the reference to "long-tailed barbarians." See George, Jr., *Life*, 80.

32 George, "Chinese on the Pacific Coast," in Winn, *Valedictory*, 18.

tional hostility toward Chinese themselves—that John Stuart Mill took issue with Henry George in an exchange of correspondence stemming out of the *Tribune* letter. In midsummer 1869, George, returning to California, assumed the editorship of the Oakland *Daily Transcript*.[33] He had earlier sent his *Tribune* letter to John Stuart Mill and, on receiving an answer, published it in the *Daily Transcript* along with his own comments. Mill's reply was generous and friendly. He concurred in George's economic argument, as indeed he might since it was based on his own book, *Political Economy*. He agreed that Chinese competition would, if continued, lower the living standards of all workingmen in the West. Restriction of imported contract labor was therefore desirable. But involved in this issue, Mill declared, was "one of the most difficult and embarrassing questions of political morality—the extent and limits of the right of those who have first taken possession of the unoccupied portion of the earth's surface to exclude the remainder of mankind from inhabiting it." Was it justified, he asked, to assume that Chinese could never change? "The institutions of the United States are the most potent means that have yet existed of spreading the most important elements of civilization down to the poorest and most ignorant of the laboring masses. If every Chinese child were compulsorily brought under your school system, or under a still more effective one if possible, and kept under it for a sufficient number of years, would not the Chinese population be in time raised to the level of the Americans?" [34]

George thought not. Bypassing the inquiry, he asserted that Mill's response had "entirely justified" his own position. As to the "purely economic view of the subject" (the phrase is Mill's),[35] George doubtless was correct in claiming endorsement by the dean of political economists. Yet the question Mill raised (and did not answer) struck directly at one of the fundamental assumptions of the anti-Chinese campaign: the proposition that Chinese were unassimilable—"an infusible element," as George had put it.[36] His son, Henry George, Jr., whose account of his father's life is included in the *Collected Works,* apparently believed that George never modified the views he had set forth in the New York *Tribune* letter.[37] But the evidence suggests that he modified them a good deal and that his subsequent political behavior may have been considerably influenced by John Stuart Mill's criticism.

[33] Barker, 131–134.
[34] Oakland *Daily Transcript*, November 20, 1869.
[35] George, Jr., *Life*, 201–202. *Daily Transcript*, November 20, 22, 1869.
[36] George, "Chinese on the Pacific Coast," in Winn, *Valedictory*, 18.
[37] George, Jr., *Life*, 202–203.

Nationalization of the Chinese Issue

After the joining of the railroad and following the onset of depression
in the East, George's predictions for California began to come true.
Agriculture sagged; industries shut down. Yet the influx of emigration
from older sections of the country continued, more than doubling
between 1872 and 1875. Unemployed workmen drifted up and down
the state congregating in the cities, especially in San Francisco. The
boom-time gains of the trade unionists were quickly lost. Wages fell;
the standard workday reverted to ten hours and longer.[38]

According to Ira Cross in his history of California's labor movement,
it was during these years that employers joined the anti-Chinese crusade:

> As long as the Chinese were willing to work under the condi-
> tions and for the wages set by white employers who had taught
> them their respective trades, the employers were satisfied. But
> when the Chinese began to establish their own shops, to hire
> their countrymen, and to enter into direct competition with
> their former employers and instructors, it was a different
> story. . . . Another source of irritation for the white employ-
> ers was that the Chinese learned to use the strike as a means
> of exacting higher wages and improved conditions of employ-
> ment.

The last point is doubtful since evidence of strike actions by Chinese
remains tantalizingly meager. As to the first point, it was noted earlier
that small manufacturers from well before the Civil War were playing
an active role in anticoolie clubs of the cigar makers, shoemakers, and
tailors. Yet Cross was undoubtedly correct in his description of the
generally broadening impact of Chinese competition.[39]

The events of 1867, moreover, had demonstrated that anti-Chinese
politics in the West were successful politics. One reason for this was
that during the war and the years immediately following, expressions
of hostility toward Negroes had acquired a secessionist connotation.
The argument against Chinese, however, remained untainted, and
within this fabric the driving emotions of racism could be woven into
a pattern of economic rationalization. The conclusions drawn would

[38] For a summary of economic developments during this decade, see Ira B. Cross,
A History of the Labor Movement in California (Berkeley, 1935), 60–72, 313 note
30.

[39] Cross, 84–85. On strikes by Chinese, see above, pp. 9–10; on small manufacturers in anticoolie clubs, see above, pp. 76–77.

then apply analogously to the Negro. Henry George's letter to the New York *Tribune* had set the matter in national terms; and labor, nationally, had adopted the issue.[40] Perhaps a portion of the favorable response to the *Tribune* letter was due to the fact that it showed a way by which antislavery men and Unionists of Jacksonian persuasion could find their way, through the anti-Chinese argument, to a repudiation of their now burdensome alliance with abolitionism. The letter, in effect, stated the theoretical grounds upon which a Republican dominated Senate, one year later, would defeat Charles Sumner on the issue of naturalization for Chinese.[41] This decision in turn predicted the abandoning of Reconstruction for the Negro; and the end of Reconstruction would seal the fate of the Chinese in the West. It was no accident then that George's letter had first appeared in Greeley's newspaper, nor that within three years of writing that letter George himself moved from Republicanism, by way of the Liberal schism, back to Democracy.

By 1876 both major parties had adopted anti-Chinese clauses in their national platforms.[42]

To California, 1876 brought the full impact of depression. But the political repercussions which followed were not due solely to hard times. In part at least they were due to the contrast between misery and affluence—of which California, and especially San Francisco, offered striking views. In March, for example, the *Alta,* commenting on the increased menace of tramps, reported that they were flooding the state, that privately supported alms houses were swamped and in any case ineffective because, with their blankets and hot meals, they were far too luxurious. The men would rather stay there than get out and look for work. What was needed, the *Alta* proposed, were municipal lodgings where board would consist of water, black bread, salt fish, and the in-

---

[40] See above, pp. 80–91; also John Swinton, *The New Issue: The Chinese American Question* (New York, 1870) [Pamphlets on Immigration], University of California Library, Berkeley. For a western statement of the theme, see M. B. Starr, *The Coming Struggle: Or What the People on the Pacific Coast Think of the Coolie Invasion* (San Francisco, 1873).

[41] See above, pp. 36–37.

[42] Kirk H. Porter and Donald Bruce Johnson, *National Party Platforms, 1840–1960* (Urbana, Ill., 1961), 50, 54. The Democratic statement, long and detailed, was based explicitly on the unassimilability of the "Mongolian race"; the Republican held merely that it was the "immediate duty of Congress fully to investigate the effects of the immigration and importation of Mongolians on the moral and material interests of the country." Inclusion even of this mild statement, however, constituted an acceptance of the anti-Chinese argument. As to the minor parties, the Independent (Greenback) platform of 1876 made no mention of the issue; and only in the Prohibition platform was there an assertion of the old abolitionist stance which Sumner had defended in 1870. (See 51–53.)

mates would sleep on bare floors. Two days later the same journal
noted the completion by "a well known stock-broker" of a "palace for
horses" on California between Jones and Leavenworth. The drinking
trough, "carved out of a solid block of white marble at an expense of
$1,000" represented a "wide mouthed lion leaning over an open vase."
Particularly gratifying to the reporter was the fact that these stables,
though costing "fully $40,000," showed no sign of "undue lavishness
of money, or garishness of color or design." [43]

With autumn and winter, the disasters of drought were added to
those of industrial depression. California rainfall for 1876–1877 was
the lowest in a quarter century. Crops failed; cattle died; and in the
mountains, as the streams ran dry, there was no water even for the
meager diggings of subsistence miners. San Francisco's Benevolent
Association, for the first half of 1877, reported more calls for relief
than at any time since its founding twelve years earlier. Hubert Howe
Bancroft estimated 15,000 unemployed in the city that spring—which
for a population of something less than 150,000 white males meant
that one-fifth to one-quarter of the available labor force was unemployed.[44]

Against this background, events moved in response to national developments. In 1876 the Democratic party, which had won its rehabilitation in California nine years earlier largely by virtue of its anti-
Chinese stance, was making its bid for rehabilitation at the national
level. The mayor of San Francisco, a Democrat propitiously named
Andrew Jackson Bryant, judged the moment ripe for official action.
He summoned the board of supervisors to name a commission of
twelve on the Chinese problem. This was done; and the commissioners,
meeting with the mayor, planned to draw up resolutions, to appeal to
the interior cities for aid, to convoke a mass meeting, and to dispatch
three citizen-ambassadors to Washington as lobbyists for an act of Congress against Chinese immigration.[45] The mayor declared:

> I think we can stop the hordes of paupers and thieves from
> taking possession of this city. I believe this is the best time to
> go to Washington. The House is controlled by one party and
> the Senate by another. We are on the eve of a presidential
> election and both parties are looking toward this coast for aid.

[43] *Alta,* March 17, 19, 1876.

[44] Cross, *History of the Labor Movement,* 71; Hubert Howe Bancroft, *Popular
Tribunals,* 2 vols. (San Francisco, 1887), II, 704; San Francisco population from
Elmer Clarence Sandmeyer, *The Anti-Chinese Movement in California* (Urbana,
Ill., 1939), 17, 19, Tables 3, 4. The figures refer only to white population. By the
Census of 1880 there were 21,745 Chinese in San Francisco. (Sandmeyer, Table 4.)

[45] *Alta,* March 21, 23, 28, April 6, 1876; Sandmeyer, 58–60.

If you can get a bill before one house and have it passed, the other will not be likely to kill it.[46]

The mass meeting was scheduled at the convenience of the governor, who was to preside. This was Governor Irwin, second of the Democratic restoration and the same, it may be recalled, who had appointed Henry George to the inspectorship of gas meters. By all reports the meeting came off successfully. The hall was jammed. There were people outside. Anticoolie clubs from all over the city, and from Oakland and South San Francisco, came marching up with signs and banners. The mayor opened, the governor took the chair, the chief of the mayor's twelve commissioners on the Chinese problem served as keynoter, while a host of ministers, colonels, generals, and distinguished citizens appeared briefly in supporting roles. From this demonstration went forth a seemingly unequivocal message: businessmen, farmers, labor were pressed beyond endurance; state and local efforts having proved fruitless, the only recourse left was an appeal to Congress and to the President of the United States. And each speaker stressed that the campaign must be confined within the framework of law and order; riotous proceedings would damage the common cause.[47]

Clearly all this was a feast of the establishment; and since Democrats at the time were presiding over the California establishment, it was they who were mainly to the fore. Moreover, because the federal administration and the Senate (though not, since 1874, the House of Representatives) were under Republican control, the tactic of appealing for federal relief held a strongly partisan content. Here was an issue which, in the coming election, promised to divide one party while solidifying the other. Yet nonetheless, the San Francisco mass meeting was essentially nonpartisan. The Republicans, ever since their Gorham debacle, had been retreating on the Chinese issue. As early as 1870, at the time of the naturalization debates, the *Alta California* had acknowledged that Republicans and Democrats from the Pacific slope were "a unit against the Chinese if in nothing else." [48] Now in 1876 there remained no possible ground on which to resist the Democratic initiative. The *Alta*, therefore, had no choice but to applaud—despite the hooks and innuendoes contained for the Republican cause nationally—and to rejoice that the mayor's commissioners were "clearheaded, sensible men, who will make all their moves with proper pre-

46 *Alta*, March 23, 1876.
47 *Alta*, April 6, 1876; Sandmeyer, 58–59. For collected clippings, see Bancroft Scraps, VI, 268–390. 105 vols. Bancroft Library, University of California, Berkeley. (On the Chinese in California, VI–IX.)
48 *Alta*, July 3, 1870.

caution, and will present the case in Congress with all the advantage to be obtained from well-conducted meetings and argumentative addresses by cool, practical and sensible speakers." [49]

If the anti-Chinese campaign had now been taken over by mayors and governors, by the "sensible" (and respectable) citizens, where were the workingmen? Doubtless there were many among the 25,000 who reportedly attended the mass meeting. But their spokesmen were not on the platform. And they came not under the banners of trade unions as they had done nine years earlier, but individually, or with neighborhood anticoolie clubs, some at least of which had apparently been newly organized for the occasion.[50] It seems from the evidence (or more accurately, lack of evidence) unmistakable that trade unionism in San Francisco—as in many other American cities—had almost ceased to exist during the depression years.[51] A case in point is the swan song of General A. M. Winn.

Winn, it may be remembered, was the rural Jacksonian from Punkinville, Virginia—carpenter, contractor, land speculator—who had organized house carpenters in San Francisco and emerged as champion of the eight-hour movement. But the eight-hour movement collapsed during the seventies and so did Winn's structure of organizations. All that survived was the Mechanics' State Council, an executive board now without membership, resurrected from time to time at the call of its chairman, who was of course General Winn.[52] One of these reincarnations occurred two days before the mass meeting of 1876. Winn had received an invitation from the mayor's board of commissioners to lend his name as a vice-president. While this was no great honor because there were to be dozens of vice-presidents, Winn, squeezing the most he could from the occasion, asked formal leave of his council to accept. Naturally this was granted and as usual he made them a speech. It was an old-timer's speech and a sad one. It began with a reference to the first public debate of the Chinese question in 1853. "Some of us," Winn said, "have been fighting against Chinese immigration ever since. . . . The Mechanics' State Council, Industrial Reformers, Anti-Chinese Associations, House Carpenters' League, and the People's Protective Alliance,[53] have all, in rotation, used their in-

---

[49] *Alta,* March 28, 1876.

[50] *Alta,* April 6, 1876.

[51] Robert V. Bruce, *1877, Year of Violence* (New York, 1959), 15–19; Foner, *History of the Labor Movement* (above, n. 12), I, 439–440.

[52] Cross, *History of the Labor Movement,* 66, 68. And see above, p. 79.

[53] Winn had taken a leading part in organizing the People's Protective Alliance which flourished in 1873. Based largely on Winn's House Carpenters' League in San Francisco, the Alliance had chapters scattered through California and Oregon, and employed a full-time lecturer-organizer, the Reverend Milton B. Starr. (*Alta,* May 25–June 22, 1873.) And see note 40, above.

fluence." In those earlier days, he continued, "the complainants were poor, wealth was against them"; for all their effort they accomplished little. More recently there had been a great change:

> There is a new element now in charge of the agitation; it is no longer the men who work by the day, but the property holders, who see—what we told them years ago—that little by little the Chinese would encroach upon their real estate and prevent it from increasing in value. I think it is policy for all classes of people to unite in the movement, and to show Congress how much they feel upon the subject, and tell how much they suffer by the introduction of Chinese cheap labor.[54]

Winn was here lumping under a single head almost a quarter century of agitation during which California workingmen had fought for higher wages, shorter hours, improved conditions, and recognition of their unions. Yet now, in the depth of depression, all issues seemed meaningless except the sole issue of the Chinese. And while he could greet as token of victory the fact that a "new element" had taken charge and attempt to accept philosophically his own displacement as leader, the real significance lay in the fact that there were so few of the old leaders to displace. The workingmen drifted into the crisis years 1877 leaderless, embittered, and disorganized. Winn himself was almost seventy, and the role reserved for him at the mass meeting was symbolic. Not only was he not on the platform, he was not even in the hall. Relegated to a street corner outside, his task was to pacify the groups of late comers turned away at the door with harangues from the old days.[55]

The Bipartisan Establishment

Official cognizance of the Chinese problem continued through the remainder of the year. First came a visitation by state senators who spent a few days in San Francisco after the mass meeting and later issued appropriate addresses and memorials to Congress and to the people of the United States.[56] In Washington, western senators and representatives, with the aid of Mayor Bryant's three citizen-ambassadors and the documentation furnished by the state Senate, were proposing several possible forms of action. None of these caught the fancy of Con-

---

[54] *Alta,* April 3, 1876.
[55] *Alta,* April 6, 1876.
[56] California Legislature, Senate, *Chinese Immigration; Its Social, Moral and Political Effect. Report to the California State Senate of the Special Committee on Chinese Immigration* (Sacramento, 1878). Sandmeyer, *Anti-Chinese Movement,* 60–62; *Alta,* April 15, 19, 22, May 27, 1876.

gress, and what resulted was a resolution for a joint investigative committee. Under the direction of senators Morton of Indiana and Sargent of California the committee held public hearings in San Francisco in October and November. Its majority report urged renegotiation of the Burlingame Treaty with China to permit American restrictions on the entrance of Chinese laborers. While for the Californians this represented a partial victory in that the committee accepted the anti-Chinese argument, they were disappointed because they had hoped for recommendation of immediate congressional action. Even more unfortunate from their viewpoint, however, was the question of timing. Made public early in 1877, the committee's report was immediately eclipsed by the Hayes-Tilden electoral deadlock.[57]

1877 was a year of crises. What came next, insofar as the foes and friends of the Chinese were concerned, was the series of strikes beginning in July on the eastern railroads. The California repercussions of that outburst will be discussed in the following chapter; but before moving on, it may be well to pause briefly with the election of 1876. The famous bargain, and the terms of the bargain within the bargain, are well known. In return for Democratic acceptance of decisions by the electoral board of Congress which awarded the ballots in dispute to Hayes, the Republicans had pledged withdrawal of federal troops from the South and abandonment of the Negro to southern home rule. This was the outer bargain, more or less publicly declared, and it doubtless accorded with what the majority of (white) Americans wished to hear. There was also an inner bargain, more sophisticated and more realistic. The inner bargain took the terms of the outer bargain as foregone conclusion, since the Democrats, who held control of the House of Representatives, would be able to force withdrawal of troops simply by withholding military appropriations. The essence of the inner bargain was a share of federal patronage to southern Democrats, and a slice of federal appropriations for internal improvements, especially railroads, in the South.[58]

---

[57] Sandmeyer, 82–88. Senator Oliver P. Morton of Indiana, a Republican founding father, was chairman of the committee. He was taken ill and died. The majority report was written by A. A. Sargent, Republican, of California. See U.S., Senate Report 689, 44th Cong., 2nd Sess. (Washington, 1877). A minority report, presumably written by Morton before his death, took the old Sumnerite stand, defending the Chinese and opposing restriction of immigration. See Oliver P. Morton, *Views of the Late Oliver P. Morton on the Character, Extent, and Effect of Chinese Immigration to the United States*, 45th Cong., 2nd Sess., Sen, Misc. Doc. No. 20 (Washington, 1878). See also, *Alta*, November 14, 15, 19, 1876; and [Frank M. Pixley], "Morton and the Chinese," San Francisco *Argonaut*, December 29, 1877.

[58] C. Vann Woodward, *Reunion and Reaction* (Garden City, N.Y., 1956); John D. Hicks, George E. Mowry, and Robert D. Burke, *The American Nation*, 2 vols., 4th ed. (Boston, 1962), II, 45–49.

Several aspects of this arrangement had an immediate bearing on events that were to follow in July. In the first place, from the fact that there had been any bargaining at all, it was obvious that the Democrats, though losing out in the presidential count, had won their national rehabilitation. This came as climax to a lengthy and painful process. Just as earlier in California, so now on a national scale, the Democracy resumed its role as left bower of a two-party establishment. In the second place, while Republicans and southern Democrats appeared to have benefited largely from the bargains, northern Democrats, and especially that line of northern Democracy which traced its descent from locofocoism, had profited very little.[59] These were the real losers; the effect of rehabilitation on the party, then, was a shift in center of gravity southward and to the right. At once involved was the stance of the Democracy as champion of the hard-pressed workingman. It had been easy and natural for politicians, cast out in the wilderness, to make promises to others likewise cast out—to craftsmen whose unions had been smashed; to slum dwellers, immigrants, unemployed; to the army of laborers who were stoking with their lives the engines of American industrialization. But once the party was back in power and respectability, once its central leadership fell into the grip of men who could form an alliance with the Republican leadership, then it was not easy to keep these promises. In fact it turned out to be impossible.

Such precisely had been the case in California. Rehabilitation there had been won through an alliance with the trade unions and with the anticoolie clubs. It had involved commitments to the eight-hour day, to a rising standard of living for workingmen, to effective action against monopoly, against corruption of government by private interest, and against Chinese immigration. On all these counts except the last, the rehabilitated Democracy had failed. Let General Winn serve once more as an example. A lifelong Democrat who labored for restoration of his party, he had seen his house carpenters' league wiped out by the impact of hard times and by the steady pressure of employers and had seen the men he claimed to champion forced back on the ten- and eleven-hour day at reduced wages; the supposedly ironclad eight-hour act turned into a lawyers' trick. And all the while the Democrats, now generally at the top of the pile in Sacramento, remained as unwilling or unable to offer protection as were their opposite numbers. Winn at least might argue before his Mechanics' Council that the party of Jefferson and Jackson was doing its best on the Chinese question; yet even here the policy of Mayor Bryant and Governor Irwin seemed to rob the issue of its function as a vehicle of

[59] Woodward, especially 179–220.

protest. To participate in the official program against the Chinese implied acquiescence in all the rest. Winn was willing; and he stood outside the gates and dutifully made his speech at the street corner. But as it turned out, a good many workingmen and a larger number of unemployed—with whom the general and his vest pocket council had long since lost touch—were not willing.

Nor were these developments in California essentially different from what occurred nationally. The spark came in July 1877 when a handful of enginemen on the Baltimore and Ohio walked out in desperate protest against one more in a series of wage cuts. The consequences of their action were unique in American labor history. Within two weeks a chain of spontaneous and unorganized uprisings spread from the Atlantic seaboard to the Pacific. Miners, mill workers, factory hands, women and teenage boys, masses of unemployed stormed into the railroad yards. They derailed trains, burned depots and boxcars, fought pitched battles at the crossings with police and with the military. The strikes were nonpartisan—and they encountered a bipartisan opposition. Democratic railroad directors were no less implacable than their Republican counterparts.[60] Democratic and Republican governors alike summoned state militia and appealed to President Hayes for federal troops; and in the cabinet, southern Democrat David M. Key —whose appointment as postmaster general had been part of the electoral bargain in order that he might guarantee a due share of federal patronage for the South—stood shoulder to shoulder with Liberal Republican Carl Schurz in support of Republican President Hayes.[61] It is scarcely surprising that the aftermath of the strikes of 1877 took the form of political revolt against the two-party establishment.

[60] Franklin B. Gowen, for example, of the Reading Railroad, and pursuer of the Molly Maguires, was a Democrat. Wayne G. Broehl, Jr., *The Molly Maguires* [Cambridge, Mass., 1964], 89–107.

[61] Bruce, *1877, Year of Violence*, 220–223.

6

THE WORKINGMEN'S PARTY

The July Days of 1877

The July days began rather quietly in California. The Central Pacific announced a wage cut, as had the eastern railroads, but prudently rescinded its action when news of the strikes came over the wire. Labor, meanwhile, was leaderless. General Winn and his superannuated colleagues, typifying what was left of trade unionism, offered no direction. The anticoolie clubs, although some had been lively enough with their bands and transparencies at Mayor Bryant's mass meeting, were, on the official level at least, mortgaged to the Democracy; and the Democratic party was not stirred with great enthusiasm by the rising of the railroad workers.

Into this hiatus stepped a group of men who had identified themselves with the Workingmen's Party of the United States. Then one year old, the party had begun in the East as an effort to reconcile Marxian and Lassallean socialists after the demise of the First International. Its members were for the most part German-speaking (this was not the case in California) and thoroughly out of touch with what was going on in the nation. At the onset of the strikes, stunned by this fulfillment of their own predictions, they suffered a brief trauma of indecision, then in several larger cities came forward and attempted to assume leadership. The effort involved more courage than wisdom. Almost everywhere (the exception was St. Louis) they failed; but they were extraordinarily successful in taking to themselves and their movement blame for most of the violence which the strikes—and suppression of the strikes—entailed.[1]

[1] Robert V. Bruce, *1877, Year of Violence* (New York, 1959), 228, 230–260; Philip Taft, *Organized Labor in American History* (New York, 1964), 76–83; Samuel Yellen, *American Labor Struggles* (New York, 1936), 3–38; John Rogers Commons et al., *History of Labour, in the United States*, 4 vols., (New York, 1918), II, 185–191.

Under such auspices, on the evening of July 23, a sizable crowd assembled in the sandlot adjacent to San Francisco's city hall. There were sensible speeches on the eight-hour day and nationalization of railroads—these being cardinal points in the socialists' program—and no mention of the Chinese. Yet before the evening was over, the socialists had lost control of the movement they had initiated. Hecklers infiltrated the crowd. A band from an anticoolie club marched by. Swirls of young men, breaking away from the main gathering, set off to hunt for victims. That night twenty or thirty Chinese wash houses were broken into. On the night following, there were murders of Chinese, incendiary fires, clashes between rioters and police. On the third night a lumber yard near the docks of the Pacific Mail Steamship Company (blamed, along with the Central Pacific Railroad, for the influx of Chinese) was set ablaze. The firemen came under attack, and there followed a pitched battle for possession of Rincon Hill in the course of which several men were killed and a large number injured.

From the beginning San Francisco authorities were frightened, perhaps with good reason. There was scarcely a fireproof building in the entire city, and arson in California had become a common pursuit during the preceding decade. Telegraphed news from the East, meanwhile, must have given the impression of a second civil war getting under way. City officials summoned aid from every possible quarter. Militia were mobilized. Federal gunboats stood by. The police went on round-the-clock duty. And under the lead of William T. Coleman, businessman and former chief of the Vigilance Committee of 1856, a pickhandle brigade of some 4,000 volunteers patrolled the embattled city. The climax came with the storming of Rincon Hill, after which the rioting tapered off.[2]

Precisely who the rioters were remained a matter of speculation. The *Examiner,* official voice of the Democracy, describing them as "lawless hoodlums," insisted that neither the true workingmen nor the anticoolie clubs had taken part in the disorders.[3] Since the paper was professionally sympathetic to labor and since a good many anticoolie clubs were indistinguishable from the Democratic ward apparatus, its judgment was understandable. Yet Coleman, who politically would have sat on the opposite side of the aisle from the *Examiner* staff, took substantially the same position. Coleman too, as will presently appear, had reasons for doing so. Neither he nor the editors, however, offered

[2] San Francisco *Examiner,* July 24–27, 1877; Henry George, "The Kearney Agitation in California," *Popular Science Monthly,* XVII (August, 1880), 437; Ralph Kauer, "The Workingmen's Party of California," *Pacific Historical Review,* XIII (September, 1944), 278–279.

[3] *Examiner,* July 25, 26, 1877.

much evidence for their conclusions; in view of the massive character of the rioting and the degree of distress and unemployment, it would seem likely that involvement must have cut deeper than any drifting contingent of "hoodlums" and transients could quite account for. And as to the anticoolie clubs, they had already a history at least fifteen years long of dual activity—with strong working-class support—on the threshold between legality and violence. There is no reason to suppose they had changed their nature in the crisis year 1877.

But though the social identity of the forces of disorder may have remained in doubt, there was no question as to the identity of the phalanx confronting them. San Francisco's municipal authorities were mainly Democratic. The Vigilance Committee, led by downtown interests, businessmen, and property owners, was largely Republican. Behind both stood the state administration of Democratic Governor Irwin and the federal administration of the Republican President Hayes.[4]

All this was made unmistakably clear, several weeks after the suppression of the rioting, when William T. Coleman released his Vigilance Committee members with thanks for their labors successfully performed. Coleman read on this occasion a letter from Governor Irwin, "a masterful paper," sent, he explained, at his own (Coleman's) request. The governor praised the work of the committee. He blamed the riot on three elements: first, hoodlums "actuated by mere wantoness"; second, thieves who sought an opportunity for looting; and third, "a small sprinkling of Communists or Internationalists who hope to usher in the millennium by a judicious use of the torch." "Diabolical" though these three groups were, they fortunately represented only a small minority. Doubtless they had expected the laboring men to join them; but the laborers, though conscious of being wronged, had not done so.[5] How long, however, could the community count on such forbearance if the laborers' grievances continued unrectified? Coming

---

[4] Ira B. Cross, *A History of the Labor Movement in California* (Berkeley, 1935), 90-92; Kauer, "Workingmen's Party," 279.

[5] Here is the same assertion made by the *Examiner* and by Coleman. The governor did offer some evidence for his conclusion—the ease with which the riots were supposed to have been controlled and the relatively small losses involved. In a sense, of course, he was right. If all the workingmen, or even a substantial portion, had been really determined to sack the city, the forces at hand would not have stopped them. But if we leave aside this comparison with total destruction, the actual events suggest a broader participation than the governor apparently cared to acknowledge. Bancroft, in his biographical sketch of William T. Coleman, estimated the property destroyed during the July rioting at half a million dollars belonging to Americans and $50,000 belonging to Chinese. (Hubert Howe Bancroft, *Chronicles of the Builders of the Commonwealth*, 7 vols. [San Francisco, 1891], I, 362.)

thus to his point, the governor asked, Would not the Committee of Vigilance, before disbanding, issue a public appeal for revision of the Burlingame Treaty and pledge the best efforts of its members to secure federal action?

> I know of no other body of men . . . so likely . . . to gain the attention of the proper officers of the Government . . . and of the people on the other side of the Continent to this important subject. This Committee, in large degree, embodies the wealth, the intelligence, and the enterprise of San Francisco. It is composed of men of all political parties. It embraces, also, those whose interests would be compromised by the check, or stoppage, of Chinese immigration. If the Committee, thus composed, adopted the course suggested, its action will command the most profound attention and respect everywhere.

Having read the communication from Sacramento, Coleman then made public the Committee of Safety's reply. This ended—after agreeing point by point with the Governor's argument—with the declaration that "in the interest of American civilization on the Pacific Coast," it was the duty of the federal administration to move at once to modify treaties with China, and with England and Portugal if need be, to halt Chinese immigration.[6]

Coleman's own statement made clear that this exchange had been prearranged. It occurred, fittingly, just one day prior to the upcoming municipal canvass in which Mayor Bryant was a candidate for re-election. He was successful. The voters also returned a Republican police chief, a mixed city administration, and a board of supervisors divided seven to five between Democrats and Republicans.[7] Here was a demonstration of the newly restored two-party establishment in action. Harmony would prevail and "the wealth, the intelligence, and the enterprise" of the community would unite (as in fact it had already done) in resisting any threat to law, order, or property. There was some heavy work ahead for the coming year.

Kearney

That was the end of the first phase. Next came the phase of political revolt, which began during the autumn with the rise of the Workingmen's Party of California—a title obviously borrowed from the socialist Workingmen's Party of the United States, though neither in program

6 *Examiner*, September 4, 1877.
7 *Examiner*, September 5, 1877.

nor in leadership was the new party socialist. Genuine socialists apparently resisted it, though most (and there were not very many) were finally swept along. The rise and fall of the Workingmen's Party of California forms one of those dramatic episodes which sometimes seem to cut across longer range patterns of historical development. The story has been told many times, the implications analyzed and reanalyzed.[8] Perhaps the simplest means of coming to what here needs to be said about the Workingmen's party will be through an examination of some of the men who shaped it and who were shaped by it. The first, inevitably, is Denis Kearney.

In the proletarian sense, Kearney was no workingman at all; he was a producer in the Jacksonian sense. Born and orphaned in Ireland, he had shipped as cabin boy and, sailing on English and American vessels, had risen to officer's rank. He arrived in San Francisco in 1868 as chief mate on the clipper ship *Shooting Star*. Then he worked for four years on steamers out of San Francisco, married in 1870, and two years later bought a draying business in the city. Henry George described Kearney as temperate in everything except speech, a middling prosperous businessman and property owner whose only experience of politics had been to march in the Hayes "Invincible" parades of 1876. This happened also to be the year of his naturalization. Clearly he was ambitious, and contemporaries afterward told of the ludicrous, slightly pathetic figure he cut at the Lyceum for Self Culture where, during the year or two prior to his transfiguration, he sometimes spoke from the floor in the course of Sunday afternoon discussions. He was apparently gripped at the time by the familiar syndrome of the self-made man: he praised diligence and individual go-getterism—by implication his own—and denounced the indolence of workingmen. As might have been expected, he volunteered for service in William T. Coleman's pickhandle brigade.[9]

It was perhaps the ordeal which prepared him for conversion. The legend of Paul on the road to Damascus was being reenacted on all sides during these years; and there seems a curious parallel between Kearney's revelation, whatever it may have been, and the experience of Henry George on the slum street of New York. Kearney too sprang to defend the oppressed; and like George, the first blow he struck was

8 George, *Popular Science*, XVII, 433–453, especially 435; J. C. Stedman and R. A. Leonard, *The Workingmen's Party of California: An Epitome of its Rise and Progress* (San Francisco, 1878), 15–95, especially 59; James Bryce, *The American Commonwealth*, 2 vols., 3rd ed., rev. (New York, 1895), II, 425–448; Commons et al., *History*, II, 252–268.

9 George, *Popular Science*, XVII, 438; Stedman and Leonard, 95–96; *Examiner*, April 5, 1878.

against the Chinese. During September and October he skyrocketed to fame as the orator of the sandlots. His, however, was not the genteel anti-Orientalism of Andrew Jackson Bryant and Governor Irwin; Kearney's style was that of a declaration of war against the two-party establishment. Not only must the Chinese go. The boodlers and monopolists and corruptionists of both parties must go with them. To this end Californians would organize a new party of their own. "We propose to elect none but competent workingmen and their friends to any office whatever. The rich have ruled us until they have ruined us. We will now take our own affairs into our own hands. The republic must and shall be preserved, and only workingmen will do it." Then, as if in direct challenge to his former chieftain, William T. Coleman:

> This party . . . will not be denied justice when it has the power to enforce it. It will encourage no riot or outrage, but it will not volunteer to repress, or put down, or arrest, or prosecute the hungry and impatient. . . . Let those who raise the storm by their selfishness suppress it themselves. If they dare raise the devil, let them meet him face to face. We will not help them.[10]

Late in October the Workingmen carried the battle into enemy territory with a meeting on Nob Hill more or less at the front stoop of the Central Pacific's officialdom. The oratory was abusive and during the following days became more so. A few fragments suffice to render the tone. "Are you ready to march down to the wharf and stop the leprous Chinamen from landing?" "Judge Lynch is the judge wanted by the workingmen of California. I advise all to own a musket and a hundred rounds of ammunition." "I will give the Central Pacific just three months to discharge their Chinamen, and if that is not done, Stanford and his crowd will have to take the consequences." "The dignity of labor must be sustained, even if we have to kill every wretch that opposes it." [11]

All this reawakened the fears of Mayor Bryant and the bipartisan structure behind him. The police were ordered to break up public meetings. Kearney and other leaders of the Workingmen were arrested and rearrested, their bail being increased as fast as it was posted. Again the militia was mobilized. The mayor proclaimed what amounted to a

[10] Workingmen's Party Platform, adopted October 5, 1877, as quoted in Stedman and Leonard, 21–27.

[11] *Examiner*, October 30, 1877. The quotations, all ascribed to Kearney, are, in order, from Bancroft, *Popular Tribunals*, II (Vol. XXXVII, *Works*, San Francisco, 1887), 722; Bancroft, *History of California*, VII, 357 n. 21; San Francisco *Evening Bulletin*, November 5 and November 1, 1877.

state of emergency; the legislature responded with a gag law making
it a felony to "suggest or advise or encourage" any riotous action, then
went on to authorize an enlarged metropolitan police force and to appropriate $20,000 for use by the governor as a special defense fund.[12]
For Kearney, however, despite these hostile preparations, political insurgency brought triumph upon triumph. He had vindicated before
audiences of thousands his stumbling earlier performances at the
Lyceum for Self Culture. Those who had mocked him, who had expressed pity or contempt, were now struck dumb. True, he had spent
a good many days in jail; but he had come forth, as had others before
him, a hero and a martyr.

From his first imprisonment Kearney was released in time to lead
the Workingmen's Thanksgiving Day parade. He rode at the head of
the procession on one of his own dray horses. The *Examiner,* though
nearly always venomous toward Kearney himself, was obviously impressed by the turnout, which it described as "a great demonstration
against coolie labor . . . orderly . . . well and cleanly clad." Presumably by exact count, there were 7,229 marchers. And here it may be
worthwhile noting the composition of the parade as the *Examiner*'s
reporter marked it down. After Kearney with his thirty mounted aides
came the band of the Second Infantry. Then followed the Plasterers'
Protective Union, the Shoemakers' Union, the German Club of the
Second Ward, the band of the French Zouaves, the Scandinavian Association, the Tailors' Union, the Third and Fourth branches of the
Workingmen's party, the Seventh Ward Club, the Pile Drivers' Asso-
ciation, the Second and Eighth Ward clubs, and the "Boys of the
Second Ward" (who carried signs saying "Discharge your Chinamen
and you will find no more Hoodlums"); then another band; then the
Twelfth Ward Club, the Cigarmakers' Association, the Eleventh and
Ninth wards, the Carpenters and Joiners, and finally the boys of the
Ninth Ward.[13]

The contrast with the parades of 1867 in which trade unionists had
set the style and dominated proceedings is at once striking. Here only
six of seventeen groups specifically named could be classified as labor
organizations, and of these three (Shoemakers, Tailors, Cigarmakers)
were probably associations of journeymen and small proprietors rather
than trade unions. The remainder were neighborhood or language-
association anticoolie clubs. In this lies the key to the political meaning behind the official acts of repression and the oratorical pyro-
technics. What Kearney was leading was a struggle for control of the

12 *Examiner, November* 5–14, 19, 21, 22, 1877.
13 *Examiner,* November 26, 28, 1877.

clubs which largely comprised the Democratic party's city machinery. For Bryant, perhaps for Governor Irwin as well, such a campaign if successful promised political disaster.[14] And the turnout for Kearney's Thanksgiving Day parade suggested that he was winning the battle.

It was at this point that the *Examiner*, official voice of the Democracy, shifted tactics from frontal assault against the Workingmen's movement to a policy of wooing the followers while endeavoring to divide and discredit the leadership. Eventually, thanks to a good deal of assistance from Kearney himself, these tactics prevailed; but for two years the Democratic party was virtually powerless in its former stronghold. The immediate effect was an exodus of minor functionaries and heelers from the old party to the new one. Under other circumstances the Republicans might have viewed these events with equanimity, but they too were alarmed at the rise of the Workingmen. This, together with their vivid recollections of the July days, and the ambiguous position of their own party nationally on the Chinese question, inhibited them from taking much advantage of Democratic difficulties. Consequently the two-party establishment—as enunciated in the joint declaration of Governor Irwin and William T. Coleman—held firm. The newspapers likewise held this line, with one exception. The San Francisco *Chronicle*, a normally Republican, albeit somewhat volatile sheet (Henry George described it as "a 'live paper' of the most vigorous and unscrupulous kind"), had already been dabbling with the new movement. Apparently, one of its staffmen had helped write some of Kearney's speeches. From this illicit collaboration, the newspaper suddenly dived into total conversion; it lionized Kearney and launched, at the expense of its class-bound competitors, a statewide anti-Chinese subscription drive.[15] By January of 1878 the Workingmen's party had become a major political force in California.

Early in January Kearney was arrested again and the second round of trials got under way. All the indictments of the previous November had been dismissed on technicalities or for lack of evidence; but in this second round Kearney and his colleagues stood full jury trial and won acquittal. The verdict came at precisely the moment to provide a grand entrance before the first state convention of the Workingmen's party which had assembled one day earlier. From jail Kearney marched directly to the platform, where Frank Roney, the trade unionist who

[14] John P. Young, *San Francisco: A History of the Pacific Coast Metropolis*, 2 vols. (San Francisco and Chicago, n.d. [1912?]), II, 551.

[15] *Examiner*, January 16, 23, February 2, 6, March 13, 18, 28, April 15, May 2, June 18, 1878; George, *Popular Science*, XVII, 440, 442; Young, *San Francisco*, II, 534.

had opened proceedings as temporary chairman, made way for him. And there was in addition one more factor to add to Kearney's triumph. Simultaneously with the courtroom vindication, the new party had won a major victory at the polls. Its candidate, J. W. Bones, running for a seat made vacant by the death of the incumbent, had been swept in as state senator from Alameda County.[16]

Roney

It was probably with no great enthusiasm that Roney yielded the chair to his countryman, Denis Kearney. Already they were rather too well acquainted. They had clashed before and would soon afterward lock in a bitter struggle for control of the Workingmen's party. Roney, it may be recalled, was the young revolutionist who had fled Ireland to avoid prison and possible hanging. He arrived in San Francisco in 1875 with wife and child, finding work almost immediately at his trade of iron molder. He was naturalized in the same year. The itinerary of Roney's political sympathies had run from Irish republicanism through American Radical Republicanism to the Liberal schism of 1872. By the time of the great railroad strikes and the July days in San Francisco, he was on the point of joining the socialists. But the arrest of Kearney so roused his anger that he joined the Workingmen's Party of California instead. Here his organizational ability and his experience in Ireland carried him to the front. He soon took over presidency of the Eighth Ward Club. And he it was, apparently, who generaled the first statewide Workingmen's convention which met in defiance of Mayor Bryant's ban on public gatherings. The opening had been announced for a particular hall; delegates were sent individually to a different address and from there were directed to a second hall in another part of town. When the police arrived, the business of the first session was almost concluded. Roney, in the chair, invited the captain to come in but leave his squad outside; and the captain told the delegates somewhat ruefully that he had spent the evening hunting for them but now, finding them at work in such orderly fashion, he doubted he had the authority to break up their assembly.[17] The next day Kearney was acquitted and the heat was off.

Roney claimed later to have drafted the party platform adopted by

[16] Stedman and Leonard, *Workingmen's Party,* (above, n. 8), 31–33, 47–62; Kauer, "Workingmen's Party," 281–282; Frank Roney, *Frank Roney, Irish Rebel and California Labor Leader* ed. Ira B. Cross (Berkeley, 1931), 206.

[17] *Examiner,* January 22, 1878; Roney 261–263, 273–274, 285–286. On Roney's background before he came to San Francisco, see above, p. 39.

the convention. Yet according to his own account he was by no means in sympathy with its position on the Chinese. The restrictions "which many were at that time advocating" seemed to him "brutal and such as no self-respecting people would dream of imposing upon the members of any race within their midst. The only objection to them that I felt had any validity was that they were cheap workers." Here Roney took substantially the same ground that John Stuart Mill in his letter to Henry George had taken: "It seemed to me that this objection would in a short time pass away, provided the Chinese were allowed the liberty, without molestation, that was accorded other immigrants." Had not Irish too been hated as cheap laborers? Yet the Irishman had "developed into a good American citizen with the vested right of jeering at the cheap laboring German who succeeded him"; these had joined to harass the Italian for the same reason and finally all together concentrated on the Chinese. "To assail and assault and oppress one portion of humanity seems to be the delight, inherent right, and practice of another portion." [18]

Roney justified his own position in the following terms:

> I . . . took as active a part as I could . . . to make the party as robust and as progressive as the times and circumstances permitted. It was essentially an anti-Chinese party as was indicated by the motto, "The Chinese must go." However, I never warmed to that feature of the agitation. I realized that the cry was superficial, but agreed to sail under the flag so emblazoned in order that I might in time have other and real subjects considered by the people, which I deemed to be of far greater importance to their permanent well-being.[19]

It was under this flag that Roney endeavored to advance what was to him, probably, the most "real" of all subjects, trade unionism. In the convention were a handful of unionists fretting under the hostility, or lack of interest, of the Kearney leadership, which denied them any role as spokesmen for labor.

What seems to have occurred emerges from the garbled reportage of the *Examiner* as follows: On the last day but one of the convention, a committee on permanent organization, of which Roney was a member, proposed that the state central committee should be named at once and should consist of five members for each state senatorial district and one for each trade union. The recommendation was adopted, and the committee as set up included representatives from the Shoemakers, Cabinet Makers, Stonecutters, Coopers, Cooks and Waiters, and Ship-

[18] Roney, 266–267, 286–287.
[19] Roney, 287.

wrights. The next day, however, Kearney stepped down from the chair to blast this action on the floor. Here was an instance of people electing themselves into office; the entire convention was being taken over by "political bummers," he charged. As a result of his tirade the structure of the state central committee was reconsidered, and San Francisco's representation, instead of being named immediately by the convention, was held over for the action of the ward clubs. What this seemed to mean (although the newspaper account leaves many ends dangling) was that, on Kearney's insistence, a plan which would have included trade unions as constituent elements of the new party was rejected; and for San Francisco at least, almost total control was handed over to the ward clubs.[20]

Final adjournment came soon after, but not before the disgruntled unionists had regrouped for a second and more modest endeavor. "A resolution was adopted," the *Examiner* reported, "urging Trades Unions to immediately organize a Mechanics' Council." This at least gave the sanction of the new party to an effort at reconstructing some kind of labor federation. According to Roney's memoirs, it was he who proposed the resolution, and the passage of the resolution in turn called into being soon afterward "the Trades and Labor Assembly, which Kearney thoroughly disliked." [21]

The party, meanwhile, had burst into full blossom. Following the success of Bones in Alameda came electoral victories in Sacramento, San Leandro, Berkeley, Redwood City, and Nevada and Santa Cruz counties. San Francisco seemed on the brink of going over. And this upsurge came at a crucial moment in state political history. After several abortive efforts, the legislature of 1875–76 had finally cranked itself up to the point of summoning a convention for the purpose of modernizing California's 1849 constitution. The election of delegates was set for midsummer; the constituent assembly itself was to gather in September. The sudden rise of the Workingmen cast a new ingredient into this situation.[22]

In February (that is, well after the first successes of the Workingmen) the legislature prescribed the method of representation. There would be three delegates for each of the state's forty senatorial districts and, in addition, thirty-two delegates-at-large to be chosen by statewide vote. These latter were thrown in as an extra bulwark against control by the

---

20 *Examiner,* January 25, 26, 1878.
21 *Examiner,* January 26, 1878; Roney, 287.
22 Stedman and Leonard, *Workingmen's Party,* (above, n. 8), 65–66; Carl B. Swisher, *Motivation and Political Technique in the California Constitutional Convention, 1878–1879* (Claremont, Calif., 1930), 17–18.

new party on the assumption that its main strength would lie in San Francisco. Yet might not even that prove inadequate? Were there not already the warnings of Paris in 1871, the railroad uprising in the East, the July days in San Francisco? The Republican *Alta* in April called for heroic measures—an extension of the Coleman-Irwin entente to embrace the entire process of constitution making. Republicans and Democrats should agree on nonpartisan tickets for each district and present a united front against the Communards. Essentially this was what was done; and the central committees of the old parties met separately to bestow their blessings on the nonpartisan candidates. Thus, the struggle for control of the constituent assembly took the form of a contest between the two-party establishment on the one hand, operating as a united front, and the Workingmen on the other.[23]

All this was heady brew for the insurgents. They began to think of sweeping the field. Kearney went on tour to spread the good word through the interior. Meanwhile, Roney, as director of organization, was hard at work in San Francisco. With the party's fortunes in the ascendant, the competition for nominations grew intense. "Those seeking office and unable to gain recognition in the older parties," Roney wrote, "flocked to the new party bringing nothing with them but the ideas acquired by previous and none too creditable association with the ward bosses of the older organizations." Contemptuous of these latecomers, Roney wanted to see the nominations go to men who had taken the lead from the beginning, many now being officers in the ward clubs. Kearney at this point became alarmed and jealous. Fearful apparently that he was losing his grip on the city, he brought forward a proposal to forbid any party officer from receiving a nomination by the party.[24]

On this issue the internal battle for power was fought out. Both the San Francisco county committee and the state central committee sided with Roney. Kearney then appealed to the Sunday crowd at the sandlots, which backed him up. The central committee deposed Kearney from chairmanship, setting Roney in his place. Kearney countered by invading the ward clubs. He had already, during the period of taking them from the Democrats, perfected the technique of bulldozing club meetings. This consisted in breaking in with his own band of followers, denouncing all who opposed him as traitors or "political bummers." Then, having claimed voting rights for all present, the intruders simply took over and installed a new panel of officers. The technique

23 *Alta California*, April 11, 1878; Swisher, 17–24.
24 Roney, 295–296; Kauer, "Workingmen's Party," 282–283.

nearly always worked, because Kearney's prestige with the rank and file, especially among unemployed, was enormous; he could rally a crowd to support him whenever he needed one.[25]

Moreover the slogan about political bummers had a good deal of meat to it. Seemingly the more ambitious any party member became on his own account, the greater the suspicion he entertained of his comrades. Then by way of demonstration came the case of J. W. Bones. This erstwhile champion of the workingmen of Alameda County had no sooner taken his place in the state Senate than he began to vote the bidding of the Central Pacific lobbyists. His constituents spoke of hanging. Kearney, displaying a length of rope, denounced Bones in the sandlots. It was Kearney who had proposed Bones in the first place; yet he was now able to use the defection as an illustration for his own text: to save the people from traitors like Bones, the party must be purged of opportunistic officials.[26] Of course this argument might better have served Roney's side than Kearney's, since Bones typified the latecomers rather than the party pioneers. But Roney and his friends, outclassed in the sandlots, were unable to exploit the logic of their case.

By Roney's account it is clear that he considered Kearney unprincipled, and doubtless Kearney held corresponding views.[27] Curiously, however, this factional fight had struck bottom on one of the fundamental problems of radical organization. In order for the participants in such organization to effect any basic change in the structure of society, it would be necessary for them somehow to throw into the field a stable cadre of leaders. This was Roney's contention. Both experience as craft unionist and his role in the Irish underground had taught him that survival depended on tough, permanent organization. In the ancient and positive sense of the term, Roney was the organization man. He spoke for a labor leadership already becoming specialized, but which had not yet crossed the threshold into professionalization. Kearney on the other hand spoke for the men down under—and for himself as their tribune. How could these nameless ones, having raised their leaders to power, prestige, public office—having given them a kind of tenure in the establishment—how could they then trust them not to act like part of the establishment? Only by direct

[25] On the bulldozing of ward clubs, see *Examiner*, May 8, 15, 1878; and Roney, 274–276. On the conflict over eligibility for nomination, see Stedman and Leonard, 72–80; Roney, 296–298.

[26] Roney, 299; Stedman and Leonard, 78–80. On the defection of Bones, see *Examiner*, March 19, 1878.

[27] Roney, 297–299.

confrontation, as in the sandlots. Only by constant short-circuiting of
any organizational apparatus before it could become self-sustained.
Although Roney, during the earlier convention dispute, had attributed
Kearney's stand on the structure of the state central committee to his
hostility toward trade unions, what was perhaps more deeply involved
was that Kearney could not tolerate any permanent officialdom responsible solely to conventions. Leaders must be subject to the rank and
file, so that he, Kearney (or anyone else for that matter), could appeal
against them to the undifferentiated membership in the clubs or to
the crowd at the sandlots.

Here, in abstract terms, was the controversy of Rousseau and John
Locke. Yet for the American West it held a very concrete meaning.
Then, and through half a century afterward, large segments of the
western labor force were migratory, relatively unskilled, often unemployed. Suspicion of stabilized leadership would be immediate and
extreme. Thus, the power struggle between Roney and Kearney became the opening round in a cycle of conflict which has characterized
both radicalism and labor organization in the West. During later years,
trade unionists and socialists have generally repeated Roney's script,
while the anarchists, the Wobblies, and nearly always the leaders of
unskilled and unemployed have repeated Kearney's. As for the Chinese
issue, which might be pressed into service for either side, it would be
invaded and reinvaded like a strategic height of land.

In 1878 Kearney carried the day. Leaving his opponents in control
of the apparatus, he moved the party base out from under them. Then
he wrote a new set of rules, the gist of which was that the party would
be guided by a council of club presidents, each president being recall-
able at any time by his constituency. Nominations for political office—
from which all party officials were excluded—would be made in the
following manner: clubs would nominate, mass meetings in each district would confirm, and the assemblage at the sandlots would render
final decision. A few weeks before the election of delegates to the
California constituent assembly, the second convention of the Workingmen's party met in San Francisco. Actually, there were two conventions, one called by the Kearney faction, the other by Roney's central
committee. Since, however, Kearney now controlled the city, it was a
foregone conclusion that delegations from the interior would go to
him. His convention approved the new rules and made final plans
for a statewide Workingmen's ticket to oppose the nonpartisans.
Roney's gathering meanwhile could do little more than observe the
formalities. It denounced Kearney; it named a third slate (which was
not heard of again); then adjourned and rapidly disintegrated. Roney

himself, out of work, discouraged and blacklisted, left San Francisco for a temporary job at a mining camp in southern Nevada.[28]

The Constitutional Convention

In the election, the Workingmen swept San Francisco's ten senatorial districts which gave them thirty seats and, in addition, picked up twenty-one from towns and counties throughout the state. The non-partisans won forty-five contests outside the city and took all thirty-two of the specially created delegates-at-large. A scattering of ten Democrats, eleven Republicans, and three independents accounted for the remainder. Since these would act with the nonpartisans, it seemed clear that the two-party establishment had successfully held the line against the insurgents.[29]

In reality the outcome was not so simple. For one thing there really was no line to hold. The Workingmen were not Communards; they were innocent of any far-reaching program for the new constitution. Henry George, chief intellectual-in-residence for the California Democracy and rhapsodist of individual enterprise, stood far to the left of anything advocated by the Workingmen. George in fact had been offered their nomination; but when he made clear that his exclusive focus would be on value taxation of land and that he would not be bound by any party caucus, they passed him by. He ran anyway, on a token slate of San Francisco Democrats, coming in at the head of his list, which however lagged 10,000 votes behind the lowest of the Workingmen's candidates.[30]

Moreover, the nonpartisans themselves were not a unified group. They ranged all the way from railroad henchmen to Grangers and antimonopoly men. Carl Swisher, in his analysis of the convention, has shown that there were not two, but three, fairly consistent voting blocs. One was conservative, business-oriented, having as its nucleus the thirty-two nonpartisan delegates-at-large. Another was the Workingmen's bloc. And there was a third rather nebulous grouping composed largely of delegates from small interior towns and rural districts. This third force held the balance. Generally it split or went with the conservatives, thus giving them overall control of proceedings; but on a set of issues which might be described as the Granger program (a

28 *Examiner*, May 2, 6–8, 15, 20, 21, 1878; Stedman and Leonard, 74–76; Roney, 309–311.

29 *Examiner*, July 5, 1878; Swisher, *Motivation and Political Technique*, 24.

30 George, *Popular Science*, XVII, 435–436, 448; and see Charles Albro Barker, *Henry George*, (New York, 1955), 261–262, for excerpts from a letter from Henry George to John Swinton; *Examiner*, July 5, 1878, and Barker, 251–252.

"tough" line toward corporations; an elective railroad commission
with power to fix rates and examine books; severe penalties on railroads and their officials for collusion, discriminatory rates, and unfair
competition; state rather than local control over the tax assessment of
railroad property), the agrarians and the Workingmen joined to defeat
the conservatives.[81]

It will hardly be necessary to examine seriatim the hundred days of
the convention. What emerged—"a mixture of constitution, code,
stump speech, and mandamus"—was, as Henry George shrewdly
pointed out, no more radical in most of its aspects than other new
state constitutions of the period.[32] The two major triumphs of the
Workingmen during the long proceedings were these: that their votes
made possible the enactment of the Granger program; and that they
took the lead in writing a set of bristling anti-Chinese clauses. These
were contained in the definition of suffrage ("provided no native of
China, no idiot, insane person, or person convicted of any infamous
crime . . . shall ever exercise the privileges of an elector of this State"),
and in the famous Article XIX which forbade employment of "any
Chinese or Mongolian" (except in punishment of crime) on state or
local public works or, directly or indirectly, by any corporation operating under the laws of California.[33] Both provisions, so far as the
convention was concerned, were cheap victories since there was no
opposition: the nonpartisans, being in fact Democrats or Republicans,
were either already in agreement or else had given the matter up as
a lost cause. In this field at least the Workingmen had free rein.

Their problem then was not one of fighting for principle, but one
of discovering some meaningful role for state action on an issue which
was now, by general agreement, viewed as within the purview of
federal government. To this dilemma there was no real answer; the
solution was a semantic one. Thus Article XIX, having verbally out-
lawed the employment of Chinese, went on to promise constitutional
sanction to almost any action that state or local authorities might
undertake. There were hints of the desirability of restrictive codes
with heavy penalties for noncompliance, of enforced ghettoization or
removal, of police action against aliens "dangerous or detrimental to
the peace or well-being of the State," on the grounds that such aliens

---

81 Swisher, *Motivation*, chap. 3, 32–44.

32 George, *Popular Science*, XVII, 445, 448–449. Kauer, "Workingmen's Party,"
285, makes a similar estimate, as does Swisher, 110–111.

33 *Debates and Proceedings of the Constitutional Convention of the State of
California, Convened at the City of Sacramento, Saturday, September 28, 1878,*
3 vols. (Sacramento, 1881), III, 1510–1521; California Constitution of 1879, Article
II, Section 1, and Article XIX, Sections 2, 3.

would be the cause of breaches of the peace directed against themselves. All this was clearly in defiance of the federal Constitution, and everyone knew the clauses would be invalidated in court.[34]

What then was the purpose of writing them? In part it was that of a stage performance for the edification of constituents. But there was a further meaning inherent in these clauses precisely *because* they would be invalidated. A plea for private violence with the implication that the authorities, being themselves hampered, would condone and welcome such assistance, Article XIX placed the state government in the traditional stance of the anticoolie clubs—at the threshold between legal and illegal means. If, as students of the convention have suggested, its labors were not, for the most part, outstandingly original, this portion at least had the distinction of being unique for its viciousness and irresponsibility.

Beyond these two achievements—support for the Granger amendments and leadership against the Chinese—it was the ineffectiveness of the Workingmen at Sacramento that was most striking. Apart from any question of long-range program, the simplest, most traditional labor demands went by default. Early in the proceedings one of the Workingmen's delegates introduced a proposal for a state bureau of labor statistics. This was seemingly a noncontroversial item which could far more suitably have been incorporated in fundamental law than a good deal of other material that found its way there. Yet it died along the roadside. The same was the fate of the mandatory eight-hour day, a goal to which California labor had been dedicated since before the Civil War. This too was proposed at the convention in many resolutions and floor speeches. But what emerged in the final document was only the following: "Eight hours shall constitute a legal day's work on all public work." [35] For practical purposes this was meaningless—as General Winn and his colleagues had learned ten years earlier—in part because most pubic work was done under contract and the clause would not be held binding on contractors; but more importantly because it made no reference to the vast majority of wage earners who worked for private employers.

Unlike the proposed bureau of labor statistics (which was adopted by the legislature only a few years later), the mandatory eight-hour day *was* controversial. The Workingmen might have fought for this and lost; but the record does not indicate that they fought for it at all.

[34] George described the anti-Chinese clauses of the Constitution as not worth the paper they were printed on (*Popular Science*, XVII, 445). They were subsequently invalidated by the federal courts. Kauer, 285; Constitution, XIX, Section 1.
[35] Constitution, XX, Section 17.

Nowhere in the proceedings is there any hint that they ever confronted the champions of the Granger program with a quid pro quo—an elective railroad commission, for instance, in *exchange* for the eight-hour day on the railroads. Or they might have felt that such a commitment was too venturesome, or certain in any case to be lost by court action afterward. But there was nothing else either. In the entire document, the only two specific references to labor (appropriately placed in an article titled "Miscellaneous Subjects") were those declaring the mechanic's lien right (which was already established) and the vacuous statement about eight hours on public works.[36] With their bloc of fifty votes—one third of the convention—it seems scarcely credible that the Workingmen could have made such a poor showing.

Generally this has been blamed on Kearney. His insistence on excluding party officials from nomination, it has been argued, resulted in sending incompetents to Sacramento. If these were not actually selected by the great corporations for their ineptitude, George wrote, they might as well have been, for they were "men utterly ignorant and inexperienced." [37] Frank Roney, who stopped off at the state capitol on his return from the temporary job he had taken in Nevada, reached an even more dismal estimate:

> As members of the Convention they sat in their places and voted for the adoption or rejection of clauses as they were directed. Only two of their number, Clitus Barbour and Charles Beerstecher, both lawyers, were distinguished from the general dumbness prevalent among them. . . . The majority of the remainder of the Workingmen's delegates studied fundamental law and what was best for their constituents in near-by saloons and played cards with a nourishing glass of foam-topped beer near by. And this was the result of so much honest effort on the part of the people hoping for reform! The worst brand of stand-pat, corporation ridden politician would have made a better showing than this primitive band of fake reformers.[38]

Both George and Roney had reason for bitterness against the Workingmen's party, and their judgment was perhaps unfair. Certainly it was true that most of the Workingmen were inexperienced in parliamentary technique. Of the thirty delegates from San Francisco, for

---

[36] In 1883: Walton Bean, *California: An Interpretive History* (New York, 1968), 285; Constitution, XX, Sections 15, 17.

[37] George, *Popular Science*, XVII, 445. This was Roney's position too. Bryce, *American Commonwealth* (above, n. 8), II, 436, Cross, *History of the Labor Movement*, 113–114, Kauer, "Workingmen's Party," 283, and Swisher, *Motivation and Political Technique* (above, n. 22), 32, repeat substantially the same argument.

[38] Roney, *Frank Roney*, 312–313.

example, all but eight were manual workers and craftsmen and only three were lawyers. Here was a case of genuine rank-and-filism in action. By contrast, the seventy-seven nonpartisans included thirty-nine lawyers. Perhaps intimidated by this array, the Workingmen generally spoke little, leaving debate to their leaders. Thus, the thirty San Franciscans averaged per man only one recorded statement on the floor for every 5.7 days of convention time, while Barbour and Beerstecher, the two lawyers mentioned by Roney, managed between them to take the floor on the average more than twice in each day. The entire delegation from San Francisco brought forward seventy-seven resolutions, of which Barbour and Beerstecher introduced thirty-three.[39] To this extent Roney and George were doubtless correct.

Yet there is evidence that the Workingmen caucused regularly, agreed on program, were disciplined in voting, and were no more prone to absenteeism than were their nonpartisan colleagues.[40] Given competent leaders, a grouping of this type would comprise a force more effective in many respects for parliamentary in-fighting than an equal number of legal virtuosi. There seems no reason to suppose that Barbour and Beerstecher lacked competence. Both were graduates of eastern law colleagues. Barbour, through two trials and under circumstances that might have immobilized many men, had successfully directed the defense of Kearney and the other party leaders. Beerstecher would subsequently serve on the first panel of State Railroad Commissioners. Even the hypercritical Frank Roney acknowledged the abilities of these two, seeing in Beerstecher an opportunistic, though clever, politician, while Barbour he rated highly as "an able and honest man." [41]

The charge of incompetence, then, is not convincing. What remains is the matter of motivation; and it seems clear that neither the taciturn nor the vocal members of the Workingmen's delegation went up to Sacramento with any intention of fighting a climactic battle. They were content simply to be there—to draw their eight dollars per diem and mileage, to be accepted as responsible participants in the governmental process.[42] The alliance in support of the Granger program went in the right direction, yet was respectable; beyond this they introduced for the record the obligatory resolutions; and as for glory,

[39] Computed from the index, *Debates and Proceedings*, III; and see Swisher, 25–27.

[40] "Leaves of Absence" for each delegate, index, *Debates and Proceedings*, III. On caucusing, see Swisher, 32–33.

[41] Barbour had studied law at Northwestern University, Beerstecher at the University of Michigan. See Stedman and Leonard, 105–108; Roney, 312, 313 note 26.

[42] Swisher, 18.

they could, without incurring any hostile fire, have all they wanted by declaiming against the insidious and pestilential Chinese.

Last Stand of the Abolitionists

During those same months in which the convention was laboring over California's new constitution, the second national confrontation on the Chinese issue (the first having been the debate of 1870 on naturalization) was shaping up in Washington. Western exclusionists, it may be recalled, had won a strategic victory two years earlier when the Joint Congressional Committee to Investigate Chinese Immigration had conceded in principle the undesirability of the Chinese influx. The committee's majority report had recommended that the president and State Department undertake revision of those clauses in the Burlingame Treaty with China which guaranteed free entrance and equal treatment for nationals of both countries.[43]

But in several respects westerners had been disappointed with the outcome. In the first place they had hoped for a recommendation of immediate congressional action to abrogate the treaty. Any other course seemed to them intolerably slow. In the second place the committee report, submitted at the onset of the Hayes-Tilden electoral crisis, had been obscured from national attention by the tumult over the disputed count. And finally, after the antiexclusionist chairman of the joint committee, the old-line Republican from Indiana, Senator Oliver Morton, lay safely dead and buried, a posthumous minority report had appeared. Written presumably by the senator just before his death, this second report argued that Chinese labor was a positive benefit to the West. Dismissing the economic objections as specious, the minority report declared that the true source of hostility to Chinese immigration lay in race prejudice and concluded in the old Sumnerian style that such prejudice had no place in a nation founded on the Declaration of Independence. The outcome of all this for the exclusionists was frustration of their hopes for victory in the session of 1877–78. What they got was merely a reaffirmation of the joint committee's majority recommendation: that the executive department be urged to see what could be done in the direction of treaty modification.[44]

But after the first post-Reconstruction election in 1878, the banquet table seemed finally set for the exclusionists. Both parties stood committed in principle to their cause. The violent events in the West, the

43 Elmer Clarence Sandmeyer, *The Anti-Chinese Movement in California* (Urbana, Ill., 1939), 78–87; and see above, p. 110.
44 Sandmeyer, 88–90.

rise of the Workingmen, the extreme measures being written into the California constitution with their implied threat of a new crisis of state's rights—all served to strengthen the hand of the Pacific Coast delegation in Congress. A bill to limit any vessel, under penalty of heavy fines upon its master, from carrying more than fifteen "Mongolian" passengers on any one voyage to the United States passed the House of Representatives almost without opposition. There, was, however, a sharp debate in the Senate with Senator Hoar of Massachusetts leading a recalcitrant minority of Republicans. They were defeated and the bill passed. But the Senate debate touched off a national reaction. William Lloyd Garrison and Henry Ward Beecher spoke in the Chinese cause, and even the flamboyant San Francisco poet, Joaquin Miller (once ousted from editorship of a Democratic newspaper in Oregon because of his Confederate sympathies), spoke in their favor. The defense of the Chinese during this second confrontation was fundamentally based, as it had been in 1870, on the old abolitionist stand. Now, however, not many politicians (Senator Hoar being an outstanding exception) cared to maintain such high ground. The champions were for the most part Protestant clergymen.[45]

Yet even the ministers apparently felt themselves under greater compulsion than previously to buttress their religious-moral stance with an economic rationalization. Or perhaps it was that such a rationalization stood readier to hand. The development of what Henry May has referred to as the school of "clerical laissez-faire" had persuaded them that a moral absolute could be improved by demonstrating its utility for the workaday world. It had also provided intellectual machinery, drawn from the classical economists, for doing so. Since, in these terms, the movement of labor must be included within the same category as movements of capital and fluctuations in supply and demand, and since all these taken together comprised a divinely self-regulating mechanism, it was not only harmful but impious for government to tamper with them.[46]

Moreover, this already old-fashioned concept could now be expanded into a more sophisticated and up-to-date model: progressive evolution-

[45] *Examiner,* February 20, 24, 25, 1879; *Bulletin,* February 25, 27, 1879; Sandmeyer, 90–91; M. M. Marberry, *Splendid Poseur: Joaquin Miller, American Poet* (New York, 1953), 44–45; Robert Seager, "Some Denominational Reactions to Chinese Immigration to California, 1856–1892," *Pacific Historical Review,* XXVIII (February, 1959), 49–66; *Examiner,* February 20, 28, 1879; Sacramento *Record Union,* February 15, 20, 1879. For a Protestant defense of Chinese immigration, see summary of the sermon of the Reverend A. L. Stone, San Francisco First Congregational Church, *Alta,* June 16, 1873.

[46] Henry May, *Protestant Churches and Industrial America* (New York, 1963), 13–16, 136–138, 292.

ism. Human destiny itself could thus be conceived as a divinely self-regulating mechanism. Through struggle for survival, the fittest and best would raise mankind inevitably toward physical and moral perfection. Seen in this light, the incursion of lean and hungry Chinese laborers, however troublesome in the short run the event might appear to non-Chinese workingmen, was a positive good and, in fact, the only possible road to future prosperity and happiness. Here, in essence, was the vision that Henry Ward Beecher, who only a few years later would horrify many of his ministerial colleagues by delivering the keynote speech at a dinner honoring Herbert Spencer, unfolded before the public in defense of Chinese immigration.[47]

The western exclusionists responded with bitter anger. Though he was by no means the only proponent of Social Darwinism among the Protestant clergy, Beecher was perhaps the most notable and, because of his religious liberalism and scandal-ridden private life, clearly the most vulnerable. He came to symbolize for them the hypocrisy of special privilege. Here was the adulterer who preached morality from the pulpit; the scholar who turned religion and science to the service of monopoly; the aristocrat of luxurious habits who, during the railroad strikes in 1877, had insisted that any honest man ought to be able to support a wife and five children on one dollar a day—and were he not willing to live on bread and water in doing so, was "not fit to live" at all.[48] "Aristocrat" is the key word in this context. Beecher appeared as the Brahmin, the half-English New Englander, spokesman for the old Protestant élite. He wrapped into one package all those resentments which had been carried to California by displaced workingmen, disappointed farmers, and immigrants, especially the Irish. That "pulpit demagogue and vile hypocrite," the San Francisco *Examiner* wrote of him,

> who has never raised his voice nor contributed a dollar in charity toward the relief of poor white men and women, or their famishing children, is profiting now by making himself the champion of the Chinese in addressing large audiences at exhorbitant admission fees almost each night in Boston and other cities. Guilty himself of the violation of almost every one of God's holy commandments, this moral leper labors to

[47] *Bulletin*, February 10, 1879; *Record Union*, February 24, 1879. On the Spencer dinner, see Henry Ward Beecher, *Lectures and Orations*, ed. Newell Dwight Hillis (New York, 1913), 312–324; and Paxton Hibben, *Henry Ward Beecher: An American Portrait* (New York, 1942), 299–300.

[48] New York *Times*, July 30, 1877, as quoted in Hibben, 288; Richard Hofstadter, *Social Darwinism in American Thought*, rev. ed. (New York, 1959), 46–48.

spread the horrors of Chinadom as another might spread contagion by purposeful contamination or inoculation.[49]

The exclusionists had not yet learned to use the artillery of Social Darwinism in their own cause, and this fact gave to their rebuttal a cogency it might otherwise have lacked. Beecher was vulnerable because of the confused logic of his own moral commitment. One need scarcely doubt the enthusiasm with which, as a young man, he had thrown himself into the antislavery cause. ("I remember distinctly," he recalled for his Sunday evening listeners at the Plymouth Church, "when Birney's press was mobbed, in Cincinnati, and dragged through the streets and thrown into the Ohio River. I remember perfectly the night when I was one of those who patrolled the streets, armed, to defend the houses of the poor colored people in that city.") And doubtless this same commitment to the brotherhood of man led him to defend the Chinese. Yet the interposition of the economic argument had somehow clouded his vision. He could see that Chinese were being abused because of their race as Negroes had been. But he could see no similarity between contract labor of Chinese and slave labor of Negroes, nor could he see that other laborers suffered through the exploitation of the Chinese. His enemies could hardly have missed this deficiency, although they failed to note, of course, that Beecher's astigmatism was due in part to the viciousness of their own manipulation of the Chinese issue. But whatever the causes may have been, the outcome was that Beecher's championship could credibly be taken for a defense of the right of employers to pursue their own interest without responsibility for the results. ("Nowhere else," Beecher had told his congregation, "does wealth so directly point toward virtue in morality and spirituality in religion as in America.") [50]

Nor were the exclusionists altogether wrong in taking Beecher for a spokesman of the Protestant persuasion as a whole, despite the fact that still in 1879 only a small number of clergymen would have joined in his endorsement of Herbert Spencer. For the doctrine of progressive evolutionism completed and in a sense laid bare the real social meaning of the much more widely held clerical economics. Its insensitivity to human suffering stood in contrast to its profession of the brotherhood of man. Thus Beecher could be used to make a mockery of the old abolitionist stance; and many Protestant ministers

[49] *Examiner*, February 20, 1879.
[50] Sunday Evening Discourse, Plymouth Church, March 11, 1874, in Beecher, *Lectures and Orations*, 190; William Drysdale, *Proverbs from Plymouth Pulpit Selected from the Writings and Sayings of Henry Ward Beecher* (New York, 1887), 74.

—who, like the Reverend Otis Gibson of San Francisco's Methodist Episcopal Mission, had labored for the Chinese in the hope of gathering them into the Christian fold—were left almost defenseless under the exclusionist attack.[51]

The immediate focus of national debate, after the Senate had approved the fifteen-passenger bill, was on President Hayes. Would he veto? "The steamers from China to this port will swarm with coolies, and as rats overrun a granary to devour the store within, these exhausting hordes will pour in upon this fated State to fatten on the feast they destroy, until this people shall be driven, by the desperation of self-preservation, to adopt heroic means to abate the unendurable evil." California stirred itself into a cresendo of activity. The Constitutional Convention, still in session, took time off from its lawmaking to adopt, by vote of 109 to 8, a resolution thanking Congress for passing the bill. The newly organized Assembly of Trades and Labor Unions held a special meeting to memorialize the president.[52]

Meanwhile, the San Francisco Chamber of Commerce proposed that Mayor Bryant summon another citizens' rally to climax the appeal for presidential signature. In Sacramento the annual Supreme Encampment of the Order of Caucasians endorsed the action of the chamber. Mayor Bryant booked Platt Hall, invited Governor Irwin down to preside, appointed the secretaries of the Republican and Democratic central committees as official secretaries, and named a slate of speakers ranging from William T. Coleman (the old hardy perennial of vigilance committees) on the right, to Philip A. Roach (one of the founders of the *Examiner*) somewhere on the left.[53] This clearly was a repetition

[51] *Examiner*, August 16, September 14, October 29, December 19, 1877; January 24, 1878; February 20, 28, 1879; July 6, 1882. Under other circumstances, Gibson, hostile to Irish and Catholics, was more than able to defend himself. See Gunther Barth, *Bitter Strength: A History of the Chinese in the United States, 1850–1870* (Cambridge, Mass., 1964), 164. For Gibson's controversy with the anti-Chinese Jesuit priest, Father James Bouchard, see Rev. Otis Gibson, *"Chinaman or White Man, Which?" Reply to Father. Buchard* (San Francisco, 1873), in Immigration Pamphlets, University of California, Berkeley; and John Bernard McGloin, *Eloquent Indian: The Life of James Bouchard, California Jesuit* (Stanford, 1949), 172–184. Gibson's *The Chinese in America* (Cincinnati, 1877) contains a full rendering of the Social Darwinist viewpoint, 110. For other statements sympathetic to the Chinese, see Samuel E. W. Becker, *Humors of a Congressional Investigating Committee. A Review of the Report of the Joint Special Committee to Investigate Chinese Immigration. Washington, 1877* (n.d., n.p.), Chinese Immigration Pamphlets, II, no. 4., Bancroft Library, Berkeley; L. T. Townsend, D.D., *The Chinese Problem* (Boston, 1876); George F. Seward, *Chinese Immigration in Its Social and Economical Aspects* (New York, 1881).

[52] *Examiner*, February 20, 21, 25, 1879.

[53] *Examiner*, February 25, 26, 28, 1879. On the Order of Caucasians, see above, p. 18. On Roach, see John P. Young, *Journalism in California*, (San Francisco, 1915), 63, and *Examiner*, June 5, 1877.

of the feast of the bipartisan establishment, first celebrated by Mayor Bryant in 1876.

Denis Kearney denounced the entire affair. He pointed out, correctly, that it was *bi*partisan rather than *non*partisan, since Republicans and Democrats had received official recognition; whereas the Workingmen (who had swept the city in the last election) were offered no place on the platform. During the rally itself a few hecklers, apparently from the ranks of the Workingmen, interrupted Coleman. But the governor strode to the podium, pledged the combined might of the police, the state, and the federal government to smash any attempt at bulldozing the gathering. Aside from this slight unpleasantness, according to newspaper accounts, the speeches were received enthusiastically by some 6,000 persons jammed into the hall.[54]

Two days later President Hayes vetoed the fifteen-passenger bill.[55]

Among exclusionists there was disappointment and anger. Yet even in California in 1879, these did not form an explosive mixture. The veto was not unexpected; and the president in his accompanying message took safe rather than high ground. The reasons he gave for his action were not those of Morton or Hoar or Beecher, but simply that the bill constituted a breach of a treaty still in force. Undoubtedly, E. C. Sandmeyer, in his study of the anti-Chinese movement, was correct when he suggested that 1879 marked the turning point of the campaign for federal intervention. That summer the American minister to China, George Seward, was instructed to open negotiations toward revision of the Burlingame Treaty. The national debate and its outcome had made clear that principled opposition to Chinese exclusion had ceased to have any political substance. It was now a matter of time, of face saving, of certain peripheral readjustments.[56]

Yet this did not mean that the labors of Senator Hoar and Reverend Beecher and their little band of Brahmins and abolitionists had been altogether without result. They had helped to forge the moral and economic arguments which for another forty years would hold open America's ports of entry for all the world except the Chinese. Long before then, however, the last of the abolitionists had succumbed, while the Brahmins had moved to the other side of the question.

54 *Examiner*, February 27, 28, 1879.
55 James D. Richardson, *A Compilation of the Messages and Papers of the Presidents* (New York, 1897–), IX, 4466–4472; *Examiner*, March 3, 1879.
56 Sandmeyer, *Anti-Chinese Movement*, 91–92.

7

WORKINGMEN AND
THE "SYSTEM"

When the California Constituent Assembly completed its labors, the Workingmen voted, as did most of their fellow delegates, to approve the final draft and submit it to the people. Kearney stumped the state in its behalf. The *Chronicle* profited from the occasion by conducting a new subscription drive. Otherwise the California press, Republican and Democratic, almost unanimously denounced the supposed radicalism of the new document. Both Henry George and Frank Roney rejected it for the opposite reason; and George was convinced that the greatest of special interests, the railroad, was by no means displeased with the work of the constitution makers. In the state referendum a slim majority, based largely on rural districts, approved. San Francisco, oddly, despite its endorsement of the Workingmen one year earlier, turned against the constitution they recommended.[1]

Who gained what out of these events remained somewhat obscure; and the obscurity was subsequently heightened as the courts gutted those articles that dealt with taxation, corporations, railroad regulation, and the status of Chinese. Yet however dubious the achievements of the constitutional convention, there was one matter upon which it was no longer possible to entertain the slightest doubt—and that was the massive public hatred directed against the Chinese. At the time of the balloting which approved the new constitution, California's voters had been offered, by order of the legislature, a referendum of

[1] *Debates and Proceedings of the Constitutional Convention of the State of California, Convened at the City of Sacramento, Saturday, September 28, 1878*, 3 vols. (Sacramento, 1881), III, 1520–1521; John P. Young, *San Francisco: A History of the Pacific Coast Metropolis*, 2 vols., (San Francisco and Chicago, n.d. [1912?]), II, 547; Carl B. Swisher, *Motivation and Political Technique in the California Constitutional Convention, 1878–79* (Claremont, Calif., 1930), 101–110; Frank Roney, *Frank Roney, Irish Rebel and California Labor Leader*, ed. Ira B. Cross (Berkeley, 1931), 301, 310; Henry George, "The Kearney Agitation in California," *Popular Science Monthly*, XVII (August 1880), 445–446.

opinion on the Chinese question. The result was a margin of 150,000 to 900 favoring total exclusion.[2]

Mayor Kalloch

The final act in this drama of the Workingmen's party hovers on the border between tragedy and restoration farce. Several years earlier a Baptist minister by the name of Isaac Kalloch had arrived on the Pacific Coast. A former New England abolitionist who came west by way of Kansas, Kalloch took San Francisco by storm. He gathered a flock, built a great institutional temple on Seventh Street (complete with auditorium, conference halls, and gymnasium), and there preached to what were undoubtedly the largest congregations west of the Great Plains. Kalloch was brilliantly competent. In addition to his triumphs in the pulpit, he had been a successful newspaper editor and later became mayor of San Francisco, an attorney, and finally a railroad promoter in the Northwest. All in all this was a kind of latter day Benvenuto Cellini, a superb craftsman at whatever he turned his hand to. And in San Francisco in the late seventies it was inevitable that he would turn his hand to the Chinese problem.

True to the abolitionist background, his first stance was that of defender of the Chinese. He soon had the largest Chinese Sunday school in the city ensconced in his Seventh Street temple.[3] But Kalloch was no more able to stand against the pricks of conscience than were those earlier travelers along the road to Damascus, Henry George and Denis Kearney. Kalloch too saw the light, and when he did had no choice but yield to it; and this occurred as a matter of fact on a public and memorable occasion. It was the Fourth of July 1878. As pastor of the city's largest congregation, Kalloch had been named chaplain of the day. He prayed as follows:

> We believe, O Lord, that the foundations of our government were laid by Thine own hand; that all the steps and stages of our progress have been under Thy watch and ward. . . . We meet together today to celebrate the anniversary of our national birth, and we pray that we may be enabled to carry out the divine principles which inspired our noble sires and others, and we pray that our rules may all be righteous; that our people may be peaceable; that capital may respect the

2 Swisher, 112–114; Elmer Clarence Sandmeyer *The Anti-Chinese Movement in California* (Urbana, Ill., 1939), 63.

3 M. M. Marberry, *The Gold Voice: A Biography of Isaac Kalloch* (New York, 1947), 50–120, 163–221, 229–238; San Francisco *Examiner*, March 23, 1878.

> rights of labor, and that labor may honor capital; that the
> Chinese must go—

At this point interrupted by a storm of applause, the Chaplain was
silent for a moment, then continued:

> and good men stay. We believe Thou wilt hear our prayer
> when we pray that we believe to be right.[4]

One year later, Kalloch burst into the ranks of the Workingmen's
party. He grasped the nomination for mayor and led them to victory
in the election of 1879. The campaign was one of the most incredible
in San Francisco's frequently incredible history. Kalloch headed a
full municipal slate pledged to solve the Chinese problem through the
use of powers already inherent in city government, to find relief for
the unemployed, and to reduce the burden on taxpayers by a voluntary
salary cut on the part of elected officials. The San Francisco *Chronicle*,
which had hitherto furnished journalistic heavy artillery for the
Workingmen's campaigns, was not happy over Kalloch's nomination.
Charles De Young, the editor and publisher, had wanted to put up
his own man. He swung into opposition and began printing accounts
of allegedly scandalous episodes in the pastor's career in Boston and
Kansas. Kalloch replied from the pulpit with a series of remarks on
the means by which De Young's mother, in less prosperous days, had
been accustomed to earn her living.

One Saturday morning toward the end of August, De Young hired
a carriage and, after stopping at the telegraph office to pick up a
messenger boy, directed his driver to Seventh Street. There he sent
the boy into the temple with a message for the pastor that a lady
awaited him outside. De Young knew his man. Kalloch, as it happened,
was not in the temple but was seated in a buggy just ahead conversing
with one Carl Browne, a henchman of Kearney's, and the editor of
the *Open Letter*, a small weekly which then claimed to be the official
organ of the Workingmen's party. Upon receiving the message, Kalloch at once left Browne; and as he stepped gallantly back toward
the carriage, now drawn up with lowered blinds at the curb, De
Young shot him down.[5]

This occurred at the very height of the campaign. The temple and
the street in front of it were full of Kalloch's supporters. They surrounded the carriage, overturned it, and De Young came within a hair's
breadth of being lynched on the spot. But a city plainclothes detective,

[4] *Examiner,* July 7, 1878.
[5] Marberry, *Golden Voice,* 250–254; Roney, 304–305; *Examiner,* June 18, 21,
August 23, 25, 1879.

happening to be nearby, broke through to him gun in hand, got De Young into another carriage, and whisked him off to the police station. There an angry throng of Workingmen converged, many of them armed—the party had several patriotic drill societies among its ward clubs—and threatened to storm the building. But party leaders now were pleading for restraint and the police were not disinclined to make concessions. They invited a platoon of Workingmen to join the special security detail posted in front of De Young's cell.[6]

The pastor, meanwhile, had been carried back into his temple. Doctors declared that he could not safely be moved, and the temple was converted into a combination hospital and fortress. Uniformed Workingmen stood watch at the doors. The street was strewn with tanbark to deaden the clatter of passing traffic. And as surgeons labored over the wounded man, they issued regular bulletins to the crowd that waited silently outside.

Kearney had been campaigning up country. Rushing back to the city, he arrived that evening on the ferry from Vallejo, marched up Market Street behind a military contingent of his partisans, and conferred at headquarters with the presidents of the ward clubs. Afterward, he spoke briefly in the sandlots. Promising that De Young would be hanged—legally—Kearney repeated the pleas for moderation made earlier by his colleagues. The city began to relax; and on the following day, Sunday, Kalloch's son, also a Baptist minister and assistant pastor at the temple, was able to tell a huge sandlot assembly that the doctors were now confident his father would pull through.[7]

The Reverend Kalloch did indeed pull through and swept the election ten days later. By the time of his inauguration in January he seemed to have regained his usual robust health. Yet while the Workingmen's party had elected a mayor, sheriff, auditor, tax collector, district attorney, public administrator, and several others, it had failed to elect a single member of the board of supervisors. Frank Roney, speculating years later on this curious event, suggested that a deal had been made whereby the obviously victorious Workingmen were given the mayoralty and a number of posts controlling patronage, while the real power centers—the board of supervisors and the police depart-

6 The shooting was on Saturday, August 23. Testimony was taken in police court on Monday and Tuesday and is summarized in the *Examiner*, August 25, 26. According to this report, Captain I. W. Lees of the city police had denied on the stand having met with De Young on the night before the shooting—this apparently in refutation of rumors that the police had collaborated with De Young. For earlier reports of military activities of the Workingmen's party ward clubs, see *Examiner*, December 20, 1877, and February 2, 1878; also Roney, 292-295.

7 *Examiner*, August 23, 25, 1879.

ment—remained in the hands of the bipartisan establishment.[8] Roney had no evidence. At this distance one can only note that tampering with vote counts was the rule rather than the exception in San Francisco; and that given the methods of tallying and recording there is no reason to assume correspondence between any announced result and a ballot actually cast. The leaders of the Workingmen, however, did not challenge the outcome of 1879. And as it turned out, Kalloch may have been thankful that the police department remained beyond his control.

What followed upon this amputation of the city's executive from its legislative and coercive faculties was a noisy deadlock of administration. The mayor vetoed the supervisors' ordinances; the supervisors declined to enact the mayor's recommendations. Each side projected programs unlikely of fulfillment and blamed the other side for blocking them. Such was the case with the promised city relief for unemployed, and so too fared Mayor Kalloch's solution for the Chinese problem. The Workingmen had won control of the board of health, of which the mayor was, ex officio, a member. After a rapid investigation the board determined that Chinatown constituted a menace to the health of the city and, early in February 1880, declared that this "nuisance" must be "abated." How and by whom such abatement was to be undertaken the health officers did not specify. The police department remained uncooperative. As for the supervisors, while understandably hesitant to take a direct negative stand, they omitted the appointment of necessary committees, refused to confer with the board of health, and adopted, then rescinded, resolutions of concurrence.[9]

The mayor lambasted them for this procrastination. Yet they were able to act with remarkable dispatch when it came to adding seventy-five men to the police force. It was whispered among the Workingmen that the police intended to smash any effort at carrying out the "abatement." Meanwhile the city's merchants and businessmen, declaring for "preservation of public peace . . . restoration of confidence in the security of life and property from all violence," had organized themselves into a Citizens' Protective Union. There were rumors that Colonel Bee, the Chinese consul, had met with these men secretly. Then there were rumors that the sandlotters intended to set Chinatown afire; and rumors that William T. Coleman's pick-handle brigade was to be rearmed and that Gatling guns were being

8 *Examiner*, September 3, 8, October 29, 1879; Roney, 302–304.
9 *Chinatown Declared a Nuisance!* (San Francisco, 1880), in *Chinese Immigration Pamphlets*, Bancroft Library, University of California, Berkeley, especially 3–6; *Examiner*, February 10, 23–25, 28, 1880.

brought to City Hall; and rumors of a plot to assassinate Kearney and Kalloch. The entire city was awash with rumors. The mayor spoke to mass meetings arguing the legality of his program, promising that the abatement of Chinatown could be peacefully carried out. The Central Committee of Presidents of Workingmen's Ward Clubs held emergency sessions.[10]

If there were substance to Roney's suggestion that a deal had been made at the time of the vote count between spokesmen for the Workingmen and those of the bipartisan establishment, then a good portion of this activity must be set down as opéra bouffe. It would be difficult to take Kalloch and his implacable board of supervisors in any other light. Yet even if this were the case, some of the players seemed not to be following their scripts. There was the *Examiner,* for example. Voice of the old Democracy, kingpin in the bipartisan establishment, the *Examiner* had, during the electoral campaign, been ruthless in its attacks on Kalloch. It now began to find merit in his proposals. Abatement of Chinatown was precisely what the paper had long clamored for. It warned, however, that the federal courts would be certain to intervene, and so shifted its fire from the mayor to the judiciary; then it turned on those traitorous white landlords who rented properties to Chinese for the sake of the gigantic rentals accruing from premises occupied "in such countless numbers." [11]

This shift of focus was hardly calculated to ease the tension. And there were those who might be ready to respond to such hints—the unemployed. Bedraggled and wretched, they stood endlessly in the winter rain. They trailed through the streets of the white men's section begging a handout at the charity kitchens; they clamored on the city hall steps for half a day's labor setting cobblestones or cleaning the city sewers. They waited in the sandlots for a word from Kearney or from Kalloch.[12]

The Unemployed

The rains always were crucial in California. In good times the rains promised a prosperous season ahead. But they made hard times worse. The onset of the winter rain closed down building activity in the city.

10 San Francisco *Evening Bulletin,* March 9, 1880, cited in Ira B. Cross, *A History of the Labor Movement in California* (Berkeley, 1935), 124–125; *Examiner,* February 25, 26, 28, 1880. On further activities of the Citizens' Protective Union, see *Examiner,* March 30, April 1, 1880.

11 *Examiner,* February 23, 24, 1880; on the newspaper's opposition to Kalloch during the mayoralty campaign, see *Examiner,* August 29, 1879.

12 *Examiner,* February 9, 10, 13, 23, 1880.

More importantly, it cut off construction projects in the countryside
and ended the seasonal demand for harvest workers. Chinese gang
labor, largely employed in harvesting and construction work *outside*
the city, would winter for the most part in the ghettoes of the rural
towns. Some might drift down for a brief holiday in the metropolitan
Chinatown, but there was no mass influx of Chinese from the country
to the city. For migratory white workers, however, just beginning to
appear as a significant element in California's labor force, the small
towns offered no refuge. They came to the cities; and most of them
came straight to San Francisco. There they joined the urban seasonally
jobless and that mass of permanent unemployed which, in depression
years, was never absent. It was from these sources that Kearney had recruited the crowds which backed him against Roney and which, during
the previous winter and spring, had marched back and forth across the
city with him, ousting his opponents from the ward clubs.[13] The
winter of 1880 brought the unemployed into action more strongly
than ever.

Now for the first time they began to develop their own leadership.
In February (while Kearney was in the East attending a conference of
labor spokesmen and Greenbackers), a man named L. J. Gannon
usurped Kearney's place in the sandlots. Gannon was apparently un-
connected with the ward apparatus of the Workingmen's party, and if
he had any trade the newspaper accounts made no mention of it. More
fiercely even than Kearney he gave expression to the dream of salva-
tion through violence. "If they start in, the city will be levelled to
ashes and the ruins filled with roasted bodies within twenty-four
hours." Gannon was jailed before the month was out.[14]

There was also a Mrs. Anna Smith whose name appeared frequently
in connection with activities of the unemployed. Of Anna Smith a
somewhat fuller picture emerges than of Gannon, and it is possible
perhaps to catch through her a glimpse of the people she spoke for.
Born in New York State in 1835, Anna Smith had been put out to
domestic service as a child. Later she found work in a shoe factory
which shut down during the depression of 1857. She drifted westward.
Almost illiterate, she seems to have craved education; in Altoona,
Pennsylvania, later in Ohio, she became caretaker and janitress in a

[13] Cross, 69–72; Stuart Jamieson, *Labor Unionism in American Agriculture*, U.S.
Bureau of Labor Statistics, *Bulletin No. 836* (Washington, 1945), 45–48; Carey
McWilliams, *Factories in the Field* (Boston, 1939), 65–72.
[14] The prediction was alleged to have been made in a sandlots speech on
February 26, 1880. (*Examiner*, March 18, 1880.)

girls' seminary, then in a public school, for room and board and the privilege of attending classes. The war came and she was a nurse for the Union Army. She married a disabled veteran who hired out as a clerk on the Pennsylvania Raiload and lost his job because of his disability. Westward again; her husband died in Missouri; Anna Smith with their child went on to Denver. She scrubbed and ironed in laundries and in 1875, just in time for another depression, arrived in California.

She tried nursing again, took service as cook and housekeeper on ranches, and slipped at last into the throng of the unemployed. But the hunger for education must still have been with her, for she was, in the words of the reporter who summarized her story, "well informed on matters connected with the labor question." [15] One newspaper at least identified her as a member of the socialistic Workingmen's party.[16] Mrs. Smith left the apocalyptic style largely to Gannon and Kearney. She herself seemed more concerned with extending the meager relief fund that came to hand from collections and with finding empty buildings where destitute women might take shelter. She had a folksy touch suggestive of later women campaigners for the Farmers' Alliance and the Populists. She would adjourn a sandlot rally by announcing that "she wanted something to keep her jaws going and give her tongue a rest," and supposed "all present felt the same." [17]

What was the relation of the unemployed movement to the ward clubs of the Workingmen's party? It is impossible to give any very precise answer to this question. The party seems to have had some thirty-five clubs functioning in San Francisco during that winter. If our earlier supposition is correct that most of these had simply been taken over from the Democrats, it would follow that their members were more or less permanent residents—shopkeepers, craftsmen, and laborers—a number of whom must have been seasonally unemployed. While many ward club members may have taken part in the sandlot demonstrations, it seems evident that the direction of the unemployed movement was outside the regular Workingmen's apparatus and that party leaders never fully controlled it. These leaders were therefore in danger of being outflanked from the left. Kearney, upon his return to San Francisco from his round of politicking in the East, felt immediately obliged to enter into competition with Gannon. Not long after

[15] *Examiner*, February 16, 1880.
[16] San Francisco *Morning Call*, February 8, 1880, quoted in Cross, 123.
[17] *Examiner*, February 18, March 6, 1880.

Gannon's arrest for filling the city with roasted bodies, Kearney was jailed for proposing the erection of a gallows in the sandlots and for calling Claus Spreckels, the West Coast sugar baron, a thief.[18]

Mayor Kalloch was too clever to be caught in any such trap. Yet his room for maneuver was narrowing and he showed himself at least as anxious over what his partisans might do as over the hostility of the supervisors and the police department. In mid-February he told a sandlot audience that he was certain things would pick up; if he were not, he would counsel differently. But he then warned:

> What I want to tell you is there is danger of some reckless and revolutionary person, some man from some hot scene in the old country that don't understand the peaceful working of our Government. We are the masters and sovereigns here and haven't got any despotism to overthrow, except the despotism of organized thieves. We are the people and the voice of the people is the voice of God, and that is the way it must be regarded. We free ourselves from any sympathy that has come from hot revolutionary scenes of the old world, and we don't want that kind of men to put their fingers into our pie.[19]

At this same gathering, the folksy Mrs. Smith was moving in a direction diametrically opposite to that of the mayor. She had discovered, she reported, during her investigations of civic iniquities, that a large building at Page and Gough streets, presumably belonging to Buckingham and Company (shoe manufacturers), actually stood on property of the city school department which received fifty dollars monthly rental. The department had endeavored to keep the matter secret; the building housed 250 Chinese. She had been thinking, Anna Smith told the crowd, that "it might be of some benefit to you to know the fact." [20]

Five days later Kalloch repeated his plea for patience to a mass meeting at Union Hall auditorium. And on the occasion of Gannon's arrest, the mayor, in denouncing the act as an abuse of police power, revealed that he had earlier requested "Mr. Gannon . . . and his friends" to call off the "daily gatherings in the sand lots," and that the leaders of the unemployed had complied.[21]

These demonstrations and the suspended threat they posed were,

18 On the number of ward clubs, see the report of the committee on by-laws, state convention, Workingmen's Party of California, as summarized in the *Examiner*, February 24, March 11, 15, 16, 18–19, 1880.

19 *Examiner*, February 18, 1880.

20 *Ibid.*

21 *Examiner*, February 23, 28, 1880.

however, the mayor's chief source of power. He dared not fail to offer some kind of hope. But hope for what? What was needed was lodging, food, jobs—and these were indeed beyond hoping for. After four depression years, the city's private agencies of relief were totally inadequate. The mayor was said to be paying out of his own pocket for a building where 150 or 200 could squeeze in for shelter at night. But there were thousands more. As for emergency public works, the supervisors stood ready to block any proposal; [22] and even had they been willing to cooperate, there were no funds in the budget. The only hope available was hope for dispossession of the Chinese, and from the beginning of winter this hung heavy in the air. Had not the new constitution, already ratified, forbidden private corporations from employing Chinese? and promised the sanction of state law to removals by local authority? And had not Mayor Kalloch and the board of health proclaimed their deadline for the "abatement" of Chinatown? Early in February a sandlot crowd resolved to demand that "the Central Pacific Railroad and all other corporate bodies . . . immediately discharge their Mongolians and give us employment." This was followed by a threat "that we have the physical means in our hands to enforce a compliance with the Constitution . . . and will not hesitate to use these means." [23]

Daily the unemployed gathered, listened to speeches, formed up behind their leaders and marched off across Market and Mission streets to the industrial districts. They would call en masse at factories and workshops, send in delegations to demand dismissal of Chinese employees, and return at last to the sandlots to hear the reports. In the beginning there seemed to be steady progress. A laundry and a shirt making establishment complied. The great Pioneer Woolen Mills shut down their factories, promising to reopen (at some later date) with white labor. The Golden Gate Mills in Potrero, already closed for the winter, made the same pledge. And across the bay, the Pacific Jute Mills discharged 800 Chinese laborers.[24] Meanwhile, the state legislature was hard at work transcribing into statute law the mandates of the new constitution. By mid-February the *Examiner* was able to editorialize enthusiastically on the "Good Effects of the Anti-Chinese Act," concluding with a note of partriotic pride: "Every country owes its first duty to its own race and citizens. This duty

[22] *Examiner*, November 28, 1877; January 5, March 12, 1878; February 10, 13, 23, March 6, 1880.

[23] *Examiner*, February 9, 1880. Another resolution two weeks later called attention to repeated violations of the constitution and laws and urged that workingmen insist upon strict enforcement; *Examiner*, February 24, 1880.

[24] *Examiner*, February 9, 10, 13, 14, 16–18, 1880.

properly observed on this Coast will cause much riddance of the
Chinese pest." [25]

But for all these brave words, it must soon have been clear to
the rain-sodden demonstrators that the show they were putting on
was no more than a bitter joke. Factory managers, in a depression
winter, were not unwilling to halt production; they simply marked
time. Their lawyers carried the issue into federal court, and before
the end of March both the Anti-Chinese Corporation law and the
constitutional clauses on which it was based had been invalidated.[26]
Dispossession of Chinese from their jobs, then, came down to the
same rock bottom as abatement of Chinatown. Technicalities of law
stood in the way; dared they take matters into their own hands?

To judge from his statements, this was precisely what Mayor
Kalloch dreaded. Yet he and other officials of the party apparatus,
including of course Kearney, kept nudging in that direction. Even in
those speeches in which he was most urgently counseling restraint, the
mayor ended by placing the blame for unemployment on the
Chinese and insisting that the only long-range solution lay in ousting
them from jobs and from their quarter of the city. At the very height
of the winter crisis, when rumors of assassination plots and of rearmed vigilance committees were at their thickest, the sheriff of San
Francisco County, elected on the Workingmen's ticket, told the party
central committee of ward presidents "that at the end of thirty
days the authorities would call on the workingmen to clear out Chinatown." [27] The leaders were thus in the uneasy stance of giving
permission, indeed encouragement, to acts which they must constantly
forbid.

How serious was the danger of a massacre of Chinese during that
winter? Probably more serious than at any other time, including even
the July days of 1877, yet not as serious as the oratory on both sides
might lead one to suppose. For Chinatown had become by this
time almost impregnable. The convergence of non-Chinese economic
interests guaranteed protection by the courts and by the city police.
This precluded the success of any legal siege operation such as Mayor
Kalloch's abatement. Then why not that *illegal* attack toward which
the Workingmen's leadership made constant innuendoes? The answer
is that there was little chance of success. Leaving aside the regular
police and state militia, both of which would certainly have intervened,
Chinatown itself had become a fortress. There were, first of all, the

[25] *Examiner,* February 14, 18, 1880.
[26] *Examiner,* March 8, 22, 1880. The test case was *In re Tiburcio Parrott.*
[27] *Examiner,* February 10, 23, 26, 1880.

"specials," a trained corps of non-Chinese on the payroll of the Chinese establishment. In this context, the function of the specials—generally depicted as thugs hired to protect the gambling and prostitution rings—appears in rather a different light. Plenty of Chinese high-binders were available for the simple purpose of protection; what the specials were wanted for was to defend Chinatown against intrusions from the non-Chinese city surrounding it. But the specials were only one line of defense. The ghetto itself was armed. While outside San Francisco's Chinatown the Chinese seldom attempted to protect themselves by force, on their own ground they would doubtless have done so. An attack on this citadel was hardly an inviting prospect. Certainly the ward clubs' marching and drill societies, which liked to escort Kearney up and down Market Street, were not up to it.[28]

But there might be other methods of attack than armed invasion. It seems to have been widely believed at the time that the Chinese quarter was peculiarly vulnerable to fire. Newspapers, city officials, visiting investigating committees were constantly warning that China-town was likely to burst into flame at any moment from its own cooking braziers and firecrackers, and might sweep the rest of the city with it. It was to this fear (or hope) that Gannon had addressed himself when he spoke of filling in the rubble with roasted bodies. Arson in California in those days was almost as commonplace as murder; and it was true that not only Chinatown but the entire city, with its high winds and steep hills, its wooden construction, its dilapidated water system, was one vast fire trap. Why then did the sandlotters, hungry and desperate as they were in the winter of 1880, not simply light fires at the borders of the ghetto and wait for the holocaust? They probably did, several times, but without success. Curiously, Chinatown seems to have been one of the least flammable areas in town. There were numerous efforts to persuade, or coerce, insurance companies to revoke fire insurance on premises occupied by Chinese

28 *Alta California*, May 5, 1876, letter to the editor signed "James C. Zabriskie"; *Examiner*, December 19, 1877; September 28, 1878; San Francisco *Daily Report*, December 23, 1885; *Alta*, November 15, 1876; *Examiner*, June 22, 1882; Sandmeyer, *Anti-Chinese Movement* (above, n. 2), 62. On the "specials," see testimony of Captain I. W. Lees, San Francisco police force, to an investigating committee of the state legislature, *Examiner*, February 4, 5, 1878. See also, *Examiner*, June 15, December 19, 1877; February 16, 1878; June 22, 1882; *Alta*, November 15, 1876; San Francisco *Truth*, June 28, November 1, 1882. On the *armed ghetto*, see *Examiner*, July 27, September 17, December 20, 1877; testimony of Captain Lees, *Examiner*, February 5, 1878. After the shooting of Kalloch by De Young, the *Examiner* (August 25, 1879) reported: "From all parts of the city an immediate rush of Chinamen was made for the shelter of Chinatown. In Chinatown itself, the excitement was as intense as elsewhere and much more visible. Many of the stores and tenements were barricaded."

for reason of the presumably greater fire hazard. But only two years
earlier an insurance underwriter had testified before Senator Morton's
Joint Congressional Committee that no large fire had occurred in
Chinatown during the previous fifteen years. Insurance carriers, he
said, charged the same rates there as elsewhere, though the risks
involved were actually lower.[29]

The witness made no effort to account for this circumstance; but
one might speculate that it resulted in part from overcrowding and
from the tight organization of social relationships. The ghetto was like
a vessel at sea. Passengers and crew slept by turn in the same set of
bunks, and there was always one shift at least on watch for stray
sparks or enemy boarding parties. But whatever the causes, the fact
was that Chinatown in San Francisco demonstrated extraordinary
durability. It survived untouched the years 1885–86 and 1893 when
small town ghettoes from San Diego to Seattle were being laid waste
by mob attack.[30] And despite predictions of plague and fire, it yielded
to neither one nor the other until finally razed by the earthquake of
1906—which "abated" most of the rest of the city as well.

It seems reasonable to conclude, therefore, that Chinatown stood
in no great danger from the Workingmen.[31] But Mayor Kalloch and
other leaders of the party were in considerable danger. And the more
intense the apocalyptic mood of their followers, the greater that
danger became. For they were compelled, in order to keep control of
the party, to incite to actions which at the same time they were
earnestly counseling against. They must all have breathed easier when
the rainy season ended and their army began to melt into the hinterland.

There was, however, before this occurred, one final episode of
symbolic catharsis. Charles De Young, when it became clear that
Kalloch had survived his assault, was released on bail. He promptly
took off for Mexico. Returning by way of Boston and Kansas, he
gathered a good deal of documentation on the mayor's earlier adventures which he arranged to have printed as a pamphlet, by way of

[29] Testimony of Fire Marshall Durkee and Captain Lees, *Examiner,* February 5,
1878. Lees regarded Chinatown as virtually invulnerable to any form of attack
except fire. U.S., Senate Report 689 (Washington, 1877), 644, 660–670; *Alta,* November 15, 1876. In 1880 a bill was introduced in the California legislature to exempt
insurance companies from payment of claims on properties where aliens ineligible
for citizenship were employed. (*Truth,* May 31, 1882. And see above, pp. 141, 144.)

[30] Sandmeyer, *Anti-Chinese Movement,* 96–98; McWilliams, *Factories in the Field,*
75–78. See below, pp. 201–213, 229–234.

[31] This was not true of Chinese outside the ghetto. Most of the cases of arson
cited by Fire Marshall Durkee were burnings of Chinese washhouses in other
sections of the city.

softening up public opinion prior to the opening of his own trial. Meanwhile, Kalloch's son, former assistant pastor of the Seventh Street Temple, had moved over to city hall as chief clerk and secretary. The son seems to have been a moody young man, existing docilely yet perhaps bitterly in the shadow of his father. On the day that the pamphlet appeared, he took a revolver from his desk drawer, spent the afternoon drinking in Market Street bars, and in the evening waited outside the *Chronicle* office. When the editor returned from dinner, Kalloch, the son, followed him into the building—an act of considerable courage since De Young was known to go armed and might have been presumed under the circumstances to have had bodyguards with him. What followed was, like so many other events of that year, played out in the high style of restoration comedy. De Young, struggling to get out of his overcoat so that he could reach his pistol, hopped about the office, wheeling behind terrified clerks, ducking around furniture. Kalloch emptied his revolver, missing every shot except the last. At the end De Young was dead.[32]

The Institutionalization of Labor Politics

That same evening Frank Roney, recently returned from Nevada, was on the platform of the Irish-American Hall at a rally called by the socialists to protest the third arrest of Denis Kearney. Describing the scene in his memoirs, Roney recalled that he was "paralyzed . . . horrified" at the "exultation" of the crowd when they heard the news of De Young's death:

> Women waved their handkerchiefs, men yelled and cheered . . . as if some great unexpected benefit had been conferred on them. . . . It seemed to me that any people who could exult at such a deed were little better than uncivilized. . . . Poor, ignorant, brutal, merciless human nature. . . . But they gave sympathy fully and freely to Kearney, whose only title to consideration was the memory of the hatred which he had instilled in them against another race. Only a short while before the man who lay murdered had been the inspirer of the man against whose imprisonment they had met to protest. De Young was practically their leader for he led the leader whom they acknowledged.[33]

For a man as shrewd as he certainly was, Roney displayed a striking obtuseness in these comments. What speaks through the moral tone is

---

[32] *Examiner*, April 24, 1880; Marberry, *The Golden Voice* (above, n. 3), 294–297.
[33] Roney, *Frank Roney* (above, n. 1), 306–307.

the contempt of the Irish republican for his politically illiterate countrymen, and of the skilled craftsman toward what he considered a shiftless proletariat. Roney seems not to have traced any connection between this exultation he found so horrifying and the frustrated hopes of mass vengeance which he himself—as well as Kearney and De Young—had helped to instill. But he was writing long afterward. What he felt at the time is perhaps something else again.

The spring came, the rains ended, Kalloch *fils* stood trial for murder and was acquitted. Kalloch the elder was impeached by his board of supervisors upon charges of malfeasance in office; but as the supervisors failed to sustain their case, the city administration continued at loggerheads. In due course the California Supreme Court reviewed the convictions of Denis Kearney and L. J. Gannon, overruled the lower courts, and set both men free. While hardly apparent at the time, it appears clear in retrospect that the Workingmen's party had seen its best days. Regrettably, perhaps, one could not yet say that the rest was silence; but the rest certainly was anticlimax. Kearney laid waste his reserves, such as they were, in futile adventures with the Greenback movement and through endless bickering with his subordinates. The mass base broke up, a few radicals like Roney went over to the Socialists, the vast majority found their way back to the old home—the Democracy.[34] By 1880 the Workingmen's party had faded from the California scene. At least, that is, the name had faded. Two basic elements of its structure, however, continued to dominate the political skyline.

One of these was the labor vote in San Francisco. The city, which in 1880 had 27 percent and in 1900 23 percent of the total population of the state,[35] played a crucial role in every convention and legislature; and the workingmen whose votes controlled certain well-defined, stable urban districts played a crucial role in the city. The brief heyday of the Workingmen's party competed the institutionalization of labor politics in San Francisco. Under varying labels, usually Democratic, sometimes Republican, workingmen and their spokesmen became a permanent fixture at Sacramento. Yet it would be mistaken to suppose that the presence of these proletarians injected any radical or revolutionary flavor into the state capital. As a matter of fact they adjusted

[34] Cross, *History of Labor Movement* (above, n. 10) 123–128; Ralph Kauer, "The Workingmen's Party of California," *Pacific Historical Review*, XIII (September, 1944), 289; Roney, 318. *Truth*, April 1, 1882, reported that the last remaining ward club of the Workingmen's Party of California had voted to change its name to the "First Democratic Club of the 11th Ward."

[35] Davis McEntire, "An Economic Study of Population Movements in California, 1850–1944" (Ph.D. diss., Harvard University, 1947), 6, 12, Tables 1 and 4.

rather comfortably into what a later generation of reformers would refer to as the "system"—that is, the domination of state government by the railroad.[36]

Part of this adjustment was the psychological response already noted among Workingmen's delegates at the constitutional convention; having no long range program of their own, they were content simply to be included as participants in the decision-making process. Another more important aspect, already abundantly evident by 1880, was corruption.

Kearney himself had been accused of selling out to the Central Pacific. Whether this was true or not, the fact that the accusations were so frequently made indicates the general anticipation. Kearney held no public office, but the record of others who did was hardly reassuring. State Senator Bones, for one, the workingman's champion from Alameda County, had demonstrated how easily an alert legislator might discover himself to have been previously mistaken on matters of concern to the railroad.[37] And from the convention itself came an even more revealing example—the case of Charles Beerstecher. Beerstecher, one of the three lawyers in the thirty-man San Francisco delegation had been outstanding as floor leader of the Workingmen's bloc. A party history, published in San Francisco in 1878, described Beerstecher as the son of an exiled German revolutionary. Born in Würtemburg in 1851, he had been brought by his parents to the United States as an infant, grew up in Philadelphia, and later moved to Michigan where he graduated from the law department of the state university. In 1877 he reached San Francisco and hung out his shingle.[33]

Long "interested in labor reforms," Beerstecher had apparently served as spokesman for a German socialist club at the various gatherings which launched the Workingmen's Party of California; and it was largely to his efforts that the new party owed "the almost unani-

36 Franklin Hichborn, "The System" as Uncovered by the San Francisco Graft Prosecution (San Francisco, 1915); Alexander Saxton, "San Francisco Labor and the Populist and Progressive Insurgencies," Pacific Historical Review, XXXIV (November, 1965), 421–444.

37 Roney, 298; George, Popular Science Monthly, XVII, 439, 441–443; Examiner, February 2, 6, March 7, 13, 19, May 7, 8, 21, 25, 1878; San Francisco Chronicle, March 11, April 1, 1878.

38 A biographical sketch of Beerstecher (probably written by himself) appears in J. C. Stedman and R. A. Leonard, The Workingmen's Party in California: An Epitome of Its Rise and Progress (San Francisco, 1878), 107–108. See also D. G. Waldron and T. J. Vivian, Biographical Sketches of the Delegates to the Convention to Frame a New Constitution for the State of California, 1878 (San Francisco, 1878), 56.

mous support which it received from the German-speaking element among our people." [39] Presumably Beerstecher was speaking for this element when, at the second party convention, he introduced a resolution (which passed) to the effect that the Workingmen of California recognized "the Socialistic Labor Party of the United States as a kindred organization, having for its purpose and end the emancipation of the workingmen." [40] The German club nominated him to the constituent assembly and later pushed him as nominee for the newly created Railroad Commission. He won this election in 1879; [41] before the end of his term, however, he was being denounced for "high crimes and misdemeanors" as a betrayer "of the public trusts confided . . . by the people of this state." The Assembly Committee on Corporations, investigating the probity of the Railroad Commission, found with respect to Beerstecher that, while "by general report and in the opinion of his associates he was without means" prior to his election, he had during tenure of office acquired property valued at $22,000, and that this increment in his fortunes remained "without adequate explanation." Beerstecher proposed an explanation: that his parents, recently deceased, had remembered him in their will. Not long afterward the parents themselves arrived in San Francisco and took up residence with him.[42]

Beerstecher's modest variation on the Horatio Alger theme sketched tne outlines of a type soon to become classic in San Francisco politics— the labor politician, riding his ethnic or religious background and working-class style, who would speak for his constituency, on certain issues at least, and simultaneously carry on a brisk business within the "system." Here precisely was the enemy, the "political bummer," against whom Kearney had so eloquently warned.

Why did voters tolerate this sort of exploitation? There may have been several compensations, but one that was always available in unlimited supply was the permission to hate Chinese. This hostility, composed of a rational economic argument mingled with and disguising an older complex of ideas and emotions, was constantly

[39] Stedman and Leonard, 108.

[40] *Examiner*, May 20, 1878; Stedman and Leonard, 84–86. The Socialistic Labor Party of the United States was the successor to the Workingmen's Party of the United States, the name having been changed by the second party convention in 1877. (Howard Quint, *Forging American Socialism* [Columbia, S.C., 1953], 13–15.)

[41] *Examiner*, June 13, 1879; Walton Bean, *California: An Interpretive History* (New York, 1968), 241.

[42] From a resolution adopted by the Anti-Monopoly League of Tulare, quoted in *Truth*, January 28, 1882; California, *Assembly Journal*, 25th Session, 450; Stuart Daggett, *Chapters on the History of the Southern Pacific* (New York, 1922), 194.

reinforced by the sense of deprivation and displacement which unified California's diverse labor force. Since the end of the Civil War, it had fueled the rehabilitation of the Democratic party, had maintained the resiliency of the anticoolie clubs, had affected national politics, and had lofted the Workingmen's party into orbit. Here was the second of the two basic elements in the makeup of the Workingmen's party which long outlasted the party itself.

Henry George, who had prophesied and helped bring about the nationalization of the anti-Chinese issue, was one of the first to recognize its negative implication for reformers. From the tone of his *Tribune* letter in 1869, one might suppose that he would have found the Workingmen's party very much to his taste. Unlike Kearney and Kalloch, George could, without repudiation of an earlier position, have taken to himself its slogan, "The Chinese must go." Given his abilities and his reputation among Democrats, he would probably have ridden high had he chosen to do so. This must have been a temptation. Yet he rejected the party's platform and its discipline; and at the very time when everyone was repeating what he himself had written eight years earlier, George focused on the politically un-alluring topic of land-value taxation. How much of this shift may have been due to his exchange with John Stuart Mill one can only guess. But certainly by 1880 George had concluded that, while the importation of Chinese labor served the interest of monopoly, the *use* of the Chinese issue in politics must also serve monopoly since it would tend to distract and immobilize potentially radical segments of the population. In a postmortem entitled "The Kearney Agitation in California," published in *Popular Science Monthly,* George declared that the Workingmen's party was "not radical" because it was "not intelligent." Its spokesmen "satisfied with some clauses about the Chinese (not worth the paper on which they were written) readily fell in with the Grangers, imagining that in piling taxation upon capi-tal and all its shadows, they were helping the poor by taxing the rich." The result was "anything but a Workingman's constitution" and was in fact an obstacle to reform.[43]

Meanwhile Frank Roney, the trade unionist, likewise confronting the ambiguities of the Chinese issue, was pursuing a course almost opposite to George's. Roney had brought to California a viewpoint rather similar to that of John Stuart Mill as expressed in Mill's letter to Henry George. The economic argument against imported contract labor Roney regarded as irrefutable; but he felt that racial proscription

[43] George, *Popular Science Monthly,* XVII, 450, 445–446.

violated the egalitarian principles of the producer ethic upon which
any meaningful organization to improve society must be based. The
logical conclusion from this opening was the one Mill had
reached—that the only way out lay through establishing communication with the Chinese, through educating and eventually *including*
them. In California, however, Roney discovered that among non-
Chinese producers the most effective organizing tool was precisely the
crusade against the Chinese. Above all an organizer, he decided to
go with the drift of things. Thus he and George, between the July
days and the death of the Workingmen's party, exchanged positions,
passing each other at center stage. From Roney's movement in this
pas de ballet stemmed in part the first real federation of trade unions
on the Pacific Coast, which will be the subject of the next chapter.

8

THE SOCIALIST ACADEMY

The Trades Assembly

The Representative Assembly of Trades and Labor Unions sprang from that caucus of disgruntled unionists which had opposed, in the main unsuccessfully, Kearney's domination of the first convention of the Workingmen's Party of California. Defeated in their effort to incorporate their locals into the new party, the labor men had been obliged to settle for a resolution authorizing a federation of unions under the party's auspices. For the time being they were not unwilling to paddle in Kearney's wake. Plans were made for an inaugural meeting. Near the end of March in 1878, Charles Pope, a shoemaker, reported to the arrangements committee that delegations from fifteen unions would attend. These, he said, "were quite as many as could be reckoned in existence." [1] Trade unionism was clearly at a low ebb.

The gathering itself slightly exceeded Pope's anticipation. Forty-four delegates took part, representing eighteen organizations, though several of these could only loosely be described as trade unions. Of those appearing, from this distance, to have been bona fide, most fell within the same groupings that had been evident during the labor activities of the late sixties. Building construction, and shipyard and metal trades accounted for eight organizations and probably a substantial majority of the membership represented. However, it seems to have been largely the printers and shoemakers who provided the initiative for the new federation. Its first president was a member of the typographical union.[2]

The Representative Council of Trades and Labor Unions—or Trades Assembly as it came to be called—adopted a constitution and imposed a per capita tax of five cents per member upon its affiliates,

---

[1] San Francisco *Examiner*, March 25, 1878.
[2] San Francisco *Chronicle*, April 1, 1878.

in return promising financial aid to resist wage cuts.[3] Little was said during these years about wage increases. Throughout 1878 and 1879 the Trades Assembly clung to a tenuous existence. One finds references to occasional resolutions, a memorial to the president, an expression of hope for national labor federation, a protest against the purchase of Chinese-made uniforms by the United States Army and Post Office, and finally a flurry of activity in support of a local cabinet-makers' strike. These activities comprised about all the organizational display the unionists could afford.[4]

At the beginning, however, the problem which centrally engrossed their attention was neither the continuance of hard times nor Chinese competition, but their own relationship to the Workingmen's Party of California. Now that they had a going thing of their own, they were not anxious for Kearney's intervention. Even at the preliminary arrangements committee meeting early in the year, there had been, according to the *Examiner,* "a general apprehension that the 'politicians of the Workingmen's Party'" might try to take over. "If these politicians," a spokesman for the Stone Cutters' Union was reported to have warned, "should come in and yell for this man and that man (I don't mention any names), why there's an end of the amalgamation." And a Mr. Purvis of the Carpenters exhorted his fellow unionists to "keep the bulldozers out." All this was so much in tune with what the *Examiner* would have wished to report that it need not necessarily be taken at face value. The outcome, at any rate, was a decision to hold the first session behind closed doors; and it seems clear that this exclusiveness, as well as a resolution adopted by the new assembly limiting itself "strictly to matters pertaining to trade and labor organizations" and pledging never to "indorse any party . . . or nominee of any party," were both aimed at the Kearneyites.[5]

Though Frank Roney had offered the resolution at the Workingmen's Convention which led to formation of the Trades Assembly, he had as yet taken no part in its activities. He seems to have been fully occupied during that spring and summer with his labors as party organizational director and with his power struggle against Kearney. Probably most of those trade unionists who had participated in the Workingmen's party sided with Roney when the showdown came in May. Of this there is little direct evidence, yet the assumption seems reasonable in view of certain clues: The *Examiner* identified Roney's faction as consisting of "resolute and respectable workingmen who con-

3 *Examiner,* April 8, 1878.

4 Ira B. Cross, *A History of the Labor Movement in California* (Berkeley, 1935), 130–131, 151; *Examiner,* November 4, 1878; February 21, March 9, August 19, November 4, 6, 15, 17–19, 24, December 8, 15, 1879.

5 *Chronicle,* April 1, 1878; *Examiner,* March 25, 1878.

stitute the bone and sinew, the brains, the worth, the integrity"—intending, one would suppose, to distinguish established skilled tradesmen from the unskilled and the unemployed. An organizational meeting of seamen, probably held under the wing of the Trades Assembly, was reported to have denied Kearney the floor and ejected his henchman, Carl Browne, the journalist (whom we last met in conversation with Reverend Kalloch half a minute before Kalloch was gunned down by De Young). Late in May (after the party split) a group calling itself the Cooks and Waiters' Anti-Coolie Association was on the verge of calling a strike. Spokesmen from the Trades Assembly pledged support, although the Cooks and Waiters were not yet affiliated with the assembly. The president of the Cooks and Waiters' Anti-Coolie Association was one John Finnerty, who was serving simultaneously as chairman of a committee set up by the Roney faction of the party to prepare charges of corruption and betrayal against Kearney. And finally, Roney himself would, within the next two years, emerge as outstanding leader of the Trades Assembly.[6]

By the end of the summer of 1878 the party and the Trades Assembly were committed to divergent paths. Kearney's men had been successfully excluded from the assembly, which took no part in the campaign for delegates to the constitutional convention. And among Workingmen elected to that convention were few if any active trade unionists. Here was one reason for Roney's low estimate of their competence, and also perhaps a factor in their failure to push for significant labor enactments. This separation of labor politics from trade unionism would divide the labor movement in California for another three decades at least and, during that time, would merge into the classic no-politics stance of the American Federation of Labor.

The year 1881 brought a temporary respite in the succession of lean years. Labor activities soon displayed a more affluent style. Unions long defunct sprang to life again. Thus a group of carpenters came together under the leadership of Edward C. Owens to apply for a charter from the newly formed national brotherhood.[7] Early in 1882 they issued an address to their fellow craftsmen: Despite technical innovations and despite the "extraordinary skill and celerity required" in the trade, wages had not increased nor had hours been shortened. The 1,000 or 1,500 carpenters of the Bay Area had "been without semblance of a union for the past ten years"; during that period their condition had "retrograded or remained passive." What then was to be done? The words that followed might have been aimed directly at Henry Ward Beecher:

[6] *Examiner*, May 2, 1878; March 30, 1878; May 21, 25, 1878.
[7] San Francisco *Truth*, February 11, 1882.

> We have . . . let the market value of our labor be regulated by chance. . . . There is no more pernicious idea than that pet theory of political economists about supply and demand; that things will regulate themselves, as water finds its own level. This is well enough for the inanimate world, but men are not sticks and stones; their social relations to each other cannot be regulated by the law of gravity. . . . Organized action is the true policy of progress.[8]

The charter arrived, and Local 22 of the United Brotherhood of Carpenters and Joiners of America was founded. Locals 35 in San Rafael and 36 in Oakland followed within the year—all three having remained in continuous existence to the present.

Ira Cross in his study of California labor listed forty-nine local unions active in San Francisco during the years 1882–1883.[9] Since Charles Pope, the shoemaker organizer of the Trades Assembly, had found only eighteen unions then existing, it follows that thirty-one had appeared (or reappeared) during the five subsequent years; and probably most of them, like the Carpenters, came into being after 1881. A majority (26) were anchored in the three old industries: building trades (10), maritime (9), and metal trades (7). Nearly all were in crafts which had been organized during the earlier heyday. In addition to the twenty-six basic industry locals, there were now twenty-three others scattered through various trades and industries. Among them was the oldest union on the Pacific Coast, that of the printers, and two more almost as venerable—the tailors and the cigar makers. But most of these were new unions recently established among draymen and carters, beer bottlers, butchers, waiters, cooks, bakers. Simply to list the categories suggests that this fourth grouping of unions which was developing outside the three basic industries was composed mainly of service trades. San Francisco now offered a great consumer market; and as something like fair economic weather returned, service tradesmen too were resolving that in "organized action" lay "the true policy of progress." [10]

Characteristic of service trades was medium or low skill. Few were apprenticeable; and since their members could readily be replaced, these unions were economically weaker than those of the three basic sectors. This, together with the fact that the consumer market had come as a secondary development, explains their delayed entrance upon the scene.[11]

8 *Truth*, February 25, 1882.

9 Cross, *History of the Labor Movement*, 134, 143–144, 325 n. 12.

10 *Truth*, February 25, 1882.

11 The generalizations of the preceding paragraph require certain modifications. Not all apprenticeable trades were in the three basic sectors, nor were all low-

Sources of Leadership

Over the burgeoning flock of local unions presided the delegated council known as the Trades Assembly. Ira Cross credits the assembly with creating most of these new, or reestablished unions; but the relationship was probably not that simple. A report of a meeting of the Trades Assembly early in April, 1882, shows only fourteen affiliates—four fewer than had attended the inaugural session four years earlier. Unions organized by a mother council would be likely to begin as affiliates to that council, even though they might later break away.[12] But the new unions were not affiliated. What this suggests is that the Trades Assembly, for the time being at least, was not playing a key role in the spread of unionism. Roney, in fact, described the assembly upon his first coming into it as "no better than a mutual admiration club." [13]

Given the temper of the times and the return of prosperity, a certain amount of spontaneous growth might be expected. But spontaneity in the organization of trade unions, like mutation in evolution, cannot be counted on for rapid results; and what was occurring in these years of the eighties was definitely rapid. Where did the drive come from? The answer seems to be that it came from two already organized groups—the socialists and the Knights of Labor.

The socialists, it may be recalled, had with somewhat more courage than wisdom rushed to the front lines during the crisis of 1877. In California they were shouldered aside within a matter of hours by the anticoolie campaigners, subsequently led by Kearney. They then circled uneasily at the fringes, torn, as radicals have been so often, between the conflicting desires to be ideologically correct and to be "where the masses are." As to that, there was scarcely any question; and the socialists soon began drifting into, perhaps consciously infiltrating, the Workingmen's party. The activities of Beerstecher, before he became a man of property, furnish a case in point. And at the

skill groupings in the service sector. The exception of the Printers' Union has already been noted; on the other side, sailoring and longshoring in the maritime sector were predominantly low-skill occupations. An indication of their relative weakness is the fact that the Sailors established the permanence of their union only in the 1890s (Paul S. Taylor, *The Sailors' Union of the Pacific* [New York, 1923]. Comparable efforts of West Coast longshoremen continued into the early years of the New Deal.

12 *Truth*, April 8, 1882. On May 24, *Truth* listed 29 unions in operation. One of the main incentives for members of a delegated council to organize new locals is to increase per capita income and active membership of the council; consequently, the organizer insists upon affiliation before anything else.

13 Frank Roney, *Frank Roney, Irish Rebel and California Labor Leader*, ed. Ira B. Cross (Berkeley, 1931), 346.

convention of 1879, Kearney himself appeared in the curious role of
champion of the French Communards. A resolution condemning
"communism and agrarianism" had been introduced, backed largely
by up-country delegates. Kearney at first spoke against the resolution,
although when it appeared likely to pass, he withdrew his opposition.
Since it would be difficult to suppose that Kearney held convictions
of his own on this matter, the evidence suggests that socialists were
assuming some importance among urban cadres of the party.[14]

Roney's account bears this out. Roney testified that he had been on
the verge of joining the socialists in 1877, but went instead into the
Workingmen's Party of California because he was incensed at the
attacks on its leaders. Also, certainly, he felt the Kearney movement to
be a more effective instrument than the tiny socialist group. After
his defeat by the Kearney faction, however, Roney, when he returned
from Nevada, finally did join the socialists. The experience left a deep
impress. "I never had so much genuine pleasure in any enterprise," he
wrote, "as I had with my German and English associates in spreading
socialist propaganda. Most of them are gone and forgotten, but the
memory of them and their work remains with me as clear as when they
endeavored night after night to arouse the people to an appreciation of
their condition and the means by which to better their lots." At first
the only available means seemed to consist in boring from within the
Workingmen's ward clubs:

> I proposed that our socialist speakers should . . . address the
> [Tenth Ward] club, whose meetings were well attended. This
> proved a success. The word "socialist" was never used, nor did
> any of the socialists show an eagerness for office, which there-
> fore made them unobjectionable to the politicians of the party
> who still hoped to land a "fat" job. The word "socialist" was
> synonymous with murder, arson, destruction, and the other
> delectable terms attributed to radical reformers. Consequently
> we were careful not to use a word which would deprive us of
> our audiences. The land for the people and the abolition of
> land monopoly . . . was our theme.[15]

But to infiltrate an organization already half perishing could hardly
have seemed, for these enthusiasts, a promising venture. Some new
channel was needed.

When, six years earlier, the predecessor to the Socialistic Labor
Party of the United States (to which Roney's group was nominally

---

14 *Examiner,* June 4, 1879.
15 Roney, 273–274; 318; 332.

attached) [16] had made its appearance, it had been as a merger of the Lassallean socialists with Marxians left over from the First International. Perhaps the principal difference between these two groups lay in their attitude toward trade unionism. For the Lassalleans, unions appeared as bulwarks of the capitalist system, obstacles in the way of socialist progress. The Marxians, on the contrary, viewed unionism as a necessary stage of working class education and organization. Roney, a trade unionist before he became a socialist, dropped naturally enough into the Marxian camp, though with him it was probably not so much any variety of theory as simple pragmatism that determined the line of action. From his rather garbled account of the ideological scene in San Francisco, one gathers that most of the Germans were rigid Lassalleans. This dovetails with what we already know of the support they had given to Beerstecher's candidacy for railroad commissioner. The English-speaking socialists, on the other hand (in addition to native Americans, the group included some English and Irishmen), were either of the Marxian persuasion or ignorant of the difference between the two.[17]

In any case they were quite ready to shuffle off the Germans. Thus, when the changing economic climate of 1881 ushered in a growing season for trade unionism, they threw themselves into this cause with a passion—and with extraordinary effectiveness. Roney's first success was the organization of a sailors' union. He belonged, of course, to the union of his own trade, the Molders' International, but was more interested for the time at least in new organization than old. During the summer of 1881 the sailors affiliated with the Trades Assembly and sent up a five-man delegation, three of whom were shoreside socialists. Roney was one of these. The assembly almost immediately elected him to its presidency. After the regular six-month term, he stepped aside (into a place on the executive board) while a fellow socialist, Henry Marsden, took over the chair.[18] Other socialists busied

16 This is a guess. When Roney spoke of being about to join the socialists in 1877, he was clearly referring to the San Francisco branch of the Workingmen's Party of the United States which had organized the ill-starred sandlot meeting of July 23, 1877. The WPUS subsequently changed its name to the Socialistic Labor Party of the United States. (Howard Quint, *Forging American Socialism* [Columbia, S.C., 1953], 13–16.) A branch of the SLP was still (or again?) functioning in San Francisco in 1882. Notice of an SLP-sponsored rally to discuss "Present Existing Political Parties" appears in *Truth,* October 11, 1882.

17 Roney, 318–319, 327–328.

18 Taylor, *Sailors' Union,* 40–64. The new sailors' union collapsed in 1882. Three years later the socialist academy made a second attempt. The result was the Coast Seamen's Union, from which through various shifts and amalgamations has emerged the present Sailors' Union of the Pacific. (Roney, 342–347 and notes 8, 9; *Truth,* February 11, 1882.)

themselves in organizing or resuscitating local unions, and they too showed up at the assembly. Among them (to mention only names that will reappear) were C. F. Burgman of the Tailors; Marsden, the president after Roney and delegate from the Bookbinders' Union; Danielewicz of the Barbers; and Thomas Poyser from the Painters. Through their labors in the field, these men came to dominate the assembly and the expanding trade union apparatus.[19] And the converse was also true: in consequence of their domination they drew to themselves active labor men. The result was the gathering, at first around Roney, of a leadership caucus, a kind of socialist academy in trade unionism. This group held together for only about four years; yet its graduates were in large measure responsible for building the framework of the modern labor movement in California.

Early in 1882, with an intuition not altogether fortunate, Roney recruited into this caucus a brilliant young attorney and journalist by the name of Burnette Haskell. At the time he crossed Roney's orbit, Haskell was neither a labor militant nor a socialist. He was the editor of a Republican weekly puff sheet financed by an uncle ambitious for power within the party machine. But Haskell was looking for some cause other than that of his uncle. A few meetings of the Trades Assembly—which he came to first simply as a reporter—and some intense conversations with Roney showed him the way. He reoriented his little weekly (entitled *Truth*) from Republican truth to the workingmen's truth, and so effectively wooed the somewhat suspicious assembly delegates that they adopted the paper as their official organ.[20] Haskell soon penetrated the academy. As Roney became engrossed in trade union responsibilities, Haskell assumed the role of chief socialist theoretician and ended by leading the caucus in directions which Roney disapproved. But as of 1882 Haskell was still in harness, Roney in the driver's seat, and harmony prevailed.

Harmony prevailed between the assembly and its locals, between

[19] For socialist identification, Cross, *History of Labor Movement*, 131, 159, 165. For union affiliations, see *Truth*, Union Directory, May 24, 1882, and list of delegates to the League of Deliverance Convention, *Truth*, May 3, 1882. Danielewicz, apparently not in the Assembly at this time, was listed as one of six Barbers' Union delegates to the League of Deliverance Convention. The Trades Assembly at its semiannual election meeting in 1882 elected five officers and five executive board members. Both the outgoing and incoming presidents (Roney and Marsden) were members of the socialist group, as were the incoming financial secretary (Poyser) and two executive board members (Roney, S. Robert Wilson). (*Truth*, February 11, 1882.) C. F. Burgman, another member of the socialist group, had just returned from Pittsburgh where he had represented the Assembly at the founding convention of the Federation of Trades and Labor Unions of the United States and Canada (subsequently the AF of L).

[20] Roney, 387–390.

socialists and nonsocialists, and even between the trade unions and the Knights of Labor. The Knights, having made their appearance on the Coast some four or five years previously, had experienced the same growth cycle as had the trade unionists. They were soon able to set up a district council for the Bay Area and by 1882 listed at least eight locals for the city alone. Several of these were mixed, which meant that they included people of various occupations. The mixed assemblies probably functioned on a neighborhood basis much as had ward clubs of the Democratic or Workingmen's parties. Their focus, however, seems to have been less directly political and more turned to self-education. It emphasized the distribution of literature, economic improvement through propagandizing for cooperatives, higher wages, and shorter hours. This enumeration suggests the activities of Socialist party branches as depicted, say, in Upton Sinclair's *Jimmy Higgins*.[21] It would probably not be difficult to trace a line of descent from the mixed assembly of the Knights, by way of the nationalist clubs of the Bellamy movement and the urban groupings of Populism, to the neighborhood branches of the Socialist party. Given the American urban environment, this organizational type was a logical expression of the impulse to radical reform. During the early eighties, at least, it seemed not incompatible with unionism; seven of the Knights' Bay Area chapters were small trade unions, several of which were affiliated with the Trades Assembly as well.[22]

The unions and the Knights of Labor were not rival undertakings. To discuss them separately is to some degree merely a matter of convenience. Everything in the house of labor in those days was interpermeable; ideas overlapped; personnel swapped places. Haskell, editing what had become the official organ of the Trades Assembly, devoted his columns to the service of the Knights with impartial enthusiasm.[23] This was still the age of innocence; it would not last long.

Before turning from this idyllic interlude, however, it may be well to glance at the functioning of the Trades Assembly. What actually did it do? That it endeavored to collect a per capita tax from its

---

21 *Truth*, Union Directory, November 22, 1882; articles on the Knights of Labor, April 15, August 2, 1882; Upton Sinclair, *Jimmy Higgins* (New York, 1919); Miriam Allen DeFord, *Up-Hill All the Way: The Life of Maynard Shipley* (Yellow Springs, Ohio, 1956).

22 The seven were Painters, Patternmakers, Pressmen, Cigar Makers, White Shoemakers' League, Harness and Whipmakers, and Telegraphers. The Painters, Shoemakers, Harness and Whip Makers, and probably the Cigar Makers, were affiliated with the Trades Assembly. (*Truth*, April 8, 1882; April 21, August 11, 1883; Cross, 153–155.)

23 *Truth*, February 11, April 8, 15, 22, May 3, August 2, 23, September 20, October 18, December 20, 1882.

affiliates has already been noted, as well as the promise of aid in case of strike or lockout. Beyond this, the reports in *Truth* offer some scattered close-ups. Under socialist leadership, the assembly's organizational effectiveness had increased. There were now planned campaigns and regular progress reports. In May, basing itself upon the already existing stronghold of the Molders' International, the assembly launched a drive to unionize the metal trades. Out of a mass rally, organizing committees of boilermakers, machinists, and foundry laborers were set in motion. Results from efforts such as these, while not spectacular, were impressive. The number of listed unions rose from twenty-nine at the end of May to forty-seven at the end of November, 1882, while total claimed membership increased from 4,554 to 7,846. The assembly also set up a legislative committee, under Roney's direction, to prepare bills for submission to the next session of the legislature. It pressed the campaign—which would remain on the agenda of California labor for many decades—against the contracting of state prisoners to private employers. It tried to raise money for a labor temple. It used its influence to advance the cause of national labor federation—in pursuit of which C. F. Burgman, the journeyman tailor who was a member of Roney's academy, traveled to Pittsburgh in 1881 as delegate to the convention which established the Federation of Organized Trades and Labor Unions of the United States and Canada, predecessor of the American Federation of Labor.[24]

All these undertakings, hallmarks of normal trade unionism, could be expected to increase (as in fact they did) with the improvement of economic conditions. But what of anti-Chinese activity? Having reached a peak, so far, during the three depression winters from 1877 to 1880, would this not tend to taper off with the return of prosperity?[25]

[24] *Examiner*, May 27, 1882; *Truth*, January 28, February 4, 11, 25, March 4, April 22, May 10, 31, 1882; Roney, 347, 351–352, 391–400. Figures on union membership appear in *Truth*, May 24 and November 22, 1882. It is safe to assume that no figures on union membership during this period were accurate, especially if they had passed through Burnette Haskell's hands. One might begin by discounting 20 percent from both tallies as the measure of Haskell's enthusiasm. The relation between the two counts (that union membership nearly doubled) seems reasonable. Figures are for the city of San Francisco.

[25] For a statement of this view, S. W. Kung, *The Chinese in American Life: Some Aspects of Their History, Status, Problems and Contributions* (Seattle, 1962), 69: "Decidedly we see a correlation in the ups and downs of the anti-Chinese movement, between periods of prosperity in California and periods of depression."

Areas of Confrontation

The line of agitation prevalent during the depression winters had been carried by the unemployed. The aims of the agitators had been thwarted; and as the economic climate improved the thrust from below dwindled. However, the same factors that dissipated the pressure of unemployment increased the vigor of trade unions. Presumably, the anti-Chinese proclivities of unionists—and of the Trades Assembly which capped their apparatus—would bear some relationship to job competition between union members and Chinese laborers. Where was such competition taking place?

This chapter opened with an analysis of trade union structure in relation to four sectors of economic enterprise—building, maritime, metal trades and a miscellaneous or service trades sector. Beyond stretched a territory largely unknown to unionism in which were to be found the city's manufactories of consumer goods. These ranged all the way from basement sweatshops to great establishments like the Mission Woolens Mills. For convenience this will be referred to as sector five. It was suggested in an earlier chapter that division of labor between Chinese and non-Chinese contingents of the California labor force had followed two main lines of cleavage: for the state as a whole, between skilled or prestigious occupations and unskilled or menial occupations; and in urban areas, especially San Francisco, between local market industries on the one hand and industries compelled to market their product under conditions of national competition on the other. It is at once evident that sector five contained most of the city's national market industries and the preponderance of its un-skilled jobs. Sectors one through three by contrast (building, maritime, and metal trades, in which were the long-established strongholds of unionism) comprised almost exclusively local market industries and industries in which the skilled, apprenticeable trades predominated. In between was sector four, mostly service trades. These trades catered to a local market and their skill levels ranged from low to medium. Union organization was taking hold in some of the service trades but remained weaker than in the three basic sectors.

We are now in a position to reexamine this industrial map with a view to locating points of confrontation between unionized working-men and Chinese competitors. In the building sector no conflict had taken place at least since 1867. In metal trades there seems no evidence that such a confrontation had ever occurred. And with one important exception, the same statement would apply to the maritime sector. In respect to sector four the situation was quite different. Here in "menial" pursuits such as domestic service, laundering, vegetable and fish peddling, the Chinese retained almost unchallenged possession. They also dominated pork butchering. Most other services outside Chinatown (restaurants, butcher and grocery shops, liquor stores, breweries, saloons, cigar stores, printing establishments, livery stables, hacks, teaming and drayage concerns, and so forth) were non-Chinese. Friction developed at the fringes of these trades: white butchers, for example, kept pressing to take over the pork trade; there were occasional flurries of alarm that Chinese typesetters might be imported from Hong Kong; and efforts were made to establish mechanized laundries for the employment of white women.[26] All these, however, were minor conflicts and seldom directly concerned trade unionists.

We come finally to sector five. Here there was a long continued and noisy confrontation, involving the small white-owned shops in cigar making, shoemaking, and tailoring. In the latter two trades, the shops were devoted primarily to custom work and repairs. Taken all together, they depended for existence on the presumed high quality of their work and upon its alleged non-Chineseness. The white craftsmen employed in these shops were organized, but their organizations could scarcely be described as trade unions. They were associations of journeymen and proprietors dedicated to product differentiation, which they endeavored to achieve by means of white labor stamps and labels. Their aim was to preserve a refuge for small entrepreneurs against the march of capitalized manufacture. Such almost certainly was the union of tailors (having a claimed membership of 180), which sent C. F. Burgman as delegate to the Trades Assembly, apparently endorsed his activities in the socialist academy, and probably paid part of his expenses when he journeyed to Pittsburgh as emissary to the first convention of Trades and Labor Unions.[27] Such likewise was the League of White Shoemakers, whose master workman, J. M. Clark,

[26] The exception is that trans-Pacific vessels were taking on Chinese crewmen in Asian ports. The first organizational ventures of the socialist academy were in coastal shipping, and here there seem to have been almost no Chinese employed except a few cooks and messmen. (Taylor, *Sailors' Union* 40–44.) A report prepared by the Trades Assembly near the end of 1881 quoted the United States Shipping Commissioner of San Francisco to the effect that on deep sea vessels under his jurisdiction some 350 Chinese were employed, and that in addition there were "many" in the coasting trade as cooks and stewards. The Assembly report described the Chinese on deep sea vessels as firemen, cooks, waiters, and servants to officers. There were also said to be Chinese as cooks and officers' servants on U.S. vessels in the Pacific. Trades Assembly, "Address on Chinese Competition," *Examiner*, January 8, 1882. *Truth*, March 18, May 10, June 7, August 2, 1882.
[27] *Truth*, May 24, 1882; Roney, 285–286.

regularly advertised his shoe sales and repair shop in the pages of *Truth*.[28] And as for the Cigarmakers' Association, this was becoming so notoriously an organization of proprietors that only a few years later it was repudiated by both the Trades Assembly and the Knights of Labor. The journeymen dropped out and joined the Cigar Workers International Union of Strasser and Gompers, which only then was able to establish itself on the West Coast.[29]

Toward the end of 1881 the Trades Assembly had prepared a statistical survey of Chinese penetration. After an introductory commentary on the Chinese as "an alien race" and "producers but not consumers of American products," the report went on to summarize its findings:

> The trades that have suffered most are the cigarmakers, tailors, boot and shoemakers, makers of male and female underclothing, brush and broom making and the manufacture of slippers. . . . We find them [Chinese] employed in the manufacture of boots and shoes, barrels, boxes, brushes, brooms, blankets, bricks, blinds, clothing, canned goods, cigars and cigar boxes, cloth, cordage, furniture, flannels, gloves, harness, jute bagging, knitted goods, leather, matches, paper, ropes, soap, straw boards, sashes, saddles, shirts and underclothing of all kinds, slippers, twine, tinware, willow-ware, wine and whips; also employed as cooks, carpenters, domestic servants, expressmen, farm laborers, fishermen, firemen on steamers, laundrymen, locksmiths, miners, painters, peddlers, sign-writers, waiters, and at repairing clocks and watches. We find them employed in breweries, chemical works, flourmills, lumber and planing mills, distilleries, smelting works, powder factories, vineyards, woolen mills, tanneries, on railroads, and as laborers in almost every department of industry.[30]

The reference above to carpenters, expressmen, and painters is particularly interesting. Later stories in *Truth*, based on the same survey, spoke of 32 "Chinese expressmen" and 225 in "painting trades." Early in 1882 *Truth* reported the incorporation of a beneficial association of Chinese carpenters. Yet all this probably should not be taken as

28 *Truth*, October 11, 1882. "PATRONIZE WHITE LABOR! J. M. Clark, 337 Hayes Street, near Gough. Warrants all his boots and shoes made by white labor. He keeps first class goods, no Chinese trash, and sells very cheap. Repairing done in first class style." In the same issue, J. M. Clark is listed as "Master Workman" of Boot and Shoemakers' White Labor League of the Knights of Labor.

29 San Francisco *Daily Report*, October 31, November 11, 18, December 18, 22, 1885; January 14, 1886. See also W. W. Stone, "The Knights of Labor on the Chinese Situation," *Overland Monthly*, 2nd ser., VII (March, 1886), 225–230.

30 Roney 358, 359; Trades Assembly on Chinese Competition, *Examiner*, January 8, 1882.

evidence that white workers in these trades were encountering Chinese
competition. What it does indicate is that *inside* Chinatown, for Chinese employers, a certain amount of construction, maintenance work,
and cabinetmaking was carried on by Chinese; and the same presumably would have applied to express deliveries.[31]

As to actual statistical data in the Trades Assembly's survey, the
rather meager findings can be tabulated as follows:

	Number in Occupation	Average Wage
Boot and shoe		
white	1,100	$9–13 a week
Chinese	5,700	$20–30 monthly
Laundry		
white	615	—
Chinese	5,107	—
Cigarmaking		
white	179	—
Chinese	8,500	—
Clothing		
white	1,000 (tailors)	$15–25 (in 1876) a week
Chinese	7,510	$20–28 monthly
Peddlers (fruit and vegetable)		
white	—	—
Chinese	513	—

The compilers of this document, C. F. Burgman the tailor and Henry
Marsden the bookbinder, did not indicate the sources of their information; nor is it necessary to inquire very deeply into its accuracy.
Taken simply as evidence of how trade unionists viewed the situation
in 1881–1882, it coincides with the analysis offered above of urban
labor division by sectors of enterprise.

The conclusion from all this is that there was extraordinarily little
confrontation between union members and Chinese competitors. In the
building, maritime, or metal trades sectors, the average craftsman
could work out his entire life without ever setting eyes on an Oriental
in his own trade. The single zone of direct conflict lay in sector five

[31] *Truth,* February 11, 18, March 4, 1882. On the division of labor in Chinatown
construction work, see California, Bureau of Labor Statistics, *Third Biennial Report*
(Sacramento, 1888), 184.

along the margin where highly skilled (apprenticeable) occupations overlapped the national market industries. On one side of this narrow margin were many trade unionists but few Chinese, while on the other were large numbers of Chinese but no trade unionists. This does not mean that there was not bitter conflict for employment in the mills and sweatshops of sector five. But trade unionists were not involved because they had never entered the territory. One might argue that the presence there of Chinese had precluded unionization or, with equal logic, that the failure of unionists to secure this area had left it open to Chinese. Actually neither statement gets to the heart of the matter; the point is that the factors rendering these national market industries unorganizable by the craft unionists of the Trades Assembly and its affiliates were the same factors that constantly pulled in the lowest bidders in the labor market, whether women, children, or Chinese. Sector five had indeed been challenged—by the unemployed under the leadership of Gannon and Mrs. Smith, with the somewhat unwilling collaboration of Kearney and Kalloch. But the trade unionists at the time had been busy with their own problems and gave no assistance. In fact it was largely through fear of such leaders as Kearney and Kalloch, Gannon and Mrs. Smith that the unionists had separated themselves from the Workingmen's movement. And that was the very time when they began seriously to preach the gospel of no-politics. There were meanings within meanings contained in the factional struggle of Roney against Kearney.

By 1882 the Workingmen's party was dead; the unemployed agitation had largely subsided. The Trades Assembly was dominant. Since its membership as a whole was only marginally engaged in competition with Chinese laborers, one might suppose that pressure against the Chinese would have receded; however, the opposite was the case. The anti-Chinese impulse overshadowed and permeated every action of the Trades Assembly and of its locals. It was characteristic, for example, that the carpenters, whose lucid critique of Social Darwinism has been quoted earlier, should have adopted at the same meeting at which they ratified their new constitution a resolution declaring themselves "unutterably opposed to further Chinese immigration." [32] When the socialists, under Roney's presidency, took over leadership of the Trades Assembly, one of their first ventures had been the statistical survey on Chinese penetration. Scarcely a meeting of the Trades Assembly went by without discussion of this topic.[33]

[32] *Truth*, March 11, 1882. See above, p. 160.
[33] Trades Assembly on Chinese Competition, *Examiner*, January 8, 1882; *Truth*, February–May, 1882, especially February 18 and March 4.

Eventually the executive committee, directed by Roney, geared its entire organizational effort to the anti-Chinese campaign by adopting a Trades Assembly white labor label. Right of use was to be leased to affiliates in good standing, the message to the public being that *union* labor was the only reliable guarantor of *white* labor. Even in the rather remote matter of national federation the Chinese issue was involved. Had it been simply a question of expressing support in principle, a letter to the founding convention of the American Federation of Labor at Pittsburgh would have sufficed. One of the prime reasons for dispatching C. F. Burgman in person was to rally the eastern brethren against the Asian menace; and on his return to San Francisco the chief burden of Burgman's accounting was that in this task he had succeeded. He made his report at a public meeting of the assembly— the very one, as it happened, first attended by Burnette Haskell.[34] Out of this coincidence sprang Haskell's conversion, followed by the enlistment of his weekly paper to the labor cause. In the fifth issue of *Truth*, dated exactly one month after the assembly meeting, the young editor set forth his credo as follows:

> There are corporate powers that do not care, so long as they can fill their coffers with extravagant profits at the expense of the blood of the Caucasian race. . . . In order to fortify ourselves against this menacing migration of the savage, vicious, idol-worshipping and barbarous race, every man in America should be at work. . . . This is a war of races and should be conducted on the same principles that have brought success in other wars.

Then, not yet having forgotten his legal training, Haskell appended to this summons the stipulation that what he referred to was "political action." [35]

The League of Deliverance

In 1880 the work of renegotiating the Burlingame Treaty was completed. The new text was not unduly onerous upon China; it gave to the United States the option to "regulate, limit or suspend" but not "entirely prohibit" entrance of Chinese laborers if and when such action seemed desirable. No limitations were to be placed on the movements of any classes other than laborers (i.e., businessmen, tourists, scholars). Chinese laborers in the United States were to be pro-

[34] Roney, 385–387, n. 27; *Truth*, January 28, February 25, April 8, July 19, 1882.
[35] *Truth*, February 25, 1882.

tected by the federal government and guaranteed the privilege of re-entry if they left the country. Labor periodicals in the West and some Democratic papers attacked these provisions as being far too mild.[36]

Meanwhile, the rate of Chinese immigration had been fluctuating dramatically. Figures kept by the San Francisco Customs House showed annual arrivals as having averaged well over 16,000 for the four years from 1873 through 1876. In 1877 the number dropped to less than 10,000 and thereafter declined steadily to less than 6,000 in 1880. The following year Chinese entries tripled and, for the first seven months of 1882, leaped to an all-time high of nearly 27,000.[37] Diverse reasons were suggested for these fluctuations. Denis Kearney, who throughout the eighties made periodic efforts to stage a comeback, argued that the decline of entry after 1877 had been due to terror inspired by the Workingmen's party, while the later increase resulted from the party's weakness.[38] On the other hand, this same increase could be explained as a last ditch effort on the part of would-be immigrants to get in before the shutting of the gates, which, since revision of the Burlingame Treaty two years earlier, had been a virtual certainty. There was undoubtedly truth to both contentions. Oddly, not much was made of the rather obvious consideration that the same economic circumstances which created jobs for white workers would also create jobs for Chinese, that Chinese immigration had fallen off during depression years and now rose with economic recovery.[39]

Treaty revision removed the last apparent obstacle to congressional restriction. Accordingly, a bill was introduced by California's Senator Miller to place a twenty-year embargo on the entrance of Chinese laborers. This moved toward passage, and the Republican and Democratic leadership in the West seemed confident of its becoming law. The Trades Assembly maintained a critical attitude. *Truth* even argued that the Miller bill was no better than a camouflage; that twenty years was not enough; that what was needed was not restriction

[36] Elmer Clarence Sandmeyer, *The Anti-Chinese Movement in California* (Urbana, Ill., 1939), 91–92; San Francisco *Weekly Stock Report*, January 20, 1881; *Truth*, May 17, November 1, 1882.

[37] Sandmeyer, 16; *Truth*, July 19, 1882.

[38] *Truth*, February 11, 1882.

[39] On second glance not so odd, since the debate was not over desirability of exclusion, but how effectively it could be achieved by the moderate methods of the bipartisan establishment. For all participants in this discussion it was a standard article of faith that Chinese immigration was the *cause* of hard times. For examples, see Trades Assembly on Chinese Competition, *Examiner*, January 8, 1882; U.S., Congress, House of Representatives, *Chinese Immigration. Report of the Select Committee on the Causes of the Present Depression of Labor*, 46th Cong., 2nd Sess., Report No. 572 (Washington, 1880); and John Rogers Commons et al., *History of Labour in the United States*, 4 vols. (New York, 1918), II, 265–266.

of a class but total exclusion of a race; and that the language of the bill contained so many loopholes that the result would be to legalize rather than restrict entry. It seems clear, however, from the general tone of the press and from the success of a bipartisan rally endorsed by the Board of Trade and Chamber of Commerce—in honor of which the governor declared a legal holiday—that this negative line was not commanding much acceptance.[40]

Near the end of March 1882 the Miller bill, already approved by the Senate, passed the House of Representatives. Twelve days later President Arthur vetoed it. The response in California was predictable: Republicans were embarrassed, Democrats indignant. There were parades, resolutions, mass rallies. *Truth* reported, perhaps accurately, that President Arthur was hanged or burned in effigy in Merced, Napa, Williams, and Tomales. California seemingly had been betrayed by the leadership of the Republican party. The president's action, Haskell wrote in *Truth*, had been brought about through "the vile influences of the Central Pacific Railroad and the monopolies, the corporations and Chinese employers of the Coast." [41] The bipartisan establishment, then, had fallen on its face. If such were the situation, it was both the duty and the opportunity of labor to seize the helm of the foundering ship. This clearly was how Roney and his colleagues of the socialist academy viewed the matter.

Early in April the Trades Assembly voted to call a convention "whereby we may unitedly deliver this Coast from Chinese competition." At the next meeting the official call was adopted, extending an invitation to "trade and labor unions, local assemblies of the Knights of Labor, Grangers, Caucasians, and all organizations of a bona fide labor character." But the call hinted that certain guests might not be welcome: "It is particularly requested that no organization will send as delegates any politician, demagogue, 'crank' or hobbyist, as such would undoubtedly create inharmony." [42]

The convention assembled on April 24 at Verein Eintracht Hall in San Francisco. A large crowd turned out for the occasion, two hundred more or less being official delegates from some fifty organizations. There was at once a dispute over credentials. It appeared that certain prospective delegates were suspected by the credentials committee of coming from organizations that were not "of a bona fide labor character" and which had in fact been created solely for the purpose of

[40] Sandmeyer, 92–93; *Truth*, March 4, 11, 1882.
[41] Sandmeyer, 93; *Truth*, April 8, 15, 1882. For a denunciation of President Arthur by the Knights of Labor, see *Examiner*, April 17, 1882.
[42] *Truth*, April 8, 15, 1882; Roney, 359.

providing an entrée into the convention. Among these were several "anti-Chinese leagues" called together some two weeks earlier under the guidance of Denis Kearney. As this issue came to a vote, an apparently hostile crowd—led by Kearney himself—was hammering at the doors of Eintracht Hall. Inside there was frightened talk of appealing for police protection against the bulldozers. But Roney, who was serving as chairman—the old antagonists were matched once again—kept a cool head. He called for a volunteer brigade of sergeants-at-arms, had them separate off that portion of the hall in which the unchallenged delegates were seated, then ordered the doors opened. The crowd came in, listened while the delegates, after taking turns in denouncing Kearneyism, cast their votes overwhelmingly to support the credentials committee. Soon afterward Kearney and his colleagues departed, leaving the Trades Assembly in undisputed control.[43]

A list of delegates published in *Truth* shows that the convention accepted credentials for 195. These represented, aside from the Trades Assembly itself, forty unions and one Grange. Of the unions, thirty-one were located in the city, while eight of the nine from outside were miners' organizations of the mountain counties and Nevada. No representatives of the Knights of Labor were listed as such, not because they were absent, but because they had chosen to come as trade unionists from their own local trade assemblies. There was, however, in addition to the purge of Kearneyites, one further exclusion; credentials had been denied to representatives of the Socialistic Labor party. It is perfectly clear from the acts of the convention and from the men it chose as officers and committee members that Roney's socialist academy held control from beginning to end. This suggests that the divergence between trade union socialists and the political (or Lassallean) tendency had widened into a formal split, and that the latter were the ones who kept up connection with the national center—the Socialistic Labor party. They must have comprised a very small group. Apparently they were collaborating with Kearney in the belief that he could provide them a link to some kind of mass base.[44] At all events they received short shrift from their erstwhile comrades of the socialist academy.

Having purified its ranks, the convention got along with the usual declarations and pronouncements. At last on the third day of its

[43] *Examiner*, April 25, 26, 1882; *Truth*, April 15, May 3, 1882; Roney, 359–360.
[44] *Truth*, May 3, 1882; *Examiner*, April 26, 1882. The *Examiner*, April 26, referred to a "Mr. D'Arcy" as a speaker at a meeting of one of the anti-Chinese leagues later denied credentials at the convention. A James D'Arcy had been organizer for the Workingmen's Party of the United States in San Francisco in 1877, according to a report in the *Examiner*, July 25, 1877.

sessions it turned its attention to the matter which, presumably, it had been called to act on. This came in the form of a report by Roney for the Plan of Action Committee. A permanent structure was to be established, known as the League of Deliverance, embracing the North American continent west of the Rockies, from the Mexican border to British Columbia. Membership would be open to all persons eligible for citizenship (of the United States, presumably) who were willing to pay ten cents initiation and pledge their "honor" not to "employ or patronize Chinese directly or indirectly" or "knowingly patronize . . . any person who does employ Chinese." [45] An executive committee quartered in San Francisco would be elected at each general convention. Here, in essence, was the old anticoolie club apparatus much as it had first appeared in 1867, though now expanded theoretically at least to cover the entire Pacific slope. But the Plan of Action Committee went on to propose several new features.

Ostracism and boycott, explicit in the membership pledge, were to become the means of financing the organization. Merchants, manufacturers, businessmen, tradesmen, and peddlers would be offered, for a fee of $1.00 per month, shop cards issued by the league (or by the Trades Assembly) [46] upon condition of adherence to the league's pledge and submission to regular inspection by its officers. Carrying out such inspections would be the task of the executive, as well as the recruitment and dispatch of white labor for employers who declared themselves willing to be rid of their Chinese hands. Thus, the anticoolie club pattern was to be transformed, under leadership of the unionists, into an instrument for trade union organization.

But this was not all. The executive committee was instructed to subdivide the Pacific slope into districts according to density of Chinese population. Singling out these districts one by one, the executive was to proceed as follows: first, to notify all Chinese to depart within a specified period of time; second, in case the order was not complied with, to declare the district "dangerous" and advise members and sympathizers of the League of Deliverance to get out of the area. Then the final step: "it shall be the duty of the Executive Committee to call upon the League to abate such danger by force. This abatement to be done with as little violence as is compatible with a certain enforcement of the order. That such course be adopted in regard to every district until no Chinese remains on our shores." [47] Roney and his colleagues had here blueprinted that dream of "abatement" by

[45] *Examiner*, April 28, 1882; *Truth*, May 3, 1882.
[46] *Examiner*, April 28, 1882.
[47] *Truth*, May 3, 1882; *Examiner*, April 28, 1882.

violence which even Kearney and Kalloch had spoken of only in the abstract language of metaphor.

After debating this program seriatim, the convention approved it without amendment and rose en masse to take the pledge of membership. Then came a few final items of business, an instruction that the executive draft a constitution which would be nonpolitical and nonpartisan; and *Truth* was "adopted as the official journal" of the organization. Throughout, the apocalyptic mood prevailed. This was summed up on the last day by an address to laboring men of the nation. Presented by Edward Owen of the Carpenters, the message thanked the workers for their support, to which was attributed the passage of the anti-Chinese bill through Congress. But one man by his veto had thwarted the will of the nation. The crisis was at hand: "further immigration of the Chinese to this country means death to American labor. Resistance is now our duty. . . . Should the time come when the workingmen of the Pacific Coast shall be obliged to unfurl the Stars and Stripes against the Chinese dragon in defense of their homes, we shall call upon you and expect your aid and comfort in the struggle. Accept from us the hand of fellowship." Roney moved the adoption.[48]

When the newly elected executive board met, it became clear that the league was to embody one further innovation. There were to be full-time paid officials. Frank Roney and William Eastman, a printer and delegate to the Trades Assembly, assumed the posts of president and secretary, their salaries being fixed at $75 a month.[49] At the time they were probably the only full-time salaried union functionaries on the West Coast.

Restriction

After the veto, Senator Miller's bill was revised and submitted with the term of restriction reduced from twenty years to ten. Again the bill passed Congress and came to President Arthur—who signed it on May 6, less than two weeks after Roney and Eastman had been installed as executive officers of the League of Deliverance. Restriction was to take effect ninety days from the date of signature. The new law applied to Chinese laborers, skilled or unskilled, from any foreign port, and was to be enforced by penalties of fine or imprisonment of shipmasters found in violation and by forfeiture of vessels. In addition

---

48 *Truth*, May 3, 1882; *Examiner*, April 28, 1882.

49 Roney, 363, wrote that the executive board set the salaries "without indicating the source thereof." Roney recalled that he gave up a job at Risdon Iron Works which "with easily earned overtime" was paying $130 a month.

state and federal courts were forbidden to naturalize Chinese. While it was not a foregone conclusion at the time that the embargo would be renewed upon expiration of the ten-year period, it must at least have seemed highly probable.[50] The act represented a near total victory for the exclusionists.

That the enactment was due to massive agreement in the West on the Chinese question is unmistakable.[51] Yet the origins of that consensus were not primarily western. Patterns of thought and organization which shaped the anti-Chinese movement had stemmed from the Jacksonian era in the East. The resurgence of these patterns in California politics deeply affected the national debate on Reconstruction. Abandonment of Reconstruction by the Republicans, together with the erosion of the abolitionist line within the party, had in effect given permission for the bipartisan anti-Chinese alliance. And there was one other factor as well. Steam transportation, especially the completion of the transcontinental railroad and the Southern Pacific network to the Gulf of Mexico, assured investors interested in the Pacific slope alternative sources of labor supply.[52] If, as suggested earlier, principled opposition to restrictions on Chinese immigration had by 1880 ceased to have much political substance, then the vetoes and revisions which intervened between 1880 and the final adoption of restriction can best be seen as a successful effort to secure the western labor supply against abrupt dislocation. The exemption, and privilege of return, for Chinese already in the United States accomplished precisely this. And in case the resident Chinese labor force dwindled more rapidly than anticipated—owing to death or emigration—or in case alternative sources of supply failed to materialize—the shortened time limit (ten years instead of twenty) provided a convenient point for review of the entire problem.

[50] Sandmeyer, *Anti-Chinese Movement,* 93–94. Restriction was renewed in 1892 for ten years and again in 1902. In 1904 all existing laws against Chinese entry were reaffirmed without time limit. In addition, by acts of Congress, by treaty revision, and by administrative measures, the enforcement mechanisms were tightened, the reentry privilege was curtailed, and restriction was extended to American insular possessions (1902). In 1904 Chinese laborers already in those possessions were barred from coming to the mainland. (Sandmeyer, 106–108.)

[51] Sandmeyer, 109–111.

[52] *Truth,* July 5, 1882, carried an editorial article charging that the Southern Pacific, with the approval of Senator Miller, was planning large-scale importation of laborers from southern and eastern Europe via New Orleans. See also September 27, 1882.

9

DEADLOCK OF LEADERSHIP

League of Deliverance: The Attack from the Left

For leaders of the Trades Assembly the enactment of legislation restricting Chinese immigration came at a most inopportune moment. They had just mortgaged their program to the League of Deliverance, and now the ground was being sluiced out from under their feet. Strategically they had two alternatives: to abandon the Chinese issue (as Henry George had already done) and climb onto the high ground of more "fundamental" social criticism; or, focusing even more narrowly on the old topic, to attack the bipartisan alliance from the "left."

Truth, typically, began to move in both directions at once. Warning against any illusions that the problem might at last have been resolved, *Truth* described the new act as "practically worthless to serve the object sought." Neither would it halt the influx of Chinese nor rid the state of those already on hand. Only direct action by the people would meet the need. "Whatever California wants done, she must do herself." At the same time the paper seemed to be struggling for broader visions. Its editor dabbled in spiritualism, pseudo-science, utopian romance. The first issue after signature of the anti-Chinese act carried an article eulogizing Charles Darwin as "soldier" of science and enlightenment and, under the headline "Beautiful," "John G. Whittier's Grand and Perfect Poem," which opened with the following stanza:

> But life shall on and upward go;
> Th' eternal step of progress beats
> To that grand anthem, calm and slow,
> Which God repeats.

On this march of progress the vanguard were to be, not the Christian churches, but workingmen organized into the Knights of Labor. In a series of articles beginning in April and continuing through the remainder of the year, *Truth* eulogized the Knights as the leading national champions of radical reform.[1]

Yet the "grand anthem" was not merely of the Pacific slope, nor of one nation; it must be worldwide. Thus, oddly, under the headline "Forgotten," the preamble to the Declaration of Independence appeared in midsummer. Subsequent issues featured Victor Hugo's salute to the Communards, essays by Henry George, John Swinton's interviews with Herbert Spencer and Karl Marx, articles on Ferdinand Lassalle, Louis Blanc, M. H. Hyndman, Krapotkin, and Bakunin—and on John Brown.[2] Haskell (for it is obvious that *Truth* must have been written and edited out of his vest pocket) had taken the whole world as his stage. Briefly, the Chinese obsession yielded to other interests. The columns of the little weekly sparked and crackled to every intellectual stimulus of those highly charged years.

But what was possible for *Truth* was altogether impossible for the League of Deliverance. The new organization was, by the circumstances of its founding, limited to a single issue. Three weeks after President Arthur's signature, the officers of the league showed themselves more than ever engrossed in the apocalyptic mood:

> The supreme moment has arrived from which shall date either the decadence of our civilization and our country, or the unimpeded glory of the one and unrestricted prosperity and happiness of the other. . . . The Chinese restriction bill is a weak and sickly invention designed to lull us into security while this silent invasion proceeds. Let us all, men and women, unite for the common purposes of race and national preservation. Let not an inch of land or habitation be leased, rented or sold to these people. . . . Interdict every business and industry they engage in.[3]

If the league was to survive, it must survive by outdoing in anti-Chineseness the authors of the anti-Chinese act. This was the task to which Roney and Eastman and their colleagues on the executive board now turned their hands.

They had, from the inaugural convention, inherited two distinct programs—first, making the league auxiliary to organizational activi-

[1] The two quotations are from San Francisco *Truth*, May 17 and May 10, 1882; and see February 4, 11, March 11, April 15, May 24, June 28, August 2, 23, September 20, October 18, November 1, December 20, 1882; and March 28, 1883.

[2] *Truth*, in the order referred to: August 2, December 13, November 8, December 13, November 15, October 11, August 9, December 13, November 9, 15, 22, December 13, November 8, 1882.

[3] *Truth*, May 31, 1882.

ties of the Trades Assembly and, second, the plan for abatement by violence. The leaguers at once set about assembling neighborhood branches on the old anticoolie club pattern. For this work the second program furnished the emotional tone. Thus, Roney (who would later write that restrictions against the Chinese had seemed to him "brutal and such as no self-respecting people would dream of imposing upon the members of any race within their midst") [4] told a Laguna district rally that all those who tolerated the Asian influx were "only worthy of being slaves and entitled to the threatened subjugation." [5]

So far as practical activity was concerned, however, the league from the beginning concentrated on the first program and ignored the second. At what was probably its initial executive board meeting, an appeal was sent out to all trade unions—"as this was essentially a labor movement"—requesting names of unionists who might be helpful in organizing branches for the league. Discussion ranged over such projects as setting up a white broom factory, encouraging retail butchers to go after the Chinese-dominated pork trade, supporting a Women's Aid Society in the operation of laundries worked by white women. Abatement by violence seems not to have been on the agenda.[6] It may be that the founding convention would never have voted for the abatement program had the delegates believed there was much likelihood of its being taken seriously. Yet even to enunciate such a program under the circumstances was a serious undertaking. To this extent the trade unionists had waded into the river, and at the crucial moment—like Kearney and Kalloch before them—had dared not cross the Rubicon.

Roney gave his attention instead to the retail shoe trade. A canvass of downtown stores showed nearly all willing to pay their dollar a month for the league shop card and to take the pledge which obligated them to dispose of all Chinese goods within ninety days and thereafter to handle only the product of white labor. There were, of course, chiselers. Two or three merchants, after signing with the league, hurriedly stocked up on Chinese-made shoes in order to be able to sell at white labor prices under the auspices of the league shop card. Since the merchants informed on one another, Roney was easily able to expose the maneuver.[7]

Given this much of an entrée, he apparently decided on a show of

[4] Frank Roney, *Frank Roney, Irish Rebel and California Labor Leader*, ed. Ira B. Cross (Berkeley, 1931), 366; see above, pp. 176–177.

[5] *Truth*, May 10, 1882.

[6] *Ibid.*

[7] Roney, 366–368.

strength. Early in July, under the heading, "League of Deliverance Attention (Official)," the following notice appeared in *Truth:* "Members of the League of Deliverance will report for active duty at the above headquarters on Wednesday morning, July 5th, 1882, at 9 A.M. None admitted without membership cards. By order—Executive Committee." [8]

The sequel to this mysterious summons came that same afternoon. An elderly man bearing sandwich boards (A. J. Starkweather, one of the most faithful members of the socialist academy) [9] stationed himself in front of Butterfield's Shoe Store on Market Street. The proprietor had refused to go along with the league—a fact now made known to the public by means of leaflets as well as by the halves of the sandwich. A crowd soon gathered and the sandwich man was arrested for obstructing traffic. Another took his place. The police confiscated the sandwich boards. A replacement then appeared clad in a linen duster with the message about Butterfield painted across his back.

Roney having arranged for posting of bail, was able to spring his pickets almost as quickly as they were locked up. For three days this round robin continued, stimulating a good deal of urban hilarity and (by Roney's account) driving Butterfield out of business. Roney himself donned the linen duster long enough to be arrested so that he could stand trial as test defendant. The result was acquittal; after which the hundred or more charges against Roney's several associates were dismissed. In his history of California labor, Ira Cross accorded to the Butterfield pickets the "distinction" of being the first persons ever arrested for boycotting in California. [10]

Pressure by the leaguers on retail outlets was to be coordinated with a drive by the Trades Assembly and the Boot and Shoemakers' White Labor League to organize the city's shoe factories, most of which employed Chinese. This campaign, too, got off to a fast start. Before the end of May, *Truth,* noting the "sudden life instilled" into the Shoemakers' League, reported that ninety-four new members had been admitted and the union had been obliged to move to a larger hall. [11] The daily *Call* referred to a "depression in the Chinese factories" and "a revival of business" for white labor establishments. "About thirty of our large factories, which were employing Chinese, have discharged them and are now employing white labor exclusively." [12]

[8] *Truth,* July 5, 1882.

[9] Roney, 318–319.

[10] Ira B. Cross, *A History of the Labor Movement in California* (Berkeley, 1935), 325 n. 9; *Truth,* July 12, 26, August 2, 1882; Roney, 368–371.

[11] Trades Assembly on Chinese Competition, *Examiner,* January 8, 1882; *Truth,* May 31, June 28, August 2, 1882.

[12] San Francisco *Morning Call,* July 31, 1882.

Nor were these results confined to the boot and shoe trade. Requests for boycotts of offending establishments, Roney wrote, came from all over the city. By the first week of June, thirteen league branches had been set in motion, and Roney, at his Market Street office, presided over Sunday meetings of branch presidents just as Kearney had done in the old days.[13] Roney was also keeping a lookout for possibilities of unionization. "I preferred organizing unions," he recalled, "to organizing branches of the League of Deliverance, for the reason that the unions were permanent, or could be made so, while I knew that branches of the League were mere transitory affairs created for a passing purpose." [14] A coopers' union and unions of laundry and cannery workers were set up out of the league headquarters. In July, Roney reported to the Trades Assembly that, thanks to the efforts of the league, Chinese servants were being replaced by white girls; employment of Chinese laundrymen in the city had been cut down by one third; and five white labor laundries had been established. Hundreds of Chinese shoemakers had been discharged to make room for white workers. Moreover, the sale of white label cigars had risen in three months from 1,800 a month to 6,000. The entire issue, Roney concluded, had been taken from the hands of "political knaves" and turned over to the "producing classes of this coast for final settlement." [15]

It was this same session of the assembly that adopted a proposal, noted earlier, for a white labor emblem. Consisting of an arm and hammer, anvil and cogwheel, and contained within the circling words, "Trades Assembly Hall and Cooperative Association—White Labor," the emblem was to be reserved for use by affiliates in good standing. These in turn must assess manufacturers within their jurisdiction not less than one-tenth of 1 percent nor more than 1 percent of the wholesale value of products to which the stamp was affixed. Roney had served as secretary to the subcommittee that prepared this plan. Several weeks earlier, the League of Deliverance, anticipating such action by the assembly, had decided that league members would be obligated not only to avoid shops failing to display the League's placards, but to refuse all goods which did not bear the Trades Assembly's stamp.[16] In blueprint at least the labors of the league would interlock with the functioning of the assembly.

At its high tide of success the league undertook a project even more ambitious than the purification of the boot and shoe trade. This was

13 Roney, 371; *Truth*, May 31, June 7, 1882.
14 Roney, 383–384.
15 Roney, 378, 384–385; *Truth*, July 19, 1882.
16 See above, p. 176; *Truth*, July 19, June 14, 1882.

an invasion of the laundry business. Roney recorded the sequence of events as follows: Two energetic young men (one of whom later became police chief of San Francisco) approached him to enlist his aid in the establishment of an up-to-date steam laundry which would employ only white labor. The young men contributed to the league; Roney helped write their advertising. Also, presumably, he threw support of the league to their enterprise, the California Laundry. It thrived. Within a few weeks they had more business than they could handle, and they found it necessary to increase the pace and the hours of labor of their employees. The employees, however, perhaps through contact with the League of Deliverance, had already absorbed certain fundamentals of trade unionism. Some walked off the job. The proprietors countered by farming out rough wash to Chinese wash houses and using their own premises for the finish work.[17]

When news of this démarche reached Roney, he was understandably displeased and saw no alternative but to turn the fire power of the league against the apostates. Space was bought in daily papers for denouncing them; 50,000 handbills were printed and distributed. Since a portion at least of the business that had brought such an embarrassing bonanza to the new laundry came from barber shops, and since most of the city's barbers were unionized and their union strongly supported the league, it is no wonder the California Laundry soon gave up the ghost under Roney's barrage. The league had thus won another victory.[18] Already its days were numbered.

The Limits of Craft Unionism

The immediate difficulty was that not enough money was coming in. Roney's mid-July report to the Trades Assembly showed that since the founding convention in April, the league had taken in only $485. Eastman, the secretary, had resigned within the first few weeks when it became obvious that income would not support two full-timers. Roney stayed till August. Later he complained that he had received no salary for his services, though his own financial report shows that he drew at least $170, or slightly more than two months' wages at the rate originally promised. That was little enough, however; and he had a family to support.[19]

In view of the League's strenuous and frequently successful undertakings, why was there such a shortage of funds? A glance at the

[17] Roney, 378–379.
[18] *Truth,* August 2, 9, 23, 1882.
[19] *Truth,* July 19, 1882; Roney, 373.

financial statement suggests the possibility that a good deal more was being collected in the field than was ever turned in at headquarters. The league's largest sources of revenue ought to have come from the sale of shop cards at $1.00 each and the renewal fees of $.50 monthly. Yet for the entire two and a half months covered by the statement, there appear under these headings only $63 and $10, respectively.[20] Roney by himself could easily have transacted that much business. If reports in *Truth* are correct, there were thirteen branches operating in the city; [21] and the *Chronicle* (among others) believed they were all engaged in gathering money. "The course they are taking is one that has a strong flavor of blackmail and unlawful intimidation. They assess merchants, for instance, so much a month. . . . Who gets this money? . . . Who accounts for the collections?" [22]

Haskell, as editor of the league's official mouthpiece, indignantly rejected the insinuation. Roney, long afterward, acknowledged the tendency of the league to degenerate into a shakedown racket. Shortly before his resignation as president, he recalled, a man had come to him, the owner of a dry-goods store known as the IXL. IXL was suffering from competition of a rival establishment across the street named XLNT. Both stores subscribed to the league, and there was ostensibly no reason to boycott either one. The proprietor of IXL, however, wished a boycott placed against his competitor and was willing to pay Roney one hundred dollars to bring this about. Roney refused; but a few weeks later, after his resignation, he noticed the boycotters out in force with leaflets and sandwich boards, in front of XLNT.[23] *Truth*, apparently not privy to Roney's information, reported this event in high style, quoting enthusiastically from the boycotters' leaflet: "Workingmen, Poor Men, and Friends of White Labor, every time you purchase Chinese made goods, you cut your own throats. . . . If you are honest in your opposition to Coolie Labor, you will not patronize the following dealers." [24]

Roney did not attribute the main difficulties of the league to dishonest stewardship. He blamed President Arthur's signature of the anti-Chinese act, which "sounded the death knell of the League of Deliverance." [25] In one sense his estimate was certainly correct. The league was an endeavor by trade unionists to rally and guide to

20 *Truth,* July 19, 1882.
21 *Truth,* June 7, 1882; the reports probably were not, but at least they indicate that several branches were active.
22 San Francisco *Chronicle,* July 14, 1882.
23 *Truth,* July 19, 1882; Roney, 371–374.
24 *Truth,* August 30, 1882.
25 Roney, 373–374, 380.

their own ends a broad mass following. In the spring of 1882 when the Trades Assembly issued its convention call, such an undertaking must have seemed highly promising. But by summer, circumstances had changed. The season and the economic upturn had eliminated the angry crowds of unemployed. Adoption of the anti-Chinese act had restored public confidence in the bipartisan alliance (this held true for trade unionists as for others). And finally, given the first two conditions, the efforts of the league and of its official paper, *Truth,* to outflank the bipartisan alliance from the left were bound to appear ludicrous and insincere. It was obvious that the league had one program for oratorical purposes (abatement by violence) and another and quite different program (consumer boycotts as an auxiliary to union organization) for real.

The relation of the Trades Assembly to the league was similar in many respects to that of union leadership in 1867 to the Central Pacific Anti-Coolie Association. In both cases the organized crafts were seeking a broader base than they could find within their own membership. But there was an important difference. In 1867 the unionists had wanted wider support for political purposes. In 1882, having disavowed partisan politics, they wanted support to help strengthen their own economic organization. This had been Roney's direction since the day at the Workingmen's convention when he had decided to "sail under the flag" of the anti-Chinese crusade.[26] And while Roney was doubtless an effective leader, he had not created this direction; he was moving with the drift.

We come then to a key question with respect to the League of Deliverance. Why did it depend so heavily upon funds from outside organized labor? If it was the creation of unionists, led by unionists, intended to further organizational aims of unionists, why did the unionists not dig into their treasuries (relatively affluent in 1882) and keep it afloat? To judge from Roney's July report, the league was accomplishing approximately what its founders had hoped. Yet the same report demonstrates the meagerness of trade union contribution. Specifically, thirteen locals (the list includes two Knights of Labor assemblies) had donated $188.75—or an average of $14.50 per local— over a two-and-a-half-month period. There were at this time at least twenty-nine, probably more than thirty, unions in the city.[27]

The Trades Assembly, by resolution, requested its affiliates to lay a per capita assessment of $.25 a month for the benefit of the league. How much this would have amounted to is impossible to determine,

26 Roney, 287.
27 *Truth,* July 19, 1882; Roney, 363–365; see above, p. 175.

though clearly it would have been greater than any sum actually collected. Of the thirteen unions, for example, listed as contributors in Roney's financial accounting, the figures of claimed membership are available for eight. Their contribution to the league totaled $103.75. Had they assessed themselves at the rate requested by the assembly, those eight unions alone over the period covered by the statement would have paid in $1,050. Haskell, in one of his euphoric phases, reported in *Truth* that four unions had "donated a monthly per capita tax of 25 cents" to the league, and that others would soon follow.[28] What Haskell probably meant was that these four had voted to comply with the request of the assembly; collection and delivery of the money was quite a different matter. "The backwardness of the unions in contributing their per capita or even to pay current expenses," Roney wrote, "was painfully evident from the start." [29]

Some reasons for this backwardness can be deduced from the two examples of league activity already cited. The campaign among retail shoe dealers had been undertaken as an aid to the Boot and Shoemakers' White Labor League in its drive to organize the shoe industry. One of the first results had been an influx into the union of new members. Who were they? Almost certainly they were small proprietors and craftsmen employed in small shops. Meanwhile, the apparent success of the boycotting had caused larger shoe factories to declare their willingness to lay off Chinese and hire whites. The next logical step would be for the Boot and Shoemakers to invite into their ranks that mass of unskilled and low-paid white laborers which would, presumably, replace Chinese in the shoe factories. To an organization of craftsmen and small proprietors, however, such a step would have seemed not only impossible but totally undesirable. The Boot and Shoemakers, therefore, after contributing a grand total of $33.20 to the endeavors of the league, ceased to cooperate. In fact they probably sabotaged the league's work.[30] There remained one other alternative: that the Trades Assembly itself organize a union of factory workers. This would have involved a huge outlay of money. Moreover, as a threat to the existence of an organized craft, it would have invited opposition from the assembly's most powerful affiliates—the unions of apprenticeable trades in maritime, metal, and construction.

28 *Truth*, in order referred to: July 19, 1882; Union Directory, May 24; November 22, July 19, August 9, 1882.

29 Roney, 365; and 363–364.

30 *Truth*, May 17, July 19, August 9, 1882; San Francisco *Daily Report*, December 7, 1885.

188   THE INDISPENSABLE ENEMY

As for the league's incursion into the laundry business, the difficulties encountered were even more formidable. Here the protagonist
was a brand new union, just organized by Roney, composed of unskilled or semiskilled workers, many of them women. When, with
Roney's blessing, the California Laundry came into being, it entered
a service trade already dominated by Chinese laundries and wash
houses. The intruder would have to be subsidized in one of two ways:
by its customers through payment of higher prices for white labor or
by its workers through acquiescence in wages and conditions which
they regarded as exploitative. Both types of subsidy were possible—but
only so long as the apocalyptic mood prevailed. In such a mood the
league and the laundry had been conceived; by midsummer, apocalypse
was yielding to normalcy.

In summary, fulfillment of the program logically implied by the
creation of the League of Deliverance would have required one or
both of the following conditions: (1) a continuing atmosphere of crisis;
(2) a willingness on the part of the craft unions of the three basic
sectors of San Francisco industry (maritime, metal, and construction)
to promote and subsidize over a long period the organization of unskilled and semiskilled workers in sectors four (service trades) and
five (manufacture of national market products). Neither condition
existed.

The evidence indicates that Roney and Haskell, and their colleagues
of the socialist academy, were unaware of these contradictions till
they were up to their necks in them. Certainly they were all deeply
committed to the organization of unskilled workers.[31] It may be that
Roney's decision to resign as league president was due as much to
his realization of its impotence for this purpose as to financial
stringency. He was, after all, only a month behind in salary; and as
the only full-time labor functionary on the West Coast, he might
not have found this delay intolerable if he had believed he was
accomplishing something of value.

The League of Deliverance, after Roney's resignation, rapidly
disintegrated. It sent to the Trades Assembly desperate appeals for

[31] For Roney's efforts to organize seamen, see Paul S. Taylor, *Sailors' Union of
the Pacific* (New York, 1923), 41–42; cannery workers, *Truth*, February 4, 1882, and
Roney, 384–385; laundry workers, Roney, 378; foundry laborers, *Truth*, May 31,
June 14, 1882. For Socialist Academy and the Coast Seamen's Union, see Taylor,
Sailors' Union, 42–48. Haskell's enthusiasm for the Knights of Labor as expressed in
the series of articles in *Truth* through 1882 was due in large part to his hope that
the mixed assemblies of the Knights would provide a means of organizing the
unskilled. For Haskell's organization of general laborers' unions, *Daily Report*,
January 6, 14, 1886.

reinforcements which apparently went unheeded. During the late summer and fall of 1882, its name appeared with decreasing frequency even in the columns of its official organ, *Truth*. Haskell, now aflame with new enthusiasms, had little time to spare for the perishing league. Others of the socialist academy struggled to keep it alive, long enough at least for decent burial.[32] That they were not altogether successful is indicated by one of the last published proclamations from a branch of the league. It will serve here for epitaph:

> Whereas, Numerous instances have been brought to the attention of this Branch, of indecent relations existing between white women and their male Chinese domestics; . . .
>
> Resolved, That this Branch do most heartily condemn such practices, as being polluting to the purity of the homes of this community, and degrading to the morals of our people;
>
> Resolved, That hereafter all families where such domestics are employed will be looked upon by us with suspicion, and that all women connected with such families will be considered as persons of doubtful character. . . .[33]

The Metal Trades

After the disintegration of the league, the Trades Assembly was not long in becoming a terminal case itself. The reasons for this decline remain something of a mystery. 1883 was a year of moderate prosperity in California; union growth and improvements in wages and working conditions continued. One catches a glimpse of the labor movement as it then was from a card issued in the summer of that year to urge a general boycott of two San Francisco newspapers which allegedly had locked out their printers. The card carried endorsements of sixteen local unions, of the Trades Assembly, and of thirteen assemblies in the Knights of Labor, representing altogether (according to a declaration in capital letters at the bottom of the card) "18,347 MEN." Leaving aside the matter of accuracy, it seems clear that the list itself constituted a fair show of strength, since fourteen of the signatory locals were in waterfront, building, and metal trades—the traditional sectors of maximum trade union effectiveness.[34] But this did not necessarily lead to success when it came to newspaper boycotting. The boycott failed; and there were soon other hints of misfortunes to follow.

[32] *Truth*, August 9, 23, 30, 1882.

[33] *Truth*, November 1, 1882.

[34] Ira Cross Labor Notes, Carton IV, folder 134, Bancroft Library, University of California, Berkeley.

In midsummer 1883 occurred the first coast-to-coast strike by a national union—that of the Telegraphers, organized as a district assembly of the Knights of Labor. Union demands were for higher wages and shorter hours; the strike was directed against all commercial telegraph companies but especially against the giant among them, Western Union, then controlled by Jay Gould. This fact alone guaranteed wide public sympathy for the strikers. In California some fifty Knights of Labor—scattered between San Francisco and Sacramento, and Yreka in the northern end of the state—were involved. The strike was lost, the union broken, and many of its members blacklisted.[35]

The year 1884 was marked by depression in the East and the beginning of a downswing in California that would continue on into 1886. Hard times triggered the inevitable employer counteroffensive. A Merchants' and Manufacturers' Association had already been organized in San Francisco, and within the next two years similar associations took shape in the maritime and metal trades industries to spearhead wage-cutting and union-breaking campaigns. The unions, thrown on the defensive, were hard pressed, although the evidence indicates that at least in the three basic sectors they suffered no major defeats.[36]

Under circumstances such as these, with local bases holding solid and an urgent need for centralized direction, it might be expected that the Trades Assembly, instead of disintegrating, would have grown stronger. But the earlier fiasco of the League of Deliverance—to which the assembly had so largely mortgaged both its enthusiasms and its personnel—had apparently stripped it of effective leadership. Roney, hurt and disappointed, had withdrawn from activity. His colleagues of the socialist academy shifted their activities temporarily to the waterfront. A number of other potential leaders, noting the rise to national prominence of the Knights of Labor, were endeavoring to build the District Assembly of the Knights into an effective center. The result was that the assembly was left in the hands of delegates from the printers, tailors, and cigarmakers—all these being small "uptown" groups, separated from the basic sectors where conflicts were developing with the newly organized employers. Affiliations dwindled; the assembly met only sporadically. And toward the end of 1884, leaving no final record, it simply ceased to function.

[35] *Truth*, July 28, September 15, 22, 1883; John Rogers Commons et al., *History of Labour in the United States*, 4 vols. (New York, 1918), II, 342–343, 348–349. District Assemblies in the Knights of Labor were normally regional delegated councils. But in some cases craft unions were organized as nongeographical district assemblies.

[36] Commons et al., *History*, II, 357–361; Cross, 142–147, 166–170.

Events of 1885 made the need for some kind of central council increasingly obvious. Yet leadership in each of the several factions which had drifted away from the Trades Assembly was by this time acquiring a vested interest in its own organizational autonomy. None cared to submit to any other; and what followed was a series of abortive efforts at grasping the initiative.

The first came from the metal tradesmen. In February 1885 San Francisco's iron-working shops announced a 15 percent wage cut. Roney's union, the Molders, took the lead in organizing resistance. Fourteen hundred men walked out, and within a month the employers gave in and restored the original scale. Almost a year earlier the Molders had called a conference looking toward the establishment of a citywide federation, but nothing had come of it. They now tried again with no better results than before. Then, under Roney's urging, they proceeded to set up a delegated metal trades council composed of Molders, Blacksmiths, Boilermakers, Machinists, and Patternmakers. The council, which has continued in existence to the present day, was certainly the first successful trades federation on the Pacific Coast, perhaps one of the first in the United States. It was in fact the implementation of a scheme Roney had proposed sixteen years earlier, and which, through the San Francisco Trades Assembly, he had offered to the founding convention of the American Federation of Labor. Ignored at the time, Roney's plan, or something very similar to it, was afterward adopted by AFL unions in many industries as a means of achieving a degree of joint action in negotiations and strikes.[37]

Roney, however, had hoped for more than this. "My plan of organization was set forth long before the formation of the trusts," he explained years later in a letter to the California labor historian, Ira Cross. "Had it been adopted when it first saw the light, it could have been a powerful instrument in shaping legislation for their control and in securing for the people *en masse* such government as would render the production of a 'big stick' president like Mr. Roosevelt an impossibility."[38] This may have been hindsight wisdom. But there can be little doubt that Roney, even in 1885, conceived the Iron Trades Council as part of a larger combination through which federations of trades in particular industries would cooperate within a statewide, or even coastwide, apparatus.

[37] *Call*, February 10, March 9, 1885; Roney, 230–233, 385–387, 410–412; Cross, 148–151, 167.
[38] Frank Roney to Ira Cross, Los Angeles, January 18, 1910, in Cross Labor Notes, Carton IV, folder 113, Bancroft Library.

There was one minor aftermath to the metal trades strike which places Roney's expectations in sharp focus. No sooner had the employers restored the original wage scale for their skilled workers than one of the larger firms imposed a 25 percent cut on foundry laborers. These unskilled hands had already been out for a month due to the stoppage just ended, and the cut was probably a trial move to see how closely the workmen could stand together. The laborers struck; the Molders came out again in support. Meanwhile, several union leaders, with Roney prominent among them, were helping the laborers to set up their own organization, which within a few days had more than four hundred members. But the other trades apparently failed to join the Molders, who then returned to work, and the strike of the laborers collapsed. Roney, in his autobiography, made no reference to this incident beyond mentioning that he had helped to organize the Foundry Laborers' Protective Association. Delegates from the new union were present at the first meeting of the Iron Trades Council which took place several weeks after the failure of the laborers' strike.[39]

It appears from this sequence of events that Roney was still searching for some method of bridging the gap between craft and industrial unionism. That essentially was what he had tried to accomplish three years earlier when he had pressed the League of Deliverance toward organization of the unskilled. Through the Iron Trades Council—and through the broader federation of councils he hoped might spring from it—he now returned to the same objective. But the road was blocked at this point because the initiative taken by the metal trades unions had received such meager response from other segments of the labor movement.

Deadlock

Nationally, the Knights of Labor in 1885 stood at the threshold of their brief moment of ascendancy. The strike against Western Union two years earlier, though unsuccessful, had won the sympathy of old Jacksonians as well as young antimonopolists. More recently, in Colorado (and these events especially caught the attention of Californians) under the leadership of Joseph Buchanan, editor of a small labor weekly in Denver, the Knights had achieved a series of victories in mining and on behalf of shop craftsmen of the Union Pacific Railroad. In March came a stunning triumph over Jay Gould in the first Wabash Railroad strike. Then followed a second round in August

[39] Roney, 411; San Francisco *Examiner*, February 9, 1885; *Call*, March 4, 5, 7, 8, 17, 1885.

and September as a result of which Gould was forced to accept a negotiated settlement. From these events and from scores of lesser conflicts, the Knights acquired the public image of a tough and aggressive association, able to trade insult for insult or blow for blow with the most powerful capitalist of them all. Membership increased tenfold over that of 1884 and by 1886 had passed 700,000.[40]

Leaders of the Knights in California doubtless anticipated a rapid expansion on the Pacific Coast. So did a number of other labor men to whom the Knights seemed to offer a form of organization potentially superior to trade unionism. Haskell for one, in his editorials in *Truth*, had argued that the Knights' mixed assemblies would unite skilled and unskilled on an industry-wide basis, and at the same time would rally other sympathetic elements to their support. Haskell, then, was groping for answers to some of the same problems that Roney sought to solve through his scheme for industrial councils of craft unions. Worth noting in this connection is the fact that one of the most successful labor organizers west of the Mississippi during this period—Joseph Buchanan, the Denver editor and Knights of Labor official—was a close friend and collaborator of Haskell. When, in 1884, Haskell was obliged for financial reasons to suspend publication of *Truth*, he turned over his subscribers' list to Buchanan.[41] Later, Haskell assumed direction of the Denver weekly while Buchanan went on to Chicago, hoping to establish there a similar radical labor paper and at the same time to use his influence toward healing the breach between the Knights and the American Federation of Labor.[42] Buchanan failed in both these missions; but his line of direction helps make clear the attraction that the Knights of Labor exerted on many western radicals.

Despite these favorable indices, however, the Knights in California experienced no upsurge of membership comparable to that of the order nationally. One reason appears to have been that the organization remained tightly controlled at the district level by unimaginative and timid men. Roney, in his autobiography, described them as

[40] Commons et al., *History*, II, 357–385; Joseph Buchanan, *The Story of a Labor Agitator* (New York, 1903), 79–241. For a more detailed account of these strikes, see Ruth Alice Allen, *The Great Southwest Strike* (Austin, Texas, 1942).

[41] *Truth*, May 15, June 28, August 2, 23, September 20, October 18, December 20, 1882. For an attack by *Truth* on the Federation of Organized Trades and Labor Unions (predecessor of the AFL) as "too timid" and "captured by the monopolists," see the issue of November 29, 1882. On December 6, 1882, *Truth* published a letter from the Detroit anarchist Joseph A. Labadie to the convention of the Federation recommending that it "dissolve the Federation with the advice to all Trades and Labor organizations to join the Knights of Labor." On Haskell's subscribers list, see Cross, 158.

[42] Buchanan, 327–372; Roney, 390 note 28. Denver *Labor Enquirer*, June 4, 1887, Cross Collection, Newspapers on Microfilm, Bancroft Library, lists Haskell as editor.

"politicians." What he presumably meant was that they were proposing electoral activities within the major party framework, in lieu
of militant labor unionism. Early in March of 1885—almost simultaneously with the unsuccessful conference sponsored by the metal
trades—the Knights convened what was billed as a general labor convention in San Francisco. It was meagerly attended. Perhaps because of
the narrowly defined political aims, trade unionists stayed away; and
before the end of the month a continuations committe set up by
the convention had proven itself so unrepresentative that its organizers
converted it into a "parliamentary training school." [43]

If the Knights are considered the right wing of the California labor
movement and the trade unionists as occupying a more or less central
position, then the spaces to the left would be filled by Haskell and
his colleagues of the socialist academy.[44] Haskell, since losing interest
in the League of Deliverance, had been experimenting with various
secret organizations. These had the greater part of their existence in
the columns of *Truth* and in his own imagination. Perpetually playing
games, Haskell was a kind of Tom Sawyer never grown up; yet the
games he played were at the shadow line of nightmare. Other men
mocked Haskell, feared him, and ended by becoming entangled one
way or another in his fantasies.

Out of his reading he resurrected the romantic names of defunct
revolutionary societies. These he wrote up in *Truth* as if they were
still extant. First came the "Invisible Republic," then the "Illuminati,"
to which he ascribed a direct continuity since before the American
Revolution. By midsummer 1883 Haskell had rolled both these into a
new package called the International Workingmen's Association and
claimed to be in direct contact with its executive in London. Actually,
the International Workmen's Association—the Marxian First International—had ended its days rather drably at a rump convention in
Philadelphia seven years earlier.[45] But this was a sort of difficulty
Haskell could easily cope with: might not the dissolution of the IWA
have been simply a camouflage, a ruse by the master conspirators of
world revolution?

[43] Roney, 437, 442, 444. In September 1886, the Knights set up a California
State Assembly, but this apparently held only one meeting. (Minutes and Proceedings, September 16, 1886, in Knights of Labor Records, Bancroft Library,
Berkeley; *Daily Report*, March 27, 1885, in Cross Labor Notes, Carton I, folder 5.)
[44] For a description of the political spectrum of the labor movement in late
1885, see Roney, 440–441.
[45] *Truth*, February 14, 21, May 19, September 15, 1883; Roney, 471–472; Ralph E.
Shaffer, "Radicalism in California" (Ph.D. diss., University of California Berkeley,
1962), 28–35; Howard Quint, *Forging American Socialism* (Columbia, S.C., 1953),
13–14.

And could anyone doubt that there were such conspirators? On the contrary, their handiwork was everywhere to be seen. Readers of *Truth* knew that in Europe at least the old order was tottering. The sappers worked there relentlessly; yet for all their dangerous labors they found time to lead marvelously voluptuous lives in those doomed capitals, and even came at intervals to America for vacations, or to raise recruits and money, or to experiment with new explosives. Haskell wanted in on this game. He wrote endlessly of dynamite. He printed directions for its manufacture. He published articles, probably written by himself, but credited to European scientists and revolutionaries, one of whom he quoted as follows: "You can learn to make tri-nitroglycerin, and if you carry two or three pounds with you people will respect you much more than if you carried a pistol. But don't use the dynamite till the government becomes autocratic, and you cannot obtain your rights at the polls." That Haskell considered such a state of affairs reasonably imminent is suggested by one of his headlines less than a month later: "DYNAMITE WILL BE USED IN AMERICA." [46]

He was, of course, right. Haskell's fantasies were never more than half an octave out of phase with reality and this was what gave them their persuasive power. Arson was already a common occurrence in California and dynamiting soon would be.[47] Traditions of terrorist activity were deeply established, and especially so perhaps in working class and immigrant segments of the population. In America, as already noted, there had been a shift of focus from violence against national or class enemies to violence against racial enemies. But though the focus shifted, the style and a great deal of the emotional dynamic remained the same. Anyone could dream of dynamite; anyone who dared could use it. And whoever used it made himself equal to the masters of the earth. Thus the man who bombed a Chinese washhouse or blew up a factory where Chinese were employed had overmastered Leland Stanford himself.

Fascinated by the abracadabra of conspiracy, Haskell worked out an

[46] *Truth*, in the order cited: April 21, 28, May 26, June 9, 23, 30, May 26, June 23, all 1883.

[47] On the arrest and trial of several members of anticoolie societies, said to be anarchists and/or socialists, charged with illegal storage of dynamite, which allegedly they intended to use for bombing Chinatown, see *Daily Report*, November 10, December 18, 1885; *Call*, December 16–18, 185; January 6, 7, 1886. According to Roney, 472–475, Haskell was involved in a plot (never carried out) to bomb the San Francisco Hall of Records. See Buchanan, 169–173, on the activities of dynamiters during the railroad strikes in Colorado. San Francisco newspapers early in 1885 carried many stories on dynamite, especially in connection with the Tower of London bombing which was charged to Irish nationalists. See, for example, *Examiner*, February 1, 3, 10, 1885.

elaborate blueprint of interlocking circles, initiatory degrees designated by different colored cards, and cells of ten members known to each other (at least for the purposes of the game) only by code number. In part, this was simply the contemporary mode of fraternal organization. In part, it was a repetition of forms that had become common to groupings of all sorts which engaged in illegal activity. Anticoolie clubs, the Order of Caucasians, the Ancient Order of Hibernians, the Molly Maguires, probably the Ku Klux Klan, had all followed similar patterns. Roncy, who regarded Haskell as one-tenth genius and nine-tenths crackpot, had himself worked within a similar system before his expulsion from the old country in 1868.[48]

Through *Truth* and by avid letter writing, Haskell made contact with other groups of radicals scattered about the country. Buchanan at Denver became chief of the IWA's "Rocky Mountain Division." During the summer of 1883, Haskell was seeking an approach to the so-called Black International, the Anarchist International Working People's Association founded two years earlier in London. American adherents (notably August Spies and Albert Parsons, both later to die for the Haymarket bombing) were planning a congress at Pittsburgh for November at which Johannes Most—another of those romantic exiles from the doomed capitals who so fired Haskell's imagination—was scheduled to be the leading spirit. Haskell had probably hoped to attend in person; unable to do so, he drew up a program on behalf of the "Pacific Division," copies of which he mailed to Spies and to the Detroit radical, Joseph Labadie. The program was intended as a basis on which to unify the American left. With a contempt for ideological refinements altogether character-istic of far western radicalism, Haskell insisted that all radicals, whether propagandists of the deed, revolutionary socialists, political socialists, or trade union socialists, were in fundamental harmony and needed only a statement of principles to bring them together. The principles he proposed were in effect a rendering of the producer ethic into a series of Jacksonian paraphrases of the Declaration of Independence.[49]

---

[48] Buchanan, 269–273, describes the IWA group system in some detail. In *Truth*, May 19, 1883, appears a long article about the IWA's Pacific Division, signed, "By Order of the Division Executive, I-41, Secretary." I-41 was of course Haskell. See Roney, 56–58, 162–168, 471–474.

[49] Buchanan, 265–269; Roney, 473; Chester M. Destler, *American Radicalism, 1865–1901: Essays and Documents* (New London, Conn., 1946), 78–81; Destler, "Shall Red and Black Unite? An American Revolutionary Document of 1883," *Pacific Historical Review*, XIV (December, 1945), 437–448; *Truth*, September 15, 1883. On Johannes Most, see Commons et al., *History*, II, 293–294, note 77.

While Haskell's efforts received a rather chilly response from the assembled anarchists at Pittsburgh, the occasion at least provided an opportunity for one of his grand perorations in *Truth*:

> The work of peaceful education and revolutionary conspiracy well can and ought to run in parallel lines. The day has come for solidarity. Ho! Reds and Blacks, thy flags are flying side by side! Let the drum beat out defiantly the roll of battle: "Workingmen of all lands unite! You have nothing to lose but your chains; you have a world to win!" Tremble! Oppressors of the World! Not far beyond your purblind sight there dawn the scarlet and sable lights of the JUDGEMENT DAY!
>
> Published by Order of the Division Executive, I-41, Division Secretary.[50]

When and to what extent the IWA changed from a fiction in the columns of *Truth* to a membership organization remains in considerable doubt. Ira Cross, while well aware of Haskell's penchant for exaggeration, concluded on the basis of a study of records in the Haskell estate that the IWA "had at least nineteen groups in San Francisco, ten in Eureka and vicinity, two in Oakland," and six others in small towns of northern California. It is not clear why Haskell's records should merit greater confidence than his newspaper reportage. A good many of these groups may have represented simply individuals who Haskell hoped might form groups. Roney, who according to his own declaration was never a member, described the IWA as he recalled it at the height of its influence (1885): "I saw that it was the usual glamor which attaches to secret societies that enhanced the importance of the International, which Haskell sedulously exaggerated. The membership consisted of less than one hundred persons and most of them were members of the Coast Seamen's Union." [51]

In this instance, as in several others, Roney's recollection is probably close to the truth. However, this by no means implies that the IWA was negligible. Its membership, small though it may have been,

50 *Truth*, September 15, 1883.

51 Roney, 472; Cross, 161, 165. Estimates of IWA membership vary widely. Perlman, in *Commons* et al., *History*, II, 300, wrote that national membership "although including some of the prominent labor leaders of the country, hardly ever exceeded a thousand." Morris Hillquit, on the other hand, placed the membership in 1887 at 6,000. (Hillquit, *History of Socialism in the United States* [New York, 1903], 230–232.) Buchanan, while acknowledging that membership centered in the Far West, claimed that it included "prominent and progressive labor men and reformers in New York, Cincinnati, Chicago and other cities of the East and middle West." Only the nine-man national executive (of which he was one) knew the numerical strength—"and we never told" (Buchanan, 269).

included most of that loose grouping of trade union socialists earlier referred to as the socialist academy. During the League of Deliverance days Roney had been one of them; and though afterward he preferred to keep his distance, he never ceased to speak of the socialists with affection and admiration. "I knew . . . how valuable they were in enthusing men to join the unions," he wrote, "how earnest . . . in the work and how ably and disinterestedly they performed it. W. C. Owen, Peter Ross Martin, J. J. Martin and Burnette G. Haskell had all done excellent work in that connection, in fact much better than the trade unionists had." [52]

A major breakthrough achieved by the IWA was organization of the West Coast sailors. There had been several prior attempts at maritime unionization (most recently in 1880, led by Roney), all of which had broken up under attack by the shipowners and their heavy-handed mates and skippers, and against the adamant hostility of the crimp boardinghouse keepers. In the mid-eighties, conditions of seamen before the mast remained much as they had been when Richard Henry Dana made his voyage to the Pacific. The depression winter of 1885 brought wage cuts to the shipping industry as it had to the metal trades; but seamen, unlike the metal craftsmen, were unprepared to resist. The IWA moved down to the waterfront. Led by Sigismund Danielewicz, the barber, and Haskell, the lawyer-editor, sailors organized, for the first time hung together, and fought an incredibly fierce and successful battle to defend their new union. During the first years, this defense hinged upon a dual leadership, half composed of sailors who would necessarily be away at sea for long periods and half of IWA shoresiders who actually administered the affairs of the organization. Thus was born the Coast Seamen's Union, subsequently the Sailors' Union of the Pacific, one of the most powerful—and conservative—of American labor organizations. [53]

But in the early days there was little hint of conservatism. The sailors trusted their socialist counselors and almost no one else. A letter published in 1886 in the daily press of San Francisco bears witness to this confidence. Apparently, Haskell had been criticized by members of a carpenters local on the grounds that he was not a workingman, and several officers of the Seamen's Union—making clear that they were themselves sailors—had come to his defense:

> The sailors have been making their fight, singly and unorganized, for many years, and on a memorable night last March, Mr. Haskell addressed a striking crowd of these sailors and

[52] Roney, 437.
[53] Taylor, *Sailors' Union*, 40–43, 46–100; Roney, 406–407.

showed them the advantages of organization, and under his
instruction the sailors have learned to assist each other and
to master many of the social problems which every workingman should understand. Eighteen times has he appeared in
court to defend their interests and secured success without a
fee. . . . He acts as our representative by compulsion on our
part, and has repeatedly offered to resign as our delegate if
we would permit him. To have lost him would have imperilled
the success of our Union. He has told us over and over again
that he is a Socialist, but we prefer him to any capitalist or
reactionary as our representative. . . . It is true he is a lawyer but for many years he has not practised except gratis for
men who could not pay for justice in the courts. He derives his
living from his work as a compositor and pressman, and is as
much a laborer as any man in the world, and we think workingmen who have watched the progress of the Sailors' Union,
which was mainly due to the efforts of Mr. Haskell, will bear
us out in our respect and esteem for him.[54]

Here was a testimonial which Roney himself might have envied. It
makes clear why the sailors during the ensuing several years often
marched, in uniform, under the IWA banner in labor parades, why
they sent large and enthusiastic delegations to vote with the IWA
at labor conventions, and why they undoubtedly furnished, as Roney
suggested, a substantial portion of IWA membership.

Organization of the sailors marked an abrupt accretion of power
for the socialists; and it may have been the exuberance inspired by
their new proletarian base which led them to summon a laboi convention in March 1885, competitive with the one already called
by the Knights of Labor. The IWA gathering met two weeks after the
other. To judge by the attendance roster one would suppose a rather
impressive representation from IWA groups, Granges, and labor
unions, though how much of this was bona fide remains in some doubt.
Roney, at least, took a dim view of the matter. He attended for the
Molders' Union, as an observer, not a delegate; and according to his
account only two or three other unions responded. "To make it appear
that he had got together a large representative gathering, Haskell
divided the Coast Seamen's Union into a boatmen's union, a mates'
union, and about a dozen other unions, all the members of which
were, of course, part and parcel of the Coast Seamen's Union." [55]

[54] Letter, Edward Crangle, secretary, Ed Anderson and Ed Carpenter, patrolmen,
Coasting Sailors, *Daily Report*, February 6, 1886, clipping in Cross Labor Notes,
Carton I, folder 6.
[55] Roney, 408; Cross, 173–175, 331 note 12.

However this may be, the IWA effort to establish a labor center met with no greater success than had similar initiatives by metal tradesmen and by the Knights of Labor. Clearly, some modicum of cooperation among the rival leaderships was going to be necessary if a knitting up of the labor movement were to be achieved.

The circumstances which made such cooperation possible—and which brought it to a successful conclusion—involved, once again, the Chinese.

10

THE FEDERATED TRADES

Eureka and Rock Springs

One Saturday evening in the winter of 1885, rival factions of Chinese came to blows on the street of their block-long enclave in the northern California lumber port of Eureka. Spectators pushed in to see the show. Some of the Chinese opened fire—at each other, not at the outsiders; but among those hit were two white onlookers. One was a boy, wounded in the foot; the other a Eureka city councilman, killed instantly. The town was crowded not only with the usual Saturday night influx, but with loggers and sawmill workers idled by the winter rains. A thousand men gathered in Centennial Hall. They elected a committee to notify the Chinese they had twenty-four hours to pack up and leave. In the morning, while the committeemen delivered this message, their fellow citizens surrounded the Chinese quarter, erecting a gallows at the main entrance. The Chinese offered no resistance. They packed what they could, marched off under guard to a warehouse at the docks. Later, when the tide permitted crossing the bar, two steamers took them down to San Francisco.[1]

The Eureka expulsion, at the time, seems to have roused relatively little interest in other parts of the state. This was perhaps because attention of newspaper readers was focused on the metal trades strike in San Francisco and on the gigantic struggle shaping up between the railroads and the Knights of Labor across Colorado and the Southwest. Yet before the end of the year, the Eureka episode took on a new dimension. "The ball that was set in motion at Eureka," the San Francisco *Call* wrote in November, "seems to be moving with accelerated speed. After years of apathy the people of almost every city and town on the Pacific Coast have simultaneously resolved to expel the Chinese

[1] San Francisco *Chronicle*, February 8, 1885; San Francisco *Examiner*, February 9, 1885; San Francisco *Morning Call*, February 10, 1885.

laborers, in order to get a chance to give the wages now being diverted by Chinese into the hands of our own needy citizens." [2] In fact, however, there was a considerable time lag between the events at Eureka and the wave of expulsions to which the *Call* had reference.

This began only in September, and outside California. The triggering incident was a fist fight between Chinese and white coal miners at a shaft operated by the Union Pacific Railroad in Wyoming Territory. There were at the time 331 Chinese and 150 whites employed in the mine. Two Chinese were pummeled and ejected. Later the white miners quit work, marched into the nearby town of Rock Springs, summoned a mass meeting for that evening at their Knights of Labor hall. During the afternoon a group armed with revolvers and Winchesters attacked the Chinese quarter. Most of the Chinese fled, some being shot down as they ran. Other whites, meanwhile, had served two of the most unpopular foremen with an ultimatum to leave town, which they did on the next train. That evening the abatement of Chinatown resumed; buildings were set afire and stragglers killed as they emerged. The next day when the bodies were picked out of the ashes and dragged in from the surrounding sagebrush, the official count came to twenty-eight Chinese killed, fifteen wounded. In addition, property amounting to $150,000 had been destroyed.[3]

The refugees, after scattering into the hills, made their way to the railroad where they were picked up by Union Pacific trains and taken to Evanston, Wyoming. There again they faced hostile crowds, while the local authorities, if there were any, vanished from sight. The territorial governor, and presumably the railroad as well, telegraphed President Cleveland for federal aid. Troops moved into Wyoming from Utah; but it was a full week before the Union Pacific was able to return its surviving Chinese miners, under military escort, to Rock Springs.

The massacre at Rock Springs became at once a cause célèbre. The local press and many newspapers in the Far West defended or excused the attackers. So did the territorial apparatus of law enforcement. Sixteen white miners were arrested; but the grand jury, declaring itself unable to elicit testimony from any witness, released the sixteen without indictment. Colonel Bee, Chinese consul at San Francisco, and

<hr/>

[2] *Call*, November 22, 1885.

[3] Paul Crane and Alfred Larson, "The Chinese Massacre," *Annals of Wyoming*, XII (January, 1940), 47–55; (April, 1940), 153–160. Union Pacific Coal Company, *History of the Union Pacific Coal Mines, 1868–1940* (Omaha, Neb., 1940), 75–86. [Isaac H. Bromley], *The Chinese Massacre at Rock Springs, Wyoming Territory, September 2, 1885* (Boston 1886).

his counterpart from New York met in Wyoming where they prepared an extensive report later submitted through the Chinese ambassador to Secretary of State Bayard. The matter was reported to Congress in a presidential message; and Congress, at the president's request, while denying any legal obligation on the part of the federal government, appropriated $150,000 to cover property losses detailed in the consul's report. No indemnity was ever paid for the lives lost. Meanwhile, Charles Francis Adams, Jr., the Union Pacific's president, wired from his Boston office to the western general manager, "We here think you too timid." Stiffened by this fortitude at headquarters, railroad officials fired approximately one-third of their white miners and reopened the shafts, again with white and Chinese labor.[4]

The white miners involved seem to have been, like the Chinese, mostly aliens. They were described as Cornish, Welsh, Irish, English, and Scandinavian.[5] Both the Chinese embassy and the federal government made a good deal of this, for somewhat different reasons—the one to discredit the anti-Chinese cause, the other to exonerate the United States. Perhaps the railroad actually knew the citizenship status of its employees; but there were besides these many other whites in Rock Springs, and how anyone could tell which of them took part in the killings is difficult to imagine. Yet whether or not the actors at Rock Springs were aliens, the drama itself was of fundamentally American origin.

Until 1875 the mines had been worked exclusively by white labor. In that year there had been a dispute over production, the company demanding higher tonnage output. The men had refused. The company then, for the first time, brought in Chinese. The white workers struck in protest, but their strike failed and a number of supposed leaders were discharged. Employment of Chinese continued; before the end of the decade they outnumbered whites by more than two to one. Between the two groups, however, there seems to have been little overt conflict during this period. Rates of payment were equal and both worked under substantially the same conditions.[6] Though without much direct evidence, it might not be difficult to reconstruct by inference the economic sequence behind these events.

<hr/>

[4] [Bromley], 7–17; Crane and Larson, *Annals*, XII, 50–51, 55, 153–159. *John Swinton's Paper* (New York), after first denouncing the attackers, repeated the justifications of the western papers: September 13, 20, 27, October 4, November 1, 1885; *Call*, March 3, 1886. James D. Richardson (ed.), *A Compilation of the Messages and Papers of the Presidents* (New York, 1897—), X, 4969.

[5] Crane and Larson, *Annals*, XII, 48–49.

[6] Union Pacific Coal Company, 77–79; Crane and Larson, *Annals*, XII, 53–55. The Chinese, however, were said to have averaged lower daily earnings.

1875 had been a depression year. That the white miners would have resisted increased production (payment was by the ton) appears unlikely, unless they felt themselves already pushed to the limit or believed that additional exertion would add little to their daily earnings. This suggests that the Rock Springs mines, in order to meet rising demands for coal on the Union Pacific system, had extended its operation into seams of lower yield. After the 1875 strike, those whites who remained would have been rewarded for their loyalty—or placated—by assignment to the richer diggings. The Chinese newcomers were probably set to work in low yield areas. On the basis of these suppositions, the ten-year period of relative peace between the two groups becomes comprehensible since it reproduced (with one important exception) [7] the traditional pattern established for Chinese in the mine camps and railroad construction crews of an earlier period—a pattern which continued to dominate the social fabric of both industries in the Far West. But why was the pattern disrupted in 1885?

Spokesmen for the Knights of Labor on the Union Pacific presented, soon after the massacre, a bill of grievances and demands. These included ouster of the labor contracting firm which recruited and supervised both whites and Chinese in the mines; removal of the superintendent; an end to favoritism in the assignment of digging surfaces, to false measure at the scales, and to coercion to buy at the company store.[8] So far, the demands were typical (*traditional* one might say again) of labor relations of the period. They identified the Rock Springs episode as one manifestation of that shock wave which during the years 1884–1886 set off collisions between workingmen and the new industrialists from Texas to Puget Sound and from New York to the Pacific.

The Chinese issue was entangled in this wider context. Thus the key demand of the Knights of Labor at Rock Springs (the order had first made its appearance there only in 1883) was for the discharge of Chinese employed by the railroad.[9] Accusations against the Chinese were specifically that they prevented the hiring of white men, that they paid kickbacks for their jobs, and that they were the prime beneficiaries of favoritism in the assignment of digging surfaces. It was this last point which had touched off the dispute that culminated

[7] The exception being that in quartz mines Chinese were generally excluded from underground work. The customs that governed coal mining were largely derived from railroad construction, not from the silver and gold mining camps. See below, note 10.

[8] Union Pacific Coal Company, 80–86.

[9] Ibid., 53. Crane and Larson, Annals, XII, 52–55.

in the attack on the Chinese quarter. Doubtless many white miners believed that Chinese enjoyed favored assignments; but in fact the opposite was more likely the case. According to company records, white miners averaged higher daily earnings than Chinese. Since tonnage scales were equal, this must have been due either to longer hours and greater effort on the part of the whites or to the fact that they were working richer seams. The second explanation appears the more plausible and tends to confirm the supposition ventured earlier as to the division of labor following the 1875 strike.

All the above suggests one further supposition: that the real cause of trouble in 1885 was not the favored position of Chinese, but a tendency to reduce the favored position hitherto enjoyed by whites. Such a tendency would have been probable for three reasons. First, high yield seams furnished a diminishing proportion of total production; second, white labor, due to the onset of depression in the East, was becoming more plentiful, therefore cheaper; and third, Chinese labor, as a result of the Exclusion Act of 1882, was becoming scarcer, therefore more expensive. The Rock Springs catastrophe was, clearly, part of the long continued and nationwide industrial conflict which reached a peak of intensity in winter 1885–86. But in Rock Springs, as generally throughout the Far West, the fund of anger and discontent building up among workingmen, by a kind of Gresham's law, converted itself into the cheaper currency of anticoolieism.

Abatement by Violence

From Wyoming the trouble center shifted to coal mines near Seattle. Washington's territorial governor, Watson Squire, informed the Department of the Interior in October that Chinese miners were being forced from their jobs, and reports from Canada told of refugees fleeing across the border. In Seattle there were mass meetings, torchlight parades, demands for immediate eviction of the Chinese.[10] At Tacoma on November 3 a committee of prominent citizens led by the mayor and fire chief put into effect their own version of the Eureka program. Several hundred Chinese were expelled from their buildings and

10 *Call*, October 22, 25, November 6, 7, 1885. One reason why coal miners were more prominent in these agitations than other types of miners is that coal mining had come west with the railroads. Therefore, instead of following patterns developed in placer and hard-rock mining (it will be recalled that Chinese were traditionally excluded from underground work in hard rock), coal had followed the patterns of railroad construction. These had permitted training the lowest ranking labor groups (Irish in the East, Chinese in the West) in techniques of tunneling and heavy construction—which equipped them perfectly for digging coal.

driven out of the city. Seattle seemed on the point of doing likewise. Federal officers arrested anti-Chinese leaders in Seattle and in Squak (also Washington Territory), where three Chinese hop pickers had been killed during a raid on their encampment. On November 7, President Cleveland exhorted all citizens engaged in unlawful assemblies in the territory to desist forthwith, warning that he would dispatch federal troops if disorders continued.[11]

The expulsion program by this time was out of control. As news of the successful action at Tacoma spread, hinterland towns in Oregon and California set up their own committees. In California, Truckee took the lead. Through a series of mass meetings, lumber mills and woodcutting contractors were pressured into rescinding their agreements for Chinese gang labor. One of the last holdouts at Truckee was the firm of Sisson, Crocker and Co.—the Crocker of this partnership being a younger brother to Charles Crocker, the Central Pacific director. Since the same firm had in fact served the railroad as a major importer of Chinese labor, its surrender took on a symbolic value. Truckee became famous; and the guiding spirit of its anti-Chinese committee, a state assemblyman by the name of C. F. McGlashan, spoke at rallies up and down the state, billed as "the hero of Truckee." [12]

But Washington soon reclaimed preeminence. Early one Sunday in February a band of Seattle citizens, led by the police chief and followed by a sizable crowd, moved into Chinatown, ostensibly to investigate violations of the health laws. While the police chief was questioning residents about their sanitary facilities, the crowd was breaking into houses and loading furnishings into wagons. Furnishings and owners both were removed forcibly to the docks where they waited, in the rain, while the *Queen of the Pacific* got up steam for its regular sailing to San Francisco. The steamship captain, however, refused to take Chinese on board except as paying passengers, and few had money for the fare. The citizens at once set about raising the necessary funds from local merchants and bankers.

While this was going on, Governor Squire heard the news and

11 *Call*, September 7, October 28, November 3, 6, 8, 12, 13, 17, 24, 1885; February 12, 1886; Clinton A. Snowden, *History of Washington: The Rise and Progress of an American State*, 4 vols. (New York, 1909), IV, 320–322; Jules A. Karlin, "The Anti-Chinese Outbreaks in Seattle," *Pacific Northwest Quarterly*, XXXIX (April, 1948), 103–129.

12 *Call*, December 16, 20, 27, 1885; January 3, February 5, 10, 12, 25, 26, 28, March 14, 1886. Truckee, like Eureka, emphasized the nonviolence of its anti-Chinese campaign. Chinese merchants were allowed time to wind up their affairs. There was, in both cases, however, an accompaniment of threats of violence in case of noncompliance.

intervened by mobilizing militia and securing a writ of habeas corpus with respect to the embarking Chinese. The writ blocked their departure, and on the following morning Squire's little group of militiamen marched them up to the courthouse. There they were informed by a federal judge that, although they were under no legal obligation to leave, means for their protection if they stayed were at best dubious. Most of the Chinese elected the voyage to San Francisco. The *Queen of the Pacific* had stood by for the outcome; but it was now clear that there were too many Chinese for the capacity of the vessel. Eventually 196 took passage, leaving some 200 at the pierhead, guarded by the handful of militia, and facing a return to what was left of Chinatown through the hostile crowd assembled to see them off. The skipper of the *Queen* reported afterward that as his steamer slipped away into the mist, he heard firing begin in the city behind him.

What had happened was that the Chinese and the militia were cut off a few blocks from the waterfront. The crowd closed around them, shouting, jostling, attempting to wrestle the rifles from the guardsmen. Several of these opened fire, and as the crowd fell back, reinforcements of militia broke through from the docks and from the courthouse. They formed a hollow square surrounding the Chinese; and while casualties of the first volley (two dead, several wounded) were dragged away and for an hour or more afterwards, the militia faced the crowd at gunpoint. Eventually this deadlock eased off sufficiently to permit the return of the Chinese to their quarters. The governor invoked martial law, declared a curfew, then proceeded with summary arrests. One day later President Cleveland ordered federal troops from Vancouver to Seattle.[13]

Eureka, Rock Springs, Tacoma, Truckee, Seattle—with precedents such as these the floodgates were open. From Los Angeles and Pasadena in the south to Olympia and Oregon City in the north, cities and towns hastened to imitate these examples. Some proceeded by legal means, some with violence, the majority by combination of the two. Through California's Central Valley, along the foothills of the Sierra Nevada, and in the coastal forest regions from Fort Bragg to the Canadian border, dozens of communities followed suit.[14] In California

13 *Call*, February 8, 9, 12, 1886.
14 A check of the *Call*, following references in the newspaper subject index, California Room, California State Library, Sacramento, indicated expulsions or removal committees in thirty-five California communities during the months January–April, 1886. Citations are too numerous to list separately, since some localities appeared more than once in news reports. Such reports took up only a minor portion of column space devoted to the Chinese issue. Taking precedence for front-page coverage were debates in Washington, activities of anti-Chinese groups in

the movement quickly acquired its own organizational apparatus. Early in February 1886, a conference at San Jose, after naming Assemblyman McGlashan as chairman, proposed a boycott of Chinese, of their products, and of all who employed Chinese to be implemented locally by those methods so successfully demonstrated at Truckee.[15] The conference adjourned upon call of its chairman.

Meanwhile, a recently organized committee at Sacramento summoned a state convention to be composed of delegates named by county boards of supervisors.[16] The method of selection was intended to impart a semiofficial character, and among delegates to the Sacramento convention were men high in the leadership of both political parties.[17] What resulted, in effect, was a reincarnation of the bipartisan establishment. But McGlashan, not to be left out, called his adjourned San Jose conference to reassemble at Sacramento simultaneously with the convention. After a good deal of bickering and fussing, the two bodies merged, uniting Republicans and Democrats with the more radical immediate actionists (even including a number of San Francisco labor men, Burnette Haskell among them, who had already established close ties with the San Jose group). [18] Thus the bipartisan

San Francisco, cases of alleged illegal entry, and charges and countercharges of malfeasance among customs officials who presumably administered the Exclusion Act. On the anti-Chinese campaign in western Washington during this same period, see Snowden, IV, 319–324.

[15] Call, February 5, 1886.

[16] Call, December 11, 19, 1885; February 25, 1886. On the Sacramento convention, Call, March 10–12, 1886; Sacramento Record Union, March 10–12, 1886.

[17] Prominent delegates were John Bidwell, pre-gold-rush pioneer, one of the largest landowners in the state (Dictionary of American Biography, II, 247–248); Andrew Jackson Bryant, former Democratic mayor of San Francisco (above, p. 106); M. M. Estee, San Francisco lawyer, president of the Republican National Convention in 1888, later U.S. judge for Territory of Hawaii (J. C. Bates, ed., History of the Bench and Bar in California [San Francisco, 1912], 189); Grove Johnson, state senator and assemblyman, U.S. congressman, for many years anchor man for the Southern Pacific at Sacramento, father of Hiram Johnson (California Blue Book [1911], 199–200, 216, 265, and George E. Mowry, California Progressives [Chicago: Quadrangle Paperback, 1963], 82, 111); George B. Katzenstein, Sacramento insurance executive, fruit grower and fruit shipping agent (Leigh H. Irvine, A History of the New California, 2 vols. [Chicago, 1905], I, 436–438); F. G. Newlands, son-in-law of William Sharon, later Democratic U.S. senator from Nevada and outstanding conservationist (DAB, XIII, 462–463); Frank M. Pixley, San Francisco Republican, editor of the Argonaut (Alonzo Phelps, Contemporary Biography of California's Representative Men, 2 vols. [San Francisco, 1881], I, 308); A. A. Sargent, former Republican U.S. senator from California (California Blue Book (1903), 489, 491); John F. Swift, San Francisco lawyer, chairman of the convention committee which drew up a long address to the U.S. Congress and president. Swift won the Republican nomination for governor the following year, 1887, but lost the election. He later served as U.S. minister to Japan: DAB, XVIII, 246–247.

[18] Jake Wolf and Herman Guttstadt of the San Francisco Cigar Makers' Union (below, pp. 216, 271), James H. Barry, San Francisco labor editor, and Volney Hoffmeier of the Musicians' Union, later state master workman of the Knights of Labor

establishment became a united front which through the Sacramento convention launched a statewide organization—the California Anti-Chinese Non-Partisan Association—committed, verbally at least, to the McGlashan program. Ratification meetings througout the state merged into and stimulated the already rapid spread of the expulsion campaign.[19]

To contemporary observers these events seemed to be working decisive changes in the social geography of the West. After the San Jose conference, but before the convention at Sacramento, the Chinese minister in Washington protested to Secretary of State Bayard that "a concerted movement [was] in progress to drive out the Chinese from all the cities and towns of California except San Francisco, and that the Governor of the State and the Sheriffs of the various counties evinced no disposition to protect the Chinese in their rights." "Bankrupt Chinese" from all over the Pacific Coast were said to be pouring into San Francisco. The *Call* estimated that the city's Oriental population had increased by 20,000 in three months. Chinese were fighting in the alleys for garbage and rotten fish, the paper reported enthusiastically, and went on to quote an unidentified officer, presumably one of the Chinatown Specials: "I'm sure I don't know what is to become of these people. They are on the verge of starvation. I know for I have been here for years." Colonel Bee, consul for the Chinese, while denying any overcrowding or starvation and minimizing the effects of the expulsion campaign in the hinterland, acknowledged that large numbers had left the Pacific Coast since passage of the Exclusion Act. The result, he predicted, would be a shortage of labor. Already orders for several hundred laborers remained unfilled because men were not available. As for the two steamer loads of Chinese brought down from Seattle and neighboring towns, they had been employed by the Southern Pacific Railroad "the moment they landed" at San Francisco. Farmers above all, he told reporters, would be facing disaster. "If you drive the Chinese out now, who is going to gather the fruit and the harvests of next summer and fall?"[20]

and president of the San Francisco Federated Trades Council, all came to the Sacramento convention with the San Jose group (*Call*, March 10, 11, 1886; Ira B. Cross, *A History of the Labor Movement in California* (Berkeley, 1935), 148, 155, 328 note 3); so did Burnette Haskell, bringing with him thirty proxies of San Francisco labor organizations, which were accepted in the convention after a sharp debate (*Record Union*, March 12, 1886); and see also San Francisco *Open Letter*, March 20, 1886, found in Cross Labor Notes, Carton IV, folder 149. The *Open Letter* was published sporadically by Carl Browne, a hanger-on-the-fringes of the labor movement, formerly Denis Kearney's henchman and "secretary." See above, p. 140.

[19] For example, *Call*, March 20, 21, 1886.

[20] *Call*, in the order cited: February 16, 9, 16, 1886; October 24, 1885; March 7, 30, 30, 7, 1886.

In the long view of census statistics results were not quite so decisive as they appeared to contemporaries. For California, comparison of returns for 1880 and 1890 shows that Chinese population reached a peak of 75,000 in 1880 (the real peak of course came in 1882, and was considerably higher),[21] fell off to 72,000 in 1890, then sloped into a long decline. This was the result of the Exclusion Act. Meanwhile white population was increasing so that the percentage of Chinese to total population dropped from just under 10 percent in 1880 to somewhat less than 6.5 percent in 1890.[22] Against this background of relative overall decline, there were significant regional variations. The percentages of total statewide Chinese population found in the mountain counties, in the north coast counties, and in the northern portion of the Central Valley declined sharply. On the other hand, corresponding percentages increased for emergent agricultural regions in the southern Central Valley, the Salinas Valley, Orange and Los Angeles counties, as well as for the six counties of the San Francisco Bay Area.[23] These figures indicate that in California's major farming regions—with the important exception of the northern Central Valley —the expulsion campaign of 1885–1886 proved relatively ineffective. As for the mountain areas and north coast, there was certainly an exodus of Chinese; but whether this resulted from anti-Chinese activities or from other factors such as the decline of placer mining would be difficult to determine. The increased percentage in the Bay Area seems unmistakably to have represented the retreat of Chinese from sections of the hinterland to the metropolis.

Out of this summary of the expulsions and of seemingly related

[21] Elmer Clarence Sandmeyer, *The Anti-Chinese Movement in California* (Urbana, Ill., 1939), 17; California Bureau of Labor Statistics, *Second Biennial Report,* (Sacramento, 1887), 55.

[22] Based on tabulation from U.S. census figures in Robert J. Pitchell, "Twentieth Century California Voting Behavior" (Ph.D. diss., University of California, Berkeley, 1955), 97, Table 15.

[23] Warren S. Thompson, *Growth and Changes in California's Population* (Los Angeles, 1955), 75, Table VII-6, shows the following variations in percentage of total Chinese population of the state found in counties grouped regionally: seventeen Sierra Nevada and Trinity Alps counties, from 23.7 percent (1880) to 10 percent (1890); five north coast counties, from 2 percent (1880) to 0.8 percent (1890); seven counties of the northern Central Valley, from 11.4 percent (1880) to 7.2 percent (1890). Increased percentages appeared in the following regions: Fresno County, 1 percent (1880) to 3.8 percent (1890); four counties of the southern Central Valley, 1.4 percent (1880) to 2.9 percent 1890); four counties of the Salinas and San Benito valleys, 1.8 percent (1880) to 4 percent (1890); Orange, and Los Angeles County, 1.6 percent (1880) to 6.3 percent (1890); six counties of the San Francisco Bay Area, 39.6 percent (1880) to 44.8 percent (1890). It may be well to reemphasize that these percentages refer to proportions of California's total Chinese population found in specified regions.

population movements, certain interconnections appear. First, it was in rather remote areas where law enforcement was at a minimum that the sharpest conflicts developed. But these locations had a second and perhaps more important characteristic in common: the dominant industries were mining (especially coal) and lumbering. News reports and eyewitness accounts almost without exception stressed the participation of workingmen from these industries in the agitation.[24] Moreover, there is evidence of widespread leadership by local assemblies of the Knights of Labor: at Rock Springs the Knights' hall served as rallying point for the attack on the Chinese quarter; at Olympia a leader of the Knights was one of the directing committee; at Seattle, Knights of Labor officials were among those arrested by federal authorities.[25] In Oregon, assemblies of the Knights were instrumental in convoking a convention which set Washington's Birthday 1886 as target date for removal of Chinese from the smaller towns.[26]

The Knights of Labor, because of its organizational form, was particularly attractive to the semiskilled, highly mobile workers drawn into mining and lumbering. Unprotected by sharply defined skills, they had characteristically found their defense against Chinese competition in those lines of status and prestige passed down from earlier mine camps and railroad construction gangs. But in the mid-eighties such traditional lines were dissolving, the chief reductive agents being increased pressure from the white unemployed and the diminishing availability (and rising cost) of Chinese labor. Whites were now demanding traditionally Chinese jobs, while Chinese were becoming too costly to be restricted to limited categories. One result was a lessening of wage differentials between white and Chinese labor, which should have worked to the advantage of whites; a second result was the breaking down of job division by caste, which if not to the *dis*advantage of white workers was very much to their distaste. It was apparently intolerable to them (especially in the face of job scarcity and falling wages) to be thrown into direct competition with a group hitherto relegated to inferior status. As noted earlier, the tensions and discontents of an era of industrial conflict tended in the West to concentrate on this issue.

[24] Secretary of State Bayard's reply to the Chinese minister, quoted in *Call*, March 3, 1886; statement of the captain of the *Queen of the Pacific*, *Call*, February 12, 1886. See also *Call*, December 6, 1885; February 12, 1886.

[25] Crane and Larson, *Annals*, XII, 47–55; *Call*, November 12, 1885; February 10, 12, 1886.

[26] Burnette Haskell to his wife, Anna Haskell, Portland, Oregon, February 10, 1886; Haskell's report to the San Francisco Federated Trades on his trip to Oregon, leaflet reprint of an article from San Francisco *Daily Report*, dated February 25, 1886 (both in Haskell Family Papers, Box II, Bancroft Library).

But involvement of white workingmen from certain extractive industries by no means fully explains the expulsion campaign of 1885–1886, especially as it developed in California. The newspapers, while generously ascribing acts of violence to the workers, spoke frequently of local businessmen as the real leaders. Unquestionably there was an element of class prejudice in this assignment of roles; yet the evidence is nevertheless conclusive. There can be no doubt that Seattle merchants and bankers raised money for passage to San Francisco of the expelled Chinese, nor that local businessmen organized and executed the Tacoma and Eureka expulsions as well as the removal at Truckee and played leading parts in many less dramatic actions in the hinterland towns of Oregon and California.[27] Why? The answer applies almost equally well for towns centered in agricultural regions and those adjacent to extractive industries. Local business people felt themselves at a disadvantage in relation to larger entrepreneurs who employed Chinese gang labor. These larger operators neither purchased supplies nor marketed their product through the town; they went directly to the city. Their Chinese employees on the other hand traded locally, but only with fellow countrymen whose stores and trading posts formed the Chinese enclave within the town. This situation became a source of mounting irritation to small-town businessmen. Their steadiest customers, in areas of extractive industry, were the white industrial workers; in agricultural regions, family-size ranchers and white farm laborers (if there were any).[28] From this community of interest sprang the expulsion campaign of 1885–1886.

[27] The expulsion committee at Eureka, after setting up permanent machinery to prevent any return by Chinese, made clear its own socioeconomic status in the following resolution: "That every man who has no visible means of support and who habituates a house of prostitution or gambling dens to be allowed until Saturday the 14th day of February to leave this city" (*Chronicle,* February 8, 1885). On participation of businessmen, bankers, property-holders, etc., Tacoma: *Call,* November 17, 1885; Seattle: *Call,* November 8, 17, 1885, February 9, 1886; Truckee: *Call,* December 20, 1885, January 3, 1886; and for other examples in California; Pasadena, Stockton, Moore's Station (near Marysville), Merced, Arroyo Grande, Sebastopol, Dutch Flat, respectively: *Call,* November 8, December 24, 1885; February 5, 12, 16, 27, March 7, 1886.

[28] Colonel Bee (above, p. 209) was doubtless correct in his insistence that, as of the mid-eighties, few white farm workers were to be found in California. This was almost certainly the reason why actions against Chinese enclaves in small towns produced (at this period) no lasting reduction in the employment of Chinese agricultural labor. It was noted above that the northern counties of the Central Valley represented an exception to this general case. One may speculate that the presence of important mining and lumbering operations in and around these counties had early created a white industrial labor force which not only toughened the anti-Chinese agitation, but moved over into agricultural work during the depression years. No corresponding process occurred in the southern agricultural regions of the state until the depression of the nineties. County farm associations during the

It will be evident that organized labor in San Francisco was foreclosed from direct participation in these exciting events. The city's Chinatown, for reasons set forth earlier, was invulnerable to attack.[29] Beyond this, urban craftsmen had few organizational links with the two main social groups pressing the campaign in the hinterland. Although it was true that Knights of Labor were active in San Francisco, these were a different type of cat from the miners and loggers of Wyoming and the Northwest; and in any case common affiliation to the national center (a very loose affiliation) made for no contact between regional branches.

The situation was a frustrating one for San Francisco labor leaders. What was being done in the back country was the carrying out of that program of abatement by violence which had been declared first by San Francisco's labor politicians through the Workingmen's party and next by San Francisco's trade unionists through the League of Deliverance. Accustomed to playing the title role of the drama, the San Franciscans could now only applaud from the sidelines. This they did vehemently; and they denounced the federal authorities, especially for the shootings and arrests in Seattle.[30] Yet what they wanted and what they kept groping for was a leading part in a movement which appeared to be gathering mass support. And here precisely they were thwarted by division within their own ranks. In an attempt to resolve these divisions and to take advantage, for organized labor, of the seemingly vast opportunities opened up by the expulsion campaign, a group of trade unionists around Frank Roney (strongly backed by Burnette Haskell's IWA) executed a kind of *coup de main* in December 1885 and took over direction of the labor movement.

To understand how this came about, it will first be necessary to glance for a moment at developments in the Pacific Coast cigar trade.

The Cigar Makers' Crusade

Cigar making, by western standards of the time, was a major industry. California production in 1886 was more than 145.5 million cigars. In

eighties were for the most part strenuously opposed to the expulsion campaign. For reactions, especially of fruit and hopgrowers, see San Francisco *Pacific Rural Press*, February 27–April 10, passim; *Argonaut*, April 3, 1886.

[29] Above, pp. 148–151. The Board of Supervisors renewed its attack on Chinatown, but without much effect. See Willard B. Farwell, *The Chinese at Home and Abroad. Together with the Report of the Special Committee of the Board of Supervisors of San Francisco, on the Condition of the Chinese Quarter of that City* (San Francisco, 1885), especially Part II, 3–76.

[30] San Francisco sandlot oratory, *Call*, November 9, 1885; meeting of IWA, San Francisco, *Call*, February 16, 1886; Haskell report on Oregon (above, n. 26).

San Francisco alone, the trade employed somewhere between 4.000 and 8,000 men, among whom were a large number of Chinese. Manufacturers, facing sharp competition from the East, complained of high western production costs and sometimes threatened to move to New York or Florida.[31] Cigar making, like many other industries during this period, was undergoing drastic rationalization. This depended in part on technical innovation (a mold had been introduced which simplified shaping the cigar), but mainly on subdivision of the production process through assignment of preliminary stages to unskilled or semiskilled hands, while the final stages were reserved to skilled journeymen. The maximum benefits of such subdivision could be achieved only in rather large and highly capitalized factories. From the beginning of the industry in the West, journeymen and small proprietors had endeavored to hold some kind of line against the encroachment of capitalization and rationalization.[32]

As noted earlier, this line generally coincided with the line between white-only establishments and those employing Chinese. Anticoolieism thus became a means of product differentiation by which small producers could cling to a toehold in the market. Since the mid-seventies an organization of journeymen and small proprietors, the White Cigar Makers' Association of the Pacific Coast, had been endeavoring to popularize its white label, granted as an endorsement to white-only establishments. Members of the association pledged to work for no manufacturer who employed Chinese.[33]

For the larger enterprises it may be that the chief advantage of Chinese labor, even outweighing its lower cost, lay in its greater amenability to the rationalization process. Despite endeavors of the White Cigar Makers' Association, Chinese rapidly permeated the trade. By 1885, three-quarters and perhaps as many as seven-eights of all cigar workers were Chinese, and of these at least half were employed by white proprietors. Periodic efforts to persuade these proprietors to forego their use of Chinese failed, in part at least, because replacements of skilled white labor were unavailable. To have obeyed the

[31] California, Bureau of Labor Statistics, *Second Biennial Report,* 439, 442; Mary Roberts Coolidge, *Chinese Immigration* (New York, 1909), 365–371; *Call,* October 24, 1885.

[32] John R. Commons et al., *History of Labour in the United States,* 4 vols. (New York, 1918), II, 71–74. Willis N. Baer, *The Economic Development of the Cigar Industry in the United States* (Lancaster, Pa., 1933), especially 80–89. On technological change in the cigar industry, see *Chronicle,* July 25, 1882; *Daily Report,* October 31, 1885.

[33] See above, pp. 5–7, 73–75; *Daily Report,* October 31, 1885.

ethic of race solidarity under such circumstances might not only have raised labor costs and narrowed profit margins, but resulted in surrendering the West Coast market to eastern competitors or to rival establishments owned by Chinese.[34]

Meanwhile Chinese wages had been rising. In 1884, two years after passage of the Exclusion Act, Chinese cigar makers in San Francisco conducted a successful strike for an increased rate per thousand. In the fall of the same year occurred a second Chinese strike not for wages this time but for what seems to have been insistence upon "union shop" conditions. Strike demands were for dismissal of two Chinese presumably not members of a Chinese union. At this critical moment, however, the newly organized San Francisco Merchants and Manufacturers' Association stepped in, stiffened the white proprietors against further concessions; and the Chinese returned to work without winning their demands. These episodes, and what followed in 1885, raise the fascinating question of whether there was a Chinese union. Cross wrote that such an organization had come into existence in 1883. Newspapers at the time debated the question at length. Given the highly integrated Chinese community, it seems reasonable to suppose that Chinese cigar makers must have been organized, but whether horizontally as wage earners or vertically into an all-Chinese guild which would function as a union only against *white* employers remains at this distance probably impossible to determine.[35]

However that may be, there seems little doubt that by 1885 the wages of Chinese and of white skilled cigar makers were beginning to overlap. And here a new and dynamic factor entered the situation—the Cigar Makers' International Union, of which Adolph Strasser was national president and Samuel Gompers the most famous son. The CMIU was one of that group of new unions which, having joined forces with older craft organizations like the Molders' and Typographical Unions, was in the mid-eighties already challenging the Knights of Labor for leadership of the organized labor movement. Characteristic of these new unions was a militant wage consciousness, only one step removed from Marxian class consciousness, and an

---

[34] Cross, 169; California, Bureau of Labor Statistics, *Second Biennial Report*, 439. In 1883 an effort to replace Chinese with white cigar makers from the East had failed. In the following year there had been an attempt to set up an apprentice school for white youngsters, which also failed. See the comments of Jake Wolf, president of the San Francisco Cigar Makers' Union, *Call*, November 21, 26, 1885.

[35] *Call*, October 24, 27, 30, November 17, 1885. The *Call* maintained that the Chinese "union" was in fact a vertical syndicate, controlled from the top by the Six Companies. I think this description is probably about right. See Cross, 147.

emphasis on organizational stability to be achieved through high dues, full-time officials, and insurance and benefit programs modeled on the trade unionism of Great Britain.[36] The CMIU would have little patience with an organization like the White Cigar Makers' Association of the Pacific Coast, which devoted itself to prolonging the existence of inefficient and undercapitalized manufacturers.

Local 228 of the CMIU was organized in San Francisco in the autumn of 1884. Unlike the association, it required no pledge of its members to refuse work for proprietors employing Chinese. On the contrary, it made every effort to place men in white-owned factories where Chinese had been exclusively employed. This was the first step of a long-range plan for driving Orientals out of the trade. Jake Wolf, president and organizer of the new local, announced that his union had 36,000 members nationally—many in the East being out of work—and could replace every Chinese cigar maker in San Francisco if the white employers would cooperate.[37] Nor would this involve any loss to employers, since white cigar makers would work at the same wages currently being paid Chinese. On this point Wolf was emphatic. "Why not?" he responded to a question from a newspaper reporter. "You do not suppose that skilled Chinese cigar makers work for starvation wages? No sir," and then explained:

> A Chinaman knows the value of his work as well as his employer. Those who employ Chinese cannot advance the plea that it is because the coolie works cheap. He does not work cheap. John gets as good wages for his skilled labor as does a white man, though I will admit that the Chinaman has caused a great decline in the scale of wages paid white cigar makers ten years ago. When John comes a raw hand into the business to learn it, he will work for almost nothing—25 cents

[36] *Call*, October 24, 26, 1885. Both the Cigar Makers' Union official and the editorial writer cited here spoke explicitly of equal wage rates. I have used the more ambiguous term "overlap" because the evidence suggests that to the extent that there was an equalization of wages, this occurred at the top skill level. It is difficult to find comparisons of the same categories of work. The California Bureau of Labor Statistics' *Second Biennial Report,* comparing weekly average earnings of white journeymen with those of Chinese cigar workers generally, found that whites averaged twice as much as Chinese (439). Earnings of white journeymen in San Francisco and in New York were shown to be approximately equal (24, 143). The trade in New York had already undergone extensive rationalization (above, n. 53). Had earnings of skilled Chinese cigar makers been taken as the basis of comparison with earnings of white journeymen, East and West, it seems likely that the earnings of Chinese would have come quite close at least to those of whites. See Commons et al., *History,* II, 301–315, 317–331, 395–411; and see below, pp. 238–241.

[37] *Call*, October 25, 1885.

a day—until he masters it, but as soon as he knows all the intricacies of the trade, and it does not take him long either, he wants his journeyman's wages.[38]

Wolf's use of the phrase "journeyman's wages" suggests something he did not say but which was implicit in the proposal to place white journeymen in factories largely manned by Chinese. This was that the union, unlike the association, was willing to accept subdivision of the trade by rationalization. Clearly the whites would move into skilled final positions, while at least for some time to come Chinese would perform the preliminary operations. Eventually they might be replaced by women and children, or by immigrant white labor, thus duplicating the pattern already worked out in New York; but certainly this was not part of the immediate program.[39]

The Cigar Makers' Union encountered opposition not only from manufacturers, but also (and most strenuously) from the White Cigar Makers' Association. At first the union made little progress but finally won a sympathetic hearing at one large plant previously worked exclusively by Chinese. This was under the management of Koenigsberger, Falk, and Mayer, who cautiously took on a few whites and gradually increased the number until their production force of 160 was almost evenly divided. Then came an event which astonished San Francisco: the Chinese walked out, demanding ouster of the whites.

Within the trade the immediate effect was to make white manufacturers even more leary of the union plan than they had been before. They feared a citywide strike by Chinese cigar makers which would have ruined many of them. But for whatever reasons no such strike occurred. Koenigsberger, Falk, and Mayer stood firm, while the Cigar Makers' Union, with vociferous support from the Knights of Labor and other organized trades, launched a boycott against all brands of cigars except those marketed by Koenigsberger, Falk, and Mayer.[40] The White Cigar Makers' Association charged that this firm had previously stored up quantities of Chinese-made cigars which it was now selling under the CMIU's label. Nonetheless the boycott hurt—or at least frightened—other manufacturers; and before the end of November there was a stampede for the CMIU program. This required a

---

[38] *Call*, October 24, 1885.

[39] The immediate program was to substitute white journeymen for Chinese skilled workers at the top level. This was why Wolf emphasized the equality of wage rates at that level. See note 36 above.

[40] *Call*, October 24, 25, 31, November 17, 1885. A leaflet issued by the San Francisco Branch, CMIU of A, urging patronage of Koenigsberger, Falk, and Mayer, will be found in Cross Labor Notes, Carton IV, folder 119 (Bancroft Library).

pledge to discharge all Chinese as of January 1, 1886, or as soon there-after as white workers were available; in return for which the union guaranteed a supply of competent journeymen willing to work for the going New York scale.[41] Wolf journeyed East at the manufacturers' expense to recruit cigar makers, who would naturally be members of his own union; and the CMIU national office agreed to advance money for railroad fares. Eventually under this arrangement more than four hundred eastern cigar makers made the trip to San Francisco.[42]

But repercussions of the Chinese strike were even more dramatic outside the cigar trade than within it. Here was a revelation of what seemed the real mind of the Chinese. "They number from 25,000 to 30,000," the *Call* wrote, "nine-tenths, or thereabouts, of whom are male adults—and they begin to feel overbearing in their strength." The labor movement, divided though it was, rallied in defense of its embattled brothers. A mass meeting assembled upon call of the Knights of Labor. This was preceded by a parade for which Roney, the trade unionist, served as grand marshall, while at the head of the parade marched 150 sailors captained by Burnette Haskell of the IWA. One of the guest orators, Colonel Stuart Taylor, a federal officeholder in San Francisco, summed up the general thrust of the proceedings in two remarkably compact sentences: "This is the old irrepressible con-flict between slave and white labor. God grant there may be a survival of the fittest."

No one seems to have intended, however, that the matter should be left altogether in divine hands. Earlier, during preparations for the mass meeting, one of the several arrangements committees had suggested that a coastwide labor congress ought to be convened. The Knights of Labor took hold of this proposal and such a congress was summoned for November 30, 1885, in San Francisco.[43]

[41] The CMIU had first offered to work for the same wages paid Chinese, then for the New York scale. San Francisco manufacturers accepted this latter offer (under some pressure). No direct evidence has come to hand as to whether it was equal to what they had been paying Chinese. When, less than a year later, San Francisco manufacturers laid off most of the eastern cigar makers, they charged that the easterners had violated the agreement by demanding an "increase of from $2 to $4 on the price paid Chinese workmen." (California Bureau of Labor Sta-tistics, *Second Biennial Report*, 438–439; *Call*, December 17, 20, 1885.)

[42] By fall of 1886 more than half the imported cigar makers had gone back east. Koenigsberger, Falk, and Mayer, the white labor champions, moved to Key West in that year. (*Call*, September 30, 1886; and Frank Roney, *Frank, Roney, Irish Rebel and California Labor Leader* [Berkeley, 1931], 381–383.)

[43] *Call*, in the order cited, October 27, November 1, October 31, November 30, all 1885.

The Federated Trades

Before the congress assembled, something in the nature of a game of musical chairs ensued. Leaders of the Knights caucused, the trade unionists caucused, the IWA caucused. Since their affiliations over-lapped, they infiltrated each other's councils. Roney, invited by all groups, attended none; yet he was busy caucusing with all of them in less formal style. The start of the congress was therefore the culmination of a great deal of diplomacy already transacted; and as in a well-played chess game, the opening gambit determined much of what was to follow.[44]

John Payne, one of the "politicians" in leadership of the Knights of Labor, rose to welcome the delegates—157 altogether from 64 organiza-tions, including trade unions, local assemblies of the Knights, and branches of the IWA and the Socialistic Labor party. Payne invited nominations for chairman. Several names were offered, among them that of Frank Roney. But Payne refused to accept Roney's nomination. There were protests from the floor. While Payne hesitated, perhaps an instant too long, J. F. Valentine, president of the Molders' Union, shouted that since the chair seemed unwilling to place the question he would do so himself. He called for a voice vote on Roney. The re-sponse was a standing ovation; and Roney, leaping to the platform, took the gavel from Payne's hand, thanked him, waved him from the podium and proceeded at once with the business of the congress.[45]

The major problem was that of inducing some kind of cooperation from a thoroughly discordant gathering. "It was the first time that so many conflicting elements had assembled in one body," Roney wrote in his autobiography:

> We had the conservative trade unionist who favored an aris-tocracy or upper-class division of labor; we had the demo-cratic trade unionist who believed that all laborers were on a common level; we had the mild socialist who believed in party discipline when not too rigidly enforced; we had the socialist who demanded nothing less than the whole socialistic program; we had the internationalist who was an advocate of expedient methods designed to bring about the social revolu-tion, and finally, we had the anarchist, an exponent of in-dividualism and a relentless foe of government in every form. It was a queer combination of heterogeneous elements that I

44 Roney, 435–438.
45 Roney, 437, 439; *Daily Report,* December 1, 1885, clipping in Cross Labor Notes, Carton IV, folder 148 (Bancroft Library).

had set myself to control and for the moment, at least, to harmonize. . . . The radicals gave me less trouble than the conservatives.[46]

This was scarcely surprising since the radicals and middle ground unionists had previously agreed on a program with which Roney was in full accord. Seizure of the chairmanship proved decisive because it gave Roney appointment of the credentials committee, thus preventing exclusion of the radicals from the congress. The conservatives had been suspected, doubtless correctly, of harboring such an intent.[47] As it turned out, what resulted was approximately the opposite.

With committee appointments out of the way, an agenda apparently worked out beforehand by the trade union caucus (and which had been approved by the IWA) was submitted and adopted. It ran as follows: (1) the Chinese question; (2) convict labor; (3) the cause of hard times; (4) shorter hours of labor; (5) miscellaneous; (6) the better federation and organization of labor. The key points, obviously, were the first and last. On the Chinese question, the chair appointed a committee of five to bring in a report; meanwhile, however, one of the Sailors' delegates, speaking from the floor, offered a resolution which demanded removal of all Chinese from San Francisco within sixty days. Upon this proposition the congress erupted into violent debate.[48]

Here, in effect, was the old maximum program of the League of Deliverance, abatement by violence, and with a two-month time fuse attached. Clearly the resolution had been authored by the IWA and planted in the Sailors' Union which the IWA at that time controlled. Adoption would place the congress at the forefront of the entire Pacific Coast expulsion movement. But it would at the same time commit the leadership either to an assault on the public authorities or to an ignominious retreat. Everyone saw the fatal alternatives; and it was on these that the major division took shape. Conservatives, led by the Knights of Labor spokesmen—who threatened to withdraw their organization if the resolution were approved—took the negative. Following Roney's lead, trade unionists and the radicals favored adoption.[49]

46 Roney, 440–441.

47 IWA Minute Book, 72–73, November 15, 22, 1885 (IWA Records, Bancroft Library); Roney, 437–438. For an account of the unsuccessful effort by conservatives to prevent seating of delegates of the Socialistic Labor party, see Call, December 1, 1885.

48 IWA Minute Book, 73, November 22, 1885; Call, December 2, 3, 1885.

49 IWA Minute Book, 72–73, November 15, 22, 1885; Roney, 443.

At this point, however, a second cleavage surfaced in the debate, not between radicals and conservatives but entirely within the radical wing. And as a matter of fact it was contained within the IWA itself. Sigismund Danielewicz, the San Francisco barber turned seaman, a leading IWA member (he was at the time secretary of the IWA Central Committee) and one of the founders of the Sailors' Union, stepped up to the stage. There he began delivery of a prepared statement which (to quote a newspaper report of what followed) "would have proved a defense of the Chinese if it had been completed." He "tried the patience of the Convention," the account went on, "by reading several pyramids of words about the equality of men. He said that he belonged to a race which had been persecuted for hundreds of years and was still persecuted—the Jews; and he called upon all of his people to consider whether 'the persecution of the Chinese' was more justifiable than theirs had been. And he left it upon the Irish to say whether it was more justifiable than their persecutions in New York had been; upon the Germans to make a similar comparison upon their condition somewhere else." [50] Danielewicz, seemingly, was in defiance of the line of his own organization.

Insiders, however, knew that his *démarche* was one that had been agreed to, or at least accepted, beforehand. Seven days prior to the opening of the congress, the IWA Central Committee had met to chart the course for all delegates under its control. The conclusion arrived at was to push for the expulsion resolution and, in case that failed, to drop back to a minimum program of pressure through legal means and selective boycotting. This decision amounted to a continuation of the tactical line West Coast socialists had been following since 1877 when they had moved into the Workingmen's Party of California because that was where the mass base was. Yet as Roney had realized at the time, for a socialist to "sail under the flag" of anticoolieism involved a fundamental contradiction between tactics and long-range goals.[51] And while Roney's ideological enthusiasms in the interim had considerably cooled, he was still pursuing precisely the same tactics, no longer toward socialist but toward trade union objectives. The IWA group was able to work with him and with trade unionists generally, because it viewed unionism as an essential step in its own direction. Theoretically, then, the IWA accepted agitation against the Chinese— though perhaps distasteful in itself—as justifiable for economic reasons (the cheap labor argument) and expedient because it tended to unite

50 *Daily Report,* December 3, 1885, in Cross Labor Notes, Carton IV, folder 148.
51 IWA Minute Book, 73, November 22, 1885; Roney, 287.

the main body of workers and educated them to a perception of their own potential strength.

By 1885, however, the conflict between tactics and strategic goals was becoming more difficult to reconcile. Though the full effects of the Exclusion Act had not yet become visible, recent developments in the cigar trade were readily apparent, and so was the increasing militancy of the Chinese. The old rationale that Chinese were unorganizable and unassimilable because they were too abject to defend themselves seemed scarcely to apply in the new situation. Considerations such as these seem to have been leading certain socialists to wonder if the time had not come for a changeover from the expedient to the principled line. And this was precisely the question Sigismund Danielewicz opened up at the IWA Central Committee by an attack on the majority decision. Socialists, he argued, must stand for working class solidarity. They ought to dissociate themselves from the anti-Chinese campaign. If they attended the congress at all, it should be to declare their position as internationalists, and to focus the attention of delegates on the real issue which was the struggle against capitalism.[52]

Of this classic division on the left, no record remains aside from the subsequent conduct of IWA delegates and a few handwritten lines in a tattered notebook, Danielewicz' minutes of the Central Committee meeting. Nonetheless it is clear that the dispute cut deep. The very wording of the expulsion resolution as introduced by the Sailors' Union bore witness to the divided counsels which informed it. The opening clause began in the language of working class solidarity: "While this Convention recognizes that the Chinese are not the cause of hard times and that the settlement of the Chinese question will not settle the labor question . . ." Throughout the entire congress, IWA members in their speeches, and Haskell especially, repeated over and again the gist of this qualifying clause: the Chinese were not to blame; the main thrust must be against the real culprits—capitalists, land monopolists, and those governmental agencies which did their bidding. "If the Chinese question were settled today in San Francisco as it was in Eureka," Haskell was reported to have said, " in five months the workingmen of the city would be as hard up as they are today." And yet . . . so the expulsion resolution continued:

> . . . yet considering their bad moral habits, their low grades of development, their filth, their vices, their race differences from the Caucasians, and their willing status as slaves,
> *Resolved,* That we demand their complete removal from

52 IWA Minute Book, 73, November 22, 1885.

all parts of the Pacific Coast, and especially that they be removed from San Francisco within sixty days.[53]

Danielewicz, in his effort to oppose this resolution, had been voted down in the IWA Central Committee. But he pressed his point and finally won agreement that he be permitted, speaking as an individual socialist, to present the internationalist argument at the congress. Perhaps the others intended this rather seriously as a test, to see how the mass base might respond to a whiff of higher principle. If that were the intent, the result was unmistakable—and not one that encouraged Danielewicz' comrades to rush to his defense. His speech against the expulsion resolution was drowned in howls and laughter. The chairman, Roney, finally ruled him out of order. Danielewicz appealed, lost by almost unanimous vote.[54]

The debate then returned to the major cleavage, that between radicals and conservatives. On the radical side the most vigorous statements came from IWA members. Some were perhaps taking pains to repudiate Danielewicz' heresy. Thus another sailor, Alfred Fuhrman, also active in the IWA and later nationally known as organizer of the West Coast Brewery Workers' Union, declared his absolute reliability on the Chinese question by criticizing the expulsion resolution "from the left." Sixty days was too long, Fuhrman argued. The time to strike was at once, during the rainy season, while employment was at its height. "By force is the only way to remove the coolie and twenty days is enough to do it in. The Nihilists in Russia and the Fenians in Ireland were once called fools, but after the Czar was blown up and after the Phoenix Park murders, they were termed fanatics. If there are fools and fanatics in Russia and Ireland, I don't see why they cannot be here too." [55]

When the vote was taken (Danielewicz abstaining), the radicals carried the day by 60 to 47. Spokesmen for the Knights of Labor then led some, though not all, of their members from the hall, leaving the congress in the hands of trade unionists and the IWA. After this victory, an adjournment of several days was agreed upon to allow the various committees time for completion of their reports.[56]

53 Daily Report, in the order cited: December 3, December 7, December 3, all 1885, in Cross Labor Notes, Carton IV, folder 148; and see, also December 3, the resolution submitted by the Committee on the Chinese Question (eventually adopted) and summary of debate.
54 IWA Minute Book, 73, November 22, 1885; letter, signed "Sigismund Danielewicz," Daily Report, December 5, 1885; Daily Report, December 3, 1885, in Cross Labor Notes, Carton IV, folder 148.
55 Daily Report, December 3, 1885, in Cross Labor Notes, Carton IV, folder 148.
56 Ibid; Roney, 443–444.

But during the recess a new set of difficulties arose. The trade unionists, delighted though they were at the departure of the Knights of Labor "politicians," were scarcely any happier with the expulsion resolution than the Knights had been. They too began to talk of withdrawal. Roney, in order to hold them, promised reconsideration of the matter. Apparently there was not much resistance from the IWA, which dropped back in good order to its minimum program of gradual removal through legal means. Discussing these events long afterward, Roney hinted that the entire sequence had been planned beforehand solely for the purpose of ousting the Knights of Labor leaders (after making use of their organizational facilities to build the congress). Roney certainly was capable of devious means if such suited his purpose, and so was the IWA; but whether the expulsion program was actually conceived as a Trojan Horse or whether Roney was making the best, in retrospect, of a partial defeat, the record does not show. What it does show is that when the congress next assembled, the chair permitted reconsideration, and the sixty-day time fuse clause, almost without debate, was deleted from the resolution. The Knights of Labor leaders then applied for readmission. They were summarily rejected; and the congress went on to its major business, which was the organization of a labor federation for San Francisco.[57]

Under the ambitious title of Representative Council of the Federated Trades and Labor Organizations of the Pacific Coast (later shortened to San Francisco Federated Trades Council), the new center began its career early in 1886. Appropriately, Frank Roney became the first president; and the first activities were those of the expulsion campaign which had given the federation birth. Haskell was dispatched to Oregon where he harangued mass meetings and helped coordinate expulsionist energies on a target date of Washington's birthday 1886—in the process picking up from unions and local Knights of Labor assemblies promises of affiliation to the new center. When Assemblyman McGlashan's anti-Chinese conference met in San Jose, the Federated Trades gave full support and later participated with the McGlashan forces in the state convention at Sacramento. Here the ubiquitous Haskell arrived, armed with thirty proxies which he claimed represented the membership of the federation. These were challenged, but McGlashan and the San Jose delegates insisted upon Haskell's right to cast them. Haskell afterward boasted that his bloc of votes had saved the Sacramento convention from falling into the

[57] Roney, 444 and note 47; *Call*, December 6, 1885; *Daiy Report*, December 7, 1885, in Cross Labor Notes, Carton IV, folder 148.

grasp of the Southern Pacific. However that may be, the Federated Trades enthusiastically ratified the anti-Chinese program declared at Sacramento and took charge of implementing that program in San Francisco. What resulted was one more in the city's long list of assembly-district-based boycotting associations led by trade unionists.[58]

Along with these undertakings, the spring of the year brought in a new growing season of trade unionism. IWA members spearhead a series of organizing drives. Workers flocked into the unions once again; the unions joined the new council which by midsummer reported a membership of 13,000. Meanwhile the Metal Trades Council, established the previous year, was functioning effectively within the larger framework of the Federated Trades. A building crafts council was launched, and there was talk of a subfederation of waterfront unions. All this seemed to be following precisely the organizational blueprint Roney had worked out twenty years before. Roney himself, for the first time in his life, was enjoying a modest political bonanza. He had been appointed to a sinecure as fireman in the boiler room of the city hall, and there with a desk of his own in the basement he was able to devote practically full time to the affairs of his flourishing union family.[59]

Even the bomb at Haymarket failed to darken these spring days in the West. In early May, partly to celebrate a victorious strike and boycott by the Printers' Union against two open shop newspapers, partly to commemorate the first anniversary of the Metal Trades Council, San Francisco's labor movement staged a triumphal demonstration. Governor Stoneman declared the day a legal holiday and came down, at Roney's invitation, to march in the procession. Roney, as grand marshal, led off, followed by an honor guard in uniform from the Sailors' Union and by some 10,000 workingmen. There were torches, music, fireworks; later a grand ball at Woodward's Gardens climaxed the occasion.[60]

[58] Cross, 176–177; Call, December 19, 1885; Roney, 445–446; IWA Minute Book, 83–84, February 23, 1886; Haskell's Report to the Federated Trades Council (above, n. 26); and see above, note 18. The boast about the effectiveness of the thirty proxies is found in a short biographical sketch of Haskell, signed "John Tyrell," on an electioneering card seeking for Haskell the Populist nomination for superior judge in 1892. (Haskell Family Papers, Box II; Call, March 6, 21, 25, 26, 1886.)

[59] California, Bureau of Labor Statistics, Third Biennial Report (1888), 114; Cross, 177–186; Roney, 230–232, 419–423, 445–451, 526–529; Daily Report, December 22, 1885; January 6, 1886.

[60] Roney, 483–488; Roney to Ira Cross, Watts, California, September 14, 1910, in Cross Labor Notes, Carton IV, folder 113; Daily Report, May 11, 12, 1886.

Representative Men

Here certainly is the moment to leave Roney. The organizational structure for which he had labored so long and hard turned out to be a sturdy one. Somewhat remodeled in the following decade and with its name changed to the San Francisco Labor Council, it survived the depression of the nineties, flourished, and continues flourishing to the present day.[61] For its first president, however, what lay ahead were defeats, not triumphs. He had helped build the foundations of the house of labor, but found no room for himself inside.[62] Returning to the iron molder's trade, Roney moved on into a bitter and disappointed old age. Twenty years later he would write to his friend Ira Cross, the University of California labor historian, angrily contrasting his "memories of the pioneers in the labor movement" to the "gang who run it now and have heaped upon it so much infamy and disgrace." [63] Yet even when he had presided at the 1885 constituent congress, Roney, then in his mid-forties, had become already a figure out of the past. With him at that time, also active in the congress, were two younger men whose rising fortunes might be taken as representative of the future.

One was Alfred Fuhrman, the sailor and IWA delegate who had repudiated Danielewicz' declaration of interracial unity. Because of his German birth, Fuhrman in 1886 was appointed by the Federated Trades Council to see what could be done about organizing brewery workers, most of whom were Germans. A brewery workers union already existed in the East and Midwest. Led by German socialists, the International Union of United Brewery Workmen of America was waging what would turn out to be a winning battle on two fronts—to maintain itself against employer opposition and to defend the privilege of existing as an *industrial* organization inside the craft-dominated AFL. Bargaining methods of the Brewery Workmen within their own industry combined militant mass strikes and local consumer boycotts. Both tactics came natually to a socialist leadership because both centered on appeals to working class consciousness. Especially this held true for the boycotts, beer being more than most

[61] Philip Taft, *Labor Politics American Style: The California Federation of Labor* (Cambridge, Mass., 1968), 14–17.

[62] Roney to Cross, Watts, California, September 14, 1910, and San Francisco, October 15, 1911, both in Cross Labor Notes, Carton IV, folder 113. See also Cross, "Editor's Introduction," Roney, xii–xxii; and Roney, 522–560.

[63] Roney to Cross, Vallejo, July 23, 1907, in Cross Labor Notes, Carton IV, folder 113.

consumer goods a workingman's commodity and one largely dispensed in premises (the neighborhood saloons) controlled by working class patronage. The bargaining power of the Brewery Workmen, therefore, while a direct function of their own organizational cohesiveness, also depended to a large measure on the working class consciousness in any given community and on the effectiveness with which that consciousness could be brought to focus through central bodies such as city or regional councils.[64]

Fuhrman, setting out to unionize the German brewery workers of the Pacific Coast, pursued the same tactics as had his colleagues in the East. These proved doubly appropriate in San Francisco, where the organizing drive originated in the central council and where working class identification was already strongly developed. Ambitious and aggressive, Fuhrman made the most of every asset. Within a few years, as chief of an alliance of brewery locals and as Federated Trades' president, he dominated the California labor movement. Though presumably acting as western agent for the national brewery union, he quickly came to grips with its officers in a power struggle that arose not so much despite as because of the political assumptions they held in common. The American Federation of Labor then moved to protect its affiliate. Fuhrman retaliated by projecting a West Coast labor league, to be independent of the Federation. Crucial to this plan was the central Trades' Council of San Francisco; but his control over the council disintegrated when the AFL revoked the council's charter until the rebellious brewery locals either returned to their "parent" organization or were ousted from the Trades' Council. The western brewery workers broke ranks under this pressure. Fuhrman, defeated, was driven out of leadership and withdrew from the labor movement.

The second representative figure was the man who had nominated Frank Roney for chairmanship of the 1885 congress, J. F. Valentine, then president of the San Francisco Molders' local. Valentine, like Fuhrman, was a man of driving ambition but did not share the other's radical viewpoint. Whereas Fuhrman had been one of the socialist academy and a member of Haskell's IWA caucus at the 1885 convention, Valentine simply had supported Roney as a moderate trade unionist. He took no special interest in mass strikes and working class boycotts, except to the extent that they might serve the trade union of which he was a member and officer. He was conse-

64 Herman Schlüter, *The Brewing Industry and the Brewery Workers' Movement in America* (Cincinnati, Ohio: International Union of United Brewery Workmen of America, 1910), especially 85–140, 171–177, 213–220, 247–250.

quently under no temptation to espouse the cause of an autonomous labor movement in the Far West. In this respect choosing more wisely than Fuhrman, Valentine linked his career to the growth of national craft unionism. In 1903 he was elected vice-president of the International Molders' Union. Concurrently with this position he served for nineteen years as vice-president of the American Federation of Labor and for fourteen years as first vice-president of the AFL Metal Trades Department. All these posts Valentine held until his retirement, full of years and honors, at the age of 67.[65]

[65] Roney, 439, 526–529, and note 76; Cross, 190–197, 330 note 2.

11

THE PROGRESSIVE ERA

Progress and Poverty

Abatement by violence, the maximum program, dwindled through a series of anticlimaxes during the depression years, 1893–1896. As in the previous decade, the locale of these actions was in small towns and rural districts, especially those where the Chinese population had increased through the late 1880s—the lower San Joaquin Valley and the new fruit-growing regions around Los Angeles. A main impetus for this final phase of the campaign seems to have come from unemployed white workingmen, who had drifted westward as wheat farming declined on the great plains and the silver crisis shut down hard rock mining through the mountain states. California already had its perennial unemployed. Together with the newcomers, they would provide a mass base for the western contingents of Coxey's Army; and some, as they wandered through California's long valleys in search of jobs or handouts, triggered sporadic demonstrations against the Chinese.

The *Pacific Rural Press*, official organ of the Granger movement in California, referred at the end of August 1893 to a "revival" of anti-Chinese agitation. Outbreaks seemed to the editor to be following a fixed pattern: rioters would "go at night to a Chinese camp," rout up the inmates, march them to a railroad, and put them on the first train out. While the agitators might claim to be workingmen, they were in reality (according to the *Rural Press*) "low tramps and bummers" who would not work if they had the opportunity. Equally specious were their efforts to justify acts of violence on the ground that federal officials had been negligent in enforcing the Chinese exclusion laws; their real motive was simply "a beastly taste for violence and plunder." [1]

1 *Pacific Rural Press* (San Francisco, August 26, 1893), 151.

The Los Angeles *Times* during August and September recorded anti-Chinese demonstrations in Riverside, Selma, Fresno, Tulare, Calistoga, Vacaville, Madera, Stockton, Bakersfield, Redlands, Compton, Huron, and San Bernardino. Several of these names were repeatedly in the news. Around Fresno, for example, agitation continued throughout the grape harvest. Chinese fled from the farms into Fresno's Chinatown. "Fully five hundred Chinamen quit work in nurseries and vineyards yesterday," the *Times* reported on August 19. "They have all become impregnated with fear and could not be induced to remain at their work." The sheriff, alarmed by rumors that a mass of unemployed men was on the road from Denver to California's "raisin districts," urged dilatory ranchers to get rid of any Chinese they might still have in their employ. Sheriffs at Bakersfield and Redlands asked the governor to mobilize the national guard. Guard units were alerted at Redlands and San Bernardino, Redlands remaining under virtual martial law for several days.[2]

The role of the federal government through these disturbances was confused and in some respects self-contradictory. As first passed in 1882, the Exclusion Act had been intended to halt further influx of Chinese laborers without disrupting the existing labor supply of the Far West. Chinese already in the United States presumably would remain, gradually diminishing as death and repatriation reduced their members. They were to be permitted to visit the old country without forfeiting their American residence; and the law, for reasons noted earlier, was limited to ten years' duration. Exclusionists, after hailing the enactment of 1882 as a victory in principle, fixed their attention on renewal and on the correction of certain alleged inadequacies. Especially they complained of widespread coolie smuggling. Since all Chinese looked alike, it was argued, and their names sounded alike, it was impossible to distinguish those legally in the United States prior to exclusion from those who might have been smuggled in afterward. To meet this difficulty the act of renewal—which bore the name of Thomas Geary, Democratic congressman from California's Sonoma County—added a system of registration with the stipulation that all Chinese found unregistered one year after passage of the Geary Act (on May 5, 1893) would be considered illegal entrants and deported. Leaders of the Chinese community, meanwhile, advised by American attorneys that the act would be held

2 Los Angeles *Times*, August 15, 19, September 1, 2, 1893; San Francisco *Morning Call*, September 22, 1893.

unconstituional because of its selective rather than general application, urged their followers to refuse compliance. The result was that few Chinese registered during the year of grace; and as the Supreme Court had, before the ending of that year, sustained the Geary law, nearly all Chinese in the country became subject to arrest and deportation. The customs authorities were unprepared for such heroic measures, and the Cleveland administration declined to initiate proceedings until Congress saw fit to provide adequate financing.[3]

This was the situation in the late summer of 1893. Exclusionists, demanding immediate enforcement, could claim to be doing the work which immigration officials ought to have done. Precisely what many of them wished, of course, was to disrupt the supply of cheap labor in the Far West. Thus at Redlands, the crisis which had led to an alerting of national guard units was finally resolved by commitments on the part of civic leaders and the federal marshal to round up all Chinese in the area for processing under the Geary law. The Los Angeles *Times* correspondent, after noting the eager hospitality with which Chinese fed and entertained those deputized citizens who had protected their ghetto from the mob, added, "But little did they suspect that those with them at that hour were evolving plans to rid the city of them, though in a legal way." And one day later, "Plans are completed for issuing warrants for the arrest of all Chinese here tomorrow." [4]

Obviously the Redlands plan would have involved serious difficulties as a general solution, since there remained more than a hundred thousand Chinese in the United States. For the federal government, the easiest way out of the dilemma was to postpone the deadline on the assumption that the Chinese, having lost their gamble on a favorable Supreme Court decision, would now be willing to comply. The Cleveland administration favored this alternative; and when Congress finally veered around to it in November with a six-month extension, the majority of Chinese did in fact register under the law.[5] In California, the drift of "respectable" opinion was clearly against mass deportation. Although most demonstrations occurred in rural districts, neither farmers nor local townspeople seem to have

[3] United States, Department of Justice, *Laws Applicable to Immigration and Nationality* (Washington, D.C., 1953), 242–249; *Call*, September 9, 14, 1892; September 10–13, 26, 1893.

[4] Los Angeles *Times*, September 3, 4, 1893.

[5] *Laws Applicable to Immigration*, 249; Roy L. Garis, *Immigration Restriction: A Study of the Opposition to and Regulation of Immigration into the United States* (New York, 1927), 294–302.

been active in promoting them. This marked a change from the earliei expulsion campaign, townspeople having then frequently taken the lead and apparently with strong backing from small farmers.[6]

One reason for this difference was the spectacular growth of fruit culture to which the economic life of many rural areas had become linked. Citrus groves, orchards, and vineyards appeared (in those days at least) to be the province of small or medium enterprisers, embattled, as were the townspeople very often themselves, against the octopus of railroad monoploy—though still largely dependent for harvesting and packing their crops on Chinese labor. United by this common interest, the Granger-oriented, Populist-tinged *Rural Press* could join hands with Harrison Gray Otis' Los Angeles *Times*.[7] To purge the Pacific slope of Orientals was, of course, in the long run devoutly to be hoped for; yet both argued the undesirability of hasty action under the Geary law. Mass deportations would prove costly and difficult. The harshness of such procedures might discredit the national image abroad and provoke retaliations against American missionaries or businessmen in China. Moreover (this being always the point most cogently stated), Chinese still furnished the "mainstay of the orchardist"; to drive them out would "utterly prostrate an interest which is doing more for the immediate and promising more for the future good of California than any other."[8] The *Times* hoped that a reliable white labor force might be settled on subsistence farms in fruit-growing regions; meanwhile, the Chinese must not be pressed too hard.[9] To prefer white help, the *Rural Press* conceded, was only natural and proper when reliable white workers could be had; but no sane orchardist would trust the task of harvesting his crop to "sandlot hoodlums and agitators," "a class who are of less value to the country than the Chinese themselves."[10]

The phrase "sandlot hoodlums" was obviously intended to evoke

[6] See above, p. 210. This account of the 1893 expulsions is substantially the same as that put forward by Carey McWilliams, *Factories in the Field* (Boston, 1939), 74–79, and Robert J. Pitchell, "Twentieth Century California Voting Behavior" (Ph.D. diss., Political Science, University of California, Berkeley, 1955), 113–114. McWilliams, however, pays little attention to the earlier wave of expulsions, while Pitchell treats the two as approximately identical.

[7] The *Rural Press* backed the Farmers' Alliance and supported the Populist party in 1891. Then, under changed management, it became nonpartisan but not hostile. Donald E. Walters, "Populism in California, 1889–1900" (Ph.D. diss. in History, University of California, Berkeley, 1952), 142.

[8] *Rural Press* (September 16, 1893), 198–199.

[9] Los Angeles *Times*, May 17, August 17, 26, 1893.

[10] *Rural Press* (September 16, 1893), 199; (October 7, 1893), 247.

memories of Denis Kearney and the Workingmen's party. While
Kearney at this late date still delivered occasional orations in San
Francisco, he had neither party nor followers to back him. An effort
was made, with Kearney's participation, to rebuild the old apparatus
of anticoolie clubs. This led into a mass meeting which memorialized
the state government and Congress and called President Cleveland "the
only Benedict Arnold" ever to disgrace "the Presidential chair." As
for organized labor, its role in the anti-Chinese activities of 1893–1894
seems to have been marginal. San Francisco's central council joined
the chorus of complaints over failure of the federal government to
enforce the Geary law. The council tried to initiate legal actions on
its own account, and the secretary, M. McGlynn, exhorted unionists
and their friends to inform against any Chinese thought to be unregistered so that they might be haled into court. The intent was to
expand the Redlands plan to statewide proportions, but not much
came of it beyond some flamboyant circulars.[11] The council's most
powerful and militant affiliate, the Sailors' Union, continued to com-
bat intrusions of Chinese seamen into American shipping. The
Coast Seamen's Journal, official organ of the Sailors' union, not only
gave regular attention to the Chinese question, but became one of
the first West Coast publications to raise an alarm over Japanese.[12]

In general, however, organized labor, based as it was in San
Francisco and composed largely of urban skilled craftsmen, had little
opportunity for leadership in activities occurring in the rural hinter-
lands and which for the most part involved unskilled migratory
workers. Labor's capabilities were less than they had been in
1885–1886 because of the shattering impact of depression. The
Federated Trades Council, created by the anti-Chinese convention of
1885, was by 1891 on the verge of shipwreck. Business failures, unemployment, attacks of newly formed employer associations worked havoc
among its constituents; and the officers turned to quarreling among
themselves. Reorganization, with a shift of leading personnel, kept
the council afloat through 1893 (the name was then changed to San
Francisco Labor Council), but its existence remained uncertain for the

11 Call, July 22, 1892, September 8, 1893. The Benedict Arnold quotation is on
page 8, September 15, 1893. On McGlynn, who would run as Populist candidate
for secretary of state in 1894, see below, p. 237. Efforts of the Labor Council to
take legal measures against Chinese are reported in the Call, September 8–10, 12,
13, 20, 24, 1893.
12 Coast Seamen's Journal, March 28, April 25, May 16, 1900; Call, July 21, 23,
31, 1892; Roger Daniels, The Politics of Prejudice: The Anti-Japanese Movement
in California and the Struggle for Japanese Exclusion (New York, 1968), 19.

next three or four years. Affiliated unions dwindled to fifteen, mem bership to barely 4,000.[13] Such adverse fortunes, of course, were not unique to the West Coast. Craft unionism rode out the nineties under bare poles, shaken and harried by the winds of that radical, utopian, apocalyptic decade. Coxey's Army, the Pullman strike, the Populist insurgency followed in rapid succession. Especially in the West the three were tightly intertwined and within this vast turmoil the survival of craft unions as well as the final phases of the anti-Chinese crusade seemed temporarily reduced to the dimension of minor details.

"We may expect to see the city overrun," the San Francisco *Chronicle* warned its readers in August 1893, "with men who have been deprived of the opportunity to labor in the mines of Nevada, Idaho, Arizona. . . . These, added to our own unemployed, will be sure to make troublous times unless . . . those most interested [the *Chronicle* was demanding financial support for a midwinter fair to be held at San Francisco] . . . assist in averting a calamity which otherwise seems inevitable." [14] In Southern California, the Los Angeles *Times,* still infused with the spirit of the recent real estate boom, endeavored to keep up a more optimistic front. Along with daily reports of business and bank failures, the *Times* insisted that the stringency was no more than a temporary state of mind which positive thinking on the part of buyers and investors would soon dispel. Yet by the end of summer even the *Times* acknowledged the depth of the crisis. "Hundreds of thousands of men" were out of work. The city must undertake measures of emergency relief. The federal government should launch a gigantic project for irrigating arid lands in the West in order to provide a job for every able bodied American. But first it would be necessary to shut off the flood of immigrants pouring into the country from abroad. "If we can keep out the Chinese, there is no reason why we cannot exclude the lower classes of Poles, Hungarians, Italians and some other European nations, which people possess most of the vices of the Chinese and few of their good qualities, besides having a leaning towards bloodshed and anarchy which is peculiarly their own." [15]

[13] Clara E. Mortensen, "Organized Labor in San Francisco from 1892 to 1902" (M.A. thesis in Economics, University of California, Berkeley, 1916), 36–39, 54–55; Ira B. Cross, *A History of the Labor Movement in California* (Berkeley, 1935), 215–218.

[14] San Francisco *Chronicle,* as quoted in Los Angeles *Times,* August 22, 1893. The San Francisco Labor Council, its own membership down to 4,000, was predicting 12,000 unemployed in the city before the end of winter. (*Call,* September 10, 1893.)

[15] Los Angeles *Times,* August 23, September 2, 1893.

The "System"

Since the contest between Roney and Kearney for control of the Workingmen's party in 1878, California trade unionists had pursued a course of avoiding overt political commitments and warning against the dangers of party entanglement. This put them in harmony with the antipolitical stance that was becoming characteristic of the American Federation of Labor nationally. Nonpartisanship among trade unionists, however, sometimes coexisted with strenuous working class politics dominated by professional labor politicians. Such was, outstandingly, the case in San Francisco where labor identification had permeated urban party structure. Of 180 San Francisco assemblymen elected between 1892 and 1910, biographical data available for 120 show that 49 were laborers or skilled or semiskilled workers, as opposed to 23 lawyers and 31 business or professional men. By way of contrast, in Los Angeles County, still largely rural but rapidly becoming urbanized at the turn of the century, 48 assemblymen elected in six elections during the same period included 19 lawyers and one workingman, a solitary carpenter.

Within San Francisco the class alignment of voters can be even more sharply delineated. As of 1892, the city contained eighteen assembly districts, eight of which comprised the traditional working class sections known as the Mission, and "South of the Slot." The biographical data referred to above show that among assemblymen chosen in these eight districts the incidence of laborers and skilled or semiskilled workmen (41 percent) was two and a half times greater than among those elected in the remainder of the city. On the other hand, the incidence of lawyers elected to the assembly was only one-quarter that prevailing in the remainder of the city.[16]

This substantial labor component, however, does not appear to have exerted any radicalizing influence at the state capital. San Francisco in the early years of the twentieth century was actually overrepresented in the legislature, since its population had declined relatively to only 18 percent of the state total whereas the city continued to fill 22.5 percent of senate and assembly seats.[17] The urban bloc could

16 Biographical data on assemblymen has been compiled from California, Secretary of State, *California Blue Book* (Sacramento, 1893–1911). See Alexander Saxton, "San Francisco Labor and the Populist and Progressive Insurgencies," *Pacific Historical Review*, XXXIV (November, 1965), 421–438.

17 Franklin Hichborn, *Story of the Session of the California Legislature of 1913* (San Francisco, 1913), 1–17. Reapportionment in 1911 reduced San Francisco to slightly less than its proportional share of seats.

normally control the legislature, while the men comprising that
bloc were in turn controlled by political bosses who sold their services
to the highest bidder, usually the railroad. Such at least was the
opinion held by several generations of Grangers, Populists, and
Progressives who gave to this symbiotic relationship the name of the
"System." [18] Franklin Hichborn, a radical journalist of muckraking
proclivities (though by no means totally hostile to labor), described its
operation as follows: "With rare exceptions the San Francisco delegation has been made up of ignorant and for the most part vicious
men, thoroughly in accord with the tenderloin and groggery interests.
. . . Such a delegation lent itself for easy manipulation . . . a
dependable trading quantity . . . readily adjustable under all conditions to corporation plans and purposes." [19] Doubtless the outstanding virtuoso at the sort of manipulation referred to by Hichborn was Abraham Ruef, who from small beginnings as a Republican ward healer made himself boss of the city by organizing the
Union Labor party in 1901. Ruef—and certainly he was in a position
to know—observed that on the San Francisco delegation "the railroad always depended for a strong voting support for its program." [20]
    The testimony of Hichborn and Ruef suggests that labor politicians
at the turn of the century were still playing approximately the same
role at Sacramento attributed to them by Frank Roney and Henry
George in the Constitutional Convention of 1878. Performance of the
role during that earlier period had depended on the rhetoric of
racial antagonism as a means of control over the labor constituency.
Depression, however, and the economic dislocations of the nineties,
while scarcely lessening the frequency of such rhetoric, temporarily
reduced its utility. Though neither lost nor forgotten, the Asian
menace was for the time being pushed back to a secondary level,
overshadowed by more urgent matters, among which was the prospect
of new political alignment.
    The depression of 1893 tended to radicalize portions of the urban
working class just as it had segments of the farm population. In
California, at least, both Coxey's Army and the Pullman strike (the
latter because it challenged everybody's villain, the Southern Pacific
Railroad) won widespread sympathy among farmers and working
people. These ground swells of discontent were caught up by the
Populist party. Actually Populism in California, far from being a

[18] Hichborn, *"The System" as Uncovered by the San Francisco Graft Prosecution*
(San Francisco, 1915).
[19] Hichborn, *Story of the Legislature of 1913*, 15–16.
[20] Abraham Ruef, "The Road I Travelled," San Francisco *Bulletin* (July 11,
1912); Walton Bean, *Boss Ruef's San Francisco* (Berkeley and Los Angeles, 1967).

spontaneous outburst, was built from the top down. Its leaders included veterans of earlier third-party campaigns, and a good many old radicals—Socialists, Single-Taxers, Bellamy Nationalists—some of whom were also active in the Knights of Labor and the trade unions. In 1890, following the pattern already taking shape through the Midwest and South, they set up a California Farmers' Alliance, which grew rapidly and was soon converted into a vehicle for third-party action.[21]

Populist leaders were keenly aware of the importance of San Francisco as a population center and the degree to which it dominated the state legislature. Their strategy in seeking support from urban workingmen was to attack the labor politicians as collaborators in the System and to demand that trade unionists abandon their traditional nonpartisanship in order to lead the working class into a politics of radical reform. The ideological framework for this program was provided by the Populists' Omaha Platform of 1892 with its declaration that all producers, "rural and civic,"[22] shared common interests and identical enemies—a text which found dramatic confirmation in the Pullman strike.

Early in 1894 a joint farmer-labor conference (arranged by San Francisco trade unionists) proposed several additional points, presumably of special interest to labor, which were included in the California Populist platform. This document in its final form advocated state inspection of workshops and factories, woman suffrage, public works for the jobless, a general eight-hour law, and total exclusion of Asian immigration. To make its working class message unmistakably clear the new party nominated a carpenter for lieutenant governor and a printing tradesman for secretary of state— M. McGlynn, who as secretary of the San Francisco Labor Council in 1893 had sent out the appeal to trade unionists to inform against Chinese. For the gubernatorial election of 1894 the results were moderately impressive. The Populist ticket carried 18 percent of the general vote; while in the eight working class districts of San Francisco it ran 5 percent ahead of its statewide average. One of those districts chose one of the only two Populist assemblymen elected in the state.[23]

21 Walters, "Populism in California" (above, n. 7), 18–50, 85.
22 John D. Hicks, *The Populist Revolt* (Minneapolis, 1931), 439–444.
23 Walters, 243–245, 276; Saxton, "San Francisco Labor," *Pacific Historical Review*, XXXIV, 421–438. It was in this same election that Adolph Sutro, a mining engineer and Jewish immigrant who became a Comstock millionaire, won the mayoralty of San Francisco on the Populist ticket. But Sutro, immensely popular as a champion of the "honest miner" and the "people" against the System, would

The New Unionism

1894 marked the climax of Populist endeavor in California. Two years later the party hitched on behind the Bryan free silver bandwagon; then followed a series of splits and fusions leading to disintegration by 1900. A principal cause of this decline was the amelioration of economic conditions which had generated the main thrust of Populist discontent. After 1896 farm and industrial indices swung to high noon, a tendency reinforced by the war against Spain, the Alaska gold rush, the long struggle for control over the Philippines. The nation thus rode into the twentieth century on a flood tide of military expansion and economic well-being. As farmers and industrialists prospered, so too did workingmen. It may be that this rapid shift from depression, with its mass discontent and radicalization of leadership, to the McKinley era of the full dinner pail provided a climate uniquely conducive to labor organization. For whatever reasons, there is no doubt that trade unionism, which in earlier periods of prosperity had put forth modest buds, now burst into luxuriant growth. Union membership, having probably fallen well below the 372,000 registered in 1890, had by the end of the decade not only recouped its losses but added half a million new members.[24]

More important than simple numerical increase was the crystallization of an organizational form, the national craft union, which would dominate the American labor movement at least through the first half of the next century. In 1901 the United States Industrial Commission reported the existence of 93 national unions. While the commission seems to have included any organization which cared to style itself as "national," it also compiled a fund of information suggesting distinctive characteristics of "national-ness." Thus 75 of the 93 were said to assert some sort of central control over local strikes;[25] 40 maintained central strike funds; and 46 conducted benefit plans of one variety or another, generally in the form of death benefits, though sometimes extending to sickness, disability, unemployment, or loss

have been elected on any ticket. His victory represented a nonpartisan tribute to a highly esteemed old man, rather than mass conversion to Populist doctrine. While Sutro polled 50 percent of the vote, the Populist candidate for governor, J. V. Webster, carried only 11 percent in the city at large. (San Francisco *Examiner*, November 4, 1894.) On Sutro, see Robert E. and Mary F. Stewart, *Adolph Sutro: A Biography* (Berkeley, 1962), and Walters, 287–290.

[24] Lloyd Ulman, *The Rise of the National Trade Union* (Cambridge, Mass., 1966), 19.

[25] Ulman, 155–187; see especially tables on 156, 177.

of tools.[26] What all such undertakings had in common was that they signified the centralization of functions previously performed locally, regionally, or (more often, perhaps) not at all. Organized labor in a small way was becoming large business, and control of that business was being consolidated within each craft union.

By 1908 the United States comissioner of labor could list 84 national unions with insurance programs. Altogether these unions were operating 163 programs which had paid out in 1908 a total of $7,829,000. The rapid and recent character of this trend was evident in part from the founding dates of the unions, but even more clearly from the dates of establishment of the various benefit plans. Of the 84 unions, one-half had been founded since 1890—25 of these after the last year of depression, 1896. As to the benefit plans, 101 of 163 had been set up after 1890—73 of these after 1896.[27]

The most significant index of labor's organizational growth is the emergence of full-time professional leadership. Unfortunately, there is no adequate statistical record of this phenomenon. The "walking delegate," or local business agent, made his first appearance in the mid-eighties and had by the turn of the century become a familiar feature of the industial scene, especially in construction trades. Though a local functionary, he depended for his effectiveness on circumstances beyond local control—on the maintenance of general rules and standards for the trade, on the power of discipline over membership, and on the availability of strike support in case of conflict with an employer. For each craft these issues were national in scope; and the prevalence of the walking delegate system at the local or district level may therefore be taken as a measure of the process of centralization. This process moved rapidly beyond the strike fund and benefit stage.[28] Unions transformed their honorary national officers into full-time salaried executives. They empowered them to hire staffs of field organizers, lawyers, journalists, and office workers. The Cigar Makers' Union, for example, increased its general expenditures from $461,000 in 1899 to almost $700,000 five years later. The Brotherhood of Carpenters nearly quadrupled its operating costs between 1898 and 1902. Simply for mileage and per diem allowances of delegates to its 1902

26 United States, Industrial Commission, *Reports of the Industrial Commission on Labor Organizations, Labor Disputes, and Arbitration, and on Railway Labor* (Washington, 1901), XVII, Tables I–III facing p. 1.

27 United States, Commissioner of Labor, *Twenty–Third Annual Report of the Commissioner of Labor. 1908. Workmen's Insurance and Benefit Funds in the United States* (Washington, 1909), 35–49.

28 Robert F. Hoxie, *Trade Unionism in the United States* (New York, 1936), 177–187, Hoxie's book was first published in 1917.

convention, the Molders' Union spent $50,000, while the United Mine Workers in that same year invested $2,000,000 in strike and organizational activities.[29] A survey of nine leading unions during this period showed an annual average outlay per union of $24,000 for the publication of official journals.[30]

Writing in 1913, Theodore Glocker, one of Johns Hopkins University's ubiquitous researchers, dramatized the transition in a sketch of two union offices, the old style and the new:

> "This is the headquarters of the international union," grandiloquently remarked the secretary of a small union, as he pointed to a dilapidated desk standing in one corner of the family living room, where nightly after his work in the factory he performed the duties of his office. In the same city a few blocks away the officers of another organization are housed in a large, modern, splendidly built office building. Here the elevator carries the visitor to the ninth story where the suite of rooms rented by the union is located. One enters a large reception room where a number of clerks are busily employed. Beyond is the private office of the president, and a nearby room is occupied by his private stenographer. In a large adjoining room the secretary, his assistant and several clerks are at work. The editor has his own little den. There is also a committee or conference room where, around a large table, meetings of the executive board are sometimes held.[31]

Samuel Gompers had begun his duties for the American Federation of Labor in just such quarters as the first of the two described above. Roney, at the apex of his career, felt himself lucky to have part-time use of a desk in San Francisco's city hall basement, where, thanks to a friendly administration, he worked as assistant furnace man. Roney would have seen the ninth floor suite as a vision of the millennium.[32] Yet within less than twenty years after the depression of 1893, such millennial establishments had become commonplace as abodes of the new labor bureaucracy. Called into existence by the rise of national craft unions, that bureaucracy would become a potent factor in their continuance and propagation.

29 Aaron M. Sakolski, *The Finances of American Trade Unions* (Baltimore, 1906), 57, 62, 122, 49 (in that order).

30 Sakolski, 116.

31 Theodore W. Glocker, *The Government of American Trade Unions* (Baltimore, 1913), 183.

32 Samuel Gompers, *Seventy Years of Life and Labor*, 2 vols. (New York, 1925), I, 269–273; Frank Roney, *Frank Roney, Irish Rebel and California Labor Leader* (Berkeley, 1931), 422–423, 446.

In the Far West a parallel process was under way. The Pacific Coast had remained in certain respects a colonial appendage to the main body of the nation, separated not only historically and psychologically, but by cost and time differentials which persisted long after the multiplication of rail connections. For this reason (perhaps some others as well) western unions lagged approximately a decade behind their eastern counterparts in the matter of national affiliation. Granted this important exception, the growth and concentration of trade unions followed much the same pattern in California as in older portions of the country.

Union membership in California expanded from 30,000 at the end of the century to 67,500 two years later. San Francisco's unionists doubled in number (20,000 to 40,000) during the same period. From its low point of fifteen affiliates in 1895, the Labor Council of San Francisco jumped to 98 by 1901. California's Bureau of Labor Statistics, reporting for 1904, listed 850 unions, 250 of them in San Francisco.[33] The old iron trades and printing trades councils took on new life; district federations were set up among locals of carpenters, painters, sheetmetal workers, machinists, team drivers, cement workers, retail clerks. In this centralizing process, the construction unions led the way after the depression and by 1900 had drawn together a spectacularly successful district apparatus—the Building Trades Council—with a full-time staff of walking delegates and elected officials, as well as its own newspaper, *Organized Labor*. In 1910 the Bureau of Labor Statistics estimated nearly 50,000 unionized workers in the San Francisco Bay area alone.[34]

Common Ground

California's burgeoning unions and councils clustered around two distinct, frequently rival, power centers—the Building Trades Council and the original San Francisco Labor Council. So complete became the rift between them that the building trades forbade their locals to send delegates to the other council, and the two customarily held separate Labor Day parades. In 1901 the Labor Council initiated a statewide federation, the California Federation of Labor, while the building

33 California Bureau of Labor Statistics, *Eleventh Biennial Report* (Sacramento, 1904), 30–45, see also *Biennial Reports* (1900), 84–122, (1902), 66–77; Mortensen, "Organized Labor" (above, n. 13), 64–65.

34 California, Bureau of Labor Statistics, *Biennial Report* (1910), 302–312; Mortensen, 36–39, 51–52, 64–65. Early issues of *Organized Labor* contain articles on the "Business Agent," the importance of the working card, and the development of district councils. (February 3, 17, 24, 1900)

trades, as counterweight, established their own state organization under the wing of their San Francisco council.[35] Both councils were based on locals of skilled craftsmen. Yet the cleavage between them, which would deeply affect California politics throughout the Progressive era, reflected significant differences in strength, membership, and policy.

The building trades comprised a set of long-established, clearly definable skills, difficult to acquire and closely interlocked within a single industry. Once building tradesmen were fully organized, as they were in the Bay Area by 1900, they achieved a leverage of bargaining power which enabled them to maintain closed shop conditions, high wages, and a general eight-hour day. Council structure centralized power in the executive committee, and especially in the hands of its president, Patrick Henry McCarthy. An Irish immigrant, a carpenter—and master craftsman of organization as well—McCarthy enjoyed for many years the position of a Lorenzo the Magnificent among West Coast labor leaders. Under his generalship, building trades power penetrated deeply into local politics. This resulted partly from the ties between construction and such city hall functions as fire and sanitary inspection, building permits, and street grading and paving, and partly from the fact that building tradesmen themselves formed a stable group of resident, and consequently *voting*, citizens. The relationship was formalized in 1900 by the appointment of McCarthy as a city commissioner of civil service.[36]

The Labor Council, on the other hand, although larger in numbers, was weaker economically and politically. Its membership, scattered through many industries, ranged from highly skilled craftsmen such as metal workers, printers, and tailors, through semiskilled service tradesmen (bakers, brewers, retail clerks) to the dockworkers, sailors, and teamsters, whose unions derived their cohesiveness not so much from irreplaceability of skill as from the disagreeableness of the work and from the locale in which it was performed. The Labor Council constituency, less protected by skills than were the building

[35] San Francisco *Labor Clarion*, September 1, 8, 1905. The *Clarion* was founded in 1902 as official organ of the Labor Council. (*Organized Labor*, September 2, 9, 1905; Cross, 234–237.)

[36] Ray Stannard Baker, "Corner in Labor: What Is Happening in San Francisco Where Unionism Holds Undisputed Sway," *McClure's Magazine*, XIII (February, 1904), 366–378. Baker noted that while McCarthy drew no salary as building trades president, he held a position, presumably something of a sinecure, as maintenance superintendent in a downtown hotel, and also received $100 a month as civil service commissioner. (Saxton, "San Francisco Labor," *Pacific Historical Review*, XXXIV, 427–428.)

tradesmen, formed a more transient and fluctuating group—especially the sailors, virtually disfranchised as they were by their occupation. Outstanding among its leaders during these years were Andrew Furuseth and Walter Macarthur, both of the Sailors Union (Macarthur edited the *Coast Seamen's Journal*), and Michael Casey of the Teamsters. Two of these at least surpassed McCarthy in national reputation, but none wielded centralized power comparable to his and none could match his influence at city hall.[37]

Often these councils worked at loggerheads both in their organizational activities and their political ventures. There was, however, a common ground upon which they could always meet, that of confronting the Oriental menace. With respect to the Chinese, one piece of unfinished business remained; for the Geary law, like the earlier expulsion act, had been limited to ten years. Renewal was to come up in 1902, and the unions, resurrected by the McKinley prosperity, turned their attention to this problem well in advance of the deadline. Their efforts were furthered by a bubonic plague scare in San Francisco. Mayor of the city at this time was James D. Phelan, a wealthy businessman, a Democrat, an advocate of municipal reform—and the political ally of Patrick Henry McCarthy, whom he had in fact appointed to the civil service commission. The panic began with discovery by the board of health of a Chinese allegedly dead from the plague. The city administration on March 6, 1900, ordered a quarantine of the Chinese quarter.

As this news was headlined across the nation, it set off anxious discussion in eastern states as to possible means of avoiding infection from the Pacific Coast. Meanwhile, proof of the diagnosis of bubonic plague remained somewhat dubious, and opponents of the Phelan administration accused the board of health of fabricating a hoax for political purposes. The mayor beat a tactical retreat under pressure; but as plague cases continued to be reported and as confirmations became more convincing, the quarantine was reimposed upon Chinatown at the end of May, together with compulsory inspection and fumigation. Efforts at purification were carried out with rigor and considerable brutality by health officers and police. San Francisco's board of trade set up a committee of businessmen to raise funds (since the city's were insufficient) and to arrange for detention of large numbers of indigent Chinese in some unused grain storage warehouses leased for the purpose. Before this final phase of purification could be

[37] California, Bureau of Labor Statistics, *Biennial Report* (1910), 302–312; Cross, 330, notes 4 and 5.

put into effect, however, a federal court enjoined the entire under-taking as a discriminatory and unreasonable exercise of power, incom-patible with the Constitution of the United States. The second quaran-tine then came to an end in mid-June 1900.[38]

Throughout this sequence of events, the city government had strong union support, especially from the newly founded building trades journal, *Organized Labor*. Picking up the keynote from recent debates over the Geary act and Chinese registration, *Organized Labor* charged that the real fault lay with the laxness of federal immigration authorities: "We believe that there is no punishment too severe for the officer of a port caught napping when the plague and the Chinese are trying to steal a march on the unsuspecting public. . . . Brothers, wake up! This is a matter of most vital importance and should receive thorough consideration in your meetings. The almond-eyed Mongolian is watching for his opportunity, waiting to assassinate you and your children with one of his many maladies." Shortly before issuance of the final court injunction against the quarantine, an editorial in *Organized Labor* defended the actions of the board of health as fully justified. The editorial ended with a declaration that the Chinese had "long since outlived their usefulness in the world's history," and the time had arrived when San Francisco must cease to be "an asylum for these silurian ghosts." [39]

During the lull between the two quarantines, the building trades journal had turned its attention to a broader (though not unrelated) topic, the dangers involved in American expansion across the Pacific. "Spain did it. Why not the victor? Our province in the Orient governed from Washington in the interest of a billion dollar trust.

---

[38] The evidence seems clear that bubonic plague did exist in San Francisco and that there was genuine cause for alarm. Many of the public health measures under-taken (cleaning up garbage and debris, flushing sewers, cementing basements, ex-terminating rats) were sensible and probably helped to avert an epidemic. On the other hand, quarantining the entire Chinese quarter, and the proposed forcible removal of indigent Chinese to detention barracks, were obviously inspired by racist attitudes and served the purposes of anti-Oriental politics. When, after the earthquake, plague cropped up in non-Chinese sectors of the city, no such measures were even considered. See United States, Treasury Department-Marine Hospital Service, *Report of the Commission Appointed by the Secretary of the Treasury for the Investigation of Plague in San Francisco, under Instructions from the Surgeon General, Marine Hospital Service* (Washington, 1901); San Francisco Citizens' Health Committee, *Eradicating the Plague from San Francisco: Report of the Cit-izens' Health Committee and an Account of its Work* (San Francisco, 1909); San Francisco *Examiner*, May 30, 31, June 1-10, 12, 16-19; San Francisco *Chronicle*, March 9, 10.

[39] *Organized Labor*, March 10, June 9, 1900; *Coast Seamen's Journal*, April 25, June 6, 1900.

. . . Our portals wide open to the Mongolian, recruited from our cheap labor nurseries in Hawaii and the Philippines. Vassals abroad and slaves at home! Ah beautiful is the fruit of imperialism!" [40] Author of this unsigned jeremiad was probably Olaf Tveitmoe, a local leader of the Cement Workers' Union and second in command within the building trades to Patrick Henry McCarthy. A Norwegian immigrant who had taught school in Minnesota before making his way to the West Coast, Tveitmoe emerges from rather meager records as one of the most paradoxical and fascinating figures in western labor history.

He was, first of all, a successful contender among the new trade union bureaucrats. Beyond his editorship of *Organized Labor*, he served as secretary of the San Francisco Building Trades Council, financial secretary of the California Building Trades, national vice-president of the Cement Workers' Union, third vice-president of the AFL Building Trades Department.[41] Despite these many titles, he remained an alienated seeker pouring into the columns of his journal the passion of a frustrated intellectual life. He tried endlessly to fabricate some coherence out of the turmoil around him. His editorials, always studded with exclamation marks, threw together fragments of Henry George and Nietzsche, Herbert Spencer and the Sermon on the Mount, Karl Marx, Darwin, Georges Sorel. Like Burnette Haskell half a generation earlier, Tveitmoe was drawn through socialism and syndicalism to the romantic aesthetic of violence. But whereas Haskell, a kind of elfin superannuated Tom Sawyer, could content himself with make-believe, Tveitmoe turned the games to reality.

He could hardly have served as McCarthy's lieutenant had he not been practical. A "gorilla," Louis Adamic described him, a "dark Scandinavian," wielding great power inside the labor movement, the direct representative of Samuel Gompers on the Pacific Coast. He had ties also with labor's underworld. The two McNamaras, and others in the Bridge and Structural Ironworkers' Union who had been studying the uses of dynamite as a counter in collective bargaining, were among his close associates. When the battle to organize Los Angeles neared its climax—upon which, seemingly, depended the fate of trade unionism in California—Tveitmoe was sent down as one of the commanders of labor's expeditionary force. Afterward, he was tried and

---

40 *Organized Labor*, March 24, 1900.

41 For a biographical sketch, see Cross, 338. *Organized Labor* began publication on February 3, 1900. Tveitmoe, at first listed as one of ten directors, appeared as editor on March 31. That he functioned as editor from the beginning is suggested by a notice from the San Francisco *Star* reprinted in *Organized Labor*, February 24, 1900.

convicted for conspiracy in connection with the 1910 bombing of the
Los Angeles *Times*.[42]

Tveitmoe's imagination, again like Haskell's, hovered constantly at
the border between utopia and catastrophe. Presenting his annual report to the California Building Trades' convention, less than one
month after indictment in the dynamite conspiracy case, Tveitmoe
declared that trade unionism, more than "any other organization of
modern times except one or two religious denominations," practiced
the "doctrine of non-resistance." Then he warned, "If Labor should
invoke as a law, 'AN EYE FOR AN EYE AND A TOOTH FOR A TOOTH,' the
world would have a deluge of human blood without a saving ark or
Mount Ararat, but with only numberless Caesar's Columns to mark
the landing points."[43] The reference was to Ignatius Donnelly's famous novel in which the final struggle between capitalism and a
tortured, maddened working class was commemorated by a huge
column of bodies encased in concrete. Tveitmoe perhaps remembered
Caesar's Column from his younger days in Minnesota, where the
book had been widely circulated as a Populist campaign tract.[44]

During his long editorship of *Organized Labor* he ranged widely in
his interests and sympathy. Woman suffrage received enthusiastic support. So did the socialists and IWW in their San Diego free speech
fight. Sun Yat-sen he described as leader of "History's Foremost
Revolution," and he defended the Mexican revolution against a
threatened United States intervention. He applauded Tom Mann, the
English dockworkers' chief, for "inciting" British soldiers to "mutiny."
"Let the workers of the world clasp hands," Tveitmoe wrote in praise
of international solidarity, "over the oceans which divide them, both
mentally and physically, from Pekin to London. Let them fight by
ceasing to toil for the drones, and the final battle is won." When
war broke out in 1914, Tveitmoe perceived it through the imagery of
Caesar's Column. Here was the apocalypse of capitalist greed and op-
pression. Would the "workers of the world clasp hands" and so win

[42] Twenty-one died in the resulting explosion. The McNamara brothers subsequently confessed and were sentenced, one to life, the other to fifteen years. Tveitmoe, with thirty-nine others, was convicted on a related conspiracy charge. He
served several months of a six-year sentence which was later reversed on appeal.
Grace Stimson, *The Rise of the Labor Movement in Los Angeles* (Berkeley, 1955),
400-423. On Tveitmoe, I have followed Louis Adamic's *Dynamite: The Story of
Class Violence in America* [New York, 1931] (rev. ed., Gloucester, Mass., 1963), 201,
206, 217, 236, 244, 264, 329. Though largely undocumented, Adamic's account seems
to me close to the truth. But Adamic was unaware of (or ignored) the agonized
intellectual life of Tveitmoe, which was not so different from his own.

[43] *Organized Labor*, January 6, 20, 1912.

[44] Alexander Saxton, "*Caesar's Column*: The Dialogue of Utopia and Catastrophe," *American Quarterly*, XIX (Summer, 1967), 224-238.

the "final battle"? [45] In an extraordinarily moving editorial titled by a phrase borrowed from Ibsen, "When We Dead Awaken," he prayed for what he doubtless knew would not happen:

> Immediately the brother toilers on the European continent ceased to be brothers. They became Russians, Germans, French, Austrians, Britons, INTERNATIONAL CANNON FOOD. . . . It is fine. So is the skyrocket. It passes in a moment and intensifies the gloom. The shell bursts. Sublime light. Hellish night of carnage. . . .
> When will we dead awaken?
> When the system dies.
> Then comes the day of social resurrection.[46]

This one was signed "O. A. Tveitmoe."

Yet he was also the same man who could describe Japanese "brother toilers" as "the most dangerous spies that have ever been allowed to exist this side of HELL." and Chinese as "watching . . . waiting to assassinate" American children by infecting them with bubonic plague.[47] He was a charter member of the Japanese and Korean Exclusion League, founded in 1905 by California trade unionists and dedicated to eradicating Oriental workingmen from the North American continent.[48] During the very years in which he had written the wide-ranging editorials quoted above, he also served the Exclusion League as president—so devotedly, in fact, that when he was himself in difficulties, the league set aside its urgent business of pursuing Koreans and Japanese to come to his assistance. The minutes of February 17, 1913, show that by motion unanimously adopted "a committee was appointed to assist in raising bonds for the liberation of President Tveitmoe . . . and the Secretary was directed to proffer the committee's services to the general committee of the Building Trades' Council, through its President, P. H. McCarthy." [49] Here certainly was a demonstration of working class solidarity since several of those who voted for the motion were delegates from the San Francisco Labor Council.

The plague scare of 1900, in furtherance of which Tveitmoe had undertaken his earliest editorial efforts, had served as a dramatic

45 *Organized Labor*, March 30, April 6, 13, 20, 27, May 11, 25, 1912; September 5, 28, 1914.
46 *Organized Labor*, November 21, 1914.
47 *Organized Labor*, December 8, 1906, and March 10, 1900.
48 Daniels, *Politics of Prejudice* (above, n. 12), 27–28.
49 The original name, Japanese and Korean Exclusion League, was changed in 1908 to Asiatic Exclusion League. I will refer to it hereafter simply as the Exclusion League. *Minutes*, San Francisco, February 17, 1913.

opener to the campaign for permanent renewal of Chinese exclusion. But since all Orientals were regarded equally as plague carriers, the scare had the effect of popularizing a new and relatively undeveloped phase of anti-Orientalism, the crusade against the Japanese. During the decade of the 1890s, Japanese in California had increased from slightly over one thousand to more than ten thousand.[50] The *Coast Seamen's Journal* had long since raised the alarm with respect to Japanese sailors, and San Francisco's *Daily Call*, in a series of articles in 1892, had endeavored to generalize the issue. Depression then postponed further elaboration until the turn of the century. Olaf Tveitmoe's *Organized Labor*, from its founding in 1900, gave increasing attention to Japanese immigration. In the spring of that year both councils and both their journals had joined in promoting the first California convention directed specifically against Japanese. Walter Macarthur, editor of the *Seamen's Journal* and spokesman for the Labor Council, served as chairman. Patrick Henry McCarthy, president of the Building Trades Council, was among the speakers, while McCarthy's ally and patron, Mayor Phelan, delivered the main political address.[51]

And there was besides an important guest, Professor Edward A. Ross of Stanford University, soon to become one of America's leading sociologists. Ross directed his remarks to the familiar argument against cheap labor, and what he said might have been little noted had it not been for the fact that it reached the attention of Mrs. Leland Stanford, widow of the late senator. Senator Stanford, it will be remembered, had served his adoptive state not only as first president of the Central Pacific Railroad and first Republican governor, but as founder of the university which bears his name. Mrs. Stanford was apparently already suspicious of Ross on account of views expressed earlier by him on free silver and municipal ownership of utilities, but it was his public fraternization with trade unionists at the anti-Japanese convention which stirred her to action. She demanded that he resign from the university. Stanford's President Jordan tried to dissuade her, but in vain, and the case escalated from a family squabble to a cause célèbre

---

[50] In the same decade, Chinese population in California dropped from 72,472 to 45,753. By 1910 there would be 41,356 Japanese as compared to 36,248 Chinese. (United States, Bureau of the Census, *Eleventh Census. Population*, Pt. 1, [Washington, 1895], 401, Table 14; *Thirteenth Census, Population*, Pt. I [Washington, 1913], 170, Table 31.) Yamato Ichibashi, *Japanese Immigration: It's Status in California* (San Francisco, 1913).

[51] *Coast Seamen's Journal* March 28, April 25, May 16, 1900; May 8, 29, 1901; Daniels, 19–20; *Organized Labor*, February 24, March 17, April 7, 14, 28, May 5, 12, 19, 26, June 2, 9, 16, July 14, 21.

of scholarship. Headed by Columbia's E. R. A. Seligman, a committee of distinguished (eastern) professors rendered a report to the American Economic Association which amounted to a condemnation of the university for violating the principles of free inquiry.[52]

Thus, what was perhaps the earliest defense of academic freedom on the Pacific Coast was undertaken to safeguard advocacy of racial exclusion. On the other hand, the spectacle of the enraged widow wheeling into line to do battle for coolie labor—upon the exploitation of which her husband's fortune had been founded—probably served the exclusionist cause better than a dozen conventions. The labor journals made the most of this incident, several times reprinting the Ross speech as pressure for permanent exclusion of Chinese drew to a climax at the end of 1901. A convention officially sponsored by Mayor Phelan's city administration in November, along with memorializing Congress on the Chinese issue, devoted a substantial portion of its energy to developing arguments for future use against the Japanese.[53] Early in 1902, the first phase of anti-Orientalism came to an end with the enactment of permanent Chinese exclusion.

The Exclusion League

Beneath these demonstrations of harmony among politicians and trade union leaders, an intense power struggle was taking shape. What brought this struggle to its final confrontation was the impact of the Progressive reform movement. California Progressivism, while taking over many slogans from the Populists, developed its main dynamic within the urban middle class. Its basic strategy was to purify the cities, then to reform the state by first capturing and reforming the Republican party.[54] Especially in San Francisco the urban vote would be decisive; and the relations between Progressive reformers and organized labor were therefore of crucial importance. The San Francisco Labor Council, driven by its own economic weakness and impotence in local politics, tended to seek remedial legislation at the state level. Thus it pressed for factory inspection, an eight-hour law, child labor restrictions, regulation of employment agencies, and expansion of the

[52] Edwin R. A. Seligman, Henry W. Farnam, Henry B. Gardner, *Report of the Economists on the Dismissal of Professor Ross from Leland Stanford Junior University* (n.p., February 20, 1901).

[53] Actually the Ross speech contained no reference to race and might easily be taken as a plea for general immigration restriction. But Ross could hardly have been unaware of the setting in which it was delivered. The speech appears in *Organized Labor*, May 19, 1900. See also November 23, 30, 1901; and Daniels, 22–23.

[54] George E. Mowry, *The California Progressives* (Chicago, 1963), 23–56, 86–104.

Bureau of Labor Statistics. One of its primary purposes in advocating statewide federation had been to strengthen labor's voice at Sacramento; by 1907 the Labor Council and the California Federation which it sponsored were able to maintain a regular labor lobby during sessions of the legislature. The Building Trades Council, on the other hand, secure in its craft skills and strongly entrenched in city politics, remained locally oriented. Toward the proponents of statewide labor unity, as well as toward advocates of state political reform, it displayed an eloquent lack of enthusiasm. For these reasons the Progressives would find their first working class allies in the San Francisco Labor Council (many of whose legislative demands they espoused at Sacramento) rather than in the building trades.[55]

Conversely, the Progressives encountered one of their most formidable adversaries in the San Francisco Union Labor Party, which would eventually be taken over (that is, after demonstrating its success) by McCarthy and the Building Trades Council. The Union Labor party, despite its name, was not the official creation of any trade union body. Organized in the aftermath of a bitterly contested teamsters' strike of 1901, it was fueled by resentment at the use which Mayor Phelan's Democratic administration had made of police and special deputies in protecting, and apparently in some cases actually aiding, strikebreakers. The party's sponsors, however, were all second stringers. Men like Andrew Furuseth, Walter Macarthur, and Michael Casey, leaders of the Labor Council which had championed the teamster strike, while sympathetic to the new party, were inhibited from taking a hand by their traditional AFL dread of overt partisanship.[56] McCarthy and the building trades, on the other hand, at most lukewarm in their support for the teamsters' strike and tied to the city administration, remained dead set against any independent ticket. Into this partial vacuum moved the aspiring young Republican politician, Abraham Ruef, and the Union Labor party was launched upon its baroque career.[57]

The new party triumphed in 1901, 1903, and 1905, electing to the mayor's office a protege of Ruef's, Eugene E. Schmitz. A native Californian of German and Irish background, Schmitz possessed almost

55 Saxton, "San Francisco Labor," *Pacific Historical Review*, XXXIV, 428–429.

56 The avoidance of partisan politics by craft unionists never included any reluctance to engage in "nonpartisan" pressure tactics to secure favorable legislation. Andrew Furuseth's long struggle for passage of the Seamen's Bill by Congress was characteristic of Labor Council and State Federation attitudes toward legislation. See Arthur S. Link, *Woodrow Wilson and the Progressive Era* (New York, 1963), 61–63. For a more general discussion, Michael Rogin, "Voluntarism: The Political Functions of an Anti-Political Doctrine," *Industrial and Labor Relations Review*, XV (1962), 521–535.

57 Saxton, "San Francisco Labor," *Pacific Historical Review*, XXXIV, 421–438.

every conceivable asset for San Francisco politics. He was Catholic, a family man, and a member of the Musicians' Union; young and handsomely black bearded, he wielded the orchestral baton in a popular downtown theater.[58] While Schmitz thus furnished an incomparable public image, Ruef, like many bosses before him, organized municipal government to maximize payoffs and bargained statewide with the System for the best available price in money and patronage. All this, of course, was nothing new. Ruef's real innovation was his direct appeal to labor voters. In the past, city bosses had been content to handle labor politicians as they came along at the ward level; Ruef, to undercut them, roused and deployed the labor constituency.[59] He was spectacularly successful. By the mid-point of Schmitz' second term, spokesmen for the two hostile councils were drawing together, albeit reluctantly, in support of the Union Labor party.

A key aspect of this rapprochement was the intensification of anti-Japanese hostility. Early in 1905, the normally conservative-Republican San Francisco *Chronicle* (which however had once backed Denis Kearney's Workingmen's party) began a series of articles, echoing those featured in the *Call* almost a decade earlier, on the menace of Japanese infiltration. The *Chronicle* series now appealed to a level of anxiety heightened by reports of Japanese triumphs over the Russians in the war then being fought in the Far East. At Sacramento the legislature responded with a resolution demanding federal action against Japanese immigrants.[60] In San Francisco, the Schmitz administration turned its attention to implementing a pledge made by the Union Labor party at the time of its first campaign in 1901 to the effect that all Asiatics would be segregated in the city schools. Such had generally been the rule for Chinese children—if they received any public education at all—but the Japanese, scattered more widely about the city, had in some cases been attending schools in districts where they lived. The board of education, dominated by labor party members (Ruef's brother-in-law served as president and the superintendent of schools was Schmitz' former trombonist), voted to transfer Japanese students to a separate school at the earliest opportunity.[61]

The board's declaration of intent, though applauded in the local press, resulted in no immediate action. Meanwhile, delegates from a scattering of organizations, for the most part trade unions, met in San Francisco to form the Japanese and Korean Exclusion League,

58 Bean, *Boss Ruef,* 20–21.
59 Ruef, *Bulletin,* June 27, 1912.
60 San Francisco *Chronicle,* February 23–March 2, 1905.
61 Daniels, *Politics of Prejudice* (above, n. 12), 24–27, 31–32, 128 note 3.

already referred to in connection with its president, Olaf Tveitmoe. Participants at this founding convention included leaders from both houses of labor—Furuseth and Walter Macarthur for the Labor Council, McCarthy and Tveitmoe for the building trades. It appeared that the building trades held the dominant interest, for Tveitmoe assumed the presidency and A. E. Yoell, listed as a member of the "Electrical Mechanics of California," was chosen to the only full time post, that of financial secretary. Throughout the following decade the league would serve as a main organizational vehicle for anti-Japanese agitation. Yoell, the secretary, salaried at $25 and later $35 a week, devoted his days to correspondence with assemblymen and representatives, rallying support for legislation favored by the league, disputing government statistics on Oriental immigration, and clipping anti-Japanese articles from the press to fill out the league's newsletter.[62]

Although the league claimed broad popular support (doubtless correctly in the sense of sympathy for its program), its actual base lay within the labor movement. Minutes of the first annual meeting listed 231 affiliates, including civic, fraternal, military, and benevolent associations, but the majority were labor organizations. Cash donations of record were credited almost exclusively to unions. The Building Trades Council in 1908 regularized its assistance by voting a monthly per capita payment. Early the following year (the minutes for March serving as sample), the league was receiving contributions from 136 donors, 105 of which were labor organizations, 68 of these being attached to the Building Trades Council. Moreover, during the active life of the league, the building trades donated the services of Tveitmoe as president and made space available for the League's lengthy reports and newsletters in the columns of *Organized Labor*.[63] Unmistakably, this was a low budget operation. Annual cash receipts ranged from $3,000 to $6,000. In one of its more vigorous years (1906–07), monthly expenditures averaged only $326.[64] Yet the significance of the league was greater than this price tag implied, because its real function was to coordinate and *harmonize* the activities of an already existing organizational system—the trade unions.

In November 1905 the Union Labor party astonished enemies and advocates alike by the totality of its triumph. Against an opposition

[62] Exclusion League, *Minutes,* San Francisco, May 6, July 1, August 5, September 16, October 28, 1906; December, 1908; on Yoell, March, 1907, p. 11. See also Daniels, 27–28, 126 note 34.

[63] Exclusion League Minutes, May 6, July 1, 1906.

[64] Compiled from Exclusion League *Minutes,* 1906–1907. See also annual financial reports in *Minutes* (May, 1909), 5; and *Organized Labor*, May 10, 1913.

for the first time united, the party not only reelected Mayor Schmitz and carried its slate of city officials, but made a clean sweep of the entire board of supervisors. Patrick Henry McCarthy, after having watched with grim hostility through two previous elections, had swung his council over to the new party during the summer. He then claimed credit for the victory and set about linking his building trades apparatus as tightly to the Schmitz-Ruef machine as formerly it had been linked to the administration of Mayor Phelan.[65] The Labor Council, on the other hand, remained, as it had been before, on the periphery, leaning more toward state politics than municipal.

Labor-Progressive Alliance

April 18, 1906, was the day of the earthquake. Three days of fire followed. Mayor Schmitz performed heroically, the city under his baton giving itself in a mood of interparty (and interclass) harmony to the symphonies of reconstruction. And as the allegro of carpenters' saws and masons' hammers filled the spring days, a similarly harmonious tone prevailed in those environs where Boss Ruef dealt with his numerous clients. Among these were agents of the city's liquor and prostitution interests, generally of working class orientation and Democratic politics, as well as spokesmen for such largely upper class Republican enterprises as street traction and telephone companies. Both groups, facing the same need for rapid rebuilding, craved favors that rested within the gift of municipal government.[66]

In this respect, urban disaster had created a sellers' market. The buyers stood ready to pay the price; and as it would soon appear, neither the labor party's newly elected supervisors nor its handsome mayor were altogether reluctant to be bought. At first there were only rumors and suppositions; yet even these were enough to demoralize the ensemble. Less than six weeks after the earthquake, the *Coast Seamen's Journal*, speaking for a segment of Labor Council leadership, repudiated all connection with the Union Labor party: "Passage of the trolley ordinance marks the point of separation between the interests of the Union Labor Party and those of organized labor and the public at large. . . . From first to last, Ruef has been the whole party and the party's candidates have been merely so many tools in his dextrous hands." [67] This was in part a blast at the rival

65 Bean, *Boss Ruef*, 61–65; *Organized Labor*, August 5, November 4, 11, 1905.
66 Bean, *Boss Ruef*, 128–144.
67 *Coast Seamen's Journal*, May 30, 1906.

Building Trades Council. But more importantly, it expressed genuine dismay at the speed and ease with which the labor party had been controlled and absorbed into the System.

Others besides the Labor Council were reading these same signs. California's Progressive reformers in 1906 stood at the threshold of their long struggle to dominate the state Republican apparatus. One of the major obstacles in their road they perceived to be the political alliance between the Southern Pacific railway and Boss Ruef's now seemingly invincible city machine. What they had failed to accomplish at the polls, however, might yet be achieved through the courts; and in October the famous graft prosecution, planned and financed by the Progressive insurgents, opened in San Francisco with Union Labor party leadership as its primary target.[68] Speaking for the Building Trades Council, Olaf Tveitmoe in *Organized Labor* denounced the prosecution as "A Conspiracy to Destroy Trade Unionism." [69] The Labor Council, on the other hand, acknowledging that a great many trade unionists believed the charges of corruption to be well founded, called for full investigation and full punishment.[70]

It was at this juncture that the anti-Japanese crusade exploded into its first international crisis. During the summer and early fall of 1906, a series of harassments and minor assaults on Japanese had taken place. On October 11, the San Francisco school board, pressured by the Exclusion League and doubtless believing that reorganization of city schools in the wake of the earthquake furnished a convenient occasion, ordered the transfer of all Japanese pupils to the Oriental school in Chinatown.[71] Nine days later angry and garbled reports appeared in the Tokyo press. Thus, by way of Tokyo the news reached Washington, where President Roosevelt, who was keenly aware of the realities of power in the Far East, intervened to muzzle the Californians. After authorizing use of the armed forces to protect Japanese nationals throughout the country and threatening a federal court suit to quash the school board order, Roosevelt conferred with the California congressional delegation, then summoned to Washington the troublesome San Francisco school board.[72]

Meanwhile, in his annual message the president had put forward the extraordinary recommendation that Congress pass an act "for the naturalization of Japanese who come here intending to become citi-

---

[68] Bean, *Boss Ruef*, 145–163.
[69] *Organized Labor*, December 1, 1906.
[70] *Coast Seamen's Journal*, November 7, 1906; *Labor Clarion*, March 22, 1907.
[71] Exclusion League, *Minutes*, September, 1906.
[72] Daniels, *Politics of Protest*, 32–42.

zens." [73] It seems unlikely that he held any serious intention of pressing this proposal, or imagined that Congress would pass it if he did so. Rather, as Roger Daniels has suggested, his aim was probably to provide himself with a forward position, the relinquishment of which might serve to placate the exclusionists, and at the same time to evoke a favorable bargaining context within which to urge on Japan that voluntary control over emigration which would come to be called the "gentleman's agreement." [74] Most Californians had no knowledge of these maneuvers. What resulted, therefore, was a long-lasting resentment toward Roosevelt himself and partial beatification of the Union Labor party, which stood sorely in need of such assistance. For by the time the presidential summons had reached San Francisco, both the mayor and Boss Ruef were under grand jury indictment.

Ruef's brother-in-law, the school board president, and Schmitz' trombonist, the superintendent of schools, declined making the journey to Washington unless Mayor Schmitz were invited to accompany them. This was eventually done, and the mayor set forth with the educators in the guise of latter day Jacksonians vowing to battle the monster of plutocracy in his own lair. In Washington, however, perhaps through comprehension of the diplomatic problems the president actually faced, perhaps simply yielding to pressure, the group agreed to rescind the segregation order. For this, of course, they were denounced at home, and the mayor returned, having lost rather than gained in prestige, to stand trial for assorted malfeasances in office. [75] What followed was melodrama in the finest San Francisco tradition. There were entrapments and confessions, inside deals, a shooting in court, and kidnapping. Ruef went eventually to San Quentin; Schmitz was convicted and removed from office; almost the entire Union Labor board of supervisors confessed to receiving bribes and resigned their posts in hopes of escaping prosecution. The Progressive reformers had thus breached the main fortress of the System. Within three years they

[73] Theodore Roosevelt, Sixth Annual Message, December 3, 1906, James D. Richardson, *A Compilation of the Messages and Papers of the Presidents* (New York, 1897-), XV, 7055.

[74] Daniels, 39.

[75] Exclusion League, *Minutes*, March, 1907. Schmitz apparently had not made up his mind whether he intended to play the role of adversary to the president or bask in the glory of being an official guest. Actually he was guest of honor at several functions including dinner with Vice-President Fairbanks and a reception arranged by Samuel Gompers. Despite these splendors, the impression in San Francisco was, as Bean puts it, that he had been "overawed by the 'Big Stick' and had backed down." Ruef, wiser than Schmitz, had advised him against forcing himself into the Washington trip. (Bean, *Boss Ruef*, 182-183.)

overran the Republican party and elected Hiram Johnson, one of their attorneys in the graft prosecution, governor of the state.[76]

Beyond this point it will not be necessary to pursue in detail the complex politics of California's Progressive era. Patrick Henry Mc-Carthy, who had not been directly implicated in the trials, took over control of the Union Labor party, ran for mayor in 1907 and was defeated, ran again in 1909 and won. Yet by 1911 his strength had ebbed so drastically that he failed even to make it through the primary. McCarthy then retired from public politics; the labor party went into permanent decline, leaving the road open for the San Francisco Labor Council and its statewide counterpart, the California Federation of Labor. Leaders of this wing of the trade union movement (many of whom, like Walter Macarthur and Andrew Furuseth, had been hostile to McCarthy and the building trades ever since the teamster strike of 1901) were meanwhile cementing an alliance with the Progressive insurgents. They succeeded in 1910 in carrying the working class districts of San Francisco for Hiram Johnson. Beginning the following year, they received their reward from the Progressive controlled state government in the form of enactments long desired by organized labor, as well as a number of secondary, though satisfying, official appointments.[77]

California's labor-Progressive alliance was in essence a relation between two leadership groups. Thus, the 1910 victory of the Progressives helped the Labor Council–State Federation leaders to win dominance inside the labor movement; and this dominance in turn helped the Progressives (since San Francisco's labor vote was so often decisive at Sacramento) to maintain control of the state. Both groups of leaders, labor and Progressive, grew rapidly less insurgent, and the narrowing of their horizons tended further to unite them. But as their social horizons narrowed, their capabilities of rousing mass enthusiasm at election times served to diminish. Consequently, after the first real bonanza of labor and social legislation, most of which was adopted by the first two Progressive legislatures, the main fruits of this alliance were bills and rhetoric directed against the Japanese.[78]

[76] Mowry, *The California Progressives* (above, n. 54), 105–134.

[77] Hiram Johnson's margin of victory in the working class assembly districts was extremely narrow, but the surprising thing was that he carried them at all, since they were traditionally Democratic, and since McCarthy, still mayor of the city, was standing in silent opposition to the Progressive candidates. In the next gubernatorial election (1914), Johnson carried these same districts by landslide proportions. (Saxton, "San Francisco Labor," *Pacific Historical Review*, XXXIV, 432–433, 436 note 45.)

[78] California State Federation of Labor, *Proceedings, 1911* (San Francisco, 1911), 80–96.

Only one law actually resulted, the Alien Land Act of 1913 which prohibited purchase or leasing for longer than three years of any land in California by aliens not eligible for United States citizenship. The phrase designated solely persons of Asian parentage and was obviously aimed against Japanese. The Japanese government protested vigorously, while two administrations at Washington—those of the Republican Taft and the Democrat Wilson—labored to forestall the enactment. All this, however, only added to the pleasurable excitement in California and enhanced those therapeutic values which sponsors of the measure hoped to extract from it. As to actual land tenure, the law had little effect, for by 1913 it had become fairly easy for Japanese purchasers to transfer title to American born children or relatives. But in laying the basis for Japanese exclusion, afterward written into the immigration law of 1924, and as a dress rehearsal for the infamous relocation camps of World War II, the Alien Land Act was a contribution of some magnitude.[79]

[79] Hichborn, *Story of the Legislature of 1911; . . . of 1913; . . . of 1915;* Daniels, 61–64. And see Jacobus tenBroek, Edward N. Barnhart, Floyd W. Matson, *Prejudice, War, and the Constitution: Causes and Consequences of the Evacuation of the Japanese Americans in World War II* (Berkeley and Los Angeles, 1968).

12

A FORWARD GLANCE

A Brief Recapitulation

From the time of the gold rush, California's labor force was divided between Chinese and non-Chinese contingents. During the seventies and early eighties, Chinese comprised one-quarter to one-fifth of those working for wages. Lines of division were sharply drawn. Throughout the state Chinese dominated the menial service trades. In rural areas they worked in mining, heavy construction, and agriculture, for the most part at tasks of low skill and minimal prestige. In the city, aside from menial trades (domestic and laundry), they worked at the manufacture of goods subject to national market competition. Their social organization was vertical from the indentured laborer to the importer-padrone. Pressure from outside tended to strengthen the cohesiveness of this nonclass structure.

The remaining three quarters of the labor force was of diverse origin. Native and immigrant, comprising many different language and cultural backgrounds, they included groups which had elsewhere been in sharp conflict. In California, however, the divergent elements were drawn together by a sense of frustration and dispossession that was common to all. Despite their own differences, they believed that a greater difference separated them from the Chinese. These two psychological factors—frustration and consciousness of non-Chineseness—welded the non-Chinese labor force into a bloc that would deeply modify the politics and social relationships of the Far West. Here, by contrast, the organizational pattern was horizontal: the workers, the producers, the dispossessed joined in self-defense against nonproducers, exploiters, monopolists. And since these producers viewed the Chinese as tools of monopoly, they considered themselves under attack on two fronts, or more aptly from above and below. But when they struck back, they generally struck at the Chinese. The result was a crusade initiated by the non-Chinese sector of the labor force, in which groups outside the labor force acquiesced or participated.

The anti-Chinese impulse has generally been presented as economic in origin and unique to the West Coast. The assertion of economic origin is probably correct, that of uniqueness probably not. First of all it is clear that the main carriers of the movement were those who came in competition with Chinese or feared possible exposure to such competition. These fears, based on the low living standard of imported Cantonese laborers and on the contract system of their importation, were by no means imaginary. A more or less free labor force was being pressed into competition with indentured labor. On the other hand, the main defenders of Chinese importation were to be found among those who benefited from the employment of contract gang labor. To this point, the division was quite simply economic. The economic division, however, coincided with a preexisting dichotomy of ideological and organizational patterns that stemmed from Jacksonian politics of the antebellum East.

For the Democratic party especially, the defense of slavery had become a condition of political survival. Essential to the defense was an assertion of black inferiority. This in turn required the denial, or at least neutralization, of the concept of the equal rights of man upon which the intellectual system of the Democracy was premised. Ideological inconsistency tended to rub smooth with time and usage; moreover, the racist addendum was constantly reinforced by social and economic insecurity among eastern workingmen, especially among Irish immigrants. And during these same years in which the Democratic party was adjusting itself to the defense of slavery, its entire structure was being infused with the emotional tones of romantic nationalism. All this was part of the manifest destiny that moved westward with the ox teams and wagons.

Hostility to slavery, on the other hand, had thrown up its barricades largely within the old Whig party. The slavery issue tore the Whigs apart. In the course of the ensuing realignment, antislavery became associated not only with the emergent Republican cause, but with the opening of western lands for settlement and finally with preservation of the Union itself. The Democrats, stripped of their nationalistic mantle, were in turn divided. Their proslavery elements were separated by secession while the antislavery and nationalistic components were drawn into coalition, for the sake of saving the Union, with the Republicans.

There had been from the beginning within the antislavery movement a dynamic but always minority phalanx of true believers: the abolitionists. Since the early thirties they had denounced slavery for its violation of those twin mandates of equality premised rationally in the Declaration of Independence and to faith revealed by the word of God. This, because of its inner cohesiveness, proved an almost indestructible line. Through crises of war and through all the political exigencies of Reconstruction (when Republican dominance seemingly depended on extension of the franchise to Negro freedmen), the abolitionist ideology had frequently seemed to be that of the Union-Republican coalition.

After Appomattox, what remained of the Democracy set about mending its shattered image. Issues which came readily to hand were restoration of the Union through quick readmission of the seceded states and maintenance of white supremacy by the restriction of blacks to a lower caste role. Both issues held powerful voter appeal; yet both had been tainted by secession as had the party itself. The problem was how to split former Democrats away from the Union-Republican coalition without at the same time giving fatal ammunition to the enemy. This required adroit tactics; and so long as the abolitionist line remained dominant within the Republican coalition, not much maneuvering ground was left open.

One of the first Democratic breakthroughs occurred on the Pacific Coast. In California, aside from European immigrants, the bulk of the citizenry were men from the Midwest and from the central and north Atlantic regions. Before the war a majority had been Democrats. Their typical thought pattern, the Jacksonian persuasion with its romantic nationalism and foreshortened egalitarianism, had become characteristic of the new state. Few blacks were to be found then in California; but there were plenty of Chinese—a people of different color and strange ways, who while not exactly slaves were not quite free either. The Chinese fitted readily enough into that mental compartment which in the East had been reserved for blacks. Already in the mines and at railroad construction camps there had been collisions of Chinese and non-Chinese; and now, during the years following the war, intense conflict was developing in the new urban areas.

But while Chinese had been identified with Negroes, hostility to Negroes was not identical with anti-Chineseness. This was of key importance; for one was tained politically, the other was not. In 1867 California Democrats launched their offensive against the Chinese. The result, as earlier noted, was a bonanza. The party laid hands on an issue of enormous potential in its own right—a new issue, uncontaminated by the sad history of civil war, yet evocative of that entire syndrome of hatreds and loyalties which still could not quite openly be declared.

As to the Republicans, given the northern whiggish origins of their movement and the fact that war had vastly stimulated Yankee enterprise in the West, it is scarcely surprising that California's new Republican élite should largely have coincided with the users of Chinese labor. Defense of the Chinese on economic grounds (though certainly the Republicans mounted such a defense) held the disadvantage of exposing their own interest. And here it was not so much a matter of concealment, for they believed their interest legitimate; it was rather that of seeking some higher ground than private profit. Under pressure of the Democratic attack, they turned (as had their colleagues in national leadership at each crisis of war and Reconstruction) to the abolitionists' twin mandates, the Declaration and the Bible.

It is clear that, while the economic circumstances which gave rise both to the importation of Chinese and to the crusade against the Chinese were unique to the Far West, the ideological and organizational patterns within which pro- and anti-Chinese interests found expression were of much older origin. In a sense these two causative sequences ran parallel. It would be possible to define, and derive, the sides of the debate either in economic or in ideological terms, although in actuality the sequences intermeshed and continually modified each other. At all events, in 1867 the Democrats swept California. One outcome of their victory was nationalization of the Chinese question, an issue which worked strongly for the Democrats by threatening to split their opponents. That most advanced (and ideologically formidable) contingent of the Republican coalition, the abolitionist phalanx, stood upon positions from which no retreat was permissible; but the main forces gave ground, and this withdrawal foreshadowed—in a sense justified and helped bring about—later evacuation of the entire southern salient which they had held since the Emancipation Proclamation.

Entanglement of an economic conflict over contract labor with older ideological and organizational cleavages precluded any single or simple solution. The racist assault on importation of Chinese guaranteed a rebuttal in abolitionist terms; and the converse also held true. Thus the abolitionist line at its latter end became tied to an economic position soon to be abandoned as indefensible; while the inevitable restriction on foreign indentured labor was achieved in purely racist terms—and carried with it a specific reaffirmation of the old racial denial of citizenship. Within the Republican and Democratic traditions what resulted was an ever more rapid erosion of the twin mandates, rational and revealed, upon which both traditions were based.

Meanwhile, the non-Chinese workingmen of California and their leaders were discovering in the anti-Chinese crusade a powerful organizing tool. Politically this had been evident since the gubernatorial campaign of 1867 when trade unions and anticoolie clubs had joined with the Democrats to upset Republican control of the state. It was displayed even more dramatically in the challenge posed by the Workingmen's party to the bipartisan establishment. Afterward the trade unionists, alarmed at the implications of Kearney's and Gannon's appeals to the unskilled and unemployed, had separated themselves from mass politics. They determined to make the most of such bargaining advantages as their skills imparted to them. The result was a focus on economic or "pure" trade unionism, comparable to the impulse in the East and Midwest which during those same years was bringing national craft unions to ascendancy within the labor movement. California, however, remained semicolonial. Craft unions, isolated from their national centers, were at best only meagerly self-sufficient. If they were to exercise any influence in California, it must still be done as it had been done earlier through the medium of the labor force as a whole. Thus, while their eastern counterparts built up centralized national unions and established the American Federation of Labor, skilled tradesmen on the West Coast were endeavoring simply to sustain (under their own leadership if possible) a regional labor center.

Pure trade unionism proved inadequate as a unifying appeal to segments of California's labor force outside the skilled trades. Unionists were therefore obliged to compete with the labor politicians, whom they had so recently brushed off, for leadership in the anti-Chinese cause. Both the Trades Assembly and the League of Deliverance represented efforts, though unsuccessful, toward impounding the anti-Chinese dynamic as an aid to trade union recruitment. Founders of the Federated Trades had better luck in this regard; for many years the council they set up managed to direct some of the fire and steam of anti-Orientalism to its own organizational purposes. A summary of the several attempts to establish an effective regional labor center in California brings these connections sharply into focus:

(1) The first such effort developed during the flush times of the Civil War. As boom conditions subsequently slacked off, the new council ventured into politics with the aim of protecting through state legislation the favorable conditions recently gained by skilled tradesmen of San Francisco. The necessary bid for mass support was made on the basis of anticoolieism, and on this same basis the council allied itself with the Democratic party in the campaign of 1867. During the ten-year postwar depression which followed, the gains of the unionists were lost and the council itself went out of existence.

(2) The second attempt, the San Francisco Trades Assembly, grew

directly out of the sandlot agitation of 1877 and the Workingmen's party. This was the point at which the trade unionists, failing to win leadership of the party, began to preach the gospel of no politics. Their assembly barely survived the depressed seventies. It flourished briefly as conditions improved in 1881–82, then wilted again with the return of slack times. Trade union leaders in 1882 endeavored to recoup the assembly's fortunes through sponsorship of the League of Deliverance. But the league failed because passage of the Exclusion Act in that year cut the ground from under it. The assembly disintegrated soon afterward.

(3) In 1885, spurred by the expulsions of Chinese from small towns up and down the Pacific Coast, San Francisco labor organizations summoned a coastwide anti-Chinese congress. The congress founded the Trades and Labor Federation of the Pacific Coast (Federated Trades), which, afterward reorganized as the San Francisco Labor Council, has enjoyed a continuous existence ever since.

(4) The crusade against Chinese terminated in 1902 with permanent exclusion. Its place was taken by the anti-Japanese campaign in large part initiated and led by trade unions through their Asiatic Exclusion League. The league served as a unifying center during the early years of the century for the rapidly growing trade union movement; and when the first political expression of that growth, the Union Labor party, faced disaster in the San Francisco graft prosecutions, its chief riposte was to provoke an international crisis over Japanese school children. Subsequently, a more enduring expression of labor's new strength took the form of alliance with the Progressive reformers—an alliance based in part on agreement as to certain legislative goals and in part on the reciprocal exploitation of anti-Oriental rhetoric.

Throughout this entire discussion, a question which keeps recurring in different contexts is that of the relation between Chinese labor and the skilled trades. The presence of Chinese in the Far West served generally to strengthen the position of white craftsmen. This was so for several closely interrelated reasons, which can most conveniently be summarized under the headings of economic, organizational, and political.

Control by craftsmen over entry into their various fields—the key to their advantaged economic position—was enhanced by racial division within the remainder of the labor force. The Chinese, always available for unskilled tasks, were excluded from entry, either as competitors or as strikebreakers, into skilled occupations. At the same time their presence inhibited immigration to California of young and aggressive unskilled workingmen. White workers actually forced into competition with Chinese in the construction gangs, harvest fields, or sweatshops, were for the most part those who were no longer capable (if they ever had been) of bidding for jobs against skilled white tradesmen.

As an organizational tool, anti-Orientalism was limited to certain users. It could serve the needs of political organizers or of craft union leaders who wished to secure the support of unskilled workingmen without assuming trade union responsibilities to them. Even under the most favorable circumstances, the unionization of unskilled or semi-skilled was difficult enough in nineteenth-century America; it remained virtually impossible so long as a large group among the unskilled were relegated to an untouchable and therefore unorganizable caste. Gains of any kind were foreclosed for all the rest. When Roney and Haskell with their socialist academy colleagues launched the League of Deliverance in 1882, they had apparently hoped for miraculous results, that the inspirational effects of the anti-Chinese slogan would transcend the boundaries of craft interest and enable them to unionize the army of the unskilled. No such miracle occurred. By 1885 Roney seems to have reconciled himself to a craft horizon; and when in that crucial year he took charge of the Federated Trades Council, he exploited the Chinese issue in a calculated and successful effort to establish skilled trades' dominance.

Beyond these economic and organizational aspects, the Chinese issue tended to reinforce the position of craft unionism through its working in mass politics. Its result, as Henry George had pointed out after the constitutional convention of 1879, was to short-circuit pressure for radical reform. On the one hand it provided a suitable instrument for labor politicians intent on doing business within the System, while on the other it freed craft unionists to exploit their advantaged position to the maximum without interference from the nonskilled and the unemployed. Though George might denounce the duplicity of anti-Chinese politicians even as Roney was futilely kicking against the harness of craft unionism, there were a host of others who would neither kick nor denounce. These were content to take things as they found them in both fields of endeavor. The Chinese question became for them an indispensable professional asset. The only real danger was that the Chinese might finally leave or die out; but happily the Exclusion Act had been written only against Chinese, and there remained a parade of Asian menaces—Hindoos, Filipinos, Japanese—waiting in the wings to provide employment for subsequent generations of craft union officials and labor politicians.

All the while, of course, the trade unionists were decrying partisanship and warning against the dangers of involvement in mass politics. Yet a kind of symbiotic relationship bound them to the labor politicians. The gist of it was that a clear field would be left the politicians to push their stock of proletarian, racist, and religious motifs in working class districts as long as their activities kept the unorganized and unemployed off the backs of union officials. When pressure for radical reform became powerful enough to upset the labor constituencies, this partnership was likely to break down. Union leaders would then be forced into mass politics in opposition to the discredited politicians. This roughly was what occurred in 1894 during the Populist insurgency, and again even more precisely in 1911 when the ascendant wing of the trade union apparatus swung labor's vote to the Progressives.

The 1911 alliance between Progressive reformers and leaders of the San Francisco Labor Council and State Federation acknowledged the power and cohesiveness achieved by the labor force in California. Throughout more than half a century labor had played a major role in state politics; and for more than ten years the metropolis of the Pacific Coast had been famed as a *union* town—the archetype of skilled trade dominance. To this result, as the forgoing pages have endeavored to show, the presence of Chinese had substantially contributed. Here one comes up against the logical impossibility of asserting that any particular situation existed because of some antecedent situation. Yet perhaps without overtaxing the argument it may be suggested that the Chinese, and the factor of anti-Orientalism which their presence occasioned, furthered the dominance of the skilled trades by enabling those trades to control and direct the energies of the entire white labor force.

Erosion of the Producer Ethic

From the foregoing it seems clear that, by the mid-eighties at least, the institutionalization of anti-Orientalism was firmly established. What did this involve in terms of thought patterns within the labor force? First of all, the long erosion in the Republican and Democratic traditions of the twin mandates of equality had been deeply influential. Experiences and responses of California workingmen had intensified this process; and to the extent that they were Republicans or Democrats, they had been in turn affected by the outcome. Beyond these two major traditions, common to the entire population, the pattern most characteristic of the labor force was the one which stemmed from the producer ethic of the Jacksonian era. Productive workers of all sorts, according to this view, regardless of whether industrial or agricultural, wage workers or self-employed, together comprised the honorable and creative elements of society. These were the value carriers; and it therefore became the mission of the labor movement, as perceived by many advocates of labor organization both before and after the Civil War, to unite them against the ever encroaching conspiracy of privilege and monopoly. Here, explicitly, was the credo of the Knights of Labor; and during the eighties trade unionism along with labor activity of all sorts was being justified largely within this framework. In the East, however, laboring men had sanctioned the exclusion of blacks from the ranks of acceptable value carriers; and in the West a similar reservation had been placed against Chinese.

The majority of American workingmen, doubtless, did not lead intense ideological lives. They were accustomed to inconsistencies in their patterns of thought and seem to have accepted without much discomfort a producer ethic from which one-tenth to one-fourth of all producers had been proscribed. Yet there were certain ideologically conscious minorities which resisted racial proscriptions. Such were the "political" labor unionists exemplified by William Sylvis and A. C. Cameron who, immediately after the Civil War, had argued for inclusion of Negroes in the National Labor Union.[1] The controversy over Negro membership in the NLU raised scarcely an echo in the Far West. But as to the exclusion of Chinese, there were some, especially European immigrants of republican revolutionary background, who held grave doubts. Most of these, probably, like Frank Roney, found their way into the socialist movement. At all events it was the socialists alone in the California labor force who mounted any criticism of the anti-Chinese crusade. Socialists took their ideology seriously; and few though they were in number, they played a crucially important role in West Coast labor. Consistently with their general view, they endeavored to redefine the producer ethic—which they considered fuzzy, agrarian, and petty bourgeois—into a wage earner ethic. But within this redefinition, any exclusion of wage earners (and who could deny that Chinese in the West, like black laborers in the East, were wage earners?) confronted the socialists with a theoretical and moral dilemma. They strained mightily over the problem and ended by agreeing, with Roney, to "sail under the flag" of anticoolieism. This was to serve merely as a tactic, a means of uniting and educating the working class.

Tactics, however, have a way of becoming habits; and so at the turning point in 1885 when, conceivably, there was a chance to have hauled down the tactical flag and raised in its stead a strategic flag of

[1] See above, pp. 40–44.

working class unity, the socialists could summon little more than a gesture. It is scarcely possible, now, to read the statement made on their behalf at the first convention of the Federated Trades by Sigismund Danielewicz, the San Francisco barber turned seamen's organizer, without believing that Danielewicz was indeed, as Roney described him, "ardent"—and totally sincere. Yet Danielewicz must have known beforehand that his comrades would permit him to be guffawed and howled and booed from the podium. Haskell the firebrand, Roney the labor statesman, who both were present, said nothing in his defense.[2]

Perhaps one reason for this passivity was that many socialists rejected, really, what Danielewicz was saying. Haskell, for one, had found his way to labor's cause through the anti-Chinese crusade. Only three months after the Federated Trades convention, W. C. Owen, another ardent socialist and a long-time colleague of Haskell and Roney in the socialist academy, wrote an article for the Denver *Labor Enquirer* (which had inherited the readership of Haskell's short-lived *Truth*) titled "The Coast Crisis: An Argument Justifying Socialists' Anti-Chinese Agitation."[3] Owen began by quoting Victor Hugo on the crusades. "It was a mighty popular movement, and all such, be the cause and design what they may, ever unchain the spirit of freedom." He proceeded then to an analogy between the crusades and the anti-Chinese agitation. Yet, as he regretfully noted, some of the "best and purest minded comrades" were standing aloof from this cause because it did not "square with their preconceived theory of fraternity." Also, and apparently for the same reason, many socialists still looked askance at the "trades union movement."

In both instances, the *Enquirer's* correspondent continued, their reluctance stemmed from failure to understand the processes of evolution. Change came only through struggle. It was therefore the duty of socialists to aid the people in acquiring habits of struggle; the goals toward which struggle might be directed were of less importance than the fact of struggle itself:

> I regard it as the adding of a fresh ring to the tree of solidarity whenever men are roused to the self-sacrifice of putting aside their selfish private interests for the sake of a common cause.

2 See above, pp. 221–223.

3 W. C. Owen in a letter dated San Francisco, February 23, 1886, printed in the Denver *Labor Enquirer*, March 6, 1886. (Cross Collection Newspapers on Microfilm, Bancroft Library.) On Owen, see Frank Roney, *Frank Roney: Irish Rebel and California Labor Leader* (Berkeley, 1931), 437, 473. On Haskell's connection with the Denver *Labor Enquirer*, see Ira B. Cross, *A History of the Labor Movement in California* (Berkeley, 1935), 158.

The workingman may not be able to explain his motives with scientific precision, but when he beats a scab, I believe that if we could see into his mind, we should discover that he is prompted to his action by an instinctive sense that th: scab is false to the cause of labor, that he is a traitor to the principle of solidarity by which alone the proletariat can hope to win. So it is with the anti-Chinese crusade; a great part of the repugnance felt to them upon this coast is that they do not act as citizens, that they have no concern in the solidarity of the nation. A precisely similar sentiment has dictated the persecutions of the Jews in Germany, Austria and Russia, persecutions which have been justified precisely on this ground. . . . It is, in short, but the public method of voicing the sentiment, "no rights without duties," or, as Comte puts it, "Man has no rights except to fulfill his duties."

In a word, I believe that we ought to welcome every opportunity which presents itself to the proletariat of developing itself in the only way, as evolution proves conclusively, in which anything ever did develop itself since the beginning of the world—that is to say, by struggle.

It would be pleasant to suppose that this argument, drawn up fifty-five years before Belsen and Auschwitz, had been naively or innocently conceived. The circumstances of its presentation scarcely permit such a supposition. During the latter part of 1885 and the early months of 1886 came that series of pogroms which resulted in the dispossession and murder of Chinese and the leveling of small town ghettoes from San Diego to Seattle. The plan of abatement by violence advocated by Kearny and Kalloch—and by Roney and Haskell—was at last being tried out in action.

The silencing of the "best and purest minded comrades" on this issue was comparable to the disintegration of the abolitionist line within the Republican coalition. General retreat followed, bringing with it a continuing restriction of the producer ethic. Just as in the major political traditions, the ideological heart of the old structure was being gnawed away. These events within the labor force of the Far West fed back to the larger national context, and especially so through their impact on the developing ideology of national craft unionism.

Race and the House of Labor

When the National Labor Union at the close of the Civil War had debated the question of black membership, speakers on both sides respected in principle that declaration of labor unity which had been set before the public in the official NLU Address: "we are of the opinion that the interests of the labor cause demand that all working-men be included within its ranks, without regard to race or nationality." [4] As noted earlier, this was an expression of the Jacksonian producer ethic adjusted to the postwar situation in which black slaves were seemingly being transformed by Reconstruction into citizens, voters, independent economic agents. To press a contrary view too diligently in 1868 might have suggested a taint of secessionist sympathies. Moreover, since the labor force had no other ideology at its disposal, groups within the labor force had little alternative but to rationalize their divergent viewpoints with reference to the producer ethic. Thus the NLU, while proclaiming the unity of labor, ended in practice by accepting exclusion of blacks at the local level.[5]

Craft unionism, then in its infancy but at the threshold of rapid growth, exhibited a similar ambivalence. Economically rather than politically oriented, the craft unionists and their leaders sought to maximize bargaining power through union control over competition for skilled jobs. To this purpose they strove to define the limits of each craft, to restrict entry by means of rigorous apprenticeship, and to establish union supervision over apprenticeship and hiring. The type of organization dictated by the craft concept was necessarily exclusive: optimum membership for each craft would be that which took in all trained practitioners of the craft, excluding all others. Since the recently emancipated black contingent of the labor force remained unskilled and inexperienced at industrial occupations, it was certain to fall largely within the excluded portion. Regardless of ideology, the logic which flowed from the practice of craft unionism tended to prohibit entry of blacks.[6]

Indeed, the preeminence of practice over ideological principle would soon become one of the seminal ideas of craft unionism. Selig Perlman, in the massive *History of Labour in the United States* on which he and John R. Commons collaborated at the University of Wisconsin, wrote that, having freed themselves of the old faith in "cooperation, social reform and politics," the craft unionists turned instead to the "wage consciousness of Marx and the International, purged of its so-

[4] Cameron, *Address* (Chicago, 1867), quoted in John R. Commons et al., *A Documentary History of American Industrial Society*, 10 vols. (New York, 1958), IX, 158–160.

[5] See above, p. 43.

[6] Alexander Saxton, "Race and the House of Labor," in Gary Nash and Richard Weiss, eds., *Race in the Mind of America* (New York, 1970).

cialist ingredients." [7] Having thus shuffled off both the producer ethic and the proletarian mission, these unions were ready to accept the industrial apparatus as they found it and do what they could for themselves. A recent study of American labor organization by the economist Lloyd Ulman has taken the drive of skilled workingmen to improve their collective bargaining potential as the chief dynamic factor in the growth of national unions. This was the decisive factor, Ulman argues, in the drawing of boundaries around particular skills. And given the mobility of American society, it was this same factor which impelled craftsmen, grasping for some means of control over entry into the various trades, to unite their separate locals into national organizations, then to permit the transfer of effective power to the national level. The result was that surge of organization and consolidation described in the previous chapter. The number of trade unions increased during the eighties by 169 percent and again the following decade by 52 percent. Membership more than quadrupled. And as indicated by the statistics referred to earlier, the new unions were now equipped with treasuries, with rather stable strike and benefit funds, and with the beginnings of full-time professional leadership.[8] And they were almost totally white.[9]

Capstone to this structure of national craft unionism was the American Federation of Labor, founded in 1881, which provided an annual convention and an executive to speak for, and serve, its affiliated organizations.[10] The Federation, whose officers liked to speak of it as the "House of Labor" and of themselves as representative of the entire American labor force, could not so conveniently disregard ideology as could the affiliated unions. What developed, therefore, was a right hand–left hand arrangement by which the national unions made their practical decisions in the field, while the Federation, created by the nationals but lacking any coercive power over them, continued to speak of (and to) Negroes in the old egalitarian language of the producer ethic. At its convention of 1894—to select one example among many—

[7] John R. Commons et al., *History of Labour in the United States,* 4 vols. (New York, 1918), II, 354.

[8] Lloyd Ulman, *The Rise of the National Trade Union* (Cambridge, Mass., 1955), 49–152, and tables on 4, 19. See above, pp. 238–241.

[9] Ray Marshall, *The Negro and Organized Labor* (New York, 1965), 14–20; Charles H. Wesley, *Negro Labor in the United States, 1850–1925* (New York, 1927); Marc Karson and Ronald Radosh, "The American Federation of Labor and the Negro Worker, 1894–1949," in Julius Jacobson, ed., *The Negro and the Labor Movement* (Garden City, N. Y., 1968).

[10] Philip Taft, *Organized Labor in American History* (New York, 1964), 92–96, 110–122. Slightly remodeled in 1886, the American Federation of Labor adopted its present name.

the Federation proclaimed its devotion to working class unity "irrespective of creed, color, sex, nationality or politics." [11] Samuel Gompers, president of the Federation for all but one of its first forty-three years, regularly denounced racial exclusiveness. Labor could never achieve its goals, he asserted, unless it struggled to "eliminate the consideration of a color line. . . ." "If we fail to make friends of [black workers], the employing class won't be so short sighted. . . . If common humanity will not prompt us to have their cooperation, an enlightened self-interest should." [12] In the early nineties, the AFL executive board refused to charter several applicant groups which insisted upon explicit antiblack clauses in their constitutions. The real point in dispute, however, was not acceptance of Negroes into these organizations (which simply transferred the discriminatory rule to the local initiation ritual) but the overt expression of exclusionary policy in a union constitution. After these semantic deviations had been corrected, the applicants soon won admission to the House of Labor.[13]

No such inhibition even at the semantic level applied in the case of Chinese. Throughout the nineties and on into the twentieth century, the Federation kept up a barrage, in openly racist terms, against Chinese and other Orientals. Thus, one year before the apostrophe to working class unity cited above, an AFL convention resolved that Chinese brought with them "nothing but filth, vice and disease"; that "all efforts to elevate them to a higher standard have proven futile"; and that the Chinese were to blame for degrading "a part of our people on the Pacific Coast to such a degree that could it be published in detail the American people would in their just and righteous anger sweep them from the face of the earth." Samuel Gompers, in his presidential report, informed the convention of 1901 that "every incoming coolie means . . . so much more vice and immorality injected into our social life." [14] That same year in a pamphlet published by the Federation for mass distribution, Gompers and Herman Guttstadt, a West Coast official of the Cigar Makers' Union, quoted with approval

[11] American Federation of Labor, *Proceedings of the 14th Annual Convention* (1894), 25.
[12] Samuel Gompers to James H. White, September 14, 1889, and to H. M. Ives, November 10, 1892, as cited in Philip S. Foner, *History of the Labor Movement in the United States,* 4 vols. (New York, 1947), II, 196.
[13] Bernard Mandel, "Samuel Gompers and the Negro Workers, 1886–1914," *Journal of Negro History,* XL (January, 1955), 34–60; Arthur Mann, "Gompers and the Irony of Racism," *Antioch Review,* XIII (Summer, 1953), 203–214; Herbert Hill, "The Racial Practices of Organized Labor: The Contemporary Record," in Jacobson, ed., *The Negro and the Labor Movement,* 286–287.
[14] AFL, *Proceedings* (1893), 73; (1961), 22.

a memorial sent to Congress by citizens of San Francisco in which they
warned the lawmakers to beware especially of the offspring of mis-
cegenation between Americans and Asiatics, for these proved "invari-
ably degenerate." [15]

It is hardly necessary to extend this recitation in order to make
the point that the Oriental issue seems to have served trade unionists
—much as it had earlier served Democratic and Republican politicians
during Reconstruction—for a language of double meaning. The language justified not only what was being done to Orientals but to Negroes; and its constant repetition paved the way for a more explicit advocacy. By the late nineties the Federation was making no fuss with its
affiliates over exclusionary practices, verbal or substantive.[16] In a report
prepared for Atlanta University in 1902, W. E. B. DuBois estimated
that some 40,000 Negroes belonged to unions affiliated to the AFL; but
75 percent of these were in three organizations of heavy black membership and semiskilled status. That left approximately 10,000 black craftsmen forming a modest 3 percent of the remaining AFL membership.
The bulk of these were in the South, in segregated locals, often receiving lower rates of pay than whites doing the same work. As of 1900 the
United States Bureau of Labor Statistics listed 82 unions affiliated to
the AFL. DuBois reported that 39 of these had no black members
and another 27 only a scattering. Gompers and his AFL colleagues—
still advocating unity of all workingmen—gave their approval to
special segregated locals which controlled the competition of blacks
and collected their dues money while denying them any effective voice
in union policy.[17]

Exclusion now came to be blamed on the blacks themselves on the
assumption that their readiness to be used as strikebreakers lay at the
root of the matter. In 1898 an article featured in the *Federationist*,
official organ of the AFL, explained that Negroes were not suitable
for trade unionism because they were "of abandoned and reckless

[15] AFL, *Some Reasons for Chinese Exclusion. Meat vs. Rice. American Manhood
Against Asiatic Coolieism. Which Shall Survive?* (Washington, 1901), 34. (Also published as U.S. Senate Document 137 (Washington, 1902).) With minor revisions,
this pamphlet was reissued in 1908 by the Asiatic Exclusion League, San Francisco.
The 1908 title page ascribes authorship to Samuel Gompers and Herman Guttstadt.

[16] Karson and Radosh in Jacobson, ed., *The Negro and the Labor Movement*,
156–158; Marshall, *The Negro and Organized Labor*, 15–18.

[17] W. E. B. DuBois, ed., *The Negro Artisan: Report of a Social Study Made
Under the Direction of Atlanta University* (Atlanta, Ga., 1902), 8–10, 157–177. U.S.
Bureau of the Census, *Historical Statistics of the United States, Colonial Times to
1957* (Washington, D.C., 1960), 67. DuBois actually listed 43 unions with total
exclusion of blacks, but four of these were railroad brotherhoods not affiliated with
the AFL.

disposition" and lacked "those peculiarities of temperament such as patriotism, sympathy, sacrifice, etc., which are peculiar to most of the Caucasian race." The best solution would be to export them to Liberia or Cuba.[18] Gompers himself completed the circle of identification: "But' the caucasians," he told a presumably Caucasian audience at St. Paul, Minnesota, in 1905, "are not going to let their standard of living be destroyed by negroes, Chinamen, Japs, or any others." [19]

The New Immigration

"Any others" doubtless referred to the "new" immigration from southern and eastern Europe. It was depression and unemployment which finally forced the Federation to turn its attention to this problem. During the eighties, there had been repeated demands for federal action to halt contract importation of foreign labor but little discussion, in national conventions at least, of the desirability of general restriction. What appears to have been the first such proposal was submitted by affiliated unions of Boston in 1889. Citing an estimate that two million American workingmen were then unemployed, the Boston unionists demanded closure of the ports for fifteen years. Their resolution was referred, without action, to the incoming executive committee.[20]

Two years later Gompers sounded the alarm in his presidential address: "We are confronted with a condition of affairs in reference to immigration which is indeed appalling, and should command the earnest attention of delegates to this convention. . . . There are ways and means by which, without bigotry, narrowness and a spirit of 'Know Nothingism,' these wrongs can be remedied." [21] The following year, he again stressed the evils of "unrestricted immigration" and urged the convention to formulate legislation which could be taken into Congress. Yet there was no action then, or in 1893. And in 1894 not only did the Federation make no demand for restriction of immigration; it resolved that no such restriction, beyond the minimum necessary for keeping out contract labor, was even desirable. Thus, into the very year of Coxey's Army and the Pullman strike, sentiment favoring free entry for all except Orientals still prevailed within the Federation.[22]

18 Will H. Winn, "The Negro: His Relation to Southern Industry," *American Federationist*, IV (February, 1898), 269–271.

19 *American Federationist*, XII (September, 1905), 636–637, quoting a report of a speech by Gompers from St. Paul *Union Advocate*.

20 AFL, *Proceedings* (1889), 38.

21 Ibid., (1891), 15.

22 Ibid., (1892), 14; (1894), 47.

On what was this sentiment based? In 1894, the December issue of the *Federationist* (edited by Samuel Gompers) carried an article over the signature of one C. Ben Johnson titled "Close the Ports." The gist of this piece was to rebuke union leaders for having lacked the courage to advocate what they knew was in labor's best interest. Nonetheless, the writer recognized serious difficulties in the way of such advocacy: "We are ourselves, the whole 70,000,000 of us, either of foreign birth or within a few generations of it. The sources of our national wealth and greatness are threefold. First—God. Second—Our form of Government. Third—Our immigrants. Up to a certain point we grew in both national and individual wealth—in exact proportion as our immigration increased." But in the face of depression and mass unemployment, he concluded, there could be no alternative. Common sense must dictate that self-preservation come first.[23]

Yet common sense was not necessarily the decisive factor. Here, as in the case of the Chinese, the economic heart of the matter— controlled importation of workers from areas of low living standard— had been overlaid by complex strata of emotion and ideology. To exclude Chinese had required their prior identification as an inferior race, congenitally unsusceptible to Americanization, and therefore beyond the pale of the producer ethic. But Europeans, presumably white and for the most part Christians of one variety or another, were definitely inside that pale. Moreover, the long tradition of hospitality to newcomers had, like the producer ethic itself, stemmed directly from the twin mandates of equality. All this clamored in the immigrants' behalf. Among working people, among trade unionists, even among full-time union officials, the kinship ties of foreign born or of the children of foreign born were still direct and powerful. To advocate barring the doors involved a kind of betrayal, and the issue took on an explosive potential. Guilt stirred by denial of such loyalties must somehow be set at rest before any reorientation on the matter of immigration would be possible. To this extent the Chinese experience had to be repeated. And as a matter of fact the process of repetition had begun more than a decade earlier.

During the summer of 1882, Burnette Haskell's little socialist weekly in San Francisco, ever alert for new styles on the left, noted that a correspondent New York paper wanted "an anti-immigration bill like the Chinese bill, against Europeans." Haskell appended the following comment:

> Query, which is best, to allow unlimited importation of the cheapest labor; then to educate that labor up to its duty, and

23 *American Federationist*, I (December, 1894), 216–217.

> so in the end civilize the world all at once; or to shut the door
> against degraded and uneducated men in every land, then
> educate in each land for itself and win the battle country by
> country? . . . This will be one of the greatest issues of the
> future.[24]

On another page of the same issue appeared a report that the Southern
Pacific Railroad was planning steamship connections between ports of
the Mediterranean and its railhead at New Orleans. The object, allegedly, was to "bring over swarms of Italians, Southern French and
Germans to take the place of the Chinese." And how would this result
for Californians?

> Voted out, drowned out with beer and gin, and pauperized out
> with the general drunkenness and misery, and beggary that
> would be entailed upon us. . . . The last thing but one this
> country wants is to be flooded by hordes of Chinese and Ma-
> lays, and that one is to be similarly flooded by hordes of igno-
> rant, barbarous, incompetent, incapable, intractable slaves
> from the Mediterranean. If we want millions of brute labor,
> the Chinaman and the donkey are the best brutes we can
> have.[25]

Two months later *Truth* reprinted an article from the Pittsburgh
(Pennsylvania) *Labor Herald* which charged that European governments had for the past twenty years been subsidizing the export of
paupers and criminals to the United States. Thanks to political ma-
chines like the Tweed ring, these "scabs on the body politic" were converted into American voters within a few hours after landing. Already
they were "elbowing aside respectable workers in the coal fields."
Whereas labor had long refrained from advocating immigration restriction because of the bad name such advocacy had acquired during
the Know Nothing period, the time had now come to think more
deeply. And then the key sentence: "The trouble with this class is not
that it does not assimilate (the objection urged against the Chinese)
but that it does, and the assimilation has the same effect as that of
poisonous weeds growing among wheat." [26]

Meanwhile, the great swing of emigration from northern and western to southern and eastern Europe had occurred. The majority of
those already in and their children, being of the "old" emigration from
the north and west, could separate themselves from the new. Clearly,

24 San Francisco *Truth*, July 5, 1882.
25 *Truth*, July 5, 1882.
26 *Truth*, September 27, 1882. See also *John Swinton's Paper* (New York), January 6, October 5, 1884; and San Francisco *Daily Report*, December 14, 1885, for
a letter to the editor criticizing the founding convention of the Federated Trades
for its exclusive emphasis on Chinese immigration.

the new was *different*, and there was impressive evidence of inferiority. Yet might not the inferiority be due simply to misfortune and lack of opportunity? How could a people be permanently inferior unless they were members of an inferior race? Racial inferiority was supposed to be marked by color. Were these people dark enough? The problem might seem reasonably simple as long as one could speak of Caucasians on one side, Orientals or blacks on the other. But was it possible to say the newcomers were not Caucasian?

One escape route from this dilemma had lately been mapped by scholars of the Germanic mystique of American history. Their view, during the nineties, was widely popularized; its impact on interpretations of the frontier and of the role of labor has already been noted. Unquestionably, the Germanic (or Anglo-Saxon) persuasion played an important part in preparing the nation for acquiescence in the restriction of immigration. Yet it was poorly devised for winning adherents within the labor force for two reasons. First, it had little to recommend it in so far as Irish or Jews were concerned; and second, it was so patently upper class in both its origins and its implications. An alliance between labor leaders and upper class spokesmen (Samuel Gompers and Henry Cabot Lodge, for example) to achieve immigration restriction might be quite possible; but the labor force would require a rationale appropriate to its own needs.

In 1894, a few days before the appearance of the *Federationist* article, "Close the Ports," Gompers delivered his presidential address to the fourteenth annual convention at Denver. A regular feature of previous addresses had been the denunciation of Chinese infiltration and demands for more rigid enforcement of the exclusion laws. Gompers in 1894 registered these points as usual; but the Chinese issue itself he handled in a curiously muted style:

> There is no antipathy on the part of American workmen to Chinese because of their nationality, but a people which have allowed civilization to pass them by untouched and uninfluenced, a people who allow themselves to be barbarously tyrannized over in their own country and who menace the progress, the economic and social standing of the workers of other countries, cannot be fraternized with.[27]

The opening clause of this sentence is so sharply at variance with attitudes generally expressed by labor spokesmen, Gompers among them, that one wonders whether some other line of thought had not intruded

[27] AFL, *Proceedings* (1894), 12.

upon the normal sequence. Here the concept of race, as usually applied to Chinese, has been transposed to *nationality*, while the role of the item itself, whatever name it be called by, has been minimized. Thus, it is not for their *nationality* (race) that the Chinese must be held to account, but for their inexcusable behavior—their acceptance of a static culture, their willing submission to tyranny. The effect of this passage is to reinterpret the permissible hatred toward Chinese into language that can be applied directly to selected peoples of Europe. Yet it would be pointless to suggest that Gompers had engaged in some sort of conspiracy to shape the thinking of the Federation. He was groping to shape his own thinking, to discover from one situation what might be taken as analogy for another. Himself an immigrant, as were most of his early friends, Gompers' visions and revisions on this question reflect the emotional and ideological conflict through which the entire labor movement was struggling.

How intense this conflict became appears from a chronology of events that followed. Two years later, in 1896, the leadership of the Federation finally dared meet the issue head-on. An endorsement of the Lodge literacy test bill was reported favorably by the resolutions committee. The report provoked bitter debate; the convention seemed at the point of deadlock; and the whole matter was referred back to the executive board. Better prepared in 1897, the board pushed through an endorsement over stiff opposition.[28] Meanwhile, Congress had passed the Lodge bill, and President Cleveland had vetoed it.[29] At the convention of 1900, under the benign influences of returning prosperity, the delegates rejected a new demand for immigration restriction but let the endorsement of 1897 stand.[30] And now the Chinese issue burst to the forefront once more, because the exclusion laws adopted originally in 1882 and extended in 1892 were due to expire in 1902.[31] Within organized labor, the Asian menace again took precedence over other menaces. The Federation in 1901 attained to heights of racist invective surpassing anything it had hitherto achieved.[32] Its efforts were rewarded by the enactment in 1902 of permanent Chi-

[28] Ibid. (1896), 81–82; (1897), 87, 90–91.
[29] Bernard Mandel, *Samuel Gompers* (Yellow Springs, Ohio, 1963), 189.
[30] AFL, *Proceedings* (1900), 120–121.
[31] Ibid. (1901), 22–23. See also *American Federationist*, VIII August, 1901), 305. On renewal of the exclusion laws, a congressional committee, after holding hearings up and down the Pacific Coast, recommended making the laws permanent. U.S., Congress, Joint Select Committee on Immigration and Naturalization, *Chinese Immigration*, Report No. 4048 51st Cong., 2d Sess. (Washington, 1891). See above, pp. 243–249.
[32] See, for example, AFL, *Meat vs. Rice* (1901), 34; and *Proceedings* (1901), 154–155.

nese exclusion.[33] Upon the flood tide of this victory, Gompers returned to his battle for general restriction and, during the latter part of that same year, lobbied for a new bill which passed the House of Representatives. But even yet, he was apparently unsure of support inside the Federation.

Part of his difficulty hinged on the nature of the restriction device which had been chosen—the literacy test. While for the population as a whole this served to lend an air of impartiality to the proposed exclusion, among working people the effect was somewhat the opposite. It was only too obvious that wealthy and privileged members of any society would always be among the literate. Was not labor then being decoyed into an anti-working class position? Gompers thought not and, in his address to the convention of 1902, went to considerable pains to explain that the literary test was not really, as it appeared, a class discrimination, but was in fact what it seemed not to be, a *national* or *racial* discrimination. "This regulation will exclude hardly any of the natives of Great Britain, Ireland, Germany, or Scandinavia. It will exclude only a small proportion of our immigrants from North Italy. It will shut out a considerable number of South Italians and Slavs and others equally or more undesirable or injurious." [34]

Labor could therefore accept such a restriction with easy conscience. No betrayal was involved. People of south and east European origin were properly excluded from the circle of the producers' loyalties because they had, through their own slothfulness and submission to tyranny, made themselves obstacles to progress. However dissimilar in appearance, they were in fact equivalent to Chinese. A reference was made earlier to the speech of Gompers at St. Paul in 1905, which, by its identification of Negro with Oriental, signaled the completion of a fifty-year thought cycle on the position of the black in American society. "But the caucasians," Gompers had said, "are not going to let their standard of living be destroyed by negroes, Chinamen, Japs, or any others." [35] There was, perhaps, no great coincidence in the fact that the same sentence marked completion of a second thought cycle as well. The new immigration, by virtue of being grouped with Negroes and Orientals, had now been officially excluded from the ranks of Caucasians. In Gompers' context, clearly, *Caucasian* had become synonymous with such hitherto tabooed terms as *Anglo-Saxon* or *Nordic*.[36]

[33] Mandel, *Samuel Gompers*, 186–187; Elmer Clarence Sandmeyer, *The Anti-Chinese Movement in California* (Urbana, Ill., 1939), 107.

[34] AFL, *Proceedings* (1902), 21–22.

[35] See above, p. 273.

[36] Tabooed, that is, in portions of the labor force that included any significant numbers of Jewish or Irish-American workingmen.

Apocalypse

The population of the Far West, among whom Chinese proscription ran its course, and the labor force, within which that proscription became elaborately institutionalized, were parts of a larger process. Both were actors and acted upon. Their experiences and responses, shaped by earlier patterns of the pre-Civil War East, in turn contributed to the developing racist fabric. Whether Gompers, when he compared the supposedly static and therefore reactionary character of Chinese culture to the supposed backwardness of southern and eastern Europeans, was acquainted with the work of the Reverend Josiah Strong does not appear from the record. The fact is, however, that the labor leader could have found his own argument almost ready-made in books published by the Protestant clergyman during the preceding decade. "In Asia," Strong had written in 1893, "there have been vast organizations of society, but the development of the individual was early arrested, hence the stagnation of everything. Oriental civilization manifests unity with but little diversity, hence the dead uniformity of many centuries." [37] Strong went on to propose two parallel tables of equivalences. The first ran: Greek, individualistic, progressive, North European, Protestant Reformation. The second was of even broader coverage: Egyptian, Oriental, Roman Catholic, highly organized, autocratic, stagnant.[38] Strong himself was anti-Irish and anti-"Latin" as well as anti-Catholic. In an earlier work he had defined his preferences as follows:

> The noblest races have always been lovers of liberty. That love ran strong in early German blood. . . . It was no accident that the great reformation of the sixteenth century originated among a Teutonic, rather than a Latin people. It was the fire of liberty burning in the Saxon heart that flamed up against the absolutism of the Pope. Speaking roughly, the peoples of Europe which are Celtic are Catholic, and those which are Teutonic are Protestant.[39]

Inherent in Strong's rough speaking was that identification toward which Gompers was simultaneously groping—though couched, of course, in language not directly acceptable to American workingmen. Yet no very extensive transposition was necessary. It would suffice to drop the invidious reference to Celts, and to express the concept of

[37] Josiah Strong, *The New Era or the Coming Kingdom* (New York, 1893), 23.
[38] Ibid., 26–27.
[39] Josiah Strong, *Our Country: Its Possible Future and Its Present Crisis* (New York, 1885), 160.

Latin-ness in geographical rather than religious terms. The Irish American, who occupied so important a place in the labor force, would find no insurmountable difficulty in sharing a Teutonic contempt for Mediterranean peoples or in believing that Catholicism of the Latin style—provided only that the papacy itself be exempted from criticism —was inferior to his own.

Strong had in fact foreseen and resolved in advance the problem of the Irish American. Truly great races, he had determined, were the products of favorable racial mixture. Mixing might be good or bad depending on the ingredients. Had not the Greek and Roman— highly mixed—been superior to pure Hebrew? As for the Anglo-Saxon, it was already a fusion to which had been added in ancient times portions of Danish and Celtic blood.[40] Afterward in America, this same fortunate combination had been repeated during the earlier period of immigration. "What took place a thousand years ago in England again transpires today in the United States." [41] But presumably by the mid-eighties the mix was perfected and the time had come to call a halt. Especially in his later writing, Strong stressed the "importance to mankind and to the coming Kingdom of guarding against the deterioration of the Anglo-Saxon stock in the United States by immigration. There is now being injected into the veins of the nation a large amount of inferior blood every day of every year." [42]

A key point at issue in the far-flung debate over restriction of entry was a racial definition of American-ness. California's curious apostle of militarism, Homer Lea, estimated in 1909 that "the foreign non-Anglo-Saxon element in this country" had increased from one-twelfth of the population in 1860 to almost one-half in 1900. "Since that time the declination of primitive Americanism has gone on at even greater speed." The outcome, if this trend continued, could only be disastrous, for "a nation may be kept in tact only so long as the ruling element remains homogenous." [43] To define implies a ruling out or circumscription. One says what one is by declaring what one is not. Thus

---

[40] Ibid., 171–172. Strong took the first part of this argument (with acknowledgment) from an article by "Canon George Rawlinson, Oxford University," titled "The Duties of Higher Towards Lower Races in a Mixed Community," *Princeton Review*, Ser. 4, II (November 1878), 804–847. Strong did not make clear to his own readers that the article from which he quoted went considerably beyond a simple declaration that certain mixed races were superior to certain pure ones. The Reverend Rawlinson's essay was in fact an assertion of the duty of Christians living in mixed communities to encourage total racial fusion through intermarriage.

[41] Strong, *Our Country*, 171.

[42] Strong, *New Era*, 79–80.

[43] Homer Lea, *The Valor of Ignorance* (New York, 1909), 124–126.

Jack London, who had grown up at the fringes of the San Francisco labor movement, imagined a hard-fisted union teamster learning the facts of life from his better educated girl friend: "they had blue eyes and yellow hair, and they were awful fighters. . . . They were the first English, and you know the Americans came from the English. We're Saxons, you and me and Mary and Bert, and all the Americans that are real Americans, you know, and not Dagoes and Japs and such." [44]

Just as in Strong's formulation, a limited degree of mixing ("not Dagoes and Japs") seems to have been recognized as acceptable. The act of exclusion would then sanctify the status of the insiders. Once safely within the gates, even the new American—taking himself (as Gompers had already implied) for an Anglo-Saxon ex officio or by adoption—could subscribe more or less wholeheartedly to the Reverend Strong's Proclamation of the Coming Kingdom:

> It seems to me that God, with infinite wisdom and skill, is training the Anglo-Saxon race for an hour sure to come in the world's future. . . . Then will the world enter upon a new stage of its history—the final competition of races, for which the Anglo-Saxon is being schooled. . . . The mighty centrifugal tendency, inherent in this stock, and strengthened in the United States, will reassert itself. Then this race of unequalled energy, with all the majesty of numbers and the might of wealth behind it—the representative, let us hope, of the largest liberty, the purest Christianity, the highest civilization—having developed peculiarly aggressive traits calculated to impress its institutions upon mankind, will spread itself over the earth. If I read not amiss, this powerful race will move down to Mexico, down upon Central and South America, out upon the islands of the sea, over upon Africa and beyond. [45]

[44] Jack London, *The Valley of the Moon* (New York, 1913), 21–22. When one notes that the speaker of these lines, the teamster's girl friend, was named Saxon Brown, it does become hard to believe that London was not attempting satire. But anyone who reads the novel will agree, I think, that on this theme London was incapable of any but a straight presentation. *Valley of the Moon* first ran as a serial in the *Cosmopolitan*, 1913.

[45] Strong, *Our Country*, 174–175. Among many renderings of this same theme were Homer Lea's secular vision: "The endless extension of the Republic, the maintenance of its ideals and the consummation, in a world wide sense, of the aspirations of its founders, constitutes the only pure patriotism to which an American can lay claim or, in defense of, lay down his life" (Lea, 25). Or Jack London's Nietzschean variation: ". . . perishing, yet mastering and commanding like our fathers before us . . . Ah well, ours is a lordly history, and though we may be doomed to pass, in our time we shall have trod on the faces of all peoples, disciplined them to obedience, taught them government" (London, *The Mutiny of the Elsinore* (New York, 1914), 148–149).

Here, the spread-eagle Jacksonian rhetoric has been unleashed again. And in one sense this search for national definition continued the Jacksonian pursuit of the American oversoul. "seest thou not God's purpose from the first?" Whitman had written in 1868:

> The earth to be spann'd, connected by network . . .
> Tying the Eastern to the Western sea,
> The road between Europe and Asia.
> (Ah Genoese, thy dream! thy dream!
> Centuries after thou art laid in thy grave,
> The shore thou foundest verifies thy dream.)
> Passage to India. . . .

Yet how different a context the intervening years imposed. Whitman had seen the American soul in transit along the great circle route homeward to the universal soul. "The races, neighbors, to marry and be given in marriage. . . . The lands to be welded together." [46] For Strong, on the other hand, as for the imperialistic Homer Lea and Jack London the Socialist, passage to India marked a rooting out of the last vestiges of the twin mandates of equality. "Can anyone doubt," Strong insisted, "that the result of this competition will be the 'survival of the fittest'?" [47]

Rather a large number, as it turned out, doubted the inevitability of the outcome or wondered at least who, under the circumstances, might finally prove fittest. Depression and unemployment in the early nineties, while forcing leaders of the American Federation of Labor to agree with Josiah Strong as to the urgency of immigration restriction, reinforced those anxieties roused by industrialization which were already causing many Americans to reject the kind of exuberant optimism expressed by Strong. Were not the monopolists firmly in the saddle? And had not inferior races always served as tools of tyrannical power? Certainly Brooks Adams was drawing heavily on recent events on the Pacific Coast when he summed up half a millennium of Roman history in the following terms:

> In the seventh century Asiatic competition devoured the Europeans in the Levant, as three hundred years before it had devoured the husbandmen of Italy; and this was a disease which isolation alone could cure. But isolation of the center of exchanges was impossible, for the vital principle of an economic age is competition. . . . Competition did its work with

[46] Walt Whitman, "Passage to India."
[47] Strong, *Our Country*, 175.

> relentless rapidity. . . . The population sank fast, and by 717 the western blood had run so low that an Asiatic dynasty reigned supreme.[48]

What was of primary concern to Adams was not the fate of Rome or Byzantium, but the abstraction of general laws of history. Economic competition, he reasoned, must always breed the banker and the cheap laborer: [49]

> As velocity augments and competition intensifies, nature begins to sift the economic minds themselves, culling a favored aristocracy of the craftiest and subtlest types; choosing, for example, the Armenian in Byzantium, the Marwari in India, and the Jew in London. Conversely, as the costly nervous system of the soldier becomes an encumbrance, organisms which can exist on less successively supplant each other until the limit of endurance is reached. Thus the Slavs exterminated the Greeks in Thrace and Macedonia, the Mahrattas and the Moslems dwindle before the low caste tribes of India, and the instinct of self-preservation has taught white races to resist an influx of Chinese.[50]

Brooks Adams' conception was precisely the opposite of Josiah Strong's. Instead of riding the Darwinian wave of the future to world supremacy, the white American might find himself hard pressed building dikes high and strong enough to keep from being engulfed. Nor was this somber view expressive simply of status anxiety among vanishing Brahmins. It was widely shared. Ignatius Donnelly, midwestern Populist leader and son of Irish immigrant parents, warned in his novel, *Caesar's Column*, of the impending destruction of America between the upper and nether millstones of a Jewish oligarchy and a debased and Orientalized proletariat. Caesar's Column, that tower of corpses encased in concrete, became the tombstone for the American nation. In the final chapter Donnelly left his hero with a group of old stock Americans, refugees from the debacle, who have barricaded themselves into a mountain valley of central Africa, and there live by tilling the soil in the old-fashioned way—while with dynamite and

[48] Brooks Adams, *The Law of Civilization and Decay* (New York, 1959), 48 (first published in London, 1895, and in New York the following year). See xl of Charles A. Beard's "Introduction" to the 1959 edition. For an earlier West Coast statement of the same theme, P. W. Dooner, *Last Days of the Republic* (San Francisco, 1880). Lea, in the *Valor of Ignorance* (1909), echoed many concepts that had appeared in Adams's work.

[49] Adams, 284.

[50] Adams, 292–293.

Gatling Guns they defend their alpine passes against the barbarian hordes of the world beyond.[51] *Caesar's Column* (later pressed into service as a Populist campaign document) sold 60,000 copies in the first year of publication and subsequently passed the quarter million mark.[52] The vision of catastrophe, through many incarnations, spread far beyond even Donnelly's readership. It had become part of the language of the times. During the nineties it would reappear in literary and propaganda efforts ranging all the way from penny pamphlets to Mark Twain's *Connecticut Yankee*. And twenty years afterward Jack London was still engrossed in the same theme.[53] "When will we dead awaken?" the labor editor Olaf Tveitmoe, on the brink of real and visible catastrophe, wrote in 1914. When the system dies, when the plutocracy and those debased races that willingly served it have both been purged from the face of the earth, "Then comes the day of social resurrection."

There were, then, in general circulation at the turn of the century two opposite forecasts of the national destiny. Not altogether lightly, these might be described as a Populist and a Progressive apocalypse. Though contradictory, they shared several elements in common. Both were molded by the long sequence of racial proscription and justification of proscription. Both took for granted a racial definition of nationality. Both, by reasserting that definition, attempted to fill in the gaps which erosion of the twin mandates of equality had left in the old ideologies.

[51] Ignatius Donnelly, *Caesar's Column: A Story of the Twentieth Century* (Cambridge, Mass., 1960), 31–32, 38, 96–98, 117, 283, 291–309.

[52] Ibid., xviii–xix of Walter A. Rideout's "Introduction"; Vernon L. Parrington, Jr., *American Dreams: A Study of American Utopias* (New York, 1964), 69–97; John D. Hicks, *The Populist Revolt* (Minneapolis, 1931), 131–132.

[53] Mark Twain's *Connecticut Yankee* was first published in 1889. Jack London's *Iron Heel* was published in 1907, *The Scarlet Plague* in 1915.

BIBLIOGRAPHIC NOTE

The people upon whom this book is mainly focused were extraordinarily articulate. They expressed themselves at length in speech and in print; but they kept few records, and the same was true of the organizations through which they moved. What records they did leave have been reduced by time, fire, and earthquake. Fortunately, however, the seventy-year period following the end of the Civil War was marked by a proliferation of locally oriented newspapers and periodicals in the West, and many complete files survive. They constitute the major primary source for the present study. A list of all newspapers and periodicals consulted forms part of this bibliographic note; most of them may be read in the University of California and Bancroft Libraries at Berkeley, in the California State Library at Sacramento (its subject index to newspapers was an invaluable aid), and in the San Francisco Public Library.

Pertinent information of considerable importance, though small in quantity, has been drawn from various manuscript, letter, and pamphlet collections. These can be located through the index under the following headings: Bancroft Scraps, Chinese Immigration Pamphlets, Charles Crocker Typescript, Cross Collection and Cross Labor Notes, Haskell Family Papers, Knights of Labor Records, Immigration Pamphlets, International Workingmen's Association Records. All other bibliographic information will be found in the footnotes. The first reference to any work in each chapter contains the full citation.

Newspapers and Periodicals

American Federationist (Washington)
Bodie *Daily Free Press*
Denver *Labor Enquirer* (Issues in

Ira B. Cross Collection. Newspapers on microfilm, Bancroft Library, University of California, Berkeley)

Dutch Flat *Enquirer*
Gold Hill (Nevada) *Evening News*
Grass Valley *Daily National*
John Swinton's Paper (New York)
Los Angeles *Times*
Oakland *Daily Transcript*
Sacramento *Record Union*
Sacramento *Union*
San Francisco *Argonaut*
San Francisco *Chronicle*
San Francisco *Coast Seamen's Journal*
San Francisco *Daily Alta*
San Francisco *Daily Report*

San Francisco *Evening Bulletin*
San Francisco *Examiner*
San Francisco *Labor Clarion*
San Francisco *Morning Call*
San Francisco *Open Letter* (Scattered issues, Cross Labor Notes)
San Francisco *Organized Labor*
San Francisco *Overland Monthly*
San Francisco *Pacific Rural Press*
San Francisco *Truth*
San Francisco *Weekly Stock Report*
Virginia City (Nevada) *Territorial Enterprise*

INDEX